THE GERMAN EVANGELICAL CHURCH AND THE JEWS
1879–1950

Richard Gutteridge

Educated at Westminster School and
Trinity Hall, Cambridge (1929-1931),
Honours Degree in History and
Theology. Studied Theology at
Tübingen University, 1933. Ordained
1935, Tutor of the Queen's College,
Birmingham, 1935-1937. Commissioned
Chaplain, Royal Air Force, 1952-1968,
Bampton Fellow in the University of
Oxford, 1969-1972.

*GUTTERIDGE, Richard. The German Evangelical Church and the Jews, 1879–1950. Barnes & Noble, a div. of Harper & Row, 1976. 374p bibl index 76-12068. 18.50. ISBN 0-06-492620-6

CHOICE   *DEC. '76*

Religion

A detailed study of the relationship of the German Evangelical (= Protestant) Church to the Jews during the Nazi regime — where "Jews," however, mainly refers to Christians of Jewish origin. Seeing how very little that Church was willing to undertake on behalf of its own "non-Aryan" members, it stands to reason that there was even less concern for the fate of Jews who had remained Jewish — particularly in view of the fact that even those very few churchmen who, *in extremis,* challenged aspects of Nazi Holocaust policy did not themselves reject the government's anti-Semitic and *völkish* presuppositions (e.g., Martin Niemöller). Exceptions, like Heinrich Grüber, stand out all the more strikingly. Gutteridge sees part of the reason for that in the contemporary understanding (or misunderstanding) of Luther's doctrine of the "Two Kingdoms" by means of which even the Nazi *Obrigkeit* was seen as divinely ordained. The book is fully documented and contains elaborate footnotes, appendixes, and a 13-page bibliography. It is indispensable for students of modern German history, theology, and the Holocaust.

THE GERMAN EVANGELICAL CHURCH AND THE JEWS 1879-1950

Richard Gutteridge

BOOKS
10 East 53d St., New York 10022
(a division of Harper & Row Publishers, Inc.)

Published in the U.S.A. 1976 by
HARPER & ROW PUBLISHERS, INC.
BARNES & NOBLE IMPORT DIVISION

ISBN 0-06-492620-6

Printed in Great Britain

'Open thy mouth for the dumb in the cause of all such as are appointed to destruction.' (Proverbs 31, verse 8.)

'The Church makes confession of her timidity, her evasiveness, her dangerous concessions. She has repeatedly been untrue to her office as watchman and her office as consoler. Thereby she has denied to the outcast and to the despised the compassion it was her obligation to show them. She was dumb, when she ought to have cried out, since the blood of the innocent was crying aloud to heaven. She has not found the right word to speak in the right manner and at the right time. . . . The Church owns that she has beheld the despotic application of brute force, the physical and spiritual suffering of countless innocent people, oppression, hatred and murder without raising her voice on behalf of the victims and without having found means of hastening to their aid. She is to be held answerable for the lives of the weakest and most defenceless of the brethren of Jesus Christ.' (Dietrich Bonhoeffer: *Ethik*, 6th edition, München, 1963, pp. 120–2, words written in 1940.)

Contents

In Acknowledgement

I wish to express my gratitude to the Bampton Electors in the University of Oxford who appointed me to the Bampton Fellowship in 1969 for a period of three years. This generous award enabled me to carry out the necessary concentrated study and research both in this country and in Germany which made the writing of this book possible. I am also most grateful for the facilities made available to me by the Cambridge University Library, the Bodleian Library, Oxford, the Wiener Library, London, the Landeskirchliches and Wilhelm Niemöller Archiv in Bielefeld, the Landeskirchliches Archiv in Stuttgart, and at the Headquarters of the World Council of Churches at Geneva. I am conscious of being greatly in debt to the remarkable unpublished dissertation by Dr. Wolfgang Gerlach entitled *Zwischen Kreuz und Davidstern*, which has the distinction of being the one and only detailed treatment in German of the attitude of the Confessing Church to the Jews. I would like to thank the Reverend Professor Owen Chadwick, the Reverend Professor Gordon Rupp and Professor John Conway, each of whom was kind enough to read through large parts of my manuscript and provided much expert advice and comment, and the Very Reverend Dr. Henry Chadwick and the Reverend Dr. Ernest Nicholson for their assistance. On various visits to Germany I received great help and encouragement from Professor Klaus Scholder and Dr. Leonore Siegele-Wenschkewitz of Tübingen, Dr. Gerhard Schäfer of Stuttgart, Dr. Wilhelm Niemöller of Bielefeld, Dr. Helmut Baier of Nuremberg and Dr. Maria Zelzer, for which I am most grateful. My warmest thanks are due to Mrs. Hazel Hedge who has shown such untiring patience and unfailing efficiency in the typing and re-typing of my manuscript.

Richard Gutteridge

I

The roots of 'Christian' anti-semitism, 1879–1918

In 1919, the very first year of the Weimar Republic, a confidential report from the police in northern Bavaria to the State Commissioner for the control of public order affirmed that anti-semitism[1] was increasing rapidly, that it was not just confined to the Right Wing, and that it was having its effect upon all sections of the population, not excluding the extreme Left.[2] The Evangelical Church[3] was certainly not immune from the anti-semitic virus. As the Republic made its uneven and chequered progress through the turbulent 'twenties, evangelical voices were to be heard unmistakably among the choir of those who did not hesitate in denouncing the Jews for their sinister part in current German misfortunes and tribulations. Before it seemed likely that Hitler was about to assume power, and before Nazi propaganda had an opportunity to give full vent to its racial prejudices and thoroughly implement its anti-Jewish programme, highly influential and much respected ecclesiastics and theologians, and not merely those within the Church who were obsessed with extreme Germanic notions, were introducing an anti-semitic content into their Christian message.

In April 1928 Otto Dibelius, writing in his capacity as General Superintendent in the Kurmark to the pastors under his care, declared that, despite the manifold evil-sounding associations of the word, he had always recognised himself to be an anti-semite. 'It cannot be denied', he affirmed, 'that in all the manifestations of disintegration in modern civilisation Jewry has always played a leading role.'[4]

In 1926 Hans Meiser, pillar of Lutheran orthodoxy, from 1933 Bishop of the Evangelical Church of Bavaria and sturdy Confessionalist fighter, published a series of articles in which he claimed that it was no exaggeration to say that the Jews had secured for themselves the lion's share of the German national wealth, and that it was astonishing to note the adroitness with which the small number of Jews who were then living in Germany were managing to dominate almost all departments of public life and to secure for themselves a decisive influence. The Jewish corruption of Press, literature and stage represented a sin against the German people that could scarcely be exaggerated. While disavowing radical anti-semitism that insisted upon regarding the Jews merely upon racial grounds as inevitably and without exception inferior beings, he had yet no hesitation in commending the demand for the preservation of the purity of German blood as entirely justifiable, and in expressing disapproval of intermarriage between those of German and Jewish descent.[5]

In 1927 Paul Althaus, regarded as one of the leading younger theologians, emphasised in a speech which won considerable attention and approval that it was essential for the Churches to keep in view and speak out against the Jewish menace. The right way, he believed, of combating the current wild version of anti-semitism was to take the Jewish problem really seriously, and, free from racial hatred and criticism of Jewish religious faith, to be prepared to speak in public about it and to resort to bold action.[6]

In 1929 Adolf Schlatter, veteran champion of biblical orthodoxy, and of Swiss origin, wrote, with undeniable relevance to the Jewish issue; 'Reverence for Race which embraces the fullest respect for the barriers which it imposes, and attention to the necessities laid down by Nature that condition our life as a People, ought for every Christian to be a matter of course.'[7]

Also in 1929, in the *Allgemeine Evangelisch-Lutherische Kirchenzeitung*, the highly respected Lutheran Church Weekly, and the one with the largest circulation, its editor, Wilhelm Laible wrote in terms of a welcome being given 'for the sake of the German people to every expression of justifiable anti-semitism'. No one, he claimed, could deny the share of the Jews in the present religious, moral and economic decline, or overlook 'the poisonous effect of the Jewish Press and Jewish literature'. These facts held good, even if Israel was to be accounted the Chosen People.

The Jews, having rejected Christ, stood under the Divine Curse, and would inevitably be a curse to many other peoples.

There certainly was an obligation to show neighbourly Christian love to the Jews, but this involved demonstrating to them that their 'predominance' in Germany was a misfortune. Anti-semitism was legitimate, when its object was to contest and break the predominance and the influence of Jewry, and should continue, as long as the German people and the Church suffered under such semitism.[8]

Such expressions of what may be termed 'Christian' anti-semitism were not just a post-war phenomenon. There was indeed a long history behind them. The Protestant tendency to anti-semitism was part and parcel of the well-established tradition of close identification between Christianity and a mystical interpretation of nationality in manifestly untranslatable terms such as *Deutschtum* and *Volkstum*.[9] The more wedded the German was to what may be described as an excessively patriotic 'volkish' ideology, the less likely would he be to prove tolerant and friendly towards those dwelling in his land who according to his reckoning were odd men out, aliens, disqualified from really sharing in his sacred experience and a potential threat to the integrity of that which he held most dear.

German Lutherans would have been greatly assisted in keeping clear of infection from the anti-Jewish virus, had they been taught by Martin Luther to have a particular regard for God's Chosen People among whom the Saviour was born. But, instead, they were encouraged, as disciples of the Reformer, to regard the Jew, unless he had been converted into a Christian, with dislike and suspicion as the inveterate enemy of Christ and His Church and carrying an inherited and awesome responsibility for the crucifixion. Luther's anti-semitism clearly had a religious and not a racial foundation, but it cannot be denied that it provided each successive Protestant generation with not only the excuse but also the sanction for animosity and persecution.[10]

The attempted emancipation and assimilation of the Jews in Germany in the nineteenth century did not provide any enduring solution for the Jewish problem. Much of the accumulated hatred and suspicion remained under the surface ready to flare up at moments of national crisis, political upheaval, or economic distress. Between 1870 and 1895 there was indeed evidence of growth in anti-Jewish feeling, fortified by the outbreak and spread of racially motivated anti-semitism.[11] In the narrowly patriotic

Protestant view the necessary condition for acceptance of the alien Jew was his radical disassociation from his hitherto national and religious peculiarity, and his readiness to become incorporated through baptism into the German Christian national community. This fundamentally illiberal insistence could not but have two ominous and unhappy results: the driving of a wedge between the conservative orthodox Jew and his liberal counterpart, and the undoubted encouragement of and connivance at many an insincere and opportunist conversion to Christianity. In Church circles there was before long widespread disillusionment at the results of assimilation. So many Jews freed from the ghetto, severed from their former religious roots and admitted to a place within the Christian community, turned out, not surprisingly, to be liberal rather than Christian, and certainly did not conform to the traditional requirements of German Christian *Bürgertum* or show an inclination to respect its accepted values.

In this situation two powerful Protestant spokesmen, Adolf Stoecker and Heinrich von Treitschke, had undoubted success in stirring up latent emotional anti-semitic feeling.

Adolf Stoecker, of quite humble origin, attained in 1874 the exalted position of Court and Cathedral Preacher in Berlin. A man of unbounded energy and of engaging and robust personality, he quickly revealed a remarkable though imperfectly disciplined flair for oratory. A conservative, fervent in devotion to Volk and Fatherland, unswerving in his loyalty to and reverence for the Monarchy, he was at the same time most sincerely concerned for both the material and the spiritual condition of the Working Class, and aspired to promote social reform from above. A conscientious preacher of the pure Word of Scripture and consistently determined to keep politics away from the pulpit, he was at the same time set upon entering with missionary zeal and responsibility into the political arena and fearlessly applying his Christian convictions in public life. Religion, he avowed, had its place every bit as much in the Chambers of Parliament as in a believer's private chamber.[12] Remarkably successful himself as an evangelist, he acknowledged the need to enlist lay co-operation to the full in what he regarded as the bridge-building apostolate of the little man.

In 1878 Stoecker launched a bold but scarcely successful attempt to oppose the Social Democratic Party which he regarded as flagrantly atheistic and materialistic and falsely liberal. He did not hesitate to try to take the wild beast by its horns, and sought to win over the proletariat of Berlin to his own newly founded Christian-Socialist Workers' Party, only to discover the working man highly suspicious of the intentions of one who was a conservative and a supporter of the Establishment 'condescending to the masses from the authoritative heights of royalty and nobility'.[13]

The following year he inaugurated a vigorous campaign against modern Jewry as being the most corrupting influence in society, complaining that 'we Germans out of cosmopolitan enthusiasm for the emancipation of the Jews are foolish enough to ruin our nation.'[14] His attack, he insisted, was not motivated by fanaticism, envy or intolerance, but was warfare in defence of what he conceived to be of supreme value in German national and religious life.

In striking the anti-semitic note he at once aroused the widest public interest. His boisterous utterances incurred bitter resentment in many circles. Countless newspaper articles and no less than two hundred pamphlets were written in protest. Theologians, pastors and Christian politicians were among those who were most disquieted by the sudden upsurge of anti-Jewish agitation in its ecclesiastical setting, and would certainly have endorsed Adolf von Harnack's judgement made over ten years later that it was 'a tragic scandal to inscribe anti-semitism upon the banner of evangelical Christianity'.[15] A Protestant member of Parliament wrote in grave disquiet, protesting at what he regarded as being Stoecker's quite unchristian attitude in daring to suggest that a persecution of the Jews could possibly be undertaken in a Christian spirit. A Berlin pastor in 1881 announced that it was high time that the Evangelical Church should disassociate itself from deceitful alliance with the anti-semites and give loud witness to the demands of Love and of the Truth, recognising that pseudo-national chauvinism was the worst enemy of the Gospel. Another pastor expressed his concern that it should be churchmen, representatives of the Christian Faith who, ostensibly on behalf of threatened Christianity, were fanning the flames of hatred in the hearts not only of the undiscriminating masses but also of educated people who had had a fine grounding in humanitarian values. Michael Baumgarten, eminent professor of Theology and

Reichstag Deputy, produced two outspoken pamphlets denouncing Stoecker. In *Stoecker's Falsified Christianity* he accused the Court Preacher of unchristian complicity in the current persecution of the Jews, and called upon the Church to shed 'tears of honest repentance' in an endeavour to wipe out the stains of anti-Jewish propaganda. In his *Christian Voice on the Jewish Question* he suggested that it was not the Jews who needed to be reformed but the Church herself. Nothing less than an officially organised Day of Repentance for all Christians was required to efface Stoecker's 'barbarous dishonour' to Christianity. It was a profane battle that was being waged with unspiritual weapons, a violently raging crusade that could well end in a blood-bath.[16]

The Church officially was uneasy, but deemed it to be prudent to keep silent, though a motion put to the Berlin District Synod recommending that Stoecker should be given a brotherly admonition to refrain from his anti-Jewish agitation, as unbefitting to his office as an evangelical clergyman, was only defeated by a narrow majority.[17] The expediency of doing nothing to risk stirring up popular passion still further was obviously a more important consideration than the public presentation of the Jewish Question as a deep-seated biblical and theological issue. In 1895 the Prussian Supreme Church Council, obviously with Stoecker very much in mind, warned against the participation of the clergy in party politics and their appearance at controversial social and political meetings. There was no divine sanction, it was declared, for the Church to attempt to be arbitrator in secular matters.[18]

On the other hand, Stoecker won a large measure of enthusiastic support. 'Not only salvoes but canonades of applause'[19] greeted his repeated eloquence, and he was hailed in certain quarters as the 'Second Luther'.[20] The petit bourgeoisie, in particular, responded fanatically, proving how much resentful feeling towards the Jews was dormant, felt but unformulated, ready to be stirred into motion by adroit manipulation. The Berlin Movement, as it came to be known, excited interest in various other parts of the Reich. Renewed impetus was given abroad to anti-semitic activity, and especially in France, Austria, and Hungary. Stoecker was uncomfortably involved in the presentation to Bismarck in 1881 of an Anti-semitic Petition, bearing more than 250,000 signatures, which urged the preservation of the German people from intolerable alien domination and called for the limitation of Jewish rights to full citizenship, which, incidentally, had only been completely realised in 1869. Restriction was demanded upon the immigration of foreign Jews, and it was recommended that Jews should be excluded from high government office and from most educational posts. Stoecker signed, though with great misgivings, and a considerable number of pastors followed suit.[21]

Stoecker and his Christian-social party flirted for a time with the radical anti-semites, but found co-operation with them increasingly distasteful and impossible, especially considering their highly critical attitude to Christianity itself. His influence with the Conservative Party was powerful enough to ensure that its revised Tivoli Programme of 1892 included an anti-Jewish paragraph 'We oppose the many-sided thrustful and disintegrating Jewish influence upon our national life. We desire to have a Christian Government for our Christian people and Christian teachers for our Christian pupils.' Stoecker was a prime mover in the rejection of an additional modifying clause—'We repudiate the excesses of anti-semitism.'[22] The Tivoli Programme with this stricture upon the Jews remained in force right up to the outbreak of the First World War.

In a letter written in December 1880 to Kaiser Wilhelm I Stoecker asserted that in all his anti-semitic utterances he was not attacking the Jews as such, but only 'the frivolous, godless, usurious, and deceitful' element among them that was in truth the misfortune of the German People.[23] These Jews had, he claimed, lost touch with the God of their Fathers, and had sold themselves completely to the worship of mammon, preferring to live in Jerusalem Street—a thoroughfare in Berlin largely populated by Jews—rather than in the streets of Jerusalem. Their brash and immodest determination at all costs to assimilate themselves into the German Community, and to exercise a corrupt influence upon German life and culture, constituted a real danger for the German people which it was urgent to recognise and combat. By means of their wide control of Press and Literature and in their claim to be advancing the cause of progress and emancipation they had no compunction in dragging through the mud so much that was sacred to the Christian. Where there was smut and immorality, there would be found the Jew. There was ever a danger of public opinion in Germany being completely controlled by the Jews.

Dietrich von Oertzen, Adolf Stoecker's biographer, writing in 1910, freely admitted that the radical racial anti-semites of that time would not have managed to make the impact that they did, had not Stoecker prepared the way.[24] This does not, however, mean that Stoecker himself should be regarded as having been racial in his outlook. He insisted that the Jewish Question was for him first and foremost a social and ethical issue, and that he was engaging in conflict with the Jews out of genuine and earnest concern for the welfare of both the German people and the Evangelical Church. Influential emancipated Jews whom he chose to describe as 'the new aristocracy' were in his eyes responsible for the present social disorders. Worshippers of mammon in impudent transgression of divine and human rights, they were at the same time highly iniquitous instigators of revolution, cashing in on the stirring up of popular agitation. The combating of the error of liberal and cosmopolitan Jewish emancipation was fundamental to Stoecker's anti-semitic utterances. He let his imagination run on the lines of an international Jewish conspiracy, and was convinced of the peril on grounds of misconceived humanity of overlooking the evil and corrupting aspect of Jewish influence. He insisted that he was not actuated by hatred or envy or desire for revenge, nor given to intolerance, insult or abuse. Rather, he professed to desire to solve the problem, if possible, in an orderly and peaceful fashion. His fight was not directed against the individual Jew but against the obnoxious Jewish system and on behalf of the sacred cause of the national and religious life of the German people. It was just because hatred for the Jews that was inimical to the Christian Gospel was beginning to flare up in Germany, and that there was grave danger of an ultimate catastrophe, that he felt impelled to speak out in time to prevent violence, brutality and bloodshed. Disaster would be inevitable, if Israel did not surrender its desire and intention to dominate Germany. He professed on occasions to be reluctant to advocate legislation, but still he could not stand by and condone the corruption of German schools and universities, the immoderate preponderance of Jewish influence in the administration of justice and the altogether disproportionate Jewish influence in economics and politics. He therefore felt bound to dispute on principle whether Jews should have equal franchise or occupy government posts, sit in Parliament or teach in German schools.[25]

Despite his insistence that he was not attacking the Jews for their religious convictions, and that he had a real regard for them as the People of the Prophets and Apostles from whom the Redeemer had emerged, he did not hesitate in one of his speeches to dismiss with disdain both Jewish Orthodoxy and reformed liberal Judaism as bankrupt and with no true message for the present time.[26] In a purple passage in another speech, much favoured subsequently for quotation, he referred to the divinely decreed Jewish fate of being obliged to roam restlessly about in the world and to have to suffer to the end of time because of failure to recognise and accept salvation. 'When the Jews', he announced, 'crucified Christ, they crucified themselves, the Revelation given through them and their History.'[27] They would never find rest, till they had become converted. His vision was that of the German people giving proof of being a truly Christian people and setting in motion a 'mighty and irresistible mission to both the orthodox and the modern Jews'.[28] His concern for the soul of his people had been a prime cause in leading him to participate in the anti-semitic movement. The fight against *Judentum* was a fight for *Deutschtum*.[29]

In his patriotic fervour—and Germanic idealism certainly played a considerable part in the forming of his point of view—he was strongly convinced that the German people could be re-garded as the 'people of God' in the Old Testament sense. It was the crime of the Jews in Germany to be contriving to destroy the 'Christian Volk-consciousness'. As an alien people on German territory they could never be at one with their German fellow-citizens except by being converted to Christianity. Having sin-cerely asked for and accepted baptism, having been admitted into the German religious community and having given proof of Christian behaviour, the campaign against them would be at an end. It has been claimed with some justification that Stoecker's vision of the conversion of Israel was conceived from the stand-point of Germanic ideology rather than that of the pure Gospel, its aim being the incorporation of Christian Jews within the Chris-tian-German people.[30]

Granted that Stoecker warmly desired the incorporation of the Jews, after conversion, into the German Volk Community, and that his approach was seriously intended to be Christian in contrast to the fanatical and vulgarly derisive racial attitude of his day, he cannot but be accused as an accredited preacher of the Gospel of raising a political battle-cry and of making political capital out of what ought to have been for him predominantly a religious issue. In his exuberance as an agitator he had but an imperfect control over his language, as is manifest in one purple passage in which he referred to Jewry as 'alien drops of blood in our people's Body' and as 'nothing else than a pernicious influence' and insisted that the false leaven that had so infectiously permeated the entire German *Volksgeist* had to be eradicated, lest the people die of it.[31] An outburst such as this certainly provided in due time grist to the Nazi mill, and lent credence to the claim that the anti-semitism of the Third Reich was indeed 'positively Christian'. It is scarcely surprising that a subsequent apologist for Stoecker felt justified in 1936 in giving his pamphlet the title of 'Adolf Stoecker—Prophet of the Third Reich'[32] and in agreeing that there was 'deep truth' in the Nazi claim that Stoecker was the forerunner of Hitler.[33]

Stoecker's influence has been assessed in widely differing terms. There have been those who have sought to play down the significance of his anti-semitism, describing it as little more than a passing episode or as an error of judgement understandable in his day and age. One writer has gone so far as to claim him to have been an adversary of racial anti-semitism, and another has felt bound to commend him for being motivated by a feeling of Christian responsibility for the avoidance of what he judged to be a threatened future catastrophe. His close friend and contemporary, the greatly revered Friedrich Bodelschwingh, insisted that Stoecker whom he regarded as 'a chosen vessel of God for the rescuing of our People from the spell of their godless seducers' was not an enemy of the Jews. In fact the Jews had had few such genuine friends as he. Such friendship was evident in the open and frank way in which he had told them the truth courageously and earnestly, and when necessary, with holy wrath, seeking to turn them from their evil ways and prevent them from injuring others.[34] In quite the other direction, it has been suggested that Stoecker appeared to be only one step removed from Adolf Hitler, and a recent critic has gone so far as to regard Stoecker as the evil genius who was responsible for 'making large sections of the Christian bourgeoisie ripe for the acceptance of the Nazi brand of anti-semitism, thus helping to prepare the path of horror which on the foundation of alleged "positive Christianity" led all the way to Theresienstadt and Auschwitz'.[35]

Johann von Leers in his assessment of the development of German anti-semitism in Theodor Fritsch's notorious *Handbuch der Judenfrage*, while conceding that Stoecker was 'no anti-semite in the usual sense of the word' claimed that he was 'nevertheless the father of German anti-semitism'.[36] This is a judgement with which it would be difficult not to agree, for Stoecker more than anyone else ensured that the Jewish problem would become and remain a passionate issue. He was as responsible as any one in bringing the whole question into the political arena. He presented his case in terms and in a manner which were readily appreciated by the less intellectual. He himself boasted that he had converted the Jewish Question from a matter of literary interest into a subject for debate in public meetings and thereby encouraged its political treatment. That so devout and orthodox a churchman, and one who was a Court Preacher into the bargain, should campaign against the Jews assisted enormously in making the cause respectable and in lending persuasion to the idea that one could without a bad conscience be a Christian and an anti-semite at one and the same time, and believe, as Stoecker himself undoubtedly did, that as a Christian one was fulfilling a moral obligation, when one went into battle upon this particular issue. Without wishing it or intending it, he had certainly undermined the future religious and ethical strength of resistance on the part of Protestant Christians to the anti-Jewish battle-cries and acts of violence produced by the radical anti-semites and the Nazis.[37]

Stoecker cannot but be accused of having helped to prepare the ground for the blossoming of radical racial anti-semitism by directing his challenging attack against Jewry (*Judentum*) as an abstract collective entity[38] rather than against the Jews as individuals, by lending on occasions weight to the suspicion that there was indeed an international Jewish conspiracy (his participation at the Anti-semitic Congress in Dresden in 1882 was a case in point), by such close identification of volkish patriotism and anti-Jewish feeling, and by at any rate indirectly encouraging the view that the Jews were a cancerous growth in the national body[39] and a ready scapegoat for what was wrong socially, economically and nationally. Stoecker must at times have been only too well aware that he had attracted to his banner, and was treating as allies, racially-minded fanatics who had quite other aims than that of making Germany thoroughly Christian. It was akin to pathetic naïvety when he proclaimed that he was 'personally assured that the whole stream of this anti-Jewish movement will ultimately flow in one channel in a broad, deep bed, and carry us into the ocean of Christian Weltanschauung and German feeling'.[40] A fellow-member of Parliament once remarked that at the end of his speeches Stoecker invariably arrived at a quite mild conclusion, but previous to his final passage one was brought to believe that he really demanded the annihilation of the Jews. Unfortunately, however, other people were encouraged to draw altogether more radical conclusions from what he had been previously saying with such aggressive fervour.[41]

While Stoecker's pronouncements had their most immediate effect upon the lower middle class, the attack upon the Jews by his contemporary, Heinrich von Treitschke, appealed rather to the intellectuals. Treitschke became renowned for his bold and incisive comments upon contemporary issues in the celebrated *Prussian Annuals* of which he was editor for a period. As professor of History and Political Science at the universities of Leipzig, Freiburg, Heidelberg and, finally, Berlin he attained a popularity with an influence upon his students which was quite exceptional.[42] They were spellbound by the power of his eloquence, the stirring pathos of his rhetoric and his unique ability to bring history to life spiced with a plentiful supply of pungent political asides. A free-thinker from an early age and much influenced by Hegel, he subscribed whole-heartedly to the ideal of the German Christian Volk State and was a tireless advocate of national unity on spiritual as much as upon political, economic, and strategic grounds.

In the late 1870s Treitschke got caught up in the current wave of anti-semitism. Hitherto his attitude to the Jews had been largely one of condescending tolerance. He was not in sympathy with Stoecker, and found the crudity and vulgarity of much that was currently being written against the Jews most distasteful. He had opposed an anti-Jewish discrimination that made it hard for them to acquire the joyful feeling of German national pride.[43] But now he became convinced that the Jews, through their dubious involvement in economic and cultural activities and through their inclination to identify themselves with the cosmopolitan liberalism of which he was a sworn enemy, were proving a threat to the nation's unity and strength. He was also perturbed that they were 'forming a clan of their own, and would exercise a negative, dissolving influence'.[44] Both the lecture room and the Annuals were to hand for the propagation of anti-semitism, and as ever his fervour and his eloquence did not allow him to do things by halves. 'In the classroom he indulged uninhibitedly in much crude ridicule of German and East European Jewry, and his eagerness for acclaim tempted him with increased frequency into sly allusions and open attacks on 'hook-nosed' and 'thin-voiced' fellow-citizens. Invariably he was greeted with frenetic applause: he was the hero again valiantly braving a deadly threat, and his listeners felt themselves spiritually uplifted by his courageous action.'[45] It is not difficult to imagine the round of applause from his students that must have greeted a remark such as, 'Whenever he finds his life sullied by the filth of Judaism, the German must turn from it, and learn to speak the truth boldly about it.'[46]

His famous anti-semitic article appeared in the Annuals on 15 November 1879.[47] While declaring himself not to be in sympathy with the form that the contemporary impassioned anti-Jewish movement was taking, he declined to dismiss it as merely an expression of coarse, rabble-rousing vulgarity and of jealousy of economic enterprise. 'Mob instinct', he wrote, 'has in point of fact correctly recognised the grave danger and the critical injury to the new expression of German life, it is no empty figure of speech, when one talks today of a Jewish problem in Germany.'[48] His intense and injured German national feeling found expression in the complaint that 'everyone is allowed to say without reserve the hardest things about the national failings of Germans, Frenchmen and all other peoples; anyone, however, who might venture to speak fairly and reasonably about an undeniable weakness in the Jewish character would straightaway be stigmatised by almost the whole of the press as a barbarian and a religious persecutor'.[49] He averred that he was only seeking to make a plain demand upon his Hebrew fellow-citizens that they should become Germans, and feel themselves to be simply and completely German.[50] This was, however, he regretted not happening in certain Jewish circles in which a presumptuous spirit damaging to German national existence was most evident. It was to be found among scholars who treated Christianity as the arch-enemy and exhibited a deadly hatred towards what was noblest in the Germanic tradition. It was to be discovered in the dishonest and grossly materialistic behaviour of a number of semitic businessmen which was having a suffocating effect upon the natural, unspoilt and joyous attitude of Germans to their work. In thousands of villages the Jewish usurer was contriving to buy out his German neighbour. Most dangerous of all was the Jewish preponderance in the daily press with the result that public opinion in many German cities was being fashioned by Jewish pens. Jewish emancipation had scarcely been achieved before the demand was being made for literal parity in just everything, overlooking the fact that the Germans were still a Christian people and the Jews a mere minority, and resulting, for instance, in a demand that in schools attended by both Christian and Jewish pupils Christian pictures should be removed and the observance of the sabbath introduced. The present noisy anti-Jewish agitation Treitschke held to be a natural reaction against the inroads of an alien element within the German community. The Jewish problem would never, he declared, be completely solved, but the antagonism could be notably diminished, if only the Jews who were so vocal themselves about tolerance would in their turn become genuinely tolerant and be prepared to show some regard for the faith, customs and feelings of the German people.

There were two sentences in this aggrieved outpouring which have acquired lasting fame, and have been endlessly quoted:

> Year after year over our Eastern frontier, from the inexhaustible Polish cradle there come, forcing their way in, a host of pushful, trouser-selling youths whose children and children's children are one day to dominate Germany's stock-exchanges and newspapers; the invasion increases visibly, and ever more serious becomes the problem as to how we can ever merge their alien Volkstum with ours.[51] . . . Right into the most highly educated circles among men who would reject with horror any thought of ecclesiastical intolerance or national arrogance, there sounds forth, as if from one mouth the cry, 'The Jews are our misfortune'.[52]

This bombshell occasioned a whole year of intensive academic strife. Treitschke seemed genuinely surprised at the furore which his utterance had created, and was deeply pained at being dubbed an anti-semite which he obviously did not regard himself as being. Both his opponents and his defenders, however, had no doubts on that score. It was a shock to the intelligent public that anti-semitism had won a foothold in Berlin University, and that anti-Jewish propaganda was now being disseminated from so distinguished a professorial chair as well as from the pulpit and the political platform. Treitschke was brought to task and answered almost entirely by Jews, both baptised and unbaptised. He had, however, no more formidable and indignant an adversary to encounter than Theodor Mommsen[53] a Gentile, who had won international renown for his History of Rome, and who incidentally also earned lasting notoriety for his unfortunate reference to the Jews as being 'an element of national decomposition',[54] a phrase which was subsequently to be quite irresponsibly torn from its context and misused. Mommsen bitterly accused Treitschke of having been responsible, where the Jewish issue was concerned, for removing the safety valve, and allowing the waves to break in and stir up the scum. He who stood deservedly high, both politically and morally, in the estimation of so many of his fellow-Germans had by his injudicious remarks made anti-Jewish feeling respectable. His alarming description of Jewish mass-immigration was a pure invention. If there were unwelcome and unscrupulous Jews in their midst, as indeed there were, were there not also highly undesirable and anti-social Germans about the place as well? Their Jewish fellow-citizens, taken as a whole, were already Germans, and as good Germans as either of them were. Nevertheless, every Jew of German nationality could do no other than conclude from his article that he was to be regarded as a second-class citizen.

Treitschke with doubtful wisdom felt bound to reply to his critics. In a further contribution to the Annuals a month later[55] he did nothing to ease matters by a disparaging reference to the Jews who had prospered in the big cities, and were therefore able to provide for their children a better education than the mass of Christians could afford. He followed this by the un-called for remark that the most beautiful and magnificent place of worship in Berlin was not a church, but a synagogue; he insisted that an influential section of Jewry was abusing the privilege of emancipation by striving to remain a nation alongside the Germans, this was a claim to which every German who held his Christianity and his Volkstum sacred could do no other than counter with a blunt 'Never'. Emigration was the only answer to those whose racial presumption defied assimilation.

Only another month elapsed before Treitschke was again on the war-path,[56] this time complaining of the arrogant objection of the authorities of a certain synagogue to the religious instruction that was being given in a local Catholic elementary school (which a small minority of Jewish pupils were attending) on the grounds that Jewish responsibility for the crucifixion of Jesus, though innocent, was being taught in the light of the evidence of the New Testament. In this further article he expressed his anxiety lest centuries of Germanic civilisation should be replaced by a period of bastard German-Jewish culture. The neo-Jewish *Geist*, if allowed independence to oppose the German *Geist* could only lead the German people astray. There could be no denial that the Germans were a Christian people, and anyone who presumed to suggest that Judaism could be reckoned to be German in the same sense as Christianity offended against the grandeur of German history. It was no valid argument to quote from the New Testament to the effect that 'Salvation is of the Jews', for that was said before the rejection and crucifixion of Christ. It was even more stupid than a Protestant declaring that salvation comes from Rome. This article concluded on a specifically religious note: 'In frivolous, unbelieving Jewish circles the opinion is firmly held that the great majority of educated Germans have finally and long ago broken with Christianity. The time will come, and maybe is close at hand, when necessity will teach us once again to pray, and when humble piety will again take its rightful place alongside pride of learning. Eventually every difficult social question leads the earnest spectator back to religion. The German Jewish Question will not come to rest, the relationship between Jews and Christians will not find a genuinely peaceful solution, until our Hebrew fellow-citizens have become convinced by our attitude that we are a Christian people, and desire to remain one'.[57]

Treitschke's anti-semitism was national not racial, in character, and only incidentally religious.[58] He complained most bitterly of the Jews who sought to promote 'a homeless world citizenship' and did 'all in their power to undo our People's national pride and their delight in the Fatherland. This element of Jewry is hostile to everything that is essentially German.'[59] He certainly played his part in bringing anti-semitism into greater prominence, though he would not have owned to be an anti-semite at all. His chief contribution was the spreading of the type of coarse, brassy, aggressive national pride which did so much to fertilise the German brand of anti-semitism. Desire to encourage hatred of and contempt for the Jews collectively was foreign to his nature and he was quite prepared to make a generous distinction between good and bad Jews. The premises of his arguments abounded with exceptions, but he could not resist generalising in his conclusions, for which he but seldom furnished any real proof and which were obviously controlled by volkish sentiments. In every volume of his magnum opus *The History of Germany in the Nineteenth Century* is to be discovered harsh and largely unfounded invective against the Jews; this has led Alexander Bein to suggest that the famous work contributed more to the spread of anti-semitism than did the avowedly radical anti-semitic literature.[60]

It is tragic indeed that this gifted historian and political thinker and brilliant man of letters should have been fated to have been known to posterity above all as the author of the slogan, 'The Jews are our misfortune' which came to be quoted on innumerable occasions by a succession of Jew-haters, and appeared as motto in monster lettering in issue after issue of that vile Nazi publication *Der Stürmer*.

The anti-semitism of Stoecker and Treitschke inspired the foundation in January 1881 of the 'Union of German Students' (*Verein deutscher Studenten*). In March of that year Stoecker addressed an enthusiastic gathering of the union on the theme of the Awakening of German Youth, and recommended the practice of what we now term 'Apartheid'. Branches of the Union were swiftly established in many of the universities. Eight hundred members of the Union met together in August on the Kyffhäuser mountain, and, in almost total disregard of the fact that they had precious little direct contact with individual Jews, issued a patriotic proclamation worthy of their distinguished mentors. 'The present threat is not from an external foe; the urgent need is the espousal of what is characteristically German, German customs, German loyalty and German faith. The sinister powers of blatant self-seeking and of cosmopolitan lack of love for the Fatherland, depravity and dechristianisation are undermining the time-honoured and sure foundations of our Volkstum.'[61] Such declaration of war upon all that was non-German left no doubt as to who were to be regarded as the real villains of the piece. Nothing less was called for than the absolute rejection of Jewish influence in German national life. Theological students were fully represented in the Union, destined to become sowers of anti-semitism in their future parishes and instigators of anti-Jewish feeling within the Church as a whole during the ensuing decades.[62]

In 1893 the Society for the Prevention of Anti-semitism discussed the problem of anti-semitic propaganda on the part of the Protestant clergy. It was obvious that it was the generation of pastors who had been at the university in the 'eighties and had joined the Union who gave most cause for anxiety. 'It is deeply to be regretted', the Society's statement ran, 'because it is no gain for the clerical profession, when these young pastors exchange the altar for the popular tribune, and win by their agitation against the Jews the applause which many of them perhaps would have failed to gain in their normal pastoral activities. We have to protest most emphatically against the dishonouring of the clerical profession by politically immature clergy. . . . Instead of a religion of love they preach one of hatred, and widen the gulf betwixt Christianity and Judaism instead of attempting to bridge it. How can the Jews respect and learn to love a religion, when they behold in its leading representatives only hatred and excess of hatred ?'[63] It can well be imagined what an unhappy influence such Jew-baiting pastors must have had upon simple-minded country congregations.

The Union of German Students was only one of a number of university organisations that at the end of the nineteenth century upheld the cause of patriotic anti-semitism. Most intolerant of all was the Academic League of Gymnasts, followed closely by a Student Assembly which in 1896 approved a motion that only students of German descent could belong to it, and that Jewish citizens of the Reich were not to be regarded as Germans.[64] A very considerable number of German students certainly carried over into their professional careers much that they had so eagerly devoured while at the university. This particularly applied to school teachers who were not above encouraging their pupils in the art of Jew-baiting.

Heinrich Class, president of the chauvinistic early twentieth-century Pan-German Association which, in promoting a united racial and cultural Germanic spirit had such an appeal to the educated bourgeoisie, attributed his anti-semitic convictions to the influence of Treitschke. 'His statement that the Jews are our misfortune', he wrote in his autobiography, 'became a flesh and blood reality to me as a 20-year-old, and has determined an essential part of my late political work. . . . We youngsters were simply and solely national; we did not want to know anything about tolerance, if it meant indulgence to the enemies of the Volk and the State. We refused to be humanitarian in every liberal sense of that term, because our own people would thereby be inevitably the sufferers.'[65]

Alongside Stoecker and Treitschke, Paul de Lagarde was regarded with veneration by the Union of German Students, as indeed he was by many another volkish group. A brilliant though erratic and rancorous scholar and philologist, Lagarde became convinced in the 1850s that without a dynamic spiritual revival the future of Germany was indeed bleak, and that the Protestant Church in which he had been nurtured was quite incapable of bringing it about. He felt the urge to fulfil the role of prophet and promoter of a revitalised new Germany; a Germany that would really find its soul. To this end a new national religion was essential, a 'cleansed version of Christianity . . . appropriate for the German character',[66] and one in which everything Jewish had been eliminated along with what he contemptuously dismissed as insipid, stale, and falsely conceived Protestant dogmas. He declared himself unable to find anything creative in the Reformation, and dismissed 'Justification by Faith' and absolute reliance upon scriptural authority as mere polemical devices against the Roman Church.[67] In this national religion full scope would be allowed for the appreciation of the creative activity of God in the individual and the nation alike, ('God is not yet finished with his Revelation') and encouragement given to the recognition that the German Volk was endowed with a more vital spiritual revelation than other peoples. In contrast to traditional Christianity, anchored in the past, and dominated by Jewish insistence upon that which had taken place once and for all, the new Germanic faith would seek to discover the object of its religious sentiments in that which was a present reality and in that which was ever happening anew. Place would be found for the historical Jesus, acknowledged to have been 'genius' in his direct perception of eternal truth,[68] a free, pure human Personality, disassociated from all connection with Judaism, not the Christ of Jewish promise, the Child of God, not the only begotten Son.[69] The significance of His Gospel-message would be appreciated, once its almost immediate corruption by the Jew Paul, and its perversion by so-called 'Christianity' had been acknowledged. Every German, with the right will, could increasingly attain to the discovery of the Gospel as incarnate in himself.[70] The Kingdom of God was to be realised in sanctified national community-life, for 'to carry out the great tasks of the Fatherland was to be about the Father's business'.[71]

Various articles in which Lagarde developed his theme were brought together and published in 1878 as the *Deutsche Schriften* and thereafter regularly reprinted to satisfy popular demand, being described as 'a foundation stone in the future edifice of German glory', their author being 'the seer of our national culture'.[72] Their appeal was tremendous to those who rejected liberalism, were dissatisfied with prevailing secularism and materialism, doubted the chances of survival of the official church, its dogmas and its institutions, and yearned for a religious sanction for their volkish aspirations. Lagarde's influence continued right into the twentieth century, and helped to inspire the effort in both the Weimar and the Nazi periods to 'convert Christianity into a polemical, anti-semitic, nationalistic faith and organisation that would supplant the old and decadent tenets of a perverted and universal Christianity'.[73]

It would have been most surprising, had not Lagarde developed a progressively contemptuous and aggressive attitude towards the Jews. His anti-semitism was not, however, racial. Though he regarded the presence of the Jews whom he scornfully described as 'asiatic pagans' as being a serious misfortune to all European nations, their offence lay for him not in their blood, but in their state of mind (*Gemut*). They comprised a nation within a nation, and constituted a constant threat to national unity and well-being.[74] Modern Jewish religion which had, in his view, lost all connection with that of the ancient Hebrews whom he professed to admire, was sterile and bereft of spiritual content, seeking to substitute materialistic ideas for living faith. In the German setting the Jews constituted a grave obstacle to the attainment of volkish regeneration. Their very presence was indeed a formidable

survival of the fittest, the racial theories of Artur de Gobineau, and Wagner-inspired emotional and mystical Germanism, he contrived to impart both intellectual respectability and spiritual depth to the racial outlook. Most attractive of all, perhaps, was his inflexible optimism, as he foretold imminent victory and 'a new splendid, light-filled future' for the Germanic race. In his view eternal life or death struggle was inevitable between the Aryan race—and that meant in particular the Germanic—symbolically representing God and responsible for every important cultural development, and the Jewish race equally symbolically representing the Devil, incapable of any truly creative activity and given over to materialistic interests.[81] The Jews, at pains to uphold the purity of their own stock (though they had become definitely bastardised through the admixture of aboriginal racial elements) had invaded the Western world as an alien people, and were out to do all they could to defile the purity of Aryan blood. The end-product was a 'herd of pseudo-hebraic half-breeds—a people beyond all doubt physically, spiritually and morally degenerate'.[82] They had to be taught that the laws of nature were holy laws. Devoid of metaphysical grace, captive to a soulless law, and out to dominate, they had to be fought with deadly seriousness. Chamberlain had also a passionate desire to dispose of the conception of the Jewish people as a religious people *par excellence*. According to him they had not been creative in the sphere of religion, because they had had their origin in the emptiness and desolation of the wilderness and were consequently poor in imagination.[83]

Jesus, in whom Chamberlain professed wholeheartedly to believe, had to be shown to belong to the Germanic and not the Jewish people. Whoever wished to see the revelation of Christ had to tear 'the darkest of veils from his eyes'. The advent of Jesus was not the perfecting of Jewish religion but its negation.[84] 'The probability that Christ was no Jew, that He had not a drop of genuinely Jewish blood in his veins was so great, that it was almost equivalent to a certainty.'[85] The presentation of Jesus as a true Aryan Galilean, and the acceptance of that element of His recorded teaching that revealed his Aryan perceptions, and the rejection of that which bore the mark of Jewish influence and emendation, led inevitably to the proposition that the norm for the faith of a German Christian Protestant was the Aryan religious

BOD

outlook.[86] St. Paul was to be regarded as not having been a racially
pure Jew.[87] 'In his breast lodged two souls',[88] a Jewish and a non-
Jewish. Indeed 'in his deepest inner nature, in his view of the
importance of religion in the life of man',[89] he could be described
as anti-Jewish. His thoroughly Aryan vein of religious mysticism,
as opposed to other aspects of his religious outlook that formed the
basis of future intolerantly dogmatic Christianity, could be warmly
acknowledged.

Luther, whose achievement of separation from Rome could be
hailed as 'the turning-point in the history of the world',[90] was
significant as a 'political hero'[91] with a fervent love for the Fatherland. The 'mighty impulse that emanated from him drove men
away from ecclesiastical religion'.[92] Luther's role as evangelical
preacher of Sola Scriptura and of Justification by Faith could be
contemptuously dismissed as a sign of his weakness as a theologian.
'No dogmatic subtleties filled his brain. They were of secondary
moment, first came the nation, "For my Germans I was born.
Them will I serve."'[93] The Reformation was to be 'regarded not
as a purely ecclesiastical affair, but as a revolt of our whole nature
against alien rule, of the Germanic soul against un-Germanic
spiritual tyranny'.[94] This revolt was still continuing.

The 'Foundations' so excited and enchanted Emperor Wilhelm
that he insisted upon reading aloud extracts from it to the Empress
and her ladies-in-waiting, and then discussing them section by
section.[95] He also promptly invited the author to be his personal
guest, assuring him subsequently that it 'was God who sent your
book to the German People, and you personally to me'.[96] In due
course a popular edition was published, and a presentation-copy
placed in all Prussian school libraries.

Chamberlain's preaching of Aryan splendour and superiority
and of Jewish degeneracy and inferiority was by no means
repugnant to many patriotic and orthodox Christians. They
appreciated his unfolding of the historical association between
the German way of life and Christianity. They welcomed both
his emphasis upon the spiritual significance of Race and the
absence in his writings of vulgar and violent anti-semitic invective. Indeed, he saw fit to register a protest against 'the perfectly
ridiculous and revolting tendency to make the Jew a general scapegoat for all the vices of our time', and added, 'In reality the
"Jewish peril" lies much deeper; the Jew is not responsible for

it; we have given rise to it ourselves, and must overcome it ourselves.'[97] If startled and mystified by some of his contentions, they were reassured by the knowledge that their author was an avowed and devout believer in Jesus Christ. In one of his published letters Chamberlain wrote: 'I know that the sun is in the Heavens; more sure and certain and meaningful, however, is my faith in Jesus Christ as my Saviour.'[98] In 1936 in *Junge Kirche*, the periodical of the Confessional Church, the very suggestion that Chamberlain was a crown witness in the Nazi case against the Church was indignantly contested with the insistence that he was outstanding among the ardent confessors of Jesus Christ at the turn of the century. A letter of his to the Emperor was quoted, in which he had declared: 'I believe in Jesus Christ. . . . That God exists, and what God is, I know through Christ alone. . . . The enemies of Christ are my enemies.'[99] Thanks initially to Chamberlain, the racial viewpoint, magnifying the noble Aryan and disparaging the ignoble Jew, could be regarded as respectable, cultured and Christian, and what was subsequently to be widely known as *artgemässes Christentum* (Christianity in tune with the Germanic character) came to have such a vogue. It is not difficult to imagine the favourable reaction to the following glowing passage in the 'Foundations': 'We need to tear away the foreign rags and tatters that still hang upon our Christianity as the trappings of slavish hypocrisy: we need the creative power to construct out of the words and the spectacle of the Crucified Son of Man a perfect religion fitting the truth of our nature, our capacities, and our present culture—a religion so directly convincing, so enchantingly beautiful, so present, so plastic, so eternally true, and yet so new, that we must give ourselves to it as a maid to her lover, without questioning, happy, enraptured, a religion so exactly suited to our highly gifted but delicate, easily injured, peculiar Teutonic nature, that it shall have the power to master our inmost souls.'[100]

Despite Chamberlain's influence and the propagation of racial and anti-Jewish ideas within nationalistic organisations such as the Association of Landowners (*Bund der Landwirte*) and the Pan-German League (*Alldeutscher Verband*) it appeared in the opening years of the new century as if anti-semitism had lost much of its impetus. Thanks to growing German imperialism, aggressive volkish feeling was finding its outlet in foreign affairs rather than in domestic issues. The official Evangelical Church Annual of 1905 reported that in most districts where anti-semitism had hitherto been markedly expanding, there were now signs of a sharp decline.[101] The Social Democrats expressed their confidence that 'anti-semitism and the classes supporting it were on the way out', and their leader, Bebel, felt able to write optimistically in 1906 that it 'had no prospect of ever exerting a decisive influence on German politics'.[102] By 1910 it apparently seemed as if the full assimilation of the Jews would only be a question of time.

Many of the protestant clergy were nevertheless still acutely troubled by the German-Jewish quandary. An eloquent example of such tension is afforded by the following testimony of Superintendent Richard Bieling of Soldin who had actually been for a number of years a prominent champion of missionary endeavour among the Jews. He wrote in 1913: 'Am I able to love the Jew? Certainly not on the natural plane! All too much separates me from him. His characteristic ways are so different from mine. He has another spirit. Not that his manner is to be deemed worse than mine, for I am far from being racially arrogant, but it is different. It is in stark contrast to my sentiments as a German. The Jewish disposition has an ever-increasing influence upon the ways of thinking and the manners of my people, and I regard this as perilous to German existence. For a German to give up his peculiar characteristics is tantamount to the abandonment of his express ego, and that is the beginning of the end for individual and nation alike. In whatever way I consider the situation I am aware of a gulf separating me from the Jew, and no argument on rational grounds will level it. . . . As a human being the Jew remains a Jew, and I am German. There is honestly no way of getting over this. If I am to love the Jew, then I must have such love bestowed upon me. There is only one person who can give me this, and it is Jesus. . . . In the love of Jesus I have learnt to love the Jew, and I think I will never lose that love.'[103]

Declaration of war in 1914 was greeted by frenzied outbursts of patriotic enthusiasm: the expression of a highly emotional communal experience of being one united Volk in defence of the Fatherland. The Evangelical Church shared wholeheartedly in such national fervour. Many a pastor could be found favouring the choice of bellicose and vengeful Old Testament passages as texts and substituting a patriotic harangue for the sober and admonitory preaching of the Scriptural Word. Chauvinistic insistences that the Germans were verily God's elect people, battling for an entirely sacred cause, sounded from evangelical pulpits up and down the country. A military chaplain excelled himself by declaring that 'God's Holy Spirit is enkindled in us anew, the spirit of fervent faith and of devotion to the Fatherland knit together by the spirit of hatred'.[104] Luther, the quatercentenary of whose Act of Reformation was due for solemn celebration in 1917 was hailed as the supreme German national prophet and Fatherland-figure. 'Germany's Sword' was described as being 'hallowed by Luther'. *Ein Fester Burg* was translated into a war anthem.[105] The evangelical clergy who were ready, as and when required, to fill the role of propaganda agents for the military High Command urged the continuance of the battle to the very end. In the spring of 1918 the following words appeared in a leading Lutheran periodical—'What God has begun He takes pains to fulfil. He does nothing by halves. If England still possessed clear-sighted Christians, they would be bound to arise and cry out in alarm to their Government: "Enough! The Lord is on Germany's side!"'[106]

The great majority of the Jews in Germany were also full of enthusiasm in 1914. They felt able to welcome the outbreak of war as bringing about a new epoch of national solidarity in which they hoped to be fully embraced. It was a unique opportunity for them to make proof of their patriotism, and Jewish organisations were unanimous in calling for devoted service to the Fatherland. A Jewish chaplain to the Forces wrote: 'At time of war a spirit of comradeship without discrimination is the order of the day. We Jews cannot but rejoice at this; if only they will learn to know us Jews, they will also learn to understand and esteem us.'[107] Despite abundant evidence of Jewish valour and the proclamation of a general war-time truce (*Burgfriede*), it was not long before the flood of volkish feeling began to overflow into anti-semitic channels. The extreme Right had certainly not shed any of its anti-semitic fervour, and was intent upon torpedoing the 'spirit of 1914'. From the very outset radical anti-semites were at work spying out for any instances of Jewish weakness or dereliction of duty. The Church Annual of 1915 recorded the complaint that the Jews were not doing their share of essential productive work.[108] Already at that time insinuations were widespread that among the Jews, and true to their outlook and nature, were unscrupulous shirkers and profiteers and a dangerous subversive element (*Volksschädlinge*). Anti-semitic circles took delight in caricaturing the image of Jewish soldiers, contemptuously contrasting the flatfooted, shortwinded little Jew, shaking at the knees with anxiety, with the brave Germanic warrior.[109] In the trenches Jewish soldiers were reported as being given the cold shoulder by their German comrades-in-arms. No doubt the close physical contact in trench-life did accentuate differences. A Jewish combatant has described his growing awareness in the trenches that there was a gulf between Germans and Jews in feeling, thinking, and attitude to moral and intellectual issues coupled with a growing awareness that they were more closely related to their fellow-Jews on the enemy side than to most of their German fellow-fighters.[110] Ostensibly for the purpose of quashing rumours of Jewish shirking, a regrettable and insulting decision was taken in October 1916 to hold a military census of Jews on active service, in order to establish how many were really in the firing-line as opposed to being, as was being frequently suggested, in safe rear-posts. As the war dragged on, the inclination grew to make convenient use of the Jews as scapegoats and whipping-boys for the reverses of the war and the distress and the hardships on the home front. They were declared responsible, especially on account of their influence upon the Press, for the mounting despondency among the population as a whole and the decline in the national will to resist. This did not stop short of the absurd accusation that numbering merely half a million or so, they were set upon utilising the growing crisis to dominate the whole nation. Until the outbreak of war organised anti-semitism had been largely a lower middle class affair, but the war saw a radical change whereby the educated and propertied classes no longer disdained to resort to vulgar anti-semitic phraseology and proved prepared to join with the small man in making a political factor out of anti-semitism.[111] The Church Annual of 1917 claimed that there was clear evidence from the Jewish side of reinforced animosity against Christianity, and prophesied that, once the war was over, an earnest and perhaps passionate debate over the Jewish Question was to be expected.[112]

NOTES TO CHAPTER 1

1. It should at the outset be made quite plain that the expression 'anti-semitism' which will be appearing on almost every page is never once employed in the sense of opposition to *all* Semites. German anti-semites have never sought to attack the genuinely semitic Arabian peoples. They have in point of fact endeavoured to embrace them in their anti-Jewish front. It refers exclusively to aversion or hostility towards the Jews. Such anti-semitism is 'concerned with something altogether other than a problem of races. Here more profound, and if it be permitted to use the term, metaphysical matters are at stake' (Karl Kupisch in *Der ungekündigte Bund*, ed. Dietrich Goldschmidt und Heinz-Joachim Kraus, Stuttgart, 1962, p. 80). We have to take into account two quite different versions of so-called 'anti-semitism', the one based upon a diabolically crude racial and nihilistic foundation, the other built upon a sincere but misinterpreted scriptural conception of a disloyal and corrupt people accursed by divine decree. These two versions were of course by no means always apart. What would now be universally regarded as bogus and fantastic national socialist racial theories were presented as *Rassenkunde*, reputed to be scientifically verified racial findings, and readily accepted in many Christian circles as largely proven and part and parcel of the welcome and disciplined New Order. The Nazis in their turn were only too prepared to cite the authority of God, Christ and Luther in religious support of their philosophy of hatred. Nazis were found describing Jesus as the greatest anti-semite of all time.

2. George Mosse: *Die deutsche Rechte* in *Entscheidungsjahr 1932: zur Judenfrage in der Endphase der Weimarer Republik*, ed. Werner E. Mosse, Tübingen, 1965, p. 184.

3. 'Evangelical' is the obvious and only translation for '*evangelisch*'. 'Protestant' is a tempting rendering, but it will not serve, if only because the term is still normally and incorrectly used by us in a negative sense as 'anti-Catholic'. An initial word of explanation seems requisite, for 'evangelical' is still popularly understood by Anglicans at any rate to carry the sense of 'low' as opposed to 'high', 'personal' and 'individual' as contrasted with 'corporate' or 'fundamentalist' over against 'modernist'. '*Evangelisch*' is, of course, in the German designed to be contrasted with '*katholisch*', the Church 'under the Word' and true to the Confessions of Faith of the Reformation, as distinct from the Church subject to the authority of the Roman Papacy. It carries, however, the positive meaning of 'obedient to the authority of the Word of God as set forth in the Gospel'.

4. Otto Dibelius: *Rundbrief*, 3 April 1928 (Wiener Library, London).

5. In *Evangelisches Gemeindeblatt*, Nürnberg, 1926, quoted in Arndt Müller: *Geschichte der Juden in Nürnberg*, Nürnberg, 1968, p. 196.

6. Paul Althaus: *Kirche und Volkstum*. Gütersloh, 1928, pp. 33–4.
7. Quoted by Wolfgang Tilgner: *Judentum und Rassenfrage in deutschen Protestantismus* in *Rasse, Kirche und Humanum*, ed. Klaus-Martin Beckmann, Gütersloh, 1969, p. 306.
8. *Allgemeine Evangelisch-Lutherische Kirchenzeitung*, 1 February 1929. (Henceforward referred to as AELKZ.) Laible's 'justifiable anti-semitism' appears to have included the propagation of the fiction about the protocols of the Elders of Zion, to the truth and significance of which he time and again made reference in his editorials (Werner Jochmann: *Die Ausbreitung des Antisemitismus* in *Deutsches Judentum im Krieg und Revolution, 1916–1923*, Tübingen, 1971, p. 481.) The importance of the Protocols, which in Germany were believed by so many to furnish an authentic disclosure of a Jewish conspiracy for world domination, was that they appeared to substantiate the Jewish peril in a concrete and terrifying form. Thanks to the purported evidence of this secret document conflict with Jewry was accepted as a life and death struggle. A conservative monthly described in 1920 the plot as being to destroy Christianity and to establish the Mosaic-Talmudic faith as the religion of the world (Norman Cohn: *Warrant for Genocide. The Myth of the Jewish Conspiracy and the Protocols of the Elders of Zion*, Penguin Books, 1970, p. 150. Cohn provides a most authoritative account of the whole story of this amazing and devastating forgery).
9. 'Germandom' is to be found as an attempted rendering for *Deutschtum*, but it is clumsy and inexpressive of what is to be conveyed. 'Nation' or 'Nationdom' is equally unsatisfactory as a translation for *Volkstum*. Following the example of George Mosse Volkish will be used throughout for the equally untranslatable *Völkisch*—pertaining to the Volk. 'Folkic' favoured by some English and American writers just will not do, and has a 'pseudoarty-crafty' ring about it. '*Volk* is one of those perplexing German terms which connotes far more than its specific meaning. *Volk* is a much more comprehensive term than "people", for to German thinkers ever since the birth of German romanticism in the late eighteenth century *Volk* signified the union of a group of people with a transcendental "essence". Fused to man's innermost nature, it represented the source of his creativity, his depth of feeling, his individuality and his unity with other members of the *Volk*' (George Mosse: *The Crisis of German Ideology*, Weidenfeld and Nicolson, 1966, p. 4). In this present work *Volk* will sometimes be given the obvious rendering of 'People', but when it has a pronouncedly mystical reference, it will appropriately be left untranslated.
10. See Appendix 1. *Luther and the Jews*.
11. The purpose of the first two chapters is to give some account of the contribution of those who were specially influential in encouraging anti-semitic ideas among their fellow-Protestants. Such particular concentration involves the risk of giving the impression that the German Evangelical Church was almost entirely dominated by such

an outlook. This is of course not true. Through the whole period under review there was dedicated missionary activity that was resolved to take most earnestly into account the essential role of the Jews in God's saving purpose and that sought in a spirit of sympathy and love to present Jesus as the Christ to contemporary representatives of the people in whose midst He was once born, and this involved countering certain false and libellous anti-semitic accusations. Appendix 2, pp. 326ff, provides a brief introduction to the *Judenmission*.

12. Karl Kupisch: *Adolf Stoecker, Hofsprediger und Volkstribun*, Berlin, 1970, p. 8.

13. Waldemar Gurian: *Antisemitism in Modern Germany* in *Essays on Antisemitism*, ed. Koppel S. Pinson, New York, 1946, p. 231.

14. Adolf Stoecker: *Christlich-Sozial. Reden und Aufsätze*, Berlin, 1885, p. 380.

15. Agnes von Zahn Harnack: *Adolf Harnack*, Berlin, 1951, p. 166.

16. Franz-Heinrich Philipp in *Kirche und Synagoge*, ed. Karl-Heinrich Rengstorf und Siegfried von Kortzfleisch, Vol. 2, Stuttgart, pp. 300–3.

17. Tilgner, 281.

18. Philipp, 304.

19. Kupisch, 90.

20. 'Contemporaries agree that Stoecker's personality and fervour— he was hailed as the 'Second Luther'—had a remarkable effect on his audiences. Indeed, they must have had, for this alone can account for his success. His arguments, read in cold blood, seem tortuous and tentative, their presentation prolix and unctuous. The liberal logic-choppers seized on the constant contradictions in his utterances so as to defeat anti-semitism with reason. That this is the weakest of arms against it was a lesson not then learnt' (P. G. J. Pulzer: *Rise of Political Anti-semitism in Germany and Austria*, Wiley, New York, 1964, p. 101).

21. Philipp, 299–300.

22. Wanda Kampmann: *Deutsche und Juden*. Heidelberg, 1963, pp. 286–7. For the Radical Racial Anti-semites see Appendix 3.

23. Dietrich von Oertzen: *Adolf Stoecker. Lebensbild und Zeitgeschichte*, Berlin, 1912, p. 160.

24. Ibid., 155.

25. *Christlich-Sozial*, 408.

26. Ibid., 438.

27. Ibid., 420.

28. Ibid., 382.

29. Walter Holsten: *Adolf Stoecker als Symptom seiner Zeit* in *Christen und Juden*, ed. Wolf-Dieter Marsch und Karl Thieme, Mainz, 1961, p. 187. *Judentum* is another word that is often difficult to translate. 'Judaism' and 'Jewry' are the two obvious renderings. When the meaning is that of a national or racial entity contrasted disparagingly with *Deutschtum*, it is perhaps best left untranslated.

30. Holsten, 200.
31. *Christlich-Sozial*, 388.
32. Paul le Seur: *Adolf Stoecker der Prophet des Dritten Reiches*, Berlin, 1936.
33. Ibid., 5.
34. In a letter from Pastor Bodelschwingh to the Crown Prince Frederick, 22 August 1885, reproduced in Walter Frank: *Hofprediger Adolf Stoecker und die christlich-soziale Bewegung*, 2nd edition, Hamburg, 1935, pp. 311–12.
35. Quoted by Gerhard Schmolze: *Der Antisemitismus Adolf Stoeckers* in *Pastoralblatt*, 1959, p. 440.
36. Theodor Fritsch ed., *Handbuch der Judenfrage*, 37th edition, 1934, p. 512.
37. Adolf Freudenberg: *Geschichtliche Wurzeln des Antisemitsmus* in *Antisemitismus, Judentum, Staat Israel*, Frankfurt, 1963, p. 24.
38. Schmolze, p. 441, quotes one of Stoecker's less controlled utterances—'They say they are Jews, and are not, but are the Synagogue of Satan, so writes the disciple of Love. . . . Regarded as a collective power the Jews are still the same today, as they then were. That they have remained unto this very day—Satan's synagogue among the peoples.'
39. In one of his speeches he declared that either the restrictive anti-Jewish measures which he advocated would be successfully applied, or else 'the cancerous sore would spread still further' (*Christlich-Sozial*, 369).
40. *Christlich-Sozial*, 105.
41. Kampmann, 252.
42. For vivid description of Treitschke's triumphs in the lecture-room see Andreas Dorpalen: *Heinrich von Treitschke*. Yale, 1957, pp. 49 and 227—'Treitschke would come in, followed by a number of his colleagues who would sit on special chairs on the lecture platform. Every few moments wild bursts of clapping and stamping, the German student's traditional sign of approval, would punctuate his oration. And, when he had finished, his colleagues, like a guard of honour, would escort him from his classroom to the thunderous applause of the audience.'
43. Dorpalen, 241.
44. Gurian, 230.
45. Dorpalen, 244.
46. Pulzer: 250.
47. The full text is to be found in *Der Berliner Antisemitismusstreit* ed. by Walter Boehlich, Frankfurt, 1965, pp. 7–14.
48. Ibid., 9.
49. Ibid., 8.
50. Ibid., 10.
51. Ibid., 9.
52. Ibid., 13.
53. Ibid., 211–27.

54. Ibid., 219.
55. Ibid., 33–47.
56. Ibid., 79–92.
57. Ibid., 92.
58. Pulzer, 250.
59. Boehlich, 230.
60. Alexander Bein: *Der moderne Antisemitismus und seine Bedeutung für die Judenfrage, Vierteljahrshefte für Zeitgeschichte*, October 1958, pp. 358–59.
61. Karl Kupisch: *Studenten entdecken die Bibel. Die Geschichte der Deutschen Christlichen Studenten-Vereinigung*, Berlin, 1964, p. 22.
62. Gerhard Kittel dedicated his highly controversial booklet *Die Judenfrage* to 'My Confederates on the fiftieth anniversary of the founding of the Union of German Students at Tübingen'.
63. Philipp in *Kirche und Synagogue II*, p. 318.
64. Pulzer, 255.
65. Quoted by Kampmann: p. 272.
66. Fritz Stern: *The Politics of Cultural Despair*, California, 1961, p. 47.
67. Robert W. Lougee: *Paul de Lagarde*, Harvard, 1962, p. 159.
68. Paul de Lagarde: *Deutsche Schriften*, First complete edition, Göttingen, 1886, p. 292.
69. Günther van Norden: *Kirche in der Krise. Die Stellung der Evangelischer Kirche zum Nationalsozialistischen Staat im Jahre 1933*, Dusseldorf, 1963, p. 31. 'Lagarde was the first to recognise clearly that which was distinctly un-Jewish in Jesus' (Max Maurenbrecher: *Der Heiland der Deutschen. Der Weg der Volkstum schaffenden Kirche*. Göttingen, 1933, p. 76).
70. Maurenbrecher, 75.
71. Lougee, 147.
72. Lougee, 277.
73. Stern, 92.
74. *Deutsche Schriften*, 30.
75. *Deutsche Schriften*, 43.
76. *Deutsche Schriften*, 31.
77. Paul de Lagarde: *Ausgewählte Schriften*, ed. Paul Fischer, München, 1934, pp. 239, 243.
78. See Alexander Bein: *Der judische Parasit* in *Vierteljahrshefte für Zeitgeschichte*, 1965, pp. 121ff. The whole article makes a most important contribution to the understanding of the horrific development of really virulent and deadly anti-semitism that ended in deliberate wholesale extermination, and stresses the devastating effect, stage by stage, of the language employed.
79. Konrad Heiden: *Der Führer*, Gollancz, 1945, p. 194.
80. William L. Shirer: *The Rise and Fall of the Third Reich*, Secker and Warburg, 1959, p. 109.
81. G. L. Mosse: *Crisis of German Ideology*, 95–7.
82. Helmut Krausnick: *The Persecution of the Jews* in *Anatomy of the S.S. State*, Collins, 1968, p. 10. Chamberlain does not appear to have

worried about contradicting himself, for in his introduction to 'Foundations' he affirmed that 'the Jew is no enemy of Teutonic civilisation and culture' (Author's Introduction, LXXVIII).

83. Eduard Lamparter: *Evangelische Kirche und Judentum* in *Versuche des Verstehens. Dokumente Jüdisch-Christlichen Begegnungen*, 1918–33, ed. Robert Geis und Hans-Joachim Kraus, München, 1966, p. 284.

84. Houston Stewart Chamberlain: *The Foundations of the Nineteenth Century*, English Edition, edited by John Lees, John Lane, 1911, Vol. I, p. 221.

85. *Foundations*, I, 211.

86. Van Norden, 29.

87. *Foundations*, II, 57.

88. Ibid., II, 65.

89. Ibid., II, 60.

90. Ibid., II, 375.

91. Ibid., II, 367.

92. Ibid., II, 376.

93. Ibid., II, 373.

94. Ibid., I, 512.

95. Tilgner in *Rasse, Kirche und Humanum*, 292.

96. Shirer, 141.

97. *Foundations*, Author's Introduction, LXXVIII.

98. H. J. Kraus in *Entscheidungsjahr*, 1932, p. 252.

99. *Junge Kirche*, 1936, p. 267. (Henceforward referred to as JK.)

100. *Foundations*, II, 134.

101. Tilgner, 295.

102. Pulzer, 269.

103. G. M. Lowen: *Die Juden und das Evangelium. Äusserungen hervorragender evangelischer Christen der Gegenwart*, Leipzig, 1913, p. 11.

104. Gottfried Mehnert: *Kirche und Politik, 117–1919*. Düsseldorf, 1959, p. 34–5.

105. Mehnert, 49.

106. Mehnert, 65.

107. Eva Reichmann: *Der Bewusstsein der deutschen Juden* in *Deutsches Judentum in Krieg und Revolution*, p. 514.

108. Tilgner, 297.

109. Philipp in *Kirche und Synagoge*, II, p. 321.

110. Reichmann, 524.

111. Jochmann, 436–7.

112. Tilgner, 298.

2
Anti-Jewish sentiment in the Weimar Period

It is no cause for surprise that the vast majority of the protestant clergy viewed the post-war democratic set-up with suspicion and dislike, as quite unacceptably international and liberal, with its origins in the French Revolution. They did not hesitate to throw in their lot with the newly formed *Deutschnationale Volkspartei* (DNVP), an amalgamation of the former conservatives, those such as the Pan-Germans who before the war had proved to be fanatical nationalists and radical anti-semites, and a certain number of non-conservatives who had changed their allegiance from left to right during the war. It has been estimated that between 70 and 80 per cent of the pastors allied themselves with the DNVP[1] and that the majority of those were German nationalists to the very core, voted quite openly for the party, and were much in demand as official speakers on numerous patriotic occasions. One of their number gave vivid expression to their attitude in announcing: 'From our Christian way of looking at life (*Weltanschauung*) we seek to act as breakwater against the democratic waves of the present time. All efforts to make the State democratic are basically designed to dechristianise the Volk. We Christians remain reactionaries by God's Grace.'[2] Cherishing their precious war-time experience of volkish solidarity and full of emotional nostalgia for the lost glories of Imperial Germany with its firm alliance of 'Throne and Altar', and only too ready to subscribe to the belief that the beloved Fatherland had been betrayed by a monstrous 'stab in the back', they rejoiced in the challenge to assist in the spiritual and moral renewal of the German Volk. Simon Schoeffel, who in 1933 became active in the abortive attempt to establish the longed for Evangelical Reich Church, declared that what mattered was to realise a new synthesis of Volkstum and Christianity. The whole shape of the future depended upon that.[3]

Sadly having to admit that the monarchy was unlikely to be restored in the foreseeable future, Volk and Fatherland were for them the obvious substitutes for the throne in the alliance with the Altar.

Anti-semitism was soon revealed to be an integral part of the DNVP programme, and was regarded as essential for its survival. The DNVP fought the first Reichstag Election against the prevailing 'disintegrating un-German spirit' and 'against the Jewish predominance in government and public life which has come to the fore more and more fatefully since the Revolution'.[4] In party propaganda much was at first made of the invasion of the Fatherland by hordes of undesirable Jews from the East, but in course of time, as the anti-semitic offensive became increasingly radical, the distinction between such semitic immigrants and well-established German Jews became blurred, and the Jew, irrespective of his origin, was declared to be the enemy.[5] In the 1924 election campaign use was made of posters calling for resistance to Jewish influence upon all fronts. A pastor in Kassel called upon Evangelical Christians to vote DNVP, because the Party had taken up the cudgels against Jewish predominance. In all probability, if the DNVP had come to power instead of the Nazis, a policy of apartheid would have been implemented.[6]

Closely allied with the DNVP was the Pan-German League, never boasting a large membership but influential as a sort of umbrella organisation for numerous other nationalistic alliances. Established in 1893, attracting support from professors, teachers, representatives of the Arts, writers, highly placed officials and right wing politicians, and designed to further nationalistic ambitions, it was, to begin with, only latently anti-semitic. But from 1908 onwards under the continuous and dictatorial presidency of Heinrich Class, a disciple of Lagarde and Chamberlain and an ardent volkish anti-semite who unhesitatingly subordinated religion to race, an increasingly hostile attitude to the Jews developed. Immediately after the war the League in its new constitution was pledged to combat 'all those forces which inhibit or detract from the volkish development of the German people, particularly . . . Jewish predominance to be found in almost all departments of the State, the economy and culture'[7] and sponsored the most radical of anti-semitic publications. Class's battle-cry to strike the Jews dead and not fear being accused of brutality by meeting force by force in the struggle for existence was greeted with rapturous applause,[8] as was also his insistence that social security and political order could only be achieved through consciousness of unity of blood kindled by the love which bound one member of a particular Volk to another. It was through its daughter-organisation the *Schutz- und Trutzbund* (Defensive and Offensive Alliance) that it had its popular appeal. In a matter of months the Alliance had a membership of 300,000 members. Its purpose was declared to be 'the moral rebirth of the German Volk through the awakening and promoting of its sound and healthy particularity (*Eigenart*)'.[9] This was affirmed to be impossible, unless Jewish influences were fought and eliminated on every possible front, every available means being adopted which inevitably led to acts of violence and incitement to pogroms. The *Schutz- und Trutzbund* was a sinister force behind every attempted assassination, and was vetoed in 1922 by the government after the murder of the Jewish Foreign Minister, Rathenau.

One of the avowed aims of the *Bund* was to influence the clergy and to encourage them in the belief that all intellectual movements that questioned Christianity were Jewish-inspired. Quite a few prominent Lutheran pastors actively supported the Pan-German League and its associate groups regardless of their marked and anti-Christian volkish tendencies. With the object of increasing their numbers and their influence Alfred Roth, the director of the *Schutz- und Trutzbund* campaigned to influence various Church elections, in order to secure the appointment of parish clergy and Church officials in key positions who could be relied upon to pursue a volkish and anti-semitic line, and who in their turn would influence the laity.[10]

Conservative and national-minded pastors in the Weimar Period were far from friendly to the Jews. They would certainly have been shocked or offended by the outburst in 1919 by a Berlin socialist pastor: 'Anyone who is an anti-semite cannot be a Christian. We desire to be revolutionaries and to fight the anti-semitic spirit for what it is—hatred, lies, godlessness and estrangement from God.'[11] Equally certainly they would have been appreciative of another pastor's recipe for what he chose to call 'Christian anti-semitism', being 'genuine Germans and convinced

Christians—the best weapon against alien infection'.[12] They would also have had ready understanding for the admission of a Bavarian pastor: 'When I make contact with a Jew, I have an instinctive repugnance, and feel myself to be uncomfortable. I say to myself involuntarily: he is one of the race that killed your Saviour,' though they would certainly have felt that he had gone too far, when he went on to stress the 'total inferiority of the Jews' and recommended 'pride in not only being a Christian but an Aryan Christian'.[13] The conservative and national-minded pastor was in fact faced by a severe dilemma. He would feel as a minister of the Gospel under an obligation to reject, if not preach against, the radical and racial version of anti-semitism, and yet he could scarcely avoid an emotion of instinctive aversion both to the Jew and to certain manifestations of the Jewish spirit. He had probably been taught in Sunday school and confirmation-class to contrast the 'wicked Jew' with the virtuous believer in Christ. Very possibly the youth organisation and student association to which he had belonged had encouraged him to regard the Jew as undesirable and alien. He was likely to have been captivated by the volkish excitement engendered by the outbreak of war only to be grievously deflated by its outcome. The yearning to re-experience that emotion in working for the spiritual regeneration of the Volk along Germanic-Christian lines and waging warfare upon the enemy within in place of the enemy without would have helped him to become resentful and suspicious of that which was modern, liberating, sophisticated and cosmopolitan, and made him desire to pin a great deal of responsibility upon the alien Jew, *zersetzend*: 'disintegrating' being as before the operative word. Prejudiced on religious, political, and moral grounds and not loath to subscribe to the idea of inevitable and incessant conflict between Christianity and Jewry, he had little hesitation in laying a substantial part of the blame upon the Jew (once again as ever 'our misfortune') for sharp and unprincipled capitalism that encouraged a materialistic attitude; and thus for successive economic crises, for the spread of both godless bolshevism and western-style democracy, for the rise in competition and in unemployment in certain professions, for the scandalously unjust treatment of Germany by the outside world, for the debasing of standards in literature, journalism and public entertainment and in the en-encouragement of sexual immorality—in fact, discovering a convenient scapegoat for a great deal of what he considered to be wrong in post-war Germany.

What was claimed to be legitimate 'Christian' anti-semitism was propagated week in week out by various organs of the Evangelical press. This is clearly demonstrated in a most illuminating dissertation by Ino Arndt[14] who made it her task to search through the pages of the principal Church weeklies which very much catered for the middle and lower-middle classes and for country folk (incidentally much the same elements in the population from which the Nazis drew their main following), were regarded by them as authoritative and without any doubt were a powerful factor in the formation of Christian opinion. The publications concerned may be estimated by 1928 to have reached as many as six million readers, and certainly had a wider and more enduring influence than the Sunday sermon. This section of the Church press was 'so nationalistically orientated that it regarded Jewry as the natural foe of the Christian-national tradition, and availed itself of every opportunity of preaching the Jewish responsibility for the collapse of the Christian and monarchial order'.[15] The unwearied reiterance that the Jews were behind all that was amiss or that was lacking in the contemporary situation had its inevitable effect in weakening the strength of moral resistance of so many Church members against the initial anti-semitic measures of the Nazis and in blunting what Arndt describes as 'their natural, their humane and ultimately also their Christian feelings'.[16] The constant plugging of the caricature of a sinister, all-powerful and degenerate Jewish minority out to corrupt and to do down the virtuous Christian majority captivated the imagination of countless readers, and provided fruitful soil for further and more radical Nazi propaganda.

Wilhelm Stählin who had become widely known and appreciated for his activity as joint leader from 1922 of the *Bund deutscher Jugendvereine* (Association of German Youth Clubs), a progressive body, a main aim of which was to encourage the rising generation in adopting a responsible Christian attitude to the issues of the day,[17] delivered in May 1924 at a Youth Leaders' Conference a stirring lecture on the subject of 'The Volkish Movement and Our Responsibility'.[18] He did not hesitate to welcome the movement in general as a counterblast to the 'abstract conception of personality stemming from the Enlightenment'.[19] 'He who does not do honour to his Volk whose blood courses through his veins and whose history is part of his being', he declared, 'fails to reverence God, the invisible Father, in whom we live and move and have our being. . . . Because we are men on earth, we cannot build the Kingdom of God, if at the same time we disdain and betray the solidarity of the Volk.'[20] This did not, however, prevent him from expressing his grave misgivings at the excessive bombast with which the volkish cause was being proclaimed, and not least by volkish pastors whose belligerent fanaticism was not calculated to promote a reverent and prayerful attitude on the part of their youthful following.[21]

It is instructive to note how uneasy Stählin was in his assessment of the Jewish problem. On the one hand, he declared that no one could deny the colossal danger that Jewish influence upon public life constituted for 'the purity and health of the Volkstum'. But on the other hand, he was equally insistent that the abject stupidity and the shameful lack of decency and discretion that were such manifest features of current vulgar anti-semitism, which gloried in hatred and which was so dangerously blind to German national failings, were not thereby justified. Such an unworthy and unchristian attitude had to be withstood, even if it meant being branded as philo-semitic and unvolkish.[22] So reprehensible a form of anti-semitism ought not, however, to be contested by a refusal to recognise that there was indeed a Jewish problem involving a formidable challenge by a completely alien culture to the German national identity and to the fulfilment of Germany's mission. That one was 'beginning to speak of "Germans and Jews" rather than of "Jews and Christians" and was recognising how misleading was talk about "German Citizens of Jewish Faith"' was positive gain, inasmuch as it aided the recognition that 'the Jew and the German represent two different types of human being'. This view could be fully endorsed without insulting the Jews collectively or resorting to idle and idiotic prattle concerning 'the offensiveness of this inferior race'.[23] There was, in his opinion, an imperative duty to resist the outcry to have descendants of Jews (who had dwelt for decades or even centuries within the German community) pilloried as citizens with inferior rights, while at the same time insisting upon a sharp distinction being drawn between them and the hordes of *Ostjuden* who since the war had streamed into Germany and preyed upon their

German hosts. He was prepared to risk being misunderstood and reviled in insisting that the Jewish people had a specially appointed task to fulfil in world history, that of furthering international solidarity, both intellectually and morally.[24]

If the Leaders of the Church did not lend positive encouragement, they did little or nothing to warn against the impropriety and danger of Christians indulging in anti-Jewish feeling. During the whole period there is no evidence whatever of any authoritative statement being issued by the Evangelical Church calling for the earnest consideration of the Jewish problem from the purely biblical standpoint and in the light of the Christian Gospel of mercy and of love. Nor can we discover any official Church warning against the mounting agitation in certain circles to treat the problem as predominantly one of race.

Serious attention to the Old Testament might have helped to redress the balance but there was an unmistakable tendency in the 1920s to conceive of the Old Testament in terms of the history and development of the ancient people of Israel rather than as being part and parcel of, as well as essential background to, the unique Divine Revelation in Christ. Such disparagement of the Old Testament can be traced back to Schleiermacher and Ritschl, and had of course been ardently propagated by Lagarde and Chamberlain. The great Adolf Harnack had questioned, in his book *Marcion*, first published in 1920, the rightness of continuing in modern Protestantism to regard the Old Testament as of canonical authority.[25] Friedrich Delitzsch in his new edition in 1921 of *Die grosse Täuschung* ('The Great Deception') insisted that 'all the Old Testament books from Genesis to Daniel have in their religious bearing for today, and especially for us Christians, absolutely no significance'.[26] The volkish-orientated theologians Emanuel Hirsch and Wilhelm Stapel who were beginning to attract considerable attention went a long way towards placing the Old Testament on a level with the record of other ancient religions, and treating it as having no direct relevance for positive Christian belief.[27]

Many of those who felt bound to defend the essential and continuing place of the Old Testament in the teaching and life of the Church did not appear to do so with any philo-semitic intention. Helmut Schreiner insisted that there was no greater witness against modern Jewry than the whole spirit of the Bible.[28] Paul

Althaus approved the description of the Old Testament as being 'semitic and yet at the same time the most anti-semitic book in the world', surpassing all volkish indignation in the earnestness and the profundity of its conflict with Judah.[29]

Althaus was indeed one of many who at this period proved unprepared to treat the current Jewish issue as essentially a biblical one. In his work *Die letzten Dinge* which attracted considerable attention he wrote: 'Since the presence of Christ among men the return of the People of Israel from the Diaspora has no further saving (*heilgeschichtlich*) actuality, for the special significance of the Holy Land, of Jerusalem, of the Kingdom of Israel and of the Temple cult has elapsed. . . . The Church is now the People of God, the Israel of God. Israel as an historical people since the Advent of Christ in Whom its saving vocation has found fulfilment is no longer a theological, *heilsgeschichtlich* factor. Israel has in the Church and for the Church no special place and no special sacred calling (*Heilsberuf*).'[30] In Althaus's view Israel in diaspora obviously constituted a theological issue as little as did the diaspora of the German people throughout the world.

In 1927 the Evangelical Church Congress (*Kirchentag*), a newly formed body of elected representatives of all the provincial Churches, the 'loudspeaker' of German Protestants, whose responsibility it was to debate social and political problems of the day and then issue a Christian word, met for the second time, in Königsberg. The theme chosen for the published message was *Volk and Fatherland*.[31] The Volkstum was declared to be of divine institution. In the present situation there was no duty more pressing than that of exalting it. German evangelical Christianity was to be recognised as possessing its own special national character. Any move to promote world-citizenship at the expense of volkish interests was quite unacceptable. The Church could not remain silent, when efforts were being made, to the deadly peril of the German people, to tear asunder Christianity and *Deutschtum*. Service to the Fatherland and service to God were identical. The opening paragraph did, it must be admitted, include the words 'There is a fellowship of faith and love which transcends national divisions and racial differences and binds together those who confess allegiance to Christ,' but this was immediately followed by the insistence that the difference among peoples was divinely ordained. This manifesto in fact revealed a heartfelt concern for volkish solidarity, an obviously less enthusiastic and a qualified desire for good relations on a mutual Christian basis and no apparent consideration of a Christian and humanitarian duty to care about those who on religious or national grounds were to be accounted as outsiders.

The principal speech at the Königsberg Kirchentag was delivered by Paul Althaus on the subject of Church and Volk. Althaus urged that the Church should strive to be sympathetic towards current volkish aspirations. The Volkstum Movement was, he believed, knocking at the door of the church. Such an approach had to be taken seriously. 'The noble glow of love for one's own Volk', he exclaimed, 'can become a wild and foul fire. All affirmation of Volkstum leads to conflict, and in such conflict the demons of arrogance, hatred and scorn for others raise their head.'[32] The cleansing power of the Christian Gospel was the necessary antidote. The speech contained a sober warning against volkish idolatry with all the exuberant talk about the 'German God' being revealed in national experience and culture, and 'the power of the demons which raged in German blood',[33] the solemn reminder that the God of the Bible 'can shatter to pieces the healthiest and most glorious of peoples and lay them in the dust of death',[34] and an insistence that 'the fate of the dismembered German people ultimately depends upon the might of Christ manifest in understanding love that heals differences and builds bridges'.[35]

Despite such words of warning Althaus ardently propagated on this as on various other occasions a distinct volkish theology. In 1919 he had not hesitated to declare that 'man's highest good is his Volk' and to dismiss both volkless individualism and supranational cosmopolitanism as 'simply impossible'.[36] In 1923 he had described Volk as 'a maternal womb . . . in which alone individuals have their life'. 'We live naturally and spiritually every moment from the inheritance of our Volk.'[37] In his Königsberg address he spoke of the Church's obligation to testify to the sanctity of identification with the life of the Volk which could lead to a new experience of God and an increased recognition of His ever fresh creative activity. 'German-Christian and Christian-German coherence stands as a clear, a transparent and an evident fact. The greatest moments and the most splendid figures in our national history bear witness to this.'[38] So nationally orientated a Church could not but be alive to the 'Jewish menace to our Volkstum'.[39]

Althaus recommended calling things by their right names and taking courageous action against the Jewish influence in the economy, the press, the arts, and literature which ran counter to the witness of the Gospel. This should not be taken as a direct expression of anti-semitic feeling. Concern for what was sincerely believed to be the welfare and the Christian interests of the German people was the paramount consideration. Althaus, as indeed many another whose attitude was akin to his, was not oblivious to the demands of the universal Christian law of love which did not exclude the alien Jews. The dilemma of how to reconcile love for one's own Volk and love for all men was very much present and felt. During the height of the Third Reich Althaus was moved to remark: 'We exist not only for our Volk, but are responsible for every one whom God causes to be our neighbour, and also for other peoples, in so far as we enter into relationship with them.'[40] It is also interesting to note that in 1932 he expressed his conviction that the presence of the Jews within Germany was of divine intention. 'However we seek to solve the problem, we shall not alter the fact that the Jews will remain in residence in our land as among other peoples of the world. It appears to me that such a destiny, notwithstanding all the attendant difficulties and exigencies, has a clear divine significance. That the Jews everywhere, and indeed especially acutely in our case, sever the bonds of volkish solidarity, has to be accepted as an indication of the limits and relativity of volkish separation, and causes us to look ahead to the coming Kingdom of God.'[41]

For Althaus the intrinsic value of the Volk lay alone in its being of divine creation and obligation. 'We love our Volk, and are pledged to stake our very lives for it, because it is indeed through God's ordinance our Volk.'[42] The struggle to preserve the Volkstum from obnoxious alien influences could be regarded as warfare in defence of the sanctity of God's creative work. It was his conviction that the First Article of the Creed, with its affirmation of God's activity as Creator, was liable to be overlooked alongside the Second Article declaring the Saving Work of God in Christ. In fact it was possible to have an altogether too exclusively christological interest. He was also convinced that the full weight of the First Article needed to be appreciated before proceeding to confession of the Second. 'Luther', he wrote, 'never spoke the second word before the first.'[43] In the zeal to redress the balance theologically he laid himself open to the accusation of having presented the Volk and other Orders of Creation as being of divine gift and origin apart from Christ. 'We live', he wrote, 'not only from the Grace of our Lord Jesus Christ. We live as individuals and peoples also from definite historical grace.'[44] As a conscientious and orthodox Lutheran theologian he was obviously aware of the danger of ending up by treating the created object as 'an absolute a supreme good in itself, an idol'.[45] He therefore took pains to stress both the free and sovereign will of the Creator and the inevitability of the sinful perversion by man of the various orders of creation, while insisting that such perversion in no wise invalidated their essential sacredness.

Althaus was the principal architect of the co-called *Theologie der Schöpfungsordnungen* (Theology of the Divine Orders of Creation) which came to exercise an ominous influence upon political as well as ecclesiastical thinking. This theology was worked out in conscious opposition to religious liberalism, Barthian dialectical theology, and unbridled heathen volkish ideology. It taught that Volk and Fatherland, alongside of Marriage, Parenthood, Family, Clan (*Stamm*) and State, were to be understood as associations instituted by God and of direct obligation for human existence. 'It is', Althaus wrote, 'God's Will to renew and to maintain the life of mankind until the Last Day. He has therefore Himself established as a means to this end the *Ordnungen* which we recognise as the indispensable conditions of the continuance of human life in history.'[46] In and through them the God of History encounters man in his natural existence, and reveals to him His creative will. This meant that the Gospel was not to be regarded as the one and only source and content of the Divine Revelation. In a letter written to an old friend after the Second World War he admitted that the narrowness of the prevailing doctrine of Revelation was intolerable to him. 'I find it both unbiblical and cramping.'[47] It was his belief that it made it impossible for the Church to adopt the right attitude towards what was happening within the Volk.

This insistence that he shared with other leading Lutheran theologians such as Hirsch, Gogarten, and Elert, in stressing the importance of the recognition of a *revelatio* and *vocatio generalis* and of a positive acknowledgement of the Hand of God in certain historical events undoubtedly had the effect of opening the door wide for the glorification, not only of the Volk, but of German Blood, Soil, Race, Language and History,[48] and encouraged the 'German Christian' element within the Church in making the presumed revelation of God in Nature, in History and in contemporary events the vital message of the moment.

In 1930 Friedrich Wieneke who took a lead in formulating such 'German Christian' theology as there was, waxed eloquent in praise of Adolf Hitler as a devout Catholic and a reverent defender of the Christian faith. He maintained that Hitler gave absolute value to Race, only because therein was revealed God's creative Will as the principle of communal life (*Gemeinschaftsleben*). 'God has not created any uniform type of human being but definite *Grundtypen* which have provided each Race and each people with its own particular stamp. Hitler regards it as a grave sin, that the will of the Creator has been annihilated by the *Humanitäts-theoretiken*'.[49] In an article appearing in 1931 in the *Deutsches Pfarrerblatt* Wieneke suggested that love of mankind in general, in the main only advocated by would-be world benefactors, was a questionable notion. One's own Volk was the prime consideration not the world, and neighbourly love found its true expression in concern for one's fellow-German.

In the lectures and writings of Althaus prior to the Nazi Revolution we shall look in vain for reference to Race. But it was inevitable that emphasis upon the importance of the purity of race would sooner or later be found in Evangelical pronouncements bracketed with stress upon the sanctity of the Volk, as volkish-orientated Christianity kept pace with developments in the political sphere. Two examples of this can be given. In 1927 at the General Assembly of the *Evangelische Bund* (Evangelical Association), a society that had been formed in 1886 for the propagation of German Protestant interests, it was stated that 'in accordance with divine provision and ordinance there is no such thing as mankind in general but only men of a particular race, a definite stock and a distinct Volkstum'.[50] In the 1931 edition of the standard Protestant encyclopaedia *Religion in Geschichte und Gegenwart* an article on the 'Volkish Movement' declared that, while rejecting a racial ideology that would lead to hatred of the Jews, 'Christianity gladly responds to the Movement's summons to assist more than hitherto and with growing consciousness in the keeping pure of Volkstum and Race. In the Church's theology there ought to be a full awareness of this need, and a form of Christianity in which the values of Volkstum and of Race have been incorporated, should be a distinct mark of its dogmatics.'[51]

The new consciousness of and concern about Race had the effect of making in certain circles the evangelisation of Jews a debatable matter. In 1928 an East Prussian Superintendent expressed anxiety at the lack of support for the Church's mission to the Jews which he regarded as a plain duty. On inquiry he was told by a certain pastor that in his view such a missionary activity was a fundamental error, if it at all overlooked the fact that the Jewish issue was a racial every bit as much as a religious one. The conversion of the Jew to Christianity was an extremely doubtful proposition, if it were taken to mean that he was no longer to be regarded as belonging to his former race but to be considered to be integrated into the Germanic race. He therefore recommended the formation of an organisation for Israelites of the Christian faith, analogous to the 'Alliance of German Citizens of Jewish faith', the existence of which would emphasize that baptised Jews still belonged to their original race.[52]

This insistence by an Evangelical clergyman that the Jewish Question was to be treated racially was by no means a lone voice. A Superintendent in Bonn wrote in 1929 that the present Jewish problem was definitely a racial issue, and he maintained that it was seriously open to argument whether missions to the Jews were justifiable at all.[53] Another clergyman who was editor of a Church paper suggested in 1926 that a Jew always remained a Jew, and that the water of baptism did not alter that fact. The converted Jew was not thereby set free from his people. 'No mission can change a man's blood or disposition. The Semite thinks, acts and speaks differently from the Aryan.'[54] A certain Pastor Pauli wrote with appreciation in the *Deutsches Pfarrerblatt* in 1927 that with the advance in racial research a 'wonderful new world' had been discovered. The clergy had a special obligation to promote racial knowledge, since it 'unveiled' the human soul. He was enthusiastic in his recommendation of the work of Hans Günther, the new leading racial authority, and he marvelled how the clergy had managed to get on for so long without such assistance.[55]

An article by Simon Schoeffel in the *Hannover Sonntagsblatt* is a telling instance of the juggling that was required to do justice to the awakened appreciation of the values of Race and Volkstum while at the same time holding fast to orthodox Christianity. Schoeffel admitted that Jesus was a Jew according to the flesh, but denied that He was one according to the spirit, for Jesus continued and fulfilled not the Jewish Volk religion but the Jewish prophetic religion. Schoeffel accepted that the German people had the task of striving to keep its racial purity inviolate, but qualified this by an insistence that other races should never be held in contempt, because it was not race as an absolute but the sovereignty of God that had to be recognised as supreme and ultimate.[56]

In similar vein an article in the *Allgemeine Evangelisch-Lutherische Kirchenzeitung* endeavoured to present the Bible, Old Testament and New Testament alike, as essentially an 'anti-Judaic book' and thereby offering a compromise between the preservation of the Bible as the essential constituent of the Evangelical Confession and a simultaneous recognition of the volkish and anti-semitic ideas of the National Socialist Party.[57] The Bible already recognised everything that was at present so detestable about the Jews.

A good example of popularised *Schöpfungstheologie* complete with racial and anti-semitic application is to be found in a 'German Christian' church election pamphlet of November 1932, and is worth quoting in full.

> In affirming the First Article of the Apostles' Creed we give unqualified recognition to God's Order of Creation, as we encounter it in Marriage, Family, Race and Volk. Just as we stand for the sanctity of marriage, so we champion the cause of the preservation of the purity of the Volk and of our Race. God does not desire monotony and uniformity but multiplicity. On the first page of the Bible we read that God did not create the tree as such but trees, 'each one according to its kind', likewise living beasts, each according to their kind. In this variety and multiplicity consists the beauty and the value of the natural world. This same order of creation also holds good in the world of man. Nowhere on this earth is there man as such, but always only German, Englishman, Frenchman, Chinaman, Jew, etc. God wills there to be Races and Peoples. And it is God's Will that we maintain our Race and our Volkstum in purity, that we remain German men, and do not become a bastard-Volk of Jewish Aryan blood. That is why we oppose unchristian humanitarianism, pacifism, the Internationale,

Freemasonry and christian cosmopolitanism, and confess with Martin Luther: 'For Germans was I born, them will I serve.'[58]

When one reads effusions such as this, and in the early part of 1933 they were multiplied through the length and breadth of Germany, one can very readily understand how optimistic the Nazis then were that they would be able to harness the Evangelical Church to their new order. Germanic fervour coupled with instinctive and sanctioned anti-Jewish feeling among Christians was already there for Hitler to make full play and use of.

The Lutheran publicist Wilhelm Stapel[59] was as responsible as any one in encouraging an increasing number of cultured Evangelicals to make room for the concept of race in their Christian outlook. Race, to be described, he wrote, as 'not merely something corporeal' but as 'soul and spirit' is an indisputable fact. 'Because there is race, it determines the embodiment of religion.'[60] Stapel was an impulsive and skilled journalist, an enthusiastic student of Luther and a practising churchman who had an ambition to evolve a persuasive theology of nationalism. He became widely known as the editor, from 1919 on, of *Deutsches Volkstum*. Based upon articles in that periodical, his work *Der christliche Staatsman: Eine Theologie des Nationalismus*, published in 1932, attracted considerable attention.[61] He was possessed, as many another, by an excessively romantic idealisation of war-time volkish experience, and a typical example of his style is to be found in his opening article in *Deutsches Volkstum*: 'Brothers in your graves, you have not fallen in vain! Brothers still alive, assist in ensuring that out of the German masses shall emerge a Volk, and that the mechanism of the State shall be imbued with German soul!'[62] During the 'twenties he developed his own peculiar brand of biological-metaphysical Volk theology. Volk, in Stapel's reckoning, was principally a biological conception, a unity of Blood, Soul, Language and Culture, into which the individual was destined at birth to be incorporated, and to which he was thereafter irrevocably bound, no matter where he eventually resided. Such an inalienable heritage he received from the Divine Creator. The denial of his biological-cum-historical communal relationship was man's intrinsic sin, 'an alienation from God as the primal source of all creative living'.[63] To reject one's Volk even in the secret recess of one's soul was tantamount to rebellion against the Divine

Will. Within the *Volkheit* there resided a Law of Life comprehended by intuition and making an absolute moral demand, this meant that the individual's share and lot as part of the Volk was ethical as well as biological. This led Stapel to a most significant conclusion: the Law as contained in Holy Scripture should no longer be regarded as the ethical authority for the German Protestant. Volk Law and Divine Law were identical, and there was therefore no call for a specific 'Christian' ethic. The individual fulfilled his moral obligations by obedience to the historically developed demands of the Volkheit. 'The morality which the Church teaches', Stapel declared, 'can be none other than that which develops in the heart of the Volk to whom the Church brings the Gospel, for morality belongs to the *Nomos* of the Volk'.[64]

In 1932 Stapel gave full publicity to his celebrated doctrine of the *Volksnomos*. His definition of *Nomos* was 'the divinely prescribed natural constitution of a community, the sanctified customs, usages, organic laws and values of a Volk'.[65] Every people not excluding the Jews had its own particular *Nomos*. The Jews had received theirs from Mount Sinai, and the Old Testament Law had validity only for them. The German did not need the Old Testament and its Decalogue to tell him how he ought to conduct himself. The Jews were instructed to have none other Gods but Jehovah, but this did not apply to other nations. For 'there is a metaphysical sphere in which the God of Heaven and Earth, the one and only true God, is none other than Jahweh, the God of Israel, Jupiter of the Capitol at Rome, Athene of the city of Athens, Woden or Thor of the Germans'.[66] 'The nomos gods and their respective national religions are the source of Volk morality. In consequence, moral customs differ from people to people, and in the moral sphere that which is national has its unassailable right.'[67] The nomos deities and their Volk religions were picturesquely described by Stapel in terms of 'the crypt which serves as the substructure of the Christian Church'.[68] If the crypt were to give way, the church would collapse. The German Church, as one of the many critics of Stapel has remarked, consisted for him of 'two storeys: ground floor pagan, upstairs Christian',[69] the former accommodating *Nomos Germanikos*, the latter enshrining the Christian Gospel, since he regarded the Church as not only Christ's but also that of the Volk:[70] a conclusion only to be arrived at by means of a bewilderingly dualistic dismemberment of the First Article of the Christian creed from the Second. Stapel went so far as to suggest that, when the Christian minister was officiating in other capacities than that of celebrant at the altar, preacher in the pulpit and baptiser at the font, he was functioning essentially as a pagan priest, and that included his functioning at marriage ceremonies, public funerals and harvest festivals.[71] Matthew 5:17 was the key text ('Think not that I am come to destroy the law, or the prophets. I am not come to destroy, but to fulfil'). This, so Stapel held, referred not only to the Old Testament law and prophets but also to the particular nomos, traditions and prophetic utterances of each and every Volk. Each national nomos found its fulfilment and its redemption, but in no wise its suspension, in the Gospel. It continued to be valid and authoritative, since through it rather than through the Gospel God made known His moral requirements, and each Volk was charged with working out its own law and ethos, customs and constitution. Stapel quoted also in eager and arbitrary fashion from Romans 2:14, 15, in which Paul wrote of the Gentiles as being a 'law unto themselves' and showing 'the work of the law written in their hearts, their conscience also bearing witness'. 'What is right and wrong we create out of the "law" of our "hearts". . . . Christ teaches no new morality, all he does is to sharpen sensitivity for the truly moral',[72] he concluded. This *Volksnomos* doctrine had a profound influence upon the outlook of many of those who chose to call themselves 'German Christians', affording sanction to their tortuous efforts to show simultaneous allegiance to the volkish Weltanschauung of the Nazis and to the orthodox Lutheran version of the Christian faith and encouraging them in restricting the Church's autonomy to the sphere of the preaching of God's word and the administration of the sacraments, while acknowledging that the volkish State should have the determining say in matters of Church order and law and be the decisive authority in various moral issues. Stapel went so far as to insist that 'to the totalitarian State belongs everything that concerns law and morals. To the Church belongs everything that concerns the Kingdom of Heaven',[73] a devastating refusal to allow the Church to regulate practical earthly affairs in the light and the spirit of the Gospel.

In application of his teaching to the Jewish problem Stapel recommended a strict separation of *Judentum* and *Deutschtum*, since both were equally committed both biologically and morally to their own specific Volk law. 'When a German loves or hates, it is a different thing than when a Jew does so.'[74] Attempts at Jewish assimilation in the name of universal humanity were nothing short of an offence against God. The Jew could grow in similarity to the member of another people, but he could never become the same. He had an exactly similar obligation as the German to avoid alien contamination. This led Stapel to appreciate the aims of Zionism and even to suggest that the banishment of the Jews from Germany could have a splendid effect in helping to bring them to their senses as a Volk. He even dared to suggest that posterity might well come to regard the year 1933 as having brought deliverance to the Jewish people.[75] To be just to Stapel, he made clear that he did not indulge in hatred of the Jews or desire their persecution, and that he objected to them being branded as inferior beings, but this did not absolve him from the responsibility of having provided additional and would-be learned encouragement to many to view the Jews as a race quite apart.

The Jew who had become a Christian through baptism was, in Stapel's interpretation, to be regarded by German Christians as 'our Christian brother but not our German brother',[76] 'as man an alien, as Christian a brother'.[77] 'As long as human beings continue to live in the flesh,' he wrote, 'the one will move through the world as a German, the other as a Jew, each with his differing nomos, a reality that baptism in no wise alters.'[78] It was a cause of offence to him that a Jewish pastor should be permitted to minister to a German congregation, for he could not possibly hope to comprehend the German soul. The Jew had a different relationship to Jesus Christ from that of a German, and it was, therefore, an embarrassment, were a Jew to administer the Body and Blood of the Crucified Christ at a German Christian altar. 'The Jew who believes in Christ is welcome to God in a Christian church. At the same time, which of us is able to suppress a shudder at the sight of him ?'[79] He found himself bound to recommend that missionary work among the Jews should be undertaken solely by Jewish Christians. He also favoured the formation of a distinct Jewish Christian Church. As there was a Roman Catholic Church, a Greek Orthodox Church, a German Lutheran Church why should there then not be as well a Jewish Christian Church ?[80]

The most extreme volkish position within the Evangelical

Church was held by the *Bund für Deutsche Kirche*[81] (Association for the Promotion of a German Church), the avowed aim of which was the Germanisation of Christianity through the cultivation of native and nordic-racial values. The *Bund* was of considerable significance as a forerunner of the 'Faith Movement of German Christians'. In 1917 a small group met in Berlin which included Professor Bartels of Weimar and Pastor Andersen of Flensburg in Schleswig-Holstein. As a contribution to the Luther celebrations of that year they published their ninety-five theses under the heading of 'German Christianity on a Pure Evangelical Foundation'. The Church was criticised as being an institution for the propagation of Judaism, the fulfilment of the Reformation was seen in a completely harmonious relationship between *Deutschtum* and Christianity, and the elimination of the Old Testament was recommended. Four years later the *Bund für Deutsche Kirche* was brought into being under the direction of a certain Dr. Joachim Niedlich, with Pastor Andersen as its chief patron. The freeing of the Church from all Jewish encumbrances was again emphasised, and the principal aim was declared to be the fashioning of a fertile form of native German Christianity, with God sought for and found in characteristic Germanic style, Jesus, whose life-work was to be appreciated in terms of conflict with the Jews, revered as an Aryan hero, and a German National Church as the ultimate goal. The whole approach was highly intellectual. The aims of the *Bund* attracted Houston Stewart Chamberlain among others, but it was of little popular appeal in the parishes. There was no real plan to organise a Church party any more than to build up a rival organisation outside the established Church. The intention was, rather, to seek to encourage the existing Church in thinking in Germanic and anti-Jewish terms. When the Nazi-inspired 'Faith Movement of German Christians' was founded in 1932, many members of the *Bund*, including Reinhold Krause, who in November 1933 was to play so ominous a role,[82] joined eagerly in the campaign to seize power within the Church. The *Bund* itself continued as an independent organisation, and in fact was still in existence in Schlesiwg-Holstein in 1938 as a recognised Church group.

Friedrich Andersen published in 1921 his book *Der deutsche Heiland*[83] ('The German Saviour') described in the sub-title of its 1932 revised edition as an attempt to present a pattern of what a German-Christian faith and a German-Christian Church should be. Captivated by Chamberlain, he had early on abandoned his orthodoxy, and had come to combine dilletante biblical criticism and extremely liberal theology with increasing German volkish dogmatism. The essence of Christianity was to him the human personality of Jesus and His teaching freed from Jewish doctrinal falsifications. Jesus he chose to regard as essentially an Aryan, both racially and intellectually altogether nordic-orientated. If He had to be regarded as belonging by blood to the Jewish race, it had to be asked why 'a beautiful flower should not grow on a muck-heap'. The Twelve Apostles, Judas naturally excepted, were obviously of Aryan origin. Whoever had heard of a Jew being a fisherman? Jesus, according to Andersen, was to be regarded as an uncompromising hero, possessed of true nobility of soul, who taught the simple messages of the fatherly Love of God, the eternal worth of the individual soul and the inward realisation of the Kingdom of God. The significance of His death lay in His readiness, just like Luther at Worms, to stand for the cause of Truth. He was himself the pledge of Victory and of Life without the need for the so-called Resurrection and Ascension.

In contrast, there was no simple, healthy humanity about the Jews; conceit, push and the service of mammon were among their most evil characteristics. They were a menace to the whole world with their capitalism, internationalism and their influence in politics, the press and the arts. They were a disintegrating (*zersetzend* again!) influence upon the peoples who offered them hospitality, and they secretly undermined their Christianity. The root trouble lay in their religion, motivated by rewards and punishments and featuring a God wrathful and biased, and indulgent only to the Jews themselves. It caused the Jew to look upon everything from the point of view of profit, and made him shameless, without conscience, self-seeking, envious, materialistic; made yet worse by the fact that he recognised no continuance of life after death. In primitive Christianity, and especially that of St. Paul, there had developed a hybrid form of Jewish Christianity, illustrated for example by the application of the Messianic title to Jesus and the identification of Him with the Suffering Servant of God in Isaiah 53, thus making a Jew out of Him. Everything evil and corrupt in the Christian Church through the centuries was, he claimed, of Jewish origin—the Inquisition, witch hunts and trials, the persecution of heretics, all manner of moral degeneracy and corruption. Luther's Reformation had missed a great opportunity of overcoming such judaising of Christianity. He was too much involved with fighting the papacy to find time and opportunity to battle for the freeing of the Church from its Jewish yoke. A fatal literal faith still prevailed among Christians, with the Old Testament regarded as of authority and attention given to Christ 'after the Flesh' rather than to Christ 'after the Spirit'. The instruction of the German people in accordance with the Old Testament was to be held responsible for the general collapse of faith at the close of the World War. The Germanic characteristics of moral purity and concern for truth, freedom and loyalty had predisposed the Germans to the acceptance of Christianity. But to achieve a real fusion of *Deutschtum* and Christianity all Jewish ingredients in the latter had to be thoroughly eliminated. They included 'the exceedingly inferior Jewish Ten Commandments', the Pauline theory of Justification, 'a pillow for moral indolence', the doctrine of the Atonement with Christ offered up as victim to the God of Wrath and the 'arch-Jewish' doctrine of Original Sin, 'this abominable product of a corrupt Asiatic spirit'. The Church could well dispense with the ungermanlike Confession of Sins every Sunday and the formal recitation of the Apostles' Creed, while the provision of chairs of Old Testament studies at the universities was unwarranted. Andersen was also fully in accord with the practical recommendations of the *Bund* that church services should be cleansed from their Alleluias and their Hosannas [84] and provide room for readings from the great German prophets and commemoration of the nation's martyrs, and that the material for religious instruction in schools should include German fairy tales and sagas.

In the *Deutsche Heiland* Andersen's unbounded hostility to the Jews was primarily directed against the Jewish way of thought and attitude to life, and not the Jewish race as such, but nevertheless it ended in a confession of allegiance to the swastika symbol as an acknowledgment of the cohesion of all Aryan peoples in warfare against the Power of Darkness. Andersen exhorted the Church to throw in her lot 'with a good conscience'. [85] He himself was active as a speaker at Nazi meetings as early as 1928, became later on a Nazi training course leader, and in 1936 defended Rosenberg in a series of lectures. [86]

COD

Pastor Falck of Berlin, who was one of the most ardent members of the *Bund für Deutsche Kirche*, launched in 1928 an attack in highly coloured terms upon the established custom of an annual collection in Prussian churches in aid of the conversion of the Jews. Missions to the Jews, in his judgement, were a thorn in the flesh of the German Volk, and, when resulting in success, encouraged and accelerated the flow of Jewish blood into the German body. The Jewish viper lay at the German nordic throat all set to imbed its lethal fangs! The following year he found the official provision of a form of Service of Thanksgiving for the tenth anniversary of the Weimar Constitution as a further occasion for energetic protest. The anniversary, in his opinion, should have been marked rather by 'funeral services', lamenting all that by poisonous Jewish contrivance had promoted the moral decline of the German Volk. In an article written in 1930 he did not shrink from debasing the Gospel of Love into an invitation to hate. The Gentile peoples had, according to him, abundant justification in returning hatred for hatred, where the Jews were concerned. To do so was not unchristian. If there was any one who could really hate, it was Jesus, not, of course, in the sense of vulgar personal animosity, but in that of positive, holy wrath. Jesus had not hesitated to call the Scribes a generation of vipers. He spoke of those for whom it would be better that a millstone should be hung about their necks, and they should be drowned in the depth of the sea. Incensed by their wretched mercenary spirit he had taken a whip and driven the rabble out of the temple courts. Thus could Jesus hate, and in the same spirit there flowed from Paul's pen the memorable words—'Abhor that which is evil'. Likewise was Luther able to hate in sincerity and in depth, when he believed himself obliged to behold the Antichrist in his opponents. [87]

There can scarcely have been any more pernicious example of anti-Jewish invective in this period than the hysterical volkish and anti-semitic tirade of a certain Pastor Gerecke, who in a pamphlet entitled 'Biblical Anti-semitism' attempted to expound the Book of Jonah. 'No one', he claimed, 'detects the mailed fist of our destroyer, the good-for-nothing revolutionary Jew so surely as the Bible-true, Pan-German churchman.' He should feel himself to be at one in fellowship with 'the anti-semitic Jonah and the anti-semite Jesus'. Our Jewish enemies 'will be made to tremble and to gnash their teeth, when we throw them into the jaws of the great fish'. Fired by what he conceived to be an Old Testament thirst for revenge, Gerecke piled threat upon threat against the 'Antichrist, Judah', urging that the death-knell should be sounded for the Jews, that they should be 'strangled' and 'thrown into the fiery furnace'. The purpose of his extreme language he avowed was to evoke 'a blazing Germanic hatred against the asiatic blood-suckers and perverters of the Volk and a blazing German Christian wrath against the anti-Christian corrupters of our people, our Churches and our schools'. These frenzied words came from a minister of the Gospel, and were published thirteen years before Hitler came to power. It would be unwise to conclude that they were such venomous and absurdly exaggerated trash that they could not be taken to heart or acted upon by the Christian readers for whom they were obviously intended, nor that they would certainly have had the opposite effect from that which was desired.[88]

It is most refreshing to turn for a moment from the chronicle of Volk-obsessed anti-semitism and to listen to a quite different voice. Eduard Lamparter, a pastor in Stuttgart, produced in 1928 a booklet entitled *Evangelische Kirche und Judentum*, which revealed him as one of the very few really courageous, uncom-promising and farsighted Protestant opponents of anti-semitism. He challenged the continuing and developing anti-semitic strain within the Church, and roundly condemned the racial theories which had no genuine scientific foundation, and which favoured, bred, and sanctioned nationalistic arrogance and will to power, and assumed the right to characterise others as ignoble and inferior. The Church was declared by Lamparter to have an obligation to provide emphatic evidence that race, colour and physical origin did not decree a man's worth but quite other realities such as free will, conscience, religion and education. 'Ought not the Church', he wrote, 'to feel it her duty to bear witness against the anti-semitic violation of Right, Truth and Love?'[89] There was need to make good old injustices and to assist in preventing new injustices from taking place. Lamparter had to admit that there was something about a typical Jew that was strange and unpleasing to the Gentile, but he went on at once to remark that it was no surprise that this should be the case, when it was remembered that the Jews had been forced for centuries to live a ghetto-existence, outlawed from their surroundings. The pressures of the

Middle Ages and the shameful treatment to which they had in more recent times been submitted, had left a distasteful mark upon the character of many Jews. But this was the result not of degenerate racial properties but rather of the injustices perpetrated upon them by Christian society. Actually, the Jews revealed a moral excellence which was a fruit of their religious inheritance. There was urgent need to overcome the appalling ignorance of the majority of the clergy and of almost all the laity of the religious and cultural history of the Jews since the time of Jesus, and to encounter the prevailing prejudice in Christian circles regarding the Jewish religion. It was just not true that the religion of the Synagogue was dry and mummified. There was much warmth and mystical feeling in orthodox Jewish religion, and in their prayers and praises there was a rich vein of true poetry and exultation. Recognition was also to be given to the kinship of liberal Judaism to the contemporary Christian attitude to life. Most serious of all was the crude and unspiritual approach which saw in the Jew nought else but the descendant of the murderers of Jesus. This worked like poison among ordinary Christian folk, and the Church just did not recognise that Palestine was the native soil from which according to God's will the Christian Family had emerged, and that there was indeed a common origin and spiritual kinship between Jews and Christians.

Lamparter's contribution was warmly sponsored by Professors Karl Barth, Martin Rade, Siegmund-Schultze, and Paul Tillich among others. In a word of introduction they declared: 'We are persuaded that the anti-semitic movement, which in the aftermath of the World War has had so mighty a boom, is irreconcilable with the Christian point of view and is incompatible with our debt of gratitude to the cradle of Christianity. While prepared to recognise the idealistic motives which lie here and there at the root of the anti-semitic movement, we maintain that the evangelical clergy both in the pulpit and in their parish work ought to be in no doubt whatever that the outlawing of a 'race' or a religious confession is an offence against Christ, who exclaimed to his zealously indignant disciples—"Ye know not what manner of spirit ye are of".'[90] In Lamparter's own Church of Württemberg an attempt in 1931 to get an official motion passed condemning anti-semitism proved unavailing.[91]

In an article in the much consulted encyclopaedia, *Die Religion in Geschichte und Gegenwart* Professor Heinrich Frick of Marburg, who had some years earlier made his witness by denouncing anti-semitism as 'one of the gravest symptoms of our present-day maladies', insisted that Christianity was to be adjudged of Jewish origin and as the fulfilment of Old Testament Revelation. Contrary to the objections of the anti-semites the religion of the Old Testament was to be regarded as an essential and inseparable element in Christianity. Frick recommended that Jewish citizens of the Reich should be integrated without any restriction whatever into German society, and be treated like any other members of the community. Christians had the duty of resisting all attempts to degrade spirit and faith into functions of blood, of promoting the cause of tolerance and equality of human rights, and of actively supporting Christian missions to the Jews on a sound intellectual basis altogether free from confused references to differences of race and blood, and calling for freedom of individual decision.[92]

There were certainly in the closing years of the Weimar Period responsible Christians in authority who, while paying serious attention to what the Nazis and others were saying about the problem, felt conscientiously bound to speak out about the quite unchristian scorn and hatred for the Jews. Hermann Kremers was one. In a lecture delivered in June 1931 to the General Assembly of the *Evangelische Bund* he did not deny that there was indeed a Jewish problem, evidenced by Jewish activity and lust for power in the political, economic, social, and intellectual life of the nation, and admitted that no one who had a love for his Volk should from humanitarian and sentimental considerations desire to disregard such facts. But he also firmly insisted that the passionate outbursts of hatred for the Jews were to be condemned. The catchword 'Perish the Jews' was an expression of coarse brutality, and employed in conjunction with 'Germany, awake' was unworthy of the German people. The reference of Jesus to the 'Israelite in whom there was no guile' still held good for the present situation. It was to a Jew that the Good Samaritan extended his neighbourly love.[93]

In December 1932 the Evangelical Church of Oldenburg issued nine theses on the theme of The Christian Faith and Racial Research.[94] The theses are of great interest, for they reveal an acceptance of the current *Schöpfungstheologie*, the extent to which considerations of race were by then being taken into account by the church authorities and an obvious Christian concern that the Gospel of Love should prevail.

The Oldenburg statement acknowledged a Christian awareness of belonging by God's Creative Law to a definite Volk. In his responsibility towards the Creator the Christian had the duty of maintaining and strengthening the good inheritance of his people. This necessitated the Church paying careful attention to the findings of scientific racial research and recognising that the irrevocable racial character of the Volk had been shaped by the sovereign rule of God in history. On the other hand, while paying due respect to Creative Order and racial research, the Oldenburg statement made no secret of a lively concern that Christian values should be upheld. The Word of God was directed to all peoples. Individual races were called by God to mutual service of one another. Through the reconciling sacrifice of Jesus Christ all men of all races were in equal fashion entitled to their share of the Love of God. Races might be irrevocably different, but that, according to the Christian view, was no warrant for any one race to regard itself as the elect one, or to look down with arrogance upon another. It was outside the province of scientific racial research to posit a so-called 'religion of blood' which was nothing short of sheer fantasy and crass idolatry. The Christian knew that religion as a spiritual good was not confined to any one single race, and racial research confirmed that an adoption of spiritual qualities by one race from another was a reality.

The Church in Oldenburg had been in the limelight in the autumn of 1932, when a Negro pastor from Togo whose work was supported by the local missionary society was invited to give an address in a central church in Oldenburg. Such an invitation evoked a storm of Nazi protest, and was declared to be both 'frivolous' and 'foolish'. A nigger pastor speaking in a German church was an outrage upon the white race, and those responsible for organising it deserved to go to prison. A Church paper commented sagely and prophetically that it was but a short step from rejecting a Negro to rejecting a Jew—and on the same grounds.[95]

The publication in 1932 in two volumes by Leopold Klotz of a series of essays on the subject of 'The Church and the Third

Reich', the majority of which revealed either deep concern at, or outright criticism of, certain aspects of National Socialism, attracted considerable attention in Church circles, and earned Nazi disapproval with the assurance that due note would be taken of the names of those who had written in such derogatory fashion. One Nazi critic condemned the first volume as a 'conglomeration of ignorance, superficiality, arrogance, and of malicious hostility against the German Freedom Movement'.[96] The contributors to the two volumes ranged from professors to young pastors and theological students. Several of the essays included direct consideration of the racial ideology and of the Jewish issue.

Ernst Bizer,[97] a promising young theologian from Württemberg, insisted that the New Testament gave no countenance to the belief that a man was damned because of his blood, or that anyone was entitled by virtue of his blood to regard himself as excused from the univeral obligation to love his neighbour. Any suggestion that a Jew could never become a Christian was as unchristlike as could be.

Paul Fiebig[98] who at that time was responsible for New Testament studies at Leipzig University, made bold application of the New Testament to the Nazi *Weltanschauung*. Jesus, Jew by birth, he declared, protested against the dangers inherent in the nationalistic attitude. The Evangelical Church and evangelical theology were likewise obliged to protest in the name of genuine religion and morality against the perils of nationalistic exclusiveness. The Cross did not point the way to bloodthirsty power, vengeance, and hatred but to peace, forgiveness, and love. The question that the German theologian and Christian had to put to the Third Reich was that as to whether the spirit of Jesus was to be dominant or not.

Paul Tillich[99] in ten crisp theses made manifest his distaste for an alliance of the Protestant Church with National Socialism. If this involved an attempted justification of the Nazi racial ideology on grounds of the Divine Creative Ordinances, it meant sacrificing the Church's prophetic principles in favour of open or veiled heathenism. Protestantism needed to preserve its prophetic and Christian character by confronting the heathenism of the Swastika by the Christianity of the Cross, witnessing that Nation, Race and Blood in their mystic sovereignty had to be brought under the judgement of the Cross.

Johannes Bruns[100] expressed his grave concern at the over-emphasis upon racial ideas in the National Socialist Movement. Blood alone decided everything. A Jew was to be rejected purely as a Jew; one who was Germanic by race was regarded as being virtually free from sin. German people were to be set free from disastrous Jewish influences; yet the national pride that inspired such a move was certainly not free from the Jewish spirit which was so sharply attacked in the Old Testament itself.

The boldest and most searching of all the various contributions to 'The Church and the Third Reich' was undoubtedly that provided by a young *Vikarin* (female curate) in Cologne, Ina Gschossl by name.[101] She enquired, as Lamparter had done, whether much of what the National Socialists claimed to find so pernicious and dangerous in the attitude and practices of the Jews was not in fact largely a result of the oppression and outlawry that they had had over many centuries to endure. Their so-called 'host-nations' shared in the guilt for such depravity. Were there not at any rate individual Jews who were courageous, kindly, pious, and obedient to God just as, on the other hand, there were cowards, weaklings, and commercially-minded characters among those who called themselves Germans? Not once in the New Testament was anyone condemned or declared to be incapable of redemption on grounds of race. Even if the Jews were really to be accounted the source and fountain of all evil, was it not a Christian duty to refrain from taking revenge upon them and rewarding evil for evil? How prophetic proved to be her further remark that those who today propagate hatred and threaten violence will tomorrow be saddled with guilt for homicide and all sorts of brutality! 'If it be claimed that such utterances are to be regarded as catch-phrases to appeal to the masses, has it been considered what influence it may have upon them, and to what actions it may drive them?'

A quite different contribution to the symposium came from Pastor Siegfried Nobiling of Berlin,[102] who had undergone a highly emotional conversion to National Socialism in 1929. It took the form of a singularly lame and inconsequent apologia for his newly developed Nazified Christianity. He expressed his firm conviction that there was a sin against the Blood, and that the Jews were to be held responsible for both the spiritual and the bodily poisoning of the Germanic race. While it could not be denied that Christianity was supranational, and that it transcended all racial theories, yet it never opposed racial purity. Socialist and liberal versions of Christianity had perverted the equality of all men before God into the equality of all men face to face with one another. Nobiling declared himself to be the sworn enemy of Jewish Christianity in so far as it stood for the attempted obliteration of racial distinctions. Any Jew could become a Christian, but not thereby a German. This did not mean that he, Nobiling, was an anti-semite in the accepted sense. He did not want to do away with the Jews altogether. His was a volkish brand of anti-semitism, which he claimed in no wise contradicted the fundamentals of Christianity, the objective Revelation of God in Christ or the subjective and inward concern of the soul.

The rapidly growing and increasingly vociferous 'Faith Movement of "German Christians"', which enjoyed the warm patronage of the Nazi Party, issued in June 1932 its Guiding Principles[103] which included the expressed desire that the Church should be found fighting in the front line in the decisive battle for the very existence of the Volk, the affirmation of Race, Volkstum and Nation as 'orders governing life given and entrusted to us by God and concern for the upholding of that which is for us God's Law'. For that reason mixture of races had to be opposed. The Christian mission to the Jews was to be regarded as a serious danger for the Volkstum, for it was 'the portal through which alien blood was infiltrated into the Volk-body' and threatened racial confusion and bastardisation. The contracting of marriages between Germans and Jews was, in particular, to be prohibited.

'By means of the Gospel a Jew may be converted into a Christian but never into a German Christian,'[104] commented the 'German Christian' Friedrich Wieneke, one of those responsible for the composition of the 'Principles'.

Another who was actively involved was Julius Kuptsch, a pastor from East Germany and former Education Minister in Latvia. The official Nazi publishing house of Franz Eher issued in January 1932 a pamphlet of his entitled *Christianity in National Socialism*, in which he sought to persuade his readers that 'the fundamentals of National Socialism and their implementation are practical Christianity and that National Socialism alone is the real champion of true Christianity'.[105] National Socialism he also regarded as professing allegiance to the Sign of the Cross, the crooked cross the token of the German after the flesh, as God desired him to be according to His Creative Order, the Cross of Christ the token of the German after the spirit, whom Christ had redeemed. 'Consequently, the National Socialists carry the Swastika on their breasts and the Cross of Christ within their breasts.'[106] As was to be expected, the pamphlet had a very marked anti-semitic emphasis. The Jewish people as an evil blend of semitic, mongolian and negro races, were dismissed by him with scorn as an international people without a fatherland, with the curse of God upon them for their rejection of Christ, and incapable of accomplishing anything permanently good for other men. Whenever God desired to punish a people that had shown scant respect for their race and fatherland, He set the Jews as a scourge for their backs. It was no solution to convert them to Christianity, for the semite remained a semite and the man who was nordic by race nordic, even if they became Christians. The Jews had to be fought, but it was a necessary battle for the preservation of life, not one of annihilation. 'National Socialism never summons its people to battle, in order to destroy other peoples, but merely in conflict for the right to existence and for its own self-preservation.'[107] A hostile attitude to the Jews of this sort he insisted was truly Christian. The New Testament, the Holy Bible of Christianity, was the most anti-Jewish book in the whole world. Did it not proclaim on almost every page that there was not a greater enemy of Christianity than the Jews? Christ Himself did not hesitate to call the Jews the children of the Devil. The Churches just did not take all that into account, and disregarded the plain distinction which the New Testament made between 'Israel after the flesh', rejected by God, and the 'Israel of God', true Christianity. It was excessively unchristian to regard the Jewish people as the Chosen People of God. National Socialism, he therefore argued, was doing no more than implementing the teaching of Christianity, when it recommended putting a check upon the enemies of Christianity, removing them from public office, and making them answerable for their misdeeds. In fact, the National Socialists would reveal themselves as the warriors of God in fighting the decisive battle on German soil on behalf of the whole world against every anti-Christian and godless enterprise of the Jews and their marxist henchmen.

NOTES TO CHAPTER 2

1. Karl Wilhelm Dahm: *Pfarrer und Politik*, Köln, 1965, p. 147.
2. Mehnert, 72.
3. Dahm, 185. Martin Niemöller in a radio interview in 1964 admitted that he was led in 1919 to seek ordination, because it appeared to be the best way in which he could serve his Volk. The national element in the Church's thinking and planning, he went on to explain, was by and large at that time much stronger than any concern for the expression of love to one's neighbour. The Church was full of solicitude for the Volk, was concerned about the individual as confirmation candidate or church member but not really geared to the fulfilment of the command to love one's neighbour as one-self (Günther Gaus: *Zur Person. Porträts in Frage und Antwort*, München, 1965, p. 109).
4. Pulzer, 303.
5. See Appendix 4, The *Ostjuden*.
6. George Mosse in *Entscheidungsjahr, 1932*, pp. 230, 237.
7. Pulzer, 305.
8. Jochmann, 452.
9. Jochmann, 455.
10. Jochmann, 479–80.
11. Mehnert, 204.
12. Tilgner, 299.
13. Quoted in Helmut Baier: *Die Deutsche Christen Bayerns im Rahmen des bayerischen Kirchenkampfes*, Nürnberg, 1968, p. 35.
14. Ino Arndt: *Die Judenfrage im Licht der evangelischen Sonntagsblätter von 1918–1933*, Unpublished Dissertation, Tübingen, 1960.
15. Arndt, 220.
16. Arndt, 220. (The *Stuttgarter Sonntagsblatt* was according to reliable sources responsible for the anti-semitic excesses in Memmingen in 1921. (Jochmann, 481).)
17. See Wilhelm Stählin: *Via Vitae, Lebenserinnerungen*, Kassel, 1968, pp. 180–7, and Manfred Priepke: *Die evangelische Jugend im Dritten Reich, 1933–1936*, Hannover, 1960, pp. 19–21.
18. Wilhelm Stählin: *Die völkische Bewegung und unsere Verantwortung*, Sollstedt, 1924.
19. Ibid., 19.
20. Ibid., 24, 29.
21. Ibid., 40.
22. Ibid., 46–7.
23. Ibid., 57.
24. Ibid., 59.
25. Tilgner, 303.
26. Kraus in *Entscheidungsjahr 1932*, p. 253.
27. Tilgner, 304.
28. Helmut Schreiner: *Das Christentum und die völkische Frage*, Berlin, 1925, p. 30.

29. Althaus: *Kirche und Volkstum*, 42–3.
30. Paul Althaus: *Die Letzten Dinge. Lehrbuch der Eschatologie*, Gütersloh, 1957, pp. 312, 313.
31. *Quellen sur Geschichte des deutschen Protestantismus, 1871–1945*, ed. Karl Kupisch, München, 1965, pp. 164–6.
32. Paul Althaus: *Kirche und Volkstum*, 17.
33. Ibid., 15.
34. Ibid., 24.
35. Ibid., 27.
36. Quoted by Ernst Wolf in Barmen: *Kirche zwischen Versuchung und Gnade*, 2nd edition, München, 1970, p. 20.
37. Paul Althaus: *Die deutsche Stunde der Kirche*, Göttingen, 1934, p. 36.
38. *Kirche und Volkstum*, 19.
39. Ibid., 33.
40. Paul Althaus: *Völker vor und nach Christus*, Leipzig, 1937, p. 9.
41. *Deutsche Stunde*, 48.
42. Ibid., 46.
43. Ibid., 8.
44. Ibid., 19.
45. Ibid., 47.
46. Paul Althaus: *Theologie der Ordnungen*, Gütersloh, 1934, p. 8.
47. Quoted by Wolfgang Tilgner in *Volksnomostheologie und Schöpfungsglaube, Arbeiten zur Geschichte des Kirchenkampfes*, Band 16, Göttingen, 1966, p. 182, note 9.
48. See Klaus Scholder: *Die Evangelische Kirche und das Jahr 1933* in *Geschichte in Wissenschaft und Unterricht*, 1945, pp. 708–9.
49. Arndt, 142–3.
50. Quoted by Wolfgang Tilgner in *Volk, Nation, Vaterland*, Gütersloh, 1970, p. 166.
51. Quoted by Tilgner in *Rasse, Kirche und Humanum*, p. 300.
52. Arndt, 80.
53. Ibid., 88.
54. Ibid., 76.
55. Ibid., 83.
56. Ibid., 149–50.
57. Ibid., 148.
58. Martin Wagner: *Die 'Deutschen Christen' im Kampf um die innere Erneuerung des deutschen Volkes*, Berlin, 1933, p. 21.
59. For Stapel and his contribution see Wolfgang Tilgner: *Volksnomostheologie und Schöpfungsglaube*, pp. 89–138.
60. Wilhelm Stapel: *Der christliche Staatsman. Eine Theologie des Nationalismus*, Hamburg, 1932, p. 17.
61. Dietrich Bonhoeffer called it a 'dangerous book full of genuine and bogus pathos, with the theological ideas contained therein not clearly thought out'. Eberhard Bethge: *Dietrich Bonhoeffer, Eine Biographie*. München, 1967, p. 1085.
62. Tilgner: *Volksnomostheologie*, 95.
63. Quoted by Tilgner in *Volk, Nation, Vaterland*, p. 164.

64. Wilhelm Stapel: *Die Kirche Christi und der Staat Hitlers*, Hamburg 1933, p. 66.
65. Wilhelm Stapel: *Sechs Kapitel über Christentum und National-sozialismus*, Hamburg, 1933, p. 13.
66. *Der christiliche Staatsman*, 183.
67. Ibid., 184.
68. Ibid., 182.
69. Martin Doerne: *Wass heisst Volkskirche?*, Leipzig, 1935, pp. 17–18.
70. Wilhelm Stapel: *Volkskirche oder Sekte?*, Hamburg, 1934, p. 52.
71. Ibid., 48–9.
72. *Die Kirche Christi*, 62.
73. Ibid., 65.
74. Quoted by Tilgner, *Volksnomostheologie*, 106.
75. Ibid., 108.
76. *Kirche Christi*, 83.
77. Ibid., 84.
78. Ibid., 83.
79. Ibid., 85.
80. Ibid., 86.
81. See Gerhard Gloege: *Die Deutschkirche* in *Die Nation vor Gott*, ed. Walter Künneth and Helmut Schreiner, 5th edition, Berlin, 1937, pp. 403–21 and Hans Buchheim: *Glaubenkrise im Dritten Reich*, Stuttgart, 1953, pp. 45–8.
82. See page 121.
83. This summary of the contents of *Der deutsche Heiland* is based upon Gloege, 405–8 and Eduard Lamparter: *Evangelische Kirche und Judentum*, 286–8.
84. So fanatical was Andersen in damning anything that could be held to have an original connection with the Old Testament, that he even recommended a ban upon the trumpet-blowing of the German Y.M.C.A. (Lamparter, 287).
85. Tilgner in *Rasse, Kirche, Humanum*, 301.
86. Buchheim 46.
87. Philipp in *Kirche und Synagoge*, II, pp. 334–5.
88. Ibid., 333.
89. Eduard Lamparter: *Kirche und Judentum* in *Versuche des Verstehens*, p. 302.
90. Ibid., 255.
91. Maria Zelzer: *Weg und Schicksal der Stuttgarter Juden*, Stuttgart, 1964, p. 132.
92. Philipp in *Kirche und Synagoge*, II, 338.
93. Hermann Kremers: *Nationalismus und Protestantismus*, Berlin, 1931, pp. 21–2.
94. Reproduced by Hans-Joachim Kraus in *Entscheidungsjahr 1932*, pp. 267–8.
95. Arndt, 166–7.
96. Leopold Klotz: *Die Kirche und das Dritte Reich*, Gotha, 1932, Vol. II, p. 9.

97. Klotz, I, 12–13.
98. Klotz, I, 25–30.
99. Klotz, I, 126–8.
100. Klotz, II, 19–24.
101. Klotz, II, 58–61.
102. Klotz, II, 79–85.
103. The full text of the 'Guiding Principles' is to be found in Kupisch: *Quellen*, 254–6, and with a revealing commentary in Friedrich Wieneke: *Die Glaubensbewegung 'Deutsche Christen'*, Soldin, 1933, pp. 14–27. An English translation is provided in John Conway: *The Nazi Persecution of the Churches, 1933–1945*, Weidenfeld and Nicolson, 1968, pp. 339–41.
104. Wieneke, 24.
105. Julius Kuptsch: *Christentum im Nationalsozialismus*, München, 1932, p. 5.
106. Ibid., 36.
107. Ibid., 34.

3
Hitler, the Church and the Jews, January–April 1933

The German Evangelical, whether he was prepared to sign on with the Nazi Party or not, had no difficulty in discovering what Hitler and his Party felt and intended regarding the Jews. *The Völkischer Beobachter* and other widely circulated Nazi papers gave ample information, as did Nazi meetings up and down the country. Long before 1933 Hitler had left no room for the slightest doubt that racial anti-semitism was an essential ingredient of National Socialist ideology.[1] It was impossible to read pages 329–62 of *Mein Kampf*[2] and not be made aware that, if Adolf Hitler came to power, a dreadful fate would be in store for the Jews as a whole. The sheer venom of his indictment, if taken seriously, as there was scant reason not to do, was fearful and chilling. The Jew was declared to be parasite, malignant germ, bloodsucking leech, 'personification of the Devil, and symbol of all evil',[3] out to 'drag everything really great in the gutter'[4] with the intention of 'enslaving and thereby destroying all non-Jewish peoples'.[5] The very existence of the Jews was held to be as calamitous as the plague. The Christian reader, in particular, was exhorted to note that the Jewish enemy made religion ridiculous, and pronounced accepted customs and morals to be outmoded.[6] The whole spirit of the Jews was declared to be 'essentially alien to that of genuine Christianity', the Founder of which in holy anger took a whip to drive them from the sacred precincts of the temple, only to be rewarded by the crucifixion.[7] Hitler's ostensibly pious assertion that in dealing with the Jews, he would be acting on behalf of the 'Almighty Creator' and doing the 'Lord's work' undoubtedly made its impression.[8]

The official Party programme plainly stated the aim to be to deprive the Jew of his privilege of German national citizenship and to subject him to special alien legislation.[9] In a much read booklet entitled *Der Deutsche Staat* written by Gottfried Feder, veteran Nazi publicist (first edition, 1924) the exclusion of all Jews from responsible positions in public life was recommended, and the influence and effect of the Jews was likened to a life and death struggle between a healthy body and the deadly poisonous germs attacking it. Either the healthy strength of the body would master the foreign invasion and eliminate it or it would no longer maintain its domination, and would suffer annihilation. There was only one alternative—exclusion of the Jews from the national body or ruin at their hands.[10]

It would have been difficult to have been unaware of the increasing acts of brutality and terrorisation aimed at the Jews. Between 1923 and 1932 125 Jewish cemeteries and 48 synagogues had been desecrated. In 1931 at the time of the Jewish New Year a thousand S.A. men took part in an anti-Jewish pogrom in Berlin. A contributor to the *Church Annual* of 1932 wrote of the crude way in which everything Jewish was vilified and the Jew personally insulted, and with, sadly enough, no express condemnation by the Evangelical Church as such.[11]

There is little doubt that the racial anti-semitism of the Nazis was not regarded with the same deadly earnestness with which it was intended. A Church that was ready to identify herself with the proposed New Order and that showed herself to be alive to the legitimate needs of the Volk, a defence of racial purity and the necessity of curbing undesirable Jewish influence, would surely have the opportunity to put in a word for a more subdued and controlled form of anti-semitism. If the virulence of what was propagated by the Nazis was viewed with concern, it was probably felt that this was something that had for the time being at any rate to be accepted along with so much else that was so attractive and desirable in the programme for national revival. There was the hope, too, that, once the Revolution had been effected, and the Nazis had their share in the responsibility of government, things would tend to settle down, and the rawness and vulgarity in the National Socialist campaign for power would have gained its purpose, and would then yield to something altogether more moderate and respectable. An interesting example is that of Professor Kuhn of Tübingen, a noted Hebraist and authority on Judaism who, in a lecture delivered early in 1933, admitted that the approval of the National Socialist recommendations for social reform and their declaration of war upon communism had encouraged him to join the Party, though he could not begin to identify himself with either its racial theories or with its particular brand of anti-semitism. He was optimistic enough, however, to believe that the extravagant notions of certain Party leaders would soon disappear, once the Party had to co-operate actively in the government of the state.[12] As well-informed and responsible a Christian observer from abroad as Dr. Visser t'Hooft still felt able to write in mid-April 1933—'While there is reason to denounce the anti-semitism which is unfortunately stronger than ever in Germany today, there is no reason to take it for granted that the worst anti-semitic tendencies will finally prevail.'[13]

Anyhow, the Church taken as a whole, was altogether too much concerned with herself, her internal affairs, and her position in a revived Germany to consider taking up the cause of the threatened Jews. Were they not, after all, an accursed people by divine decree? It would be difficult to exaggerate the general emphasis within the Churches upon the curse upon Israel rather than upon God's choice and promise, an emphasis that was neither evangelical nor Christian. The statement made in 1936 by Dr. Kühlewein, Bishop of Baden, expresses accurately the view that was generally held three or four years earlier, 'When the Jews crucified Jesus, they crucified themselves, their revelation and their history. Thus the curse came upon them. Since then that curse works itself out from one generation to another. This people has, therefore, become a fearful and divinely ordained scourge for all nations, leading to hatred and persecution.'[14] In sermons and in religious instruction there appeared time and again the assertion that the Jews are the murderers of Christ, such statements being made 'in forgetfulness of the recognition by the Reformers that the excommunication of the Son of God takes place in the midst of the Church—time and again, yesterday, today and tomorrow'.[15]

The earliest days of Nazi power with Hitler's calculatedly benevolent assurance of recognition of and respect for the status and contribution of the Churches had encouraged the great majority of leading churchmen to speak enthusiastically of the decisive break-through in German history, thanking God for the

new state so manifestly built upon 'positive Christian' foundations.[16] Typical was the summons of the venerable conservative
Bishop of Saxony, Dr. Ihmels, to the Church to advance with joy
and courage to make the old Gospel a new force in the life of the
people. 'A complete renewal of feeling for the Fatherland has
taken possession of wide circles of the people. The Church must
on no account keep silent. The order of the day is a Church
identified with the deep needs of the Volk. It is an especial cause
of rejoicing that the National Socialist Movement both seeks and
deliberately cultivates association with God.'[17] Such almost
universal volkish enthusiasm did not promise much consideration
for the Jewish misfits in the new society.

In Bavaria an enthusiastic statement was drawn up to be read
from all Lutheran pulpits on Easter Sunday, 1933. It included the
following eulogy of the New Order. 'A state which brings into
being again government according to God's Laws should, in
doing so, be assured not only of the applause but also of the glad
and active co-operation of the Church. With gratitude and joy
the Church takes note that the new State bans blasphemy, assails
immorality, establishes discipline and order with a strong hand,
while at the same time calling upon men to fear God, espousing
the sanctity of marriage and Christian training for the young,
bringing into honour again the deeds of our fathers and kindling
in thousands of hearts, in place of disparagement, an ardent love
for Volk and Fatherland. We welcome with particular gratitude
the indication that the new State will be going to crown its endeavours by the creation of a genuine Volk community (*Volks-
gemeinschaft*) with the result above all, as the Church has with
such especial ardour advocated, that the cause of the needy, the
oppressed, the poor and the destitute will be commended to the
care of the whole people.'[18] Evangelical statements such as these
two which were not of 'German Christian' origin were multiplied
throughout Germany. If the Jews were not actually mentioned,
their suppression was accepted as the inevitable and justifiable
accompaniment of volkish purification and renewal, with tacit
approval that the Nazis now in power would be taking certain
practical steps to implement what so many Protestants had been
recommending on and off ever since Adolf Stoecker's original
agitation. That Adolf Hitler had assumed the mantle of Adolf
Stoecker was a naïve and disastrous assumption!

There were varied reactions from the Jews themselves. It has been claimed that in the first days of 1933 most Jews regarded the paraded anti-semitism of the new regime as largely propaganda tactics and a transitory phenomenon. Many were of the opinion that there would be in due course a similar development to that in Italy, where the Jews in their great majority were supporters of Mussolini and valued as a loyal element of the population. Many of the Jews at that time in Germany felt themselves to be the most German of Germans and completely part and parcel of the Fatherland, and could scarcely credit that there was a danger that they would be proceeded against, cruelly persecuted, and outlawed. Some hoped that, once the new Germany was securely established, and the initial revolutionary excitement had passed, a place would be found for them to continue to live in peace and make their contribution. Some seemed quite optimistic at first that outside opinion would cause the Nazis to modify their campaign, or that economic difficulties at home and economic pressures from abroad might oblige the new rulers in Germany to change their tune.[19]

The Zionists who disapproved of Jewish emancipation in so far as it encouraged anonymity and denial of Jewishness believed that Hitler's advent to power could herald the beginning of a return to a sound appreciation of the particularity of the Jewish people as such.

There were those who were actually enthusiastic about the national awakening[20] and who were prepared to vote for and to support Hitler. There were even certain among them who would have been genuinely pleased to have been admitted into membership of the National Socialist Party. Such a one was Rabbi Elie Munk who declared, 'From the Jewish standpoint I reject the doctrines of Marxism and profess allegiance to National Socialism without its anti-semitic components. Indeed, minus anti-semitism, National Socialism would find those Jews devoted to tradition among the most loyal of their supporters.'[21] Talks did actually take place during 1933 between official German Jewish organisations and the Nazis regarding co-operation and the integration of Jews into the Third Reich.[22] Hans Joachim Schoeps who has subsequently been described as the most radical, original, phantastic, and loyal to Hitler of all Jewish reformers of this particular period,[23] optimistically sought an interview with the Führer,[24] and managed to make contact with the 'Brown House' in an effort to arrange for the incorporation within the S.A. of a special detachment of Jewish volunteers.

In his recently published book on the patriotism of the German Jews Schoeps insists that 'from 1933 to 1935 it was impossible for anyone to anticipate in the remotest way the criminal acts upon which the Nazis would one day embark. Anyone who suggests otherwise is a liar.'[25] Nevertheless, there were certainly a number who from the very beginning were astute enough to read the writing on the wall, and lost no time in making their plans to emigrate.

Without question there were those who were filled with deep sadness and despair, as they quickly came to realise that there was no place for them in the New Order. Such a one was Fritz Rosenfelder, popular sportsman and respected businessman, who early in 1933 shot himself. He left behind him a letter, in which he declared that he no longer desired to live as a German, and anyhow he would no longer be permitted to do so. He could not, and would not, allow himself to be accounted a traitor to the Fatherland. He preferred to choose death at his own hand, and trusted that thereby he might shake and arouse his Christian friends.[26]

It would, however, be a mistake to suggest that in the first days of National Socialist rule the Evangelical Church was in a state of volkish intoxication, giving vent to almost universal anti-semitic feeling. Things were more complicated than that. There were those who were concerned that the Church should not delay in making public protest regarding the treatment that was already being meted out to the Jews. Theophil Wurm, President, and shortly to become Bishop, of the Church of Württemberg, took the opportunity of presenting on 2 March to a meeting of the Central committee of the German Evangelical Church a petition submitted by a number of ladies, including Adolf Harnack's widow, asking that concern should be shown for the treatment of the Jews in Germany. It was stated in the petition that the 'campaign being waged against our Jewish fellow-citizens could be regarded in no other way than that of a continuous transgression of the supreme Law of Christianity. The German Evangelical Church is requested to raise her voice with full publicity against these abuses.' Lack of time at that particular meeting to discuss the petition did not permit of any action being taken.[27]

At the end of March Wurm wrote to Dr. Kapler, President of the Church Federation (*Kirchenbund*), stressing the mounting gravity of the situation, and Freiherr von Pechmann, a long-standing and revered lay member of the Central Church Committee, also urged Kapler on no account to keep silent, but in the name and for the sake of the Church to speak out on behalf of the Jews.[28]

At the same time as these calls were being made for open protest the German section of the World Alliance of Protestants had sent a telegram to Church leaders in the United States, in which they gave an assurance upon their honour that there was to date no pogrom against the Jews, and urging that public opinion should not be falsely influenced by atrocity propaganda, and that a right regard should be given to Christian righteousness and love of the Truth.[29] This was followed three days later by a similar message from the German Methodists to their opposite numbers in England and America ending with the words—'Apart from the misdemeanours of a few irresponsible persons, against whom the new government has at once taken the sternest of measures, quiet and order have never been endangered.'[30]

Kapler himself was obviously a troubled man. He was no doubt alarmed by the early reaction of the 'best ecumenical friends of the German *Kirchenbund*', the Federal Council of the Churches of Christ in America and the Swedish Ecumenical Committee. The president of the Federal Council had written personally to him on 24 March inquiring whether he thought it would be possible or wise 'for the *Kirchenbund* and the Federal Council to issue a manifesto denouncing anti-semitism as un-Christlike'.[31] There could be no question of his co-operation in this, but he had no desire for any disruption of ecumenical good relations. His immediate response was to wire to the Federal Council urgently begging them to use their influence in preventing the issue of manifestoes against Germany based upon false reports and calculated to cause grave damage to Church co-operation.[32] Kapler obviously felt bound to defend the measures that were being taken by the government against the Jews and to use such influence as he had to prevent Christians abroad from condemning such actions. He was apparently ready to subscribe to the official view that foreign criticism was an example of 'atrocity propaganda' —a phrase which carried overtones from the First World War. He was doubtless much influenced in doing so by fear of the adverse effect that any attempted outside Christian interference would have upon the prospect of harmonious relations between the Church at home and the new government. There was the temptation to make use of the Jews as a pawn in the contest for the independence of the Church, an issue that was of such moment to him, and to do so by suggesting that only a Church that had retained her freedom would be credible abroad, when she set out to defend government policy. And yet it would appear that Kapler had no illusions that the Jews were being subject to unchristian treatment. He 'admitted to severe pangs of conscience, and asked government officials to show humanity and moderation'.[33]

It seems highly relevant to mention at this point what had happened on 18 March in Öhringen, a small town in Württemberg. Communists and Jews had been arrested, brutally handled and whipped without any necessity or justification. They were marched through the streets and forced to make a degrading public declaration. One of the Jews concerned was compelled to hold a Communist banner over his shoulder, while it was solemnly burnt. A crowd, including many youngsters witnessed the scene, and photographs of the persecuted were taken, and afterwards offered for sale, and passed round among the children at school. The local pastors felt as ministers and representatives of the Church that they could not keep silent, and they, therefore, wrote in protest to the authorities saying, 'It contradicts our sense of right, that punishment should be executed, before a verdict in court of law has been pronounced, and we request that there shall be no repetition of this behaviour.'[34]

There were varied reactions to the Jewish Boycott[35] on 1 April, which the Nazi Party chose to advertise in terms of a purely defensive operation against Jewish 'atrocity propaganda' (*Greuelhetze*). The Berlin Church authorities did not appear to have regarded it as of any decisive significance, and deemed that they had fulfilled their responsibility by sending the following terse and tepid wire to the Reich Agency of German Jews—'Following development with greatest vigilance. Hope Boycott measures will come to conclusion today.'[36]

Bishop Wurm made it known in Berlin that the Württemberg churchpeople had in no way been in agreement with the boycott manœuvre, and urged that the Church should speak out and make her criticisms known. He expressed his confidence that, if only Dr. Kapler were to make an appropriate public statement, it would be gratefully welcomed throughout the Church.[37] This was very different from the impression given by one of the Württemberg pastors, Heinrich Pfisterer, who reported that he was in Stuttgart on Boycott Day, and that he had not heard one single malicious remark directed against the Jews. He took issue with the Swiss Evangelical Press Service on the question why the Church had kept silent over the whole affair. He declared it as his view that the action taken was carried out in disciplined fashion, and was thoroughly justified. The Church had no business to oppose the attempt of the government through economic pressure upon the Jewish community to silence the foreign outcry against Germany. 'I have', he wrote, 'in company with my colleagues an altogether good conscience regarding our silence. But I would not have a good conscience, if we had fought a rearguard action against our people. We would, in doing so, have deprived ourselves of the right to have raised our voices on other occasions, when a protest might be unquestionably called for.'[38]

Freiherr von Pechmann sought to convince the central church authorities that a firm stand by the Evangelical Church at this particular time would be widely welcomed in Christian circles. It would also serve to underline the Church's independence. For the Church to keep silent in such an hour would be fateful.[39] In a letter to Kapler, dated 12 April, he referred to the indescribable suffering of countless Jewish families, the members of which had every right to call themselves Christians and who were anxiously waiting day after day for a word from their Church promising them protection. He did not, however, just call for the championing of such persecuted fellow-Christians, but also insisted that the Church could not and should not keep silent in face of the violation of Christian justice and love so patent in the treatment being meted out to Jewish fellow-citizens (*Volksgenossen*). The Church had in this altogether wider responsibility a mission to fulfil. Failure at last to speak out would imperil the standing of the German Evangelical Church throughout the whole of Christendom.[40]

Johannes Kübel, a leading church official in Frankfurt-on-Main, claimed to be representing widespread local concern in his expression of profound dismay at the silence of the Church. The honourable name of Christian and the very basis of Christian ethics were at stake, when those who were purely Jewish were being defamed. Still more intolerable was it, when families which had belonged for three generations to the Evangelical Church were nevertheless suddenly having to endure the slur of being accounted thoroughly Jewish.[41] Hugo Hahn, Chief Pastor in Dresden, and soon to become leader of the Confessing Church in Saxony, and after the war Bishop of Saxony, admits in his memoirs that it had been his habit to avoid giving custom to Jewish businesses, but that, finding the boycott unchristian and objectionable, he began out of sympathy and in protest to patronise Jewish shops. It was touching to discover what pleasure he gave, and how nice those behind the counter were to him.[42]

Otto Dibelius, on the other hand, had no hesitation in supporting this Nazi demonstration. In a broadcast he assured the protesting outside world that the government was quite right in staging the boycott as a means of encountering lying foreign propaganda. The result would be the curtailing of Jewish influence in the public life of Germany. No one could seriously object to that![43] 'The Church', he declared, 'cannot, and ought not to, prevent the State from creating order by hard measures. . . . My friends, you know that we are a People of Order, Right and Discipline.'[44] In his weekly column in a church Sunday paper, which frequently dealt critically with the Jewish peril, Dibelius wrote: 'Despite every Christian obligation not to do injustice to anybody, there is no doubt whatever that in all the murky happenings of the last fifteen years, the Jewish element has played a leading role.' The surest way of meeting the Jewish problem, he suggested, lay in the firm German determination not to succumb to an alien race. To solve the problem, it was necessary that the Christian conscience should serve in fortifying the feeling of responsibility in the life of each individual German for the welfare of the God-given Volkstum.[45]

At about the same time a journal of the German Reformed Church crossed swords with the *Church of Scotland Observer* regarding the ridiculous and unnecessary reference to the religious persecution by Hitler of the Jews, stating that no decent Jew has had a single hair of his head tweaked. There had been, it was true, a voluntary exodus of those who saw that there was no longer a place for them in a Germany restored to decency, as for instance Emil Ludwig, *né* Cohen, Leon Feuchtwanger, and Albert Einstein.[46]

During the month of April highly critical reactions to the boycott and the persecution of the Jews were voiced by Protestants in Britain, France, Belgium, Holland, Italy, Portugal, and Switzerland, the last-named inquiring what the Evangelical Church contemplated doing to counteract the destitution of innocent persons. There was an anxious awaiting to see whether in Germany itself there was not an ecumenical personality who would raise his voice and 'open his mouth for the dumb'. Wilhelm von Pechmann and Dietrich Bonhoeffer made their feelings known, as also did Friedrich Siegmund-Schultze, well-known for his social work in East Berlin (where he founded in 1911 a highly successful Settlement after the pattern of Toynbee Hall in London) his pioneer ecumenical activity as the leading German collaborator in the work of the World Alliance for Promoting International Friendship through the Churches, and his editorship of the *Eiche* in which periodical he threatened to publish authenticated details of anti-Jewish excesses. His arrest on grounds of having on as many as ninety-three instances given assistance to Jews and his consequent expulsion from Germany prevented this.[47]

Pastor Wilhelm Menn, engaged in Christian social work in the Rheinland, was one who had certainly not fallen under the spell of Hitler, and had grave misgivings as to the direction that events were taking since the National Socialists had assumed power. On 1 April he wrote to his General Superintendent, Dr. Stoltenhoff, expressing his misgivings that what had been organised that day was the opening round of a deliberate campaign of brutal persecution. 'I am horrified', he wrote, 'at the cold hatred and the devilish cocksureness of the methods employed. . . . The persecution of men whose "guilt" consists of their belonging to a different race and of nothing else, this persecution with the clear intention of annihilating their very existence, is an act in defiance of the most elementary of moral judgements. It demonstrates that one cannot day in day out be allowing the masses to cry "Perish the Jews" without providing practical scope for this brutal will to persecute. And our Christian people are jubilant. I have never felt such inward despair of my own people as I do now. Who will

have the courage to say what is necessary? Have we not an obligation, above all, to speak on behalf of the Christians of Jewish
origin? I know how difficult it is at the present moment to give
an answer. It is not in the power of the individual to do so, for
freedom of expressing our own opinion has been entirely taken
away from us. But the Church can still find its voice, and at any
rate address its own members. If there is no longer a journal that
can fulfil the function, what about the pulpit?'[48] This was certainly
no lonely voice, but expressed without doubt the feelings of a
considerable number of those who the previous year had made no
pretence of their disapproval of National Socialist aims and
methods, and who before very long would be throwing in their lot
with the Pastors' Emergency League and the Confessing Church.

It was not until 26 April that the Central Church Committee
finally found the opportunity, at the invitation of Dr. Kapler, to
devote an extraordinary session to a detailed consideration of the
Jewish issue.[49]

Freiherr von Pechmann was the first to speak, and he took up
the cudgels on behalf of the members of the Evangelical Church
who were of Jewish extraction and who had become convinced
Christians. The Church had an obligation to come to their protection, not allowing them cause to feel that in their most terrible
distress they were being left in the lurch by a dumb and silent
Church. The Church owed it to them to utter a word of comfort
and consolation. 'We shall indeed have something to answer for',
he exclaimed, 'if the Committee adjourns without having arranged
to issue such a message.' The public statement which he recommended that the Committee should issue had the following
wording: 'We profess our solidarity with all members of the
Church irrespective of their descent, and at this present time
especially with those of complete or partial Jewish descent. We
sympathise with them and will espouse their cause. We earnestly
exhort those bearing authority in public life and intent upon
taking steps to remedy certain abuses, not to exceed the limits
set by the requirements of righteousness and of Christian love.'[50]
Although a very large majority of those present were entirely in
agreement with this proposition, they were not finally able to
come to a decision to recommend the making of a requisite public
statement. The discussion that took place is most instructive on
three counts:

1. The concern that was shown appeared to be largely confined to the plight of the non-Aryan[51] evangelical Christians, such being obviously regarded as the really legitimate ground upon which the Church could take issue.

2. The manifest fear that any statement that they might publish would prove to be fuel for hostile propaganda against the New Germany.

3. The taking altogether seriously of the Nazi-propagated and statistically fortified indictment of the unfair, sinister and in many instances immoral influence of the Jews in the cultural, economic, and political spheres, which forbade criticism of necessary State measures, and made anti-Jewish legislation appear to be a basic act of righteousness despite the cruel hardship suffered in individual cases.

In the course of the discussion Professor Titius of Berlin insisted that it would not be easy to make out a special case for the Jewish Christians, since that could well result in a fateful increase in would-be converts to Christianity; besides which he felt that public advocacy of a different treatment of the Jews would be extraordinarily difficult, since scarcely anything could be said which would remain uncontested. Pastor Walther Michaelis felt that the Church was in such tremendous danger at the present time that she had better keep her mouth shut. There were moments when it was not right to say everything. Heinrich Rendtorff, at that time Bishop of Mecklenburg and noted for his pronounced nationalistic sympathies, but later to become a revered leader of the Confessing Church, was apprehensive lest the Church should damage her relations with the new state by challenging a central point of its programme. He felt bound to question the categorising of the current accepted assessment of the Jewish problem as being unevangelical. For 1,700 years the Jews had with the full approval of the Church been subjected to special restrictive legislation. Their emancipation then came about as a product of the Enlightenment. Such progressive ideas should not be identified as evangelical norm.

Dr. Kapler gave an account of the various opportunities that he had already taken of raising the whole matter at the highest level. This had included an audience with the Führer himself, in which he, Kapler, had not felt it advisable to mention the Jewish issue specifically, but had expressed in general terms the Church's plea and prayer that the harsh methods that the State had felt bound to employ in establishing the new Reich might soon be alleviated, and peace and reconciliation promoted.

The upshot of the long discussion was that any idea of issuing a public pronouncement was abandoned. It was decided, instead, that Pechmann's proposition should serve as material that the President could make use of in subsequent contacts with the authorities;[52] a not very effective decision when it is recalled that Kapler was almost at once to become so heavily involved not only in the framing of the new Church Constitution but also in the conflict as to who should be appointed the new Reich Bishop, and then to retire completely from the scene. Kapler did on 23 May confer with a representative of the government who requested that the Church leaders should intervene against foreign Church criticism of German measures against the Jews calculated to have damaging results for Germany. Kapler assured him that the Church would do what was serviceable for the German Reich without specifying what that would be. He proceeded to make quite clear how disturbed he felt in his conscience when contemplating the indiscriminate handling of the Jews that allowed no distinction between the recently arrived *Ostjuden* and the long-established German Jews, and having to look on while thousands were suddenly rendered destitute. As a result it was no easy matter to appeal to other Christian Churches on Germany's behalf, when the Churches concerned shared his conscientious scruples.[53]

NOTES TO CHAPTER 3

1. Klaus Scholder: *Die Kirchen im Dritten Reich, Beilage zur Wochenzeitung 'Das Parlament'*, B15/71. 10 April 1971. Scholder opens this article, which is to be recommended as providing a singularly lucid, balanced and well-informed survey of the whole process of the Church Conflict, with a consideration of Hitler's Weltanschauung, which he claims to have been basically built upon a single idea, that of a dualism between a superior and inferior race of human beings. The superior so-called 'Aryan' race, in Hitler's view, was destined to dominate the whole world. Everything that had been hitherto achieved that was of real positive good was due to Aryan influence. The aim of the inferior Jewish race was to usurp this dominant role,

and to sabotage the Aryan race biologically, politically, economically, and culturally. Engagement in the subsequent life and death struggle for domination of the world was the very *raison d'être* of National Socialism. What class conflict was to the Communists, racial warfare was to the Nazis. Scholder is convinced that Hitler really and truly believed in this racial ideology, and that he never made an important political decision that would have contradicted it. Once this basic doctrine of the cosmic encounter between the two races is grasped, there can be no doubt as to the central function that anti-semitism possessed for Hitler and National Socialism. Anti-semitism in this Weltanschauung was not one element among others that could be interchangeable, nor just a kind of rudimentary aversion to 'aliens' or a serviceable target for the diversion of feelings of aggression but the determining basic principle of the entire Movement. The fight against the alleged 'Jewish World Menace' was the sole struggle which Hitler never abandoned—not even for the sake of tactical advantages. In this fight alone he never permitted any compromise. Anti-semitism was, strictly speaking, for Hitler not a means to the end of world domination, but the other way round. The mastery over Germany and Europe was a means to the end of fighting the Jews. This racial Weltanschauung, Scholder points out, was the decisive consideration from Hitler's very first political document, a letter written in September 1919, right up to his Last Political Testament, the concluding sentence of which was a charge to the Leaders of the Nation and those under them to scrupulous observance of the laws of race and to merciless opposition to 'the universal poisoner of all peoples—international Jewry'.

It should be added that to Hitler there could be no neutrality over and against this fundamental struggle, and that this affected inevitably and decisively his attitude to Christianity, rooted as it was in the Jewish Old Testament (Scholder: *Die Kirchen im Dritten Reich*, 3–5).

2. The following quotations are taken from Adolf Hitler: *Mein Kampf*, Chapter 9, *Volk und Rasse*, 29th edition, München, 1933.

'In this exposure the various assaults that past anti-semitism had levelled against the Jews were effectively recapitulated. In doing so, no effort whatever was made to check facts, to ascertain the truth or to make any objective judgment upon the Jews. On the contrary, an ideology was devised, according to which human worth was determined solely according to descent by blood. This "Blood myth" inspired the task of fighting the Jew, the arch-enemy of the Aryan, to the utmost. If possible, he was to be exterminated just as one would seek to annihilate germs which had penetrated into a healthy body. This racial doctrine was central to the National Socialist Weltanschauung. The warfare against the Jews cannot, therefore, be assessed as a regrettable misdevelopment caused by various sorts of wrong misunderstanding. It was inexorably and conclusively planned from the beginning, and was then carried through to its fearful conclusion' (Eduard Lohse: *Israel und die Christenheit*, Göttingen, 1960, p. 44).

3. *Mein Kampf*, 355.
4. Ibid., 358.
5. Ibid., 351.
6. Ibid., 358.
7. Ibid., 336.
8. Ibid., 70.
9. Points 4 and 5 of the 25 Points. See *Das Programm der NSDAP*, München, 1932, pp. 19, 20, and 43–4.
10. Gottfried Feder: *Der deutsche Staat auf nationaler und sozialer Grundlage*, München, 1933, p. 49.
11. Otto Harling in *Kirchliches Jahrbuch*, 1932, p. 484.
12. Richard Fischer Sammlung: *Landeskirchliche Archiv*, Stuttgart, I, 141. Pastor Fischer devoted his years of retirement to assembling and ordering a whole mass of invaluable material concerning the Church Struggle in Württemberg. This he edited with a lively and judicious commentary upon events and what lay behind them, placing them, when necessary in a wider context. The result, covering several thousand pages of typescript, contained in eighteen files, is certainly one of the most valuable sources available to the student of the *Kirchenkampf*. Use of this material has helped greatly to enrich this present study.
13. Armin Boyens: *Kirchenkampf und Oekumene*, München, 1969, p. 83.
14. AELKZ, 1936, p. 299.
15. Hans-Joachim Kraus in *Der ungekündigte Bund*, p. 92.
16. Point 24 of the Party Programme, which in the months and years ahead was to be quoted almost *ad nauseam* from all sides, declared that the Party as such stands for a positive Christianity, but does not bind itself confessionally to any one definite denomination. The obvious meaning of this most important affirmation would seem to be that of reverent acknowledgement of Christian fundamentals as opposed to any specific Catholic or Protestant interpretation or application, and in direct contrast to Marxist atheism. The explanation most frequently given was that it meant practical Christianity in contrast to dogmatic Christianity, a form of Christianity made evident by deed rather than by word, and which was concerned with the welfare of the whole community in contrast to any self-interested piety. Goebbels' propaganda Department defined it as a readiness to live and work and sacrifice oneself for the good of the German people. Nazi leaders in their speeches delighted in contrasting Nazi good works such as *Winterhilfe* that were manifestly 'Christian' with the unedifying doctrinal squabbles of the professional pastors. 'Positive Christianity' for the Nazis was an extremely serviceable slogan that sounded so convincing and so respectable, while it really said so little. It could be quoted for or against almost anything, if it appeared to be opportune. The German people as a whole were so conscious of this slogan that they were slow to believe that the Churches were really being persecuted, and were all too ready to discount any reports of maltreatment of Christians as being grossly

exaggerated. Many good Christians who took comfort and inspiration from this avowal of Christianity by the Party failed to ponder upon the words that immediately preceded it. 'We demand freedom for all religious denominations within the State, in so far as they do not endanger its existence, or militate against the morality and the moral sense of the Germanic Race.' 'Positive Christianity' in the light of that proved all too readily to be nothing more or less than a pseudo-religious sanction for the political endeavours and racial policy of the Nazis. The concluding words of Point 24—'The Party is engaged in a struggle against the Jewish materialistic spirit both within and without and is convinced that an enduring recovery of our People can result only from within on the basis of service of the community before self-interest' (*Gemeinutz vor Eigennutz*) indicate both that anti-Jewish measures to come would be claimed to be 'positively Christian', and that Nazi-inspired 'good works' would be advertised as being altogether more 'Christian' than theological and doctrinal affirmations.

17. Quoted by Wilhelm Niemöller: *Die Evangelische Kirche im Dritten Reich*, Bielefeld, 1956, pp. 72–3.

18. Quoted by Althaus: *Deutsche Stunde*, p. 5.

19. The optimistic view was expressed in the *Jewish Chronicle* of 11 August 1933 that 'the economic interests of Germany will suffer by too ruthless extirpation of Jewish influence from trade and industry,' and that, therefore, 'a reversal or a slowing down of anti-Jewish policy may be expected. It seems only a matter of a very little time before finis is written to this chapter of the history of the National Socialist Movement.'

20. Leo Baeck had declared in March 1933 that there was a longing within German Jewry for the renewal of Germany, and the 'Reich Representation of Jews', which he was mainly responsible in calling into being in September 1933, recommended, despite the experience of Boycott Day and the discriminatory legislation, that loyal Jews should vote *Ja* in the November plebiscite, and steer clear of involvement in foreign anti-German protests and boycotts (Hans-Joachim Schoeps: *Der Patriotismus Deutscher Juden und der National-sozialismus*, Berlin, 1970, p. 12).

21. Ibid., 12.

22. Ibid., 22.

23. Ibid., 257.

24. Ibid., 24 and 258. Schoeps founded in February 1933 the *Deutsche Vortrupp* which he himself described as the pick of the educated Jews of the young generation with an aptitude for future leadership and a conservative attitude to German affairs. Schoeps and his band, professing that religious decline was the root cause of the political catastrophe, were outspoken opponents of liberal-inspired Assimila-tion and of Zionism and sought to further a vital new religious orthodoxy in opposition both to the painfully legalistic old orthodoxy and to liberal ethical humanitarianism. Their battle-cry was *Bereit*,

(In Readiness) *für Deutschland !*. They were anxious to be given the chance to prove their *Deutschheit*, and declared that, whatever might happen to them, they would pursue their German course, and remain Germans to their lives' end. While unable on religious grounds to accept Nazi totalitarianism with its *Führerprinzip*, they were whole-heartedly in favour of an authoritative State, and yearned for a renewal of German life based upon former conservative values. They stood in readiness to serve their German Fatherland loyally, even if branded as rejects. They were resolved to bear their fate manfully, striving to live as worthy Jews, giving a new hue and lustre to the Jewish image, in the belief that the Nazis had afforded them an opportunity to make proof through the endurance of privation and suffering of their *Deutschheit* in the knowledge as Jews that spirit was stronger than blood. Also, recognising that National Socialism had rescued Germany from collapse and provided the opportunity for volkish renewal, they were desirous of adding their peculiar contribution in the belief that the time would come with a change of policy towards the Jews, when they would indeed be permitted to do so. With their hearts beating for Germany they waited in readiness to serve. In the meantime by making clear as German Jews that they were, and would remain, identified with the destiny of the German people, they would be able on Germany's behalf to raise valid objections to the treatment of the so-called non-Aryans.

Such patriotic outpourings continued to be given publicity till 1938, when Schoeps' writings were finally banned. Even in 1938-9, Schoeps ruefully remarks, very many Jews including himself and his young collaborators did not consider it possible that a civilised nation in the centre of Europe to which their whole-hearted love was dedicated, would set out to annihilate them with mass murder in the gas chambers. Self-deception and wishful thinking combined with deliberate deception and intended confusion on the part of the Nazis certainly promoted this tragic error.

25. Ibid., 11.
26. Zelzer, 160.
27. Klaus Scholder: *Die Kapitulation der evangelischen Kirche vor dem nationalsozialischen Staat* in *Zeitschrift für Kirchengeschichte*, 1970, p. 190.
28. Scholder, 190.
29. Boyens, 39.
30. Niemöller: *Evangelische Kirche im Dritten Reich*, 376.
31. Boyens, 38. An answer was finally sent to the American Federal Council in June 1933. It came in the form of an anonymous memorandum from 'an ecclesiastical personage'. Armin Boyens claims Dr. Hans Wahl, an official on Kapler's staff with special responsibility for ecumenical affairs, as the author. Richard Fischer attributes it to another higher official, Johannes Gisevius. The full text of the memorandum is to be found in Boyens, pp. 299–308. The recipients of the memorandum were reminded that a profound and necessary

revolution had taken place in Germany, which had greatly excited the population and had made inevitable isolated acts of violence against the Jews, but not solely or principally against them. These had been disapproved of and regretted not only by the Churches but also by the government, but could not in any respect be compared with the brutal and shameful happenings of the 1918 Revolution. By and large it could be testified that the German population had given proof of a discipline which had seldom been revealed elsewhere in similar circumstances of revolutionary change. The discipline of the population on Boycott Day was cited as an example, and it was claimed that the boycott had achieved its purpose, and was strictly enough organised for violent excesses to be prevented. The order had been given from Party Headquarters to shoot at any one caught plundering. Measures taken to decrease the number of Jewish officials in public service and of Jewish doctors and lawyers was declared to have been a positive contribution to the solution of the Jewish problem while not causing hard and grievous suffering to those displaced. It was not to be overlooked that previous governments in Germany with the approval of the Jewish press had removed individuals from office merely because they happened to belong to the National Socialist Party, and this had incurred no protest in Christian circles. It was wrong to contend that there was at the present time a persecution of the Jews in Germany 'aimed at economic or personal annihilation (*Vernichtung*)'. There was, rather, a justifiable reduction as a security measure for the well-being of the German people of exorbitant and disproportionate Jewish influence. It had not the slightest to do with the issue of freedom of religion, and there was no trace of an onslaught against the Jewish religion or freedom of Jewish worship. It was just a national, political exercise. The German Evangelical Churches aware of their subjection to God's Word strictly condemned every act of violence and every affront against members of another race. In preaching, pastoral work and Christian instruction they were, and would continue to be, unwearying in raising their voices against all expressions of hatred and actions arising from such hatred.

It was scarcely possible for the Church to pass a general judgement in public upon the handling by the State of the Jewish issue, and it was doubtful whether the Church was called upon to attempt to do so. The most that could be expected—and that indeed on frequent occasions had been done—was to express to the State authorities a Christian desire that hardships necessarily inflicted upon the Jews should, whenever possible, and with due regard for the safeguarding of the Fatherland, be mitigated.

The concluding paragraph of the memorandum emphasized the need for a deeper and more earnest theological consideration of the problem. One should within and outside Germany not be content with treating it from a mere humanitarian point of view, but should be seeking to develop an attitude from out of the depth of the Gospel and looking at the problem and taking action over it in the light of the Word of God.

In relation to these last words, though, of course, from a thoroughly different angle, Armin Boyens writes: 'The question of the relation between the Church and Israel was not thought out theologically. Protests were consequently made against the National Socialist persecution of the Jews in the name of Christian fundamentals, religious tolerance, humanity, civilisation, culture and the most elementary fundamentals of toleration and fair play. The assertion that Israel is God's People and that those who persecute the Jews raise their hand against God's People did not emerge in the official ecumenical protests of 1933' (p. 79).

32. Boyens, 39.
33. Jonathan Wright: *The Political Attitudes of the Protestant Church Leadership, November 1918–July 1933.* Unpublished D.Phil. Thesis, Oxford, 1969, p. 297.
34. Fischer, II, 101.
35. A precedent in the recommending of a boycott of Jewish shops is to be discovered in an anti-semitic broadsheet issued at Christmas-time in 1892: 'German Men! German Women! You will soon be celebrating the sacred festival of Christmas. Is it right that your Christmas presents should be bought from Jewish shops? You want to give Christian presents not Jewish presents. German Men, German Women, reflect that you are in conflict with your own people, when you support Jewish shops. Can the Jews who belong to an alien, oriental nation, and who observe different festivals from us and pour scorn upon our own customs, take an honourable share in our most glorious national festivals?'
36. Quoted by Peter Neumann: *Die Jungreformatorische Bewegung. Arbeiten zur Geschichte des Kirchenkampfes,* Vol. 25, Göttingen, 1971, p. 154.
37. Scholder: *Kapitulation der Evangelischen Kirche* 190.
38. Fischer, II, 106.
39. Wright, 299.
40. F. W. Kantzenbach: *Widerstand und Solidarität der Christen in Deutschland, 1933–1945. Eine Dokumentation zum Kirchenkampf aus den Papieren des D. Wilhelm Freiherr von Pechmann,* Nürnberg, 1971, p. 37.
41. Neumann, 154, note 1.
42. Georg Prater ed.: *Kämpfer wider Willen, Erinnerungen des Landes-bischofs von Sachsen, D. Hugo Hahn,* Metzingen, 1969, p. 30.
43. Kurt Meier, *Kirche und Judentum,* Göttingen, 1968, pp. 25–26.
44. Boyens, 42.
45. Arndt, 191.
46. Van Norden, 177.
47. Boyens, 44–5. See Hermann Maas: *Friedrich Siegmund-Schultze. Ein Bahnbrecher christlicher Solidariät* in *Ökumenische Profile,* ed. Günther Gloede, Stuttgart, 1961, Vol. I, pp. 253–63.

48. Van Norden, 59.
49. Boyens, 45 and 295–9 and Scholder:, 191–2.
50. Quoted in Kantzenbach, p. 17, note 1.
51. *The Jewish Chronicle* (11 August 1933) quotes Gordon Childe, Professor of Prehistoric Archaeology at Edinburgh University, as having remarked that 'Herr Hitler's views about Aryans are arrant nonsense, Aryan being originally a linguistic term denoting the speakers of a certain group of languages. Max Müller once said that to speak of an Aryan race was as absurd as to talk of a brachy-cephalic dictionary. Race, on the contrary, is a physical term. Nazi philosophy makes a quite arbitrary confusion of the two quite distinct concepts.'

There appeared in the issue of the *Doberaner Nachrichten* (Mecklen-burg) of 18 October 1933, an illuminating article entitled *Was ist arisch?*. In it the point is made that the terms 'Aryan' and 'non-Aryan' were brought into official and general use by the Nazis to meet an obvious special need. It was necessary to avoid contrasting Christians and Jews, since there were both very many baptised Jews and also a considerable number of non-Christian non-Jews. It would also not do to contrast Germans and Jews, because the intention was to make the attempt to distinguish between races, not peoples.

There were real complications, when it was necessary to work out who was in fact a non-Aryan. Was the answer—anyone who was not a German, any not purely Nordic person, anyone with alien blood in him, anyone possessing alien characteristics (*artfremde*) or merely anyone Jewish? The lack of clarity in this negative descrip-tion certainly gave a lot of trouble to the Nazi authorities. To be logical, the derogatory term 'non-Aryan' meant that the Third Reich had to regard and treat as second-grade all persons and nations that were not to be reckoned 'Aryan' in the National Socialist usage. This, however, as was in due course realised, was going to cause grave embarrassment in the relation of Germany to certain foreign states. The German Foreign Office sought in 1934 to have the Aryan legislation confined to the Jews by means of exclusion of non-Aryans from other countries and those of foreign parentage. This was not agreed to on principle, but exceptions were permitted, when foreign policy made it requisite. This proved to be expedient, where Turks, Persians, Indians, and Japanese were concerned. When the Nurem-berg Laws were published in 1935, for the negative 'Non-Aryan' was substituted the positive 'Jewish', and a new classification *artverwandt* (kindred in character) was introduced to cover those whom the Nazis were prepared to accord acceptance to alongside the Germans. The question, of course, remained—Who was *artverwandt*? In this present study 'non-Aryan' may be taken to mean all those who were reckoned to have Jewish blood in them, of Jewish or of Christian or of no religious confession. This paragraph is based upon an article by Jørge Glenthøj: *Die nicht-jüdischen Nicht-Arien im Dritten Reich* in *Junge Kirche*, 1965, pp. 138ff.

52. Klaus Scholder comments as follows: 'There is scarcely any other example that makes clearer the limitations of the Central Church Committee, and indeed that of the contemporary Church than this resolution. Here were two basic points of orientation in conflict; obligation towards the Gospel and obligation towards the authority of the State. That the Church was not capable from her own resources of detecting and resolving this conflict demonstrated her limitations, and at the same time substantiates from the Church historian's angle the legitimacy and the necessity of the Confessing Church (*Kapitulation der evangelischen Kirche*, p. 192).

53. Boyens, 54.

4

The Aryan Clause, 1933-1935

On 7 April 1933 a law was passed to purge the Civil Service of officials of non-Aryan descent, unless they had already served the State before August 1914, or had fought in the front line, or had lost father or son in the war.[1]

On 12 May a new movement, the Young Reformers (*Jungreformatorische Bewegung*),[2] led by Martin Niemöller and two most resolute representatives of the Lutheran renaissance, Walter Künneth and Hans Lilje, and which, over against the 'German Christians', stood for Reformation rather than Revolution and insisted that 'Church must remain Church', published its programme for ecclesiastical reconstruction. It was advocated that any ecclesiastical changes should be 'simply and solely derived from the essence of the Church', and that 'the Evangelical Church in joyful affirmation of the new German State should fulfil the commission given to her by God in complete freedom from all political influence, at the same time committing herself irrevocably to the service of the German people'.[3] It was declared to be the duty of the Church to seek to furnish the Gospel answer to the issues of Race, Volk and State and, anticipating the controversy that was so soon to be raging over the application within the Church of National Socialist discrimination against the Jews, it was affirmed that the exclusion of non-Aryans from the Church was irreconcilable with belief in the Holy Spirit. There should be no confusion regarding the differing responsibilities of State and Church. A week later in a further declaration it was emphasised that the Church had the obligation 'to share in the shouldering of the hard lot of those who are shattered in their spiritual and social existence by their inevitable political fate. The Church is aware that the State must "bear the sword", and that this calls for tough measures. Because of this the Church has all the more the task in obedience to the command of Jesus to practise neighbourly love and to be an abode of reconciliation for all who require her services.'[4] This recommendation of the Young Reformers did not wish in any way to be regarded as criticism of measures taken by the Nazi State. They were as anxious to emphasise their political loyalty alongside that of the 'German Christians', as they were to insist upon the independent status of the Church.

Dietrich Bonhoeffer, as his biographer Eberhard Bethge remarks,[5] was one of the very few who sat down at his desk straightaway in April, in order to work out theses for publication on both the political and ecclesiastical consequences of the new legislation. He had already in February 1933 remarked in a letter to his friend Erwin Sutz that the Church was very much occupied with the Jewish Question, and that the most sensible and intelligent of people had lost their heads and mislaid their Bibles.[6] He was apparently the first to insist that the question was no side-issue to be gingerly handled, but was absolutely fundamental in any future controversy between Church and State. In his lecture in April 1933 entitled *Die Kirche vor der Judenfrage*[7] Bonhoeffer began by pointing out that it was a fact unique in history that the Jew was being made subject to special laws by the State solely because of the race to which he belonged and quite apart from his religious beliefs. This raised new problems for the theologian. What should the Church's attitude be to this action by the State, and what should the Church do about it? What attitude should the Church adopt towards its members who were baptised Jews? In answering the first question Bonhoeffer subscribed to the prevailing Lutheran view that the Church had no right to address the State directly in its specifically political acts. The Church had neither to praise nor to censure the new laws, but rather, had the duty to affirm the State to be God's order of preservation in a godless world. The Church had to recognise the State's ordinances, bad or good as they might appear from a humanitarian point of view, as based upon the sustaining Will of God. The State was justified in adopting new methods of dealing with the Jewish Question. Individual Christians, and indeed the Church herself, could remind the State of the moral aspect, but were not permitted to criticise its history-making actions from the standpoint of some humanitarian ideal.

The Church, however, was permitted to ask the State whether its actions were justifiable in the name of law and order. It was quite definitely the duty of the Church to aid the victims of State measures, even if they did not belong to her membership. The Church might possibly have to go altogether beyond just bandaging the victims beneath the wheel, and actually put a spoke in the wheel. This would mean direct political action, rendered necessary, were some group of subjects to be deprived of their rights, or the State to chose to interfere with the very essence of the Church and demand the forced expulsion from her membership of baptised Jews or prohibit the work of missions to the Jews. An Evangelical Council would be required to decide upon the necessity of this. As regards the second issue, the State could not be permitted to prescribe what should be the Church's treatment of her baptised members, for the Jewish problem was not the same for the Church as for the State. *Judentum* was for the Church a religious, not a racial or biological concept. Jews found their way into the Church through the call of God through His Word in Christ. The splitting off of Gentile Christianity and Jewish Christianity would be an intolerable heresy and schism. Nothing ecclesiastically could stand in the way of a voluntary gathering of Jewish Christians into a congregation of their own, but this would not mean a breach of Church fellowship between German and Jewish Christians, for alone where Jew and German stood together under the Word of God was the Church to be found.

The 'German Christians' left no doubt that they would press for the introduction of the Aryan legislation within the Church. 'German Christian' theology, such as there was, laid tremendous stress upon what were regarded as the scandalously overlooked Divine Creative Ordinances which, as a matter of great jubilation, had become so evident in the awakened recognition of the sanctity of Race, Blood and Volk.

At their mass rally in Berlin in April rapturous assent was given to statements such as the following—'In the impossible existence side by side of Germans and Jews God demands that we once more pay due respect to the Laws that govern Life. . . . God did not create Man, but a man and a woman, a mother and her child, a Chinaman, a Negro, a Jew, and a German.'[8] 'Those of Jewish descent can no longer be tolerated in the pulpit and in ecclesiastical office,'[9] 'We will allow no person of alien blood, and especially no Jew, to assume the office of elder or parochial church councillor.'[10] 'It is more important that a theological student should know something about eugenics, heredity, and science than that he should have his head stuffed with the names and dates of Jewish kings.'[11] 'All Church work is merely work for the Volk.'[12] On 6 May the 'German Christians' made public announcement of their conception of the forthcoming Reich Church, and demanded that it should be the Church of German Christians, namely of Christians of Aryan race. The preaching of the Gospel among those of alien origin was a matter for foreign missions.[13] This is proof that their declared aim was not only to eliminate non-Aryan office-bearers but also to exclude ordinary non-Aryans from membership.

The State-sponsored elections in July resulted in a substantial 'German Christian' majority, and it was no surprise, when, on 5 September, the Synod of the Old Prussian Church, to be known as the Brown Synod[14] because of the profusion of S.A. uniforms and the Nazi atmosphere of the proceedings, adopted the Aryan clause, which was worded as follows—'Anyone not of Aryan descent or who is married to a person of non-Aryan descent may not be appointed as minister or official. Ministers or officials of Aryan descent who marry non-Aryans are to be dismissed. The State Law decides who is to be reckoned non-Aryan. Ministers of non-Aryan descent or married to non-Aryans are to be retired. The exceptions are the same as those laid down in the State Law.'[15] It was also decided that a necessary qualification for ministry in the Prussian Church was unreserved support of the National Socialist State and the newly planned united German Evangelical Church. Ludwig Müller, Reich Bishop-designate, who on 4 August had been elected Bishop for the whole of the Prussian Church, expressed his satisfaction that members of congregations would in future appreciate knowing that those who occupied their pulpits were men of their own flesh and blood.

The General Superintendents who were present at the Synod voted against the dismissal of non-Aryans and those married to non-Aryans who were currently in office, but were at the same time prepared to accept the ineligibility of non-Aryans in the future from office in the German Evangelical Church. General Superintendent Kalmus, their spokesman, said: 'We understand

and appreciate the value of the measures taken by the State, and recognise that the Evangelical Church also has cause to be vigilant in the preservation of what is characteristically German.'[16] Pastor Koch of Westphalia was the spokesman at the Synod for the non-'German Christian' minority. He complained that the state legistation governing the Civil Service had been adopted for application in the Church in the most arbitrary fashion without any allowance for careful theological consideration and without any kind of preparatory discussion. He was deeply disturbed at the use of force in matters that concerned not only the outward form of the Church but also her very essence.[17]

The introduction of a similar Aryan Clause was discussed in various provincial churches. In Saxony, quite the largest of the Lutheran churches, the 'German Christian' Bishop, Friedrich Coch, gave unqualified welcome to the new legislation. Its complete adoption was a pledge of the loyalty of the Church to Hitler's new State. In future anyone holding office had of necessity to be of Aryan race.[18] In Mecklenburg it was agreed that non-Aryans already ordained should be allowed to remain in office.[19] In Hannover, despite repeated 'German Christian' pressure, Bishop Marahrens successfully secured the postponement of restrictive legislation.[20] At the meeting of the *Landeskirchentag* in Württemberg a majority voted for the introduction of the Clause. Bishop Wurm, however, was not prepared to accept the decision, and consequently it was not implemented. Actually it was seen to serve no practical purpose, since the only pastor to whom it could possibly apply was an Aryan married to a baptised Jewess.[21] In Schleswig-Holstein the ruling of the Prussian Synod was adopted in almost identical language, but included the proviso that an exception could be made in the case of those who had given meritorious service to the Church. It appears that acting upon this saving clause none of the non-Aryan pastors were removed from office.[22] In Bavaria, in order to avoid difficulties and embarrassment, steps were taken to remove the very few pastors affected from their parishes and give them non-parochial appointments. Pastor Jordan, for instance, a half-Jew, was given a post in the *Innere Mission*.[23]

The new regulation actually affected only six out of the seventeen non-Aryan pastors within the Prussian Church, the other eleven coming under the saving clause. Were the legislation to be applied to the whole of the German Evangelical Church, it was calculated that it would only involve another twelve pastors.[24] This did not, however, include pastors who were married to a non-Aryan. Furthermore, by virtue of other legislation the right of non-Aryans to attend universities was restricted. This was taken to apply to theological students, and made it doubtful if more than a very occasional non-Aryan would in the future qualify for admission to the ministry. It is hard to escape the conclusion that to the great majority of churchmen this was a matter of no real concern, if not indeed to be welcomed in that it would save much possible future embarrassment.

Martin Niemöller and Dietrich Bonhoeffer lost no time in taking the offensive by issuing a concise and uncompromising joint declaration on behalf of the Berlin opposition-group, in which it was claimed that a situation had arisen in which fundamental wrong was being proclaimed as ecclesiastical law, and the Church's Confession violated. 'Anyone giving his consent to such an infringement of the Confession thereby excludes himself from the fellowship of the Church. We demand therefore that this Law which cuts off the Evangelical Church in Prussia from the rest of the Christian Church be repealed forthwith.'[25] Bonhoeffer, encouraged by his non-Aryan friend and colleague Franz Hildebrandt, considered that a state of schism already existed, and felt impelled to recommend a refusal to minister any longer within the officially recognised Church and a transfer into an Evangelical Free Church. The majority view proved, however, to be that this would be too hasty a resolution, and that it would be wiser to wait and see whether the legislation were adopted throughout the German Evangelical Church. So momentous and irrevocable a decision to break away from the official church, it was also felt, required an altogether more solid foundation than outrage, however justifiable, at gross anti-semitic discrimination. The forthcoming National Synod would provide the right occasion for a resounding protest which, to have its maximum effect, should come from the whole non-'German Christian' front.[26] Bonhoeffer sought the advice of both Hermann Sasse, a Bavarian Lutheran theologian renowned for his criticism of Nazi religious policy, and Karl Barth. Sasse agreed with Bonhoeffer that the new legislation indeed cut off the Prussian Church from the rest of Christendom, and designated it as a blasphemy against the Holy Ghost, for which there was no forgiveness in this world and in that to come, and which had the effect of outlawing Jesus Christ Himself, the Son of David after the Flesh, from the preaching ministry. He recommended united action on the fullest scale led by the still autonomous Lutheran bishops, if, as expected, the National Synod applied the restriction to the whole of the Church.[27] Barth in his reply counselled against precipitate action. If there were to be schism, then it should come from the other side. It would be rendered more inevitable and more justifiable in the end by other still worse deviations and corruptions. The desertion of what was regarded as a sinking ship and escape into a Free Church was to be considered as a last resort rather than a prime necessity.[28]

Walther Künneth, Director of the Central Institute for Apologetics in Berlin, produced in the summer of 1933 an essay entitled 'The Problem of the Jews and the Church' which was included in the much read collective work, *Die Nation vor Gott*, in later editions of which this particular essay had to be adapted to meet the developing anti-Jewish campaign. The main substance of his treatment of the problem remained, however, unaltered, since he claimed that the solution had of necessity to be based upon biblical and ecclesiastical insights 'divorced from consideration of the particular situation in which the Church might find herself during the period of national rebirth'.[29]

In Künneth's view any move that insisted upon taking away from non-Aryans the right to minister or hold office in the German Evangelical Church or that sought to deprive non-Aryans of full and equal privileges of Church membership was a depreciation of the sacrament of Baptism. To permit non-Aryans to hear the preaching of the Word and to receive the sacraments but to disallow them full and direct participation in the community life of the Church was a violation of Christian love. It would mean making an empty phrase of the doctrine of the Priesthood of All Believers, if Race and Volk rather than Faith in Christ were made a determining factor in practical Church membership.

This admirable evangelical protestation did not, nevertheless, prevent Künneth from recommending that due regard should be given to the contemporary national and political situation. The German Evangelical Church was avowedly *Volkskirche*, with an express vocation to serve the German people; and that same people, which had been stirred to its very depths, felt that to have

Jews in a leading position was an intolerable imposition. The Church on missionary grounds had to take this objection seriously, and was obliged to recommend that Jewish Christians should, to avoid offence and out of regard for the 'weakness' of others, exercise a voluntary measure of restraint, and not impede 'the Volk-missionary task in the Third Reich'.[30] Such restraint did not require hard and fast legislation but called for sympathetic charity, and could be achieved without doing violence to Church principles. Any hiving off of Jewish Christians into a church of their own, separate from the Gentile Christians would be only tolerable if achieved in a voluntary and mutually agreed fashion. The aping of the State in forcibly isolating Jewish Christianity would bear the blatant mark of uncharitableness, cause brutal havoc to brotherly fellowship and effect an ominous split in parish after parish.

Recognising that reiteration of Stoecker's claim that Jews who had become Christians had also become Germans would now fall on deaf ears, Künneth still did not hesitate to make a radical distinction between thorough-going Jews who remained radically and culturally an alien body within the Christian German Nation and Jewish Christians who had removed themselves not only from the Jewish religion but also from the Jewish people, and had, through being rooted in the Christian Church, entered into a close relationship with German culture. He nursed the hope that the State could be persuaded to acknowledge such a demarcation, and to treat Jewish members of the Church differently from the adherents of the Synagogue and those of liberal Jewish persuasion. True to Luther, the German evangelicals were led to regard the sins of the Jews as not racially determined but as resulting from their aversion to becoming converted. They advanced a messianic claim to world domination, because they denied the messiahship of Jesus of Nazareth. They remained under the Divine Curse, and were not surprisingly an accursed element within the people among whom they dwelt. This caused Künneth to conclude that the orthodox and the liberal Jews, but not the genuinely believing Jewish Christians, were 'a ferment of disintegration' for the German Volkstum.[31]

In Künneth's penultimate paragraph in the 1934 edition, which significantly had altogether disappeared in the 1937 edition, the claim was made on behalf of the Church to be the 'conscience of the Nation', jealous for the reputation both at home and abroad of the new State, and eager to use her influence to ensure that the elimination of Jewish influence in the life of the German people should be accomplished in a manner that was not contrary to the Christian ethics to which the State repeatedly affirmed its adherence. 'The Church regards herself as being at one with the will of the Reich Chancellor who has clearly expressed the view that a proud victor is free from feelings of hatred and instinct for revenge.'[32]

The impressive and widespread protest of the coming months was founded primarily upon principle and inspired by a determination to defend certain fundamental doctrines. The ensuing fight was in no wise undertaken upon humanitarian or ethical grounds. This was proved by the lack of intention to espouse at the same time the cause in general of evangelical non-Aryans dismissed from the Civil Service. Still less was any urge felt to question or to oppose non-Aryan legislation as a whole[33] or to criticise national socialist racial philosophy. Notwithstanding such limitations the controversy regarding the introduction of the Aryan clause was of pre-eminent importance, and may rightly be claimed to have set alight the Church Conflict. The very fact of so widespread an opposition to the application of the Aryan Clause within the Church did constitute an undeniable challenge to the Nazi racial outlook and totalitarian system. Here was something quite clear and definite, that put the very substance of the Christian Gospel in question in a way that such injustices and outrages as the Church had already suffered at the hands of the State certainly did not.

As was readily and robustly pointed out, the introduction of the Aryan clause within the Church was a violation of certain of her most basic doctrines. The validity of Holy Baptism was at stake. Nonsense would be made of ordination, if holders of spiritual office were to be reckoned as officials subject to State dictation, the State not the Holy Spirit determining who might be accounted a pastor.[34] It was blasphemy against the free and sovereign activity of the Holy Spirit. The basic doctrine of Justification by Faith Alone would be compromised. An attempt was being made by law to limit the Gospel. The very existence of the Church was at issue, and the Communion of Saints would be deprived of its essential meaning. In fact in such resolute opposition to the Aryan clause there was a genuine break-through in the theological consideration of the essential nature of the Church.[35]

There were some at any rate who were far-sighted enough to realise that in the long run it was unlikely that those who held office within the Church would alone be outlawed. An attempt would be made sooner or later—as indeed happened—to exclude ordinary non-Aryans from membership of and participation in the life and worship of the German Evangelical Church. It would not stop at that. The Christ of Holy Scripture, born of a Jewish maiden and declared to be the King of the Jews, was Himself the ultimate offence, and, unless Aryanised, would be banished. Prominently on the front page of an issue of the *Evangelischer Ruf*, a Breslau Church weekly, appeared the following:

VISION. Scene—A Church Service. The introit comes to an end. The pastor stands at the altar. His opening words are, 'Non-Aryans are requested to leave the church'. No one makes a move. 'Non-Aryans are requested to leave the church', he repeats. Again there is no movement. 'Non-Aryans are required to leave the church at once.' At this Christ comes down from the cross on the altar and quits the church.[36]

It was of profound significance that in the initial act of resistance a clear and bold challenge was being made to the National Socialist plan to commit and to co-ordinate the Church to the new racial programme. The principle was now enunciated, and to be repeatedly re-emphasised throughout the ensuing conflict, that the severance of external Church order from inner Church faith and doctrine was impermissible, with the former regulated according to expediency or criteria of politics and racial philosophy. The church in obedience to the Word insisted upon the right to order her own affairs. Membership of the congregation and the holding of office were no mere matters of organisation, but were of the very essence of the Church.[37] This non-Aryan issue, therefore, ensured that the fight would continue, and with the virtual certainty that neither side would give way.

On 21 September 1933 Martin Niemöller took the initiative in calling into existence a Pastor's Emergency League (*Pfarrernotbund*) the members of which were required to sign a solemn undertaking to acknowledge the binding authority of Holy Scripture and the Reformation Confessions, and to protest vigorously and whole-heartedly whenever the scriptural and confessional integrity of the Church were violated, and to be prepared to give material assistance to all who were suffering for their loyalty and to witness to their sense of outrage at the introduction of the Aryan Clause within the Church. The Emergency League began with a member-ship of 1,300. By 1934 the peak figure of 7,000 was attained, more than a third of all the clergy.[38]

Martin Niemöller, whose theological approach in 1933 was certainly coloured by reverence for the Divine Creative Ordinances and fervent enthusiasm for Volkstum and Fatherland, obviously had an understanding for the argument that the character of the presentation of the Gospel had to vary according to the people to whom it was being addressed, and that it should ideally be presented by representatives of the race concerned. There is evidence that, to begin with, he had seriously considered the possibility of two separate and parallel Aryan and non-Aryan churches, provided that they were of equal standing, and that there was a voluntary Jewish Christian acceptance of such a solution.[39] The unprincipled and unevangelical behaviour of the 'German Christians' and the influence of Barth and Bonhoeffer soon convinced him that there was a fundamental scriptural principle involved. In a letter written in October 1933 to a friend he declared that 'on the basis of Holy Scripture the Jewish people has no prerogative before the final consummation (Romans 9–11) to form its own exclusive Volk Church. God has not abrogated His promise to Israel, and He gives proof of this by allowing individual Jews to attain to faith. These individual Jews must be permitted to have in the Christian Church to which they belong full rights of domicile and full access to office and ministry. There is no real parallel to the Negro and other missionary churches, for they have the possibility of fashioning a people's church of their own, whereas the Christian Jew forfeits member-ship of his people, when he becomes a Christian.'[40]

Scriptural and theological insight, indeed, rather than any natural warmth of feeling for them caused him to espouse the cause of his Jewish fellow-Christians. In his *Sätze zur Arierfrage*,[41] published in November 1933, he made it clear that he was taking his stand in defence of the Faith, since the Aryan clause when applied to the Church conflicted with the essential basic doctrines of Holy Baptism and the Communion of Saints. 'Contrary to what we may desire, a fundamental stand is required of us, whether it be agreeable to us or not.' 'We as a people', wrote Niemöller, 'have been made to suffer considerably under the influence of the Jewish people, and it is a matter of real self-denial to champion their cause.' The attractive solution of letting the Jewish Christians form their own Jewish Christian Church he now declared to be a sheer utopia; it would be a denial of the Will of God, for the Jews had a place in God's scheme of salvation quite different from that of any other people. 'Whether it be congenial or not, we have to recognise the Jews as members of the congregation fully authorised by the Holy Ghost.' Nevertheless, anxious that offence should be avoided, he urged that appropriate restraint should be shown. It would not help matters, were a pastor of non-Aryan extraction to occupy an executive position in the Church or fulfil a prominent role in home missions. A few weeks later in an interview Niemöller went further, and suggested that non-Aryan pastors should only minister in parishes in which there would be no risk of scandal.[42]

Niemöller's concern about the non-Aryan issue was in the first place scriptural, ecclesiastical and theological rather than ethical or humanitarian. He frankly admitted this, when he told a student audience in January 1946 that he had kept silent when he was first made aware of the increasing persecution of the Jews, and only broken silence when there was an ecclesiastical problem concerning the non-Aryans. In private correspondence in September 1933 he counselled 'avoidance of involvement in moralistic speculation upon things for which the State as such bears responsibility' and treating the State to a sermon upon the justice or injustice of its forcible measures.[43] There were, we may presume, also tactical considerations in not inviting a conflict with the secular authorities which could well have done severe damage to the ecclesiatical campaign of the Emergency League. Niemöller appears to have confined himself to an exhortation from the pulpit to the faithful to care for the persecuted and outlawed and to exercise neighbourly love to all men irrespective of whether they were Christians, heathen or Jews.[44]

In the ensuing years Niemöller avoided making public pronouncements upon National Socialist anti-Jewish policy. In 1935

ne expressed his doubts as to whether the Church had the right
o sit in judgement over the State in reference to this particular
ssue, for the State was every bit as much subject to the Creator
as the Church was to her Lord.[45] A witness at his trial testified in
1937 that he knew of no instance in which the accused had
criticised the Aryan legislation in general.[46] In his self-defence at
the hearing of his trial in February 1938 Niemöller made a point
of emphasising his desire not to interfere in political issues. His
sole concern was about the Gospel. Applying this to the Jewish
Question he reiterated his former attitude that the Jews were alien
and uncongenial to him, though he added that from the scriptural
standpoint it was nevertheless not permissible to substitute for
baptism a genealogical tree. It had, he added, to be accepted
that God had seen fit to reveal Himself in the Jew, Jesus of
Nazareth. 'This painful and grievous stumbling-block has to be
accepted for the sake of the Gospel.'[47]

While certainly not, as an earnest Christian, approving of the
prevailing anti-Jewish barbarity and calumny, his upbringing in a
typical Westphalian country parish, in which many of the peasants
were in debt to Jewish money-lenders and cattle dealers, and his
years of service as a naval officer had encouraged in him, as he
himself admitted,[48] an anti-semitic attitude. He was a ready heir
to the Luther-Stoecker tradition that the Jews were subject to
divine censure and condemnation that could alone be abrogated
by conversion and baptism. In the world outside racial discrimination and hatred were understandable if not inevitable, and
the differences and distinctions could only be overcome in Christ
and within the fellowship of the Church. He revealed after the
war that it was only at a later date, when he was confined in a
concentration camp that it came home to him with conviction
that he as a Christian had not to base his attitude upon feelings of
sympathy or antipathy. It was incumbent to behold in every
fellow-man, no matter how uncongenial he might still be to him,
a brother for whom Christ hung upon his Cross, just as He did
for him, an attitude which without further ado excluded all
rejection of an animosity against a human group of whatever
race, religion, or colour.[49]

In 1935, preaching on the Gospel for the Tenth Sunday after
Trinity, Niemöller proclaimed that this 'is a day which for
centuries has been dedicated in the Christian world to the memory

of the destruction of Jerusalem and the fate of the Jewish people, and the passage of Scripture provided for this Sunday throws light upon the dark mystery that envelopes the sinister history of this people which can neither live nor die, because it is under a curse which forbids it to do either. We speak of the "Eternal Jew" and conjure up the picture of a restless wanderer who has no home and who cannot find peace, and we see a highly gifted people which produces idea after idea for the benefit of the world, but whatever it takes up changes into poison, and all that it ever reaps is contempt and hatred, because ever and anon the deluded world notices the deception and avenges itself in its own way. I say "in its own way", for we know full well that we have no licence empowering us to supplement God's curse with our hatred. Even Cain receives God's mark, that no one may kill him; and Jesus's command "Love your enemies!" leaves no room for exceptions. We cannot, however, alter the fact that until the end of time the Jewish people must go its own way under the burden which the Word of Judgement of Jesus has laid upon it: "Behold your house is left unto you desolate. For I say unto you, Ye shall not see me henceforth, till ye say, Blessed is He that cometh in the Name of the Lord". . . . What then is the real reason for this manifest penal judgement which continues in force century after century? Dearly beloved, the answer is evident, the Jews have caused the crucifixion of God's Christ. . . . They bear the curse, and, because they rejected the forgiveness, they drag about with them as a fearsome burden the unforgiven blood-guilt of their fathers.'[50]

The use of such familiar anti-semitic terminology as 'Poison', 'Deception', 'Curse', 'Blood-guilt' could be interpreted as acceptance of the Nazi persecutions as in fulfilment of biblical prophecy and as divinely ordained. But, to be just to Niemöller, it should be added that the sermon included a warning to the congregation that this did not warrant Christians following up the divine curse with expressions of hatred. 'Who can keep on hating, when God's Judgement is in full swing?'

Dietrich Bonhoeffer had obviously been meditating upon the significance of the Aryan clause, if and when introduced into the Church. About a month before the meeting of the Brown Synod he produced a short pamphlet that may be claimed to be the most lucid answer that was given to the German Christian arguments, written in simple style and yet so profound in its interpretation of the testimony of the New Testament.[51] The threatened exclusion of Christian non-Aryans was to Bonhoeffer nothing more or less than the undoing of the work of St. Paul, who, recognising that through the Cross of Christ the wall of partition had been broken down, had ensured that Jewish and Gentile Christians should be altogether one. A church that would impose racial regulations for entry into her fellowship would be acting in Jewish fashion and converting Gospel into Law. The finding of a place alongside him for the uncongenial Jew would be a sign that the German Christian understood what Church really was. The true Church was constituted of strangers and aliens who through the Word of God and faith had been called into fellowship. Organised exclusion of baptised Jews would have the effect of making of the sacrament of initiation a ceremony empty of obligation. Exclusion from the empirical church meant in fact exclusion from the Church of Christ itself. The exclusion of Jewish Christians from the ministry involved the denial of the Priesthood of All Believers and contempt for the commission given by Christ Himself. Bonhoeffer's answer to the 'German Christian' contention that German church people felt that they should be ministered to by Aryans, was that they should concern themselves about the message given by the pastor rather than about his person. If Paul the Jew, free from concern about any national or racial susceptibilities, had not proclaimed Christ in the Gentile world, there would have been no German Church. Bonhoeffer also emphasised the political character of the 'German Christian' arguments. There was a desire to copy what the State had done. The true loyalty of the Church to the State lay, however, not in the blind imitation of the latter's methods, but in the faithful proclamation of her own message and in the development of her particular ecclesiastical formation.

The opponents of the Aryan Clause looked to the theologians for support. Karl Barth in his trenchant pamphlet *Theologische Existenz Heute*, published in July 1933, had not wasted any words in announcing his view. If the German Evangelical Church were to exclude the Jewish Christians or treat them as second-class Christians, she would cease to be a Christian Church.[52] Heinrich Vogel wrote in his *Eight Articles of Evangelical Doctrine* 'Because we become Christians not through birth or through race and blood, but through the Holy Spirit, Baptism and the Word of God, we reject the demand that only Aryan Christians shall be permitted to become members of the German Evangelical Church. In particular, we reject the outlawing of Jewish Christians or the depriving them of their rights in a Church which acknowledges herself to be the Church of Jesus Christ, Who according to the flesh was a Jew, as were the prophets and apostles called, according to God's eternal decree, out of this same people. Israel is not as race or nation the Chosen People, but as the people in which the Saviour of mankind was born and the people by whom He was destined to be crucified. Not the Jew alone, however, but all the peoples of the world, we Germans included, share in the guilt of the Cross.'[53]

The Marburg Theological Faculty was requested to pronounce, and came down with full weight on the opposition side, affirming that the non-Aryan legislation within the Church was irreconcilable with Scripture and the Reformation Confessions. Nothing parallel was to be found in the Concordat between the Roman Catholic Church and the Nazi State. Evangelical clergy and Church officials were certainly pledged by God's Word to obedience to the State as well as to the Church. But this was nevertheless subject to an all-important reservation, namely that the Church's commission was in no wise political. In certain given circumstances there could be an obligation to adopt an appropriately criticial standpoint towards both political and ecclesiastical proceedings. The Aryan legislation without any doubt converted Church members of non-Aryan origin into Church members of lesser rights and inferior worth. The message of Jesus Christ as the Saviour of the world was directed to all people, and thereby to all races, consequently all who believed in that message and were baptised into such a faith were brought into brotherly relationship one with another that excluded inequality of rights and avoidable differentiation. In the whole past history of the Church and in secular and ecclesiastical law alike the term 'Jew' did not have a racial content, but had an exclusively confessional usage to denote one who did not recognise Jesus to be God's Christ. The converted and baptised Jew, was in the reckoning of the Church no longer a Jew, and from the *Church's* point of view should not be made subject to civil restrictions. The *State* had now seen fit to introduce certain limitations on racial grounds and from national and political considerations. Such restrictions could, however, not be claimed to be of validity within the sphere of the Church, since the Church was a fellowship of those who believed in Christ and were baptised in His Name, and nothing else, and could not sacrifice or surrender her unity as the Body of Christ. Unbelief and heresy were the only recognisable grounds for separation within the Church. It was indisputably true that God proclaimed His Word not only in the Old Testament but also in the New through Jews, and elected that His son should be born a Jew. There was no historical foundation to the efforts to make an Aryan out of Jesus, and any such endeavour was ineffective, since His Message took the Jewish law and prophets for granted as God's revelation, and His Apostles were without any doubt Jews. It was a pharisaical misjudgement to treat the Crucifixion as an attempted justification for the depriving of Christians of Jewish descent of their rights.[54]

A statement by a group of New Testament professors and lecturers, which included Bultmann, Deissmann, Jeremias, Lietzmann, and Karl Ludwig Schmidt, stressed that anti-semitism and the whole concept of race in the contemporary sense had no place at all in the New Testament. Human perversion emanated from original sin in the denial, by both Jew and Gentile alike, of the one and same God, and not as a result of hereditary and biological factors. 'All have sinned—without distinction.' An attitude to life (Weltanschauung) grounded upon racial biology had no significance within the New Testament horizon. The notion that religion as the soul's deepest power existed to develop the natural human properties was as foreign to the New Testament as any reflection upon the utility of the Christian faith in the ordering of such natural and historical associations as Family, People, Society, and State. According to the New Testament, the Christian Church was a church composed of Jews and Gentiles, visibly drawn into one congregation, with faith and baptism the conditions of membership. Natural, this-worldly differences ceased to count and complete parity of membership was recognised. According to the New Testament Jews and Gentiles were equally eligible for appointment to office within the Church, the qualifications being measure of faith, standard of conduct and personal suitability and the call coming solely from the Church herself. According to the New Testament the Church owed her existence in the world solely to the Holy Spirit.[55]

The Theological Faculty of the University of Erlangen was also

invited to pronounce, and a statement was issued under the
signature of the two professors of systematic Theology, Werner
Elert and Paul Althaus, well-known for their advocacy of volkish
theology and a Volk church within the limits of strict, traditional
Lutheran theology. The statement affirmed that, while it was true
that there was, in union with Christ, no difference between Jew
and non-Jew, yet biological and social differences were certainly
not to be left out of consideration. According to I Corinthians
7:20, every man was to 'abide in the same calling in which he
was called'. The Christian had to give due regard to the fact of his
inescapable share in the destiny of a particular Volk. According
to Reformation teaching, and in contrast to Roman Catholic
doctrine, the outward ordering of the Christian Church had to
conform, not only to the universality of the Gospel, but also to the
historical and volkish associations to which Christians belonged
In the primitive Church the Jewish Christians were to be found
following a different Church Order from that of the Gentile
Christians. For the Lutheran oneness in Christ was a matter of
inward faith, not of outward organisation. The holders of spiritual
office needed to be completely identified with the members of
their congregation, not only spiritually but also temporally. The
contemporary issue as to whether the Jews now inhabiting Germany belonged in full sense to the German people or to their own
Jewish people was a question which the Church as such could not
decide for herself. In the case of Jewish Christians reference to
their baptism was not conclusive. The question of the desirability
of marriage between Germans and baptised Jews who believed in
Christ was not to be decided in terms of the Saving Grace of
Baptism. Biological and historical considerations had to be taken
into account in any determination of the relationship between
Germans and Jews. The German people had come to recognise
the threat to them from the emancipated Jews in their midst, and
had taken appropriate steps to combat it by removing Jews and
half-Jews from office. The Church had to recognise the fundamental right of the State to take such legislative measures.
Conscious of her call and her task to be the German Volk Church,
she recognised the severe handicap in appointing to office those of
Jewish origin. The Church had, therefore, to require those concerned to stand back, while of course retaining in full measure
their membership of the German Evangelical Church. As if

uneasy at such a recommendation, the statement went on to admit that no hard and fast rule could be made. The State itself allowed exceptions. The Church would err in just adopting the State legislation. She had to act in conformity with her character as Church. Those already in office ought not to be affected unless there were special reasons for their removal such as, for instance, insurmountable differences between pastor and congregation.[56]

Among those who attempted to justify the introduction of the Aryan Paragraph were three professors, Hans Michael Müller, Professor of Systematic Theology at Jena, Georg Wobbermin, Professor of Systematic Theology at Göttingen and later at Berlin, and Gerhard Kittel, Professor of New Testament at Tübingen.

Müller's argument was based upon a consideration of the Lutheran doctrine of the General Priesthood of All Believers. He contended that before God there was no essential difference between pastor and layman. What he termed the 'substance of the Church', the Divine Promise, Faith, Sanctification, was made completely available to all members of the Church, partakers of one and the same Grace. Such grace was not divisible among clergy and laity, Aryans and non-Aryans. The introduction of the Aryan Clause, with its consequent depriving of certain individuals of office, did not in any way, as the opponents of the new legislation complained, destroy the substance of the Church. It was neither necessary for salvation or in any way detrimental to salvation. The non-Aryan pastor deprived of his official position preserved his priesthood intact. Indeed, the priestly authority which the preacher exercised was not the result of his ordination but of his faith. The bringing into effect of the Aryan legislation was not a doctrinal but a legal decision, that brought about such clarification and change as was demanded by the political situation. Religious faith was neither promoted nor hindered by such a canonical measure. Whether non-Aryans were Church officials or not did damage neither to their faith nor to that of their Aryan fellow-Christians. Müller came finally to his desired conclusion that the only really valid opposition of an evangelical believer to the Aryan Clause was a straightforward political one unadorned by theological arguments. As far as he was concerned, its introduction into the Evangelical Church was theologically feasible and politically necessary.[57]

Professor Wobbermin produced what must be regarded as lame and most unconvincing defence of the action taken by th Prussian Synod. Rudolf Bultmann in a powerful criticism of hi arguments expressed his indignation that in so serious an issu anyone could write so superficial an article.[58] Wobbermin pro fessed to write in his capacity as an expert in the psychology o religion, and chose to view the question from the angle of th present concrete situation rather than in the light of the Nev Testament. He claimed that the 'Brown Synod' had not acte upon its own initiative, but had felt it right and logical to adop within the Church the State-regulations regarding non-Arya officials, since it wholeheartedly accepted the new Nationa Socialist order and recognised that the extent of the non-Arya menace constituted an emergency situation. The opposition, i contrast, lacked both consistency and determination in failing t counter the whole State policy instead of merely confining it protest to the sphere of the Church. Wobbermin declared th matter at issue to be, if not exclusively, at any rate first and fore most, a racial one. He praised the Führer for having made th population as a whole conscious of the gravity of the Jewisl problem. The opposition, so concerned with its interpretation o the New Testament, did not give due consideration to the presen concrete historical situation. It was all very well, and all ver true, to declare that the category and the problem of race wei foreign to the New Testament; but surely that meant that th contemporary Jewish problem could not be answered conclusivel from out of the New Testament! Wobbermin refused to accep the conclusion that had been drawn from Galatians 3:28 an 1 Corinthians 12:13 concerning the absence of difference betwee Jew and Greek, male and female. He agreed that pastoral cai (*Seelsorge*) and fellowship in the Holy Communion were to b equally available to all and without exception. But the same di not apply to the exercise of the ministry. This was a matter c external order. Office within the Church was of human institutio and subject to concrete, historical considerations. Paul ha declared that there was 'neither male nor female', but that di not put men and women upon a completely equal footing. It di not prevent him from ruling that women were not to be permitte to speak in church. Similarly, Jew and Greek, Aryan and non Aryan, could indeed be 'one in Christ' and yet on a point of orde be treated differently. The Church, Wobbermin affirmed, by taking a different line from that of the State, endangered the newly acquired German unity of spirit, so important at present, and not least for the Church herself. A delicately awkward situation could be imagined, if in one and the same parish different treatment were accorded to a non-Aryan pastor and a non-Aryan teacher of religion. Exclusion of non-Aryans from the ministry of the German Evangelical Church was not really a matter of penalisation or of infringement of rights. It was an acceptance of an emergency situation, with an admission from the Church of her share of the blame for the present intolerable situation by her free and easy and often unworthy admission in the past of Jews into the fold. The Church had to accept her part in the task, however burdensome and hurtful, of putting to right a situation that had got out of hand. It was by no means always easy for a 'German Christian' to do full justice to both his National Socialist and his Christian convictions, and the professor revealed his scruples in allowing that a partial mitigation of the severity of the proposals was desirable, and in admitting that in individual cases the result could be tragic and painful.[59]

Gerhard Kittel's booklet *Die Judenfrage*, an expanded version of a lecture delivered in Tübingen in the summer of 1933, which had passed into its third amended edition by 1934, attracted considerable attention both in Germany and also abroad, where it met with a critical and unfriendly reception. Kittel, in contrast to both Müller and Wobbermin, was a distinguished New Testament scholar and a leading authority on ancient Judaism. He was also an enthusiastic member of the Nazi Party and a supporter of the 'German Christian' Movement until November 1933. He combined advocacy of a specifically German theology with a conscientious objectivity in his New Testament work, and revealed great reverence for and sympathy with the orthodox Jew coupled with antipathy towards the secularised and emancipated Jew. His particular kind of biblical theology rather than his political allegiance was basic to his attitude which he himself always insisted was a direct outcome of his biblical studies, maintaining that it echoed the true teaching of Scripture which recorded 'not only the history of redemption (*Heilsgeschichte*) but also the history of rejection (*Unheilsgeschichte*)',[60] telling both of the Chosen People and of the cursed and cast-off People. *Die*

Judenfrage, whatever else it may not have been, was a sincere and courageously independent contribution to the argument. It succeeded in angering the Nazis by its reference to the 'Israelite in whom there was no guile', to salvation being from the Jews, and in its note of affectionate understanding for the believing Jew who should be afforded honourable guest-status.[61] It also shocked much Christian and Jewish opinion by its sweeping and seemingly uncharitable condemnation of the assimilated and emancipated Jew as responsible for all manner of decadence, with the recommendation that he should be forced into a ghetto kind of existence, and its arguments for the establishment of a separate Jewish Christian Church. Regrettably, this sensitive and erudite scholar made considerable use of the jargon of current anti-semitism without embracing the vulgar racial standpoint of which he was in fact a formidable opponent, joining in the chorus of racial hatred or subscribing to the Nazi doctrine of the inherent inferiority of the Jewish character. Unhappily, in the first edition of the booklet, in discussing how the Jewish problem might best be solved, he ruled out the idea of a pogrom as not a serious consideration but without any word of condemnation, appearing to suggest, as one critic remarked, that such an idea was impracticable rather than monstrous.[62] Kittel insisted that the real answer to the Jewish problem was to be found by looking at it from the religious rather than the racial angle. It was a problem of a people rather than that of individuals, and to be solved neither by slogans nor by sentimentalities.[63] The assimilated Jew was the villain of the piece, in so many cases having been baptised, in order to become a Gentile rather than a sincere believing and practising Christian, certainly not an altogether unjustified complaint. Assimilation Kittel sincerely regarded as an accursed transgression of the Divine Will.[64] 'One of the fundamental laws that the Old Testament never wearied in proclaiming is that intermixture with other peoples is the gravest sin for Israel. The Old Testament penalty for this sin is extermination. This struggle for the purity of Israel is a thread running through the whole of the Old Testament from the time of Moses right down to the post-exilic period. Genuine *Judentum* has recognised at all times, and still knows today, that such intermixture of peoples and races means the loss of self-identity and decadence.'[65] The resulting decadence had become manifest from Stoecker's time onwards in a rootless, secularised internationalism that had exercised its poisonous influence upon German life. The emancipated Jew was the enemy of traditional values and standards. Kittel's solution was a complete halt to assimilation and the reintroduction of guest and minority status, with every encouragement to the Jew to take his Jewishness really seriously, and not to expect or to aspire to become a German citizen or to influence the formation and direction of German culture. He should no longer be permitted to teach in German schools or universities or hold a position in any of the professions. Marriages between Jews and Gentiles should be forbidden. He should be accorded generous rights as guest, not being treated as an inferior being but as one of a different character. Kittel's exhortation to the assimilated Jew was to have 'the courage to be a Jew again, and desire to be one, to renounce the fateful dream of assimilation . . . to have the courage to return to the sources of Jewish religion . . . to the Living God proclaimed by Moses, the Prophets and the Psalms' and to accept the divinely prescribed role of a 'restless and homeless alien wandering over the earth, waiting patiently for the Promised Day of the Lord.'[66] The Christian had his duty to do what he could to see that the necessary struggle against corrupt Jewish influences was conducted in a righteous fashion and not with barbarity, and with the privilege of acting the Good Samaritan.[67] His further duty was to point to Christ as the fulfilment of Jewry. That meant active missionary work on the understanding that the convert became not a German but a Jewish Christian. He still remained a Jew after his baptism. The purport of such missionary endeavour, Kittel wrote in a subsequent article, is not 'the obliteration of racial and volkish differences but solely that of the bringing of peace to Israel in the discovery of her Messiah'.[68] Jewish Christians required Jewish Christian theology and customs and liturgy. Therefore a Christian Jewish Church was called for, led by Jewish pastors and elders who would not presume to preside over a German congregation any more than would an Anglican living in Germany, or, in a different context, a Negro within a white American congregation, or for that matter a white within a Negro congregation.[69] Despite such limitations a Christian Jew would remain in the fullest sense 'my Christian brother' though never 'my German brother'. The resultant Jewish Christian Church would in no wise consist of second-grade Christians, but would form a full and honourable part of the Holy Catholic Church. Indeed, just because 'the Jewish Christian personifies in his existence God's *Heilsgeschichte* he has a unique role to fulfil within Christianity as a whole. He provides a necessary corrective to "National Churches" which only through association with him can become the "true Church"'[70] There would be no longer a true Church in existence, if any attempt were made to distinguish between first and second class Christians.

On the practical issue of the implementation of the Aryan Clause within the Church Kittel emphasised that 'the fundamental question was not whether a Jewish Christian can be a pastor or not, but whether, through the exercise of his ministry, his preaching or his pastoral work will in any way be hampered, edification be lessened or an occasion be provided for the enemies of the Church to launch an attack upon the Church'. If there were signs of such disadvantages, surely it would be reasonable and in no wise unchristian to expect that a Jewish Christian pastor 'out of warm love for the Church' would of his own initiative feel bound to 'make a personal sacrifice and eliminate any cause of offence!'[71] There was in Kittel's view clear Pauline sanction for this. There were in point of fact only a handful of Jewish pastors available, and they would anyhow be fully absorbed in the task of ministering to Jewish Christian congregations.

The Faculty of Evangelical Theology at Tübingen saw fit to endorse Kittel's recommendation of a distinct Jewish Christian Church, and to issue on 1 November 1933 a statement to all theological teachers in Europe and America. A covering note asserted that, although nearly all theological opinion outside Germany seemed to be opposed to the recommended Aryan legislation within the German Evangelical Church and to be united in regarding the issue as a matter of Faith and Confession involving the purity of the biblical proclamation. The Tübingen Faculty did not share such a view, and requested that their statement should be accorded serious scholarly examination. The text of the statement was as follows:

In the belief that the Revelation of Old Testament *Heilsgeschichte* has found its fulfilment in Christ, the Christian Jew is our brother in Christ, and every Jewish Christian congregation is a fully recognised part of the *Una Sancta*. Whether Jewish Christians can hold ecclesiastical office in a Volk Church which has become aware of its own peculiar character is an administrative issue for this particular Church which has to be determined in accordance with its basic pastoral concerns and with wisdom, love, and tact. Jewish Christian membership of the Body of Christ and Jewish Christian capacity for spiritual office remain fundamentally undisputed. Should it prove possible for Jewish Christians, in however modest a measure, to construct their own parishes within our Church, such a contribution to the realisation of the unsearchable riches of Christ and to the understanding of the Saving Dispensation of God would prove to be of great gain to the whole of Christendom.

Richard Fischer, in comment, makes the highly pertinent remark that 'the call for the establishment of a Jewish Christian Church should in no circumstances be allowed to be published on grounds that Aryans desire to remove Jewish Christians from their Aryan Church, but solely for the sake of the Jewish Christians themselves, and in order that they may be able to make their voice heard in new—and yet old—fashion within the *Una Sancta*'. 'God', he adds, 'is not just Lord of a History of Peoples but God also of a History of Salvation (*Heilsgeschichte*). Paul's view in Romans chapters 9–11 can be all too readily overlooked.' Fischer also asks 'whether it is possible to harmonise full brotherhood of Germans and Jewish Christians with exclusion from spiritual office on racial grounds. A tough task for Systematic Theology!'[72]

Die Ziele der Deutschen Christen[73] ('The Aims of the "German Christians"'), a booklet written in 1934 by Fritz von der Heydt, a pastor in the Rhineland, furnishes an interesting but strained example of an attempt to reconcile orthodox evangelical belief with the National Socialist volkish outlook, and do justice to both. Von Heydt could be described as a moderate 'German Christian' fired with volkish missionary ardour. He was evidently conscious of one overriding purpose—that 'the German people might become a Christian people'. Christianity, he emphasised, was not to be conceived of in the form of a doctrinal system, a code of morals, a church constitution that was fixed once and for all. It was the work of the Living God as Creator and Holy Spirit to bring the Gospel to life in each individual Christian. The same divine creative activity was to be discerned, where Christian peoples were concerned. In fact, Christianity was rooted in Volk;

hence the difference between Anglican and German piety or between German and Swedish Lutheranism. The enlightened modern worker in the mission field recognised the necessity of building up a genuine Volk Church rather than attempting to reproduce a copy of his own home church. In the light of the newly recognised national and racial insights, which were assuredly God-given and not just of human invention, there was a clear call to work out afresh the relevance of the Gospel. The individual had no choice of the Volk to which he belonged. He could not renounce or deny his volkish adherence at will. Just as a human being was either man or woman, and could not himself alter that fact, so he was a German, a Pole, a Chinaman, and was obliged to be so, because God had created him as such. Against this background von der Heydt went on to discuss the Jewish Question. It was not, he maintained, primarily, a religious issue, for the Jew did not alter either his blood or his characteristic ways (*Art*) by accepting another faith. It was simply a racial issue, made specially acute by the fact that the Jewish people had no country of their own, and were compelled to live among other peoples with the fateful result of infiltration and assimilation. The new German State was quite rightly taking steps to limit and to control such invasion. It was the responsibility of the Church to be assuring the State of the divine creative ordinances and to be true to them in her own sphere. There was no objection whatever to Jewish baptisms, provided they were not put-up jobs, nor to a church wedding of two Jewish Christians; but marriage between a German Christian and a Jewish Christian should not receive the Church's blessing, since the ensuing racial mixture could be a cause of real danger. Baptism had not obliterated racial distinctions, nor did fellowship in Christ make them to be no longer of any account. Faith in Christ should indeed serve to increase a man or woman's reverence for what the Creator had designed. Provided such racial restrictions were recognised, Jewish Christians should be permitted full enjoyment of all the privileges of Church membership in brotherhood with their German fellow-members. The universality of salvation demanded this. This was what Paul meant, when he proclaimed that there was 'neither Jew nor Greek'. Regarding the holding of office in the Church, ministers of the Gospel ought as a general rule to be of the same Volk as those who made up the congregation. But, seeing that he Jewish evangelical pastors were so very few in number, they could well be tolerated, and indeed serve to advertise the univer- ality of the Church. Still, the obvious field of work for them lay n missionary activity among the Jews. Von der Heydt concluded ais section on the Jewish issue with a resolute affirmation that Jesus was Himself a Jew and not an Aryan. This was an un- deniable fact of history. God, the Lord of History, had revealed Himself in the One born in Bethlehem. Jesus was the Son of the Jewish people. God had decreed it to be so, and it had to be accepted. This involved an acceptance of the Old Testament, which was indeed essential, if God's saving action in its entirety was to be understood. He had specially chosen, as well as rejected, Israel. The Old Testament told of the fate of a people who pro- nounced their sentence upon Jesus. Those who imagined that the Old Testament glorified the Jewish people did not know their Bible.

Another prominent 'German Christian' who looked to the Old Testament for substantiation of what was being perpetrated against the Jews was Fritz Engelke, who was for a period in 1934 Reich Bishop Müller's right-hand man. He declared in October 1933 that the Old Testament was a book of destiny revealing the awful fate of a people, and from it alone was to be derived the true explanation of what had been happening to the Jews in the past months. Destiny had found its fulfilment. As a Christian minister he felt the pastoral urgency of helping the Jew to learn from his own Bible what had been consummated. How far removed, how- ever, he was from seeking to develop a biblical or Christian attitude to the proceedings against the Jews is shown by his insistence that what was happening to them should in no wise be made the subject of moral censure. What had taken place was 'a biological eruption, a biological protest such as does not ask leave of us moral theologians but is a destined outburst'—leading, it had to be admitted, to gruesome tragedy. Worst of all in his opinion was not the fate of the racially pure Jew but that of the eager young Storm-trooper who discovers to his horror that he is the possessor of a non-Aryan grandmother or great-grandmother. How grateful, he added, was he himself to his parents, grand- parents and forbears that they all had such 'healthy instincts' which had saved them from profanation of Race and Blood![74]

It is of considerable interest to learn how a non-Aryan pastor

reacted. Paul Leo, at work in the Church of Hannover, presented
to Bishop Marahrens in May 1933 a memorandum entitled *Kirche
und Judentum*.[75] It proved to be a remarkably original, thoughtful
and objective composition. Leo freely admitted that there was a
Jewish problem which required to be ventilated and taken really
seriously, that Germany had been suffering from harmful Jewish
influences, and that certain restrictive measures against the Jew
were needed. He acknowledged that there were emphatic differences between Jews and Gentiles, and he rejected the process of
assimilation that had been developed, recommending in its stead
a regulated existence of the two peoples side by side with attendant
restrictions upon the Jewish element in the population. Such
restrictions the Jews should be prepared, as non-Germans, to
accept without resentment or bitterness, especially those converted to Christianity who had to recognise that they were still
Jewish according to the flesh, and were pledged as Christians to
show all due obedience to those in authority, or else be prepared
to emigrate. Leo expressed criticism of the extravagant racial turn
which had been given to the former German anti-semitism, and
which was causing such terrible hardship to those of Jewish race.
From the standpoint of 'blood materialism' the Jews were looked
down upon as beings of inferior worth, and the high ethical values
resident in Judaism were ignored. The Church had something of
great importance to say to the State, and it was much to be
regretted that the Evangelical Church had so far not made up its
mind to take issue with the present government on the subject of
the maltreatment of the Jews. Many Jews of evangelical faith, and
also some who were unbaptised, felt themselves to be deserted
and betrayed by the Church, because such an utterance had not
been made. It was the duty of churchmen publicly to champion
the cause of their persecuted fellow-men, and sharply to condemn
the insults and slanders directed against them. The Church ought
earnestly to demand that the State in its political campaign against
Jewry should respect the honour and the person of individual Jews.
Ecclesiastically, the problem was simple. No difference should be
made within a congregation between converted and baptised Jews
and Aryan Christians. For the Church there could be only one
question, whether a Jew was baptised or not. The unbaptised
were subjects for the Church's missionary love, the baptised were
fully valid members of her fellowship.

Leo shortly after in a further communication opposed the complete exclusion of non-Aryan pastors from the ministry of the Church, but was prepared to accept as justifiable a *numerus clausus* which would limit their number in fair proportion.

It does not appear that the various statements that dealt in theological terms with the application of the Aryan legislation within the Church had any real effect upon the outlook and policy of Ludwig Müller who was largely impervious to such coherent argument. He must, of course, have been in no real doubt that, if he were in the long run to continue to be *persona grata* with Hitler and the other Nazi leaders, he would certainly have to take definite steps sooner or later to Aryanise the Church as an essential part of the overall plan to co-ordinate it within the framework of the Nazi regime. Müller none the less had to recognise that how, when, and to what extent the implementing of the Aryan clause was to be achieved was a highly tricky issue of Church politics involving also attention to the reaction of the churches abroad. It would call for the tortuous exercise of unprincipled opportunism, temporary accommodation and deliberate deceit, so painfully characteristic of his inglorious episcopate.

It is not altogether easy to follow the see-saw fate of the Aryan Clause. At the meeting of the National Synod at Wittenberg on 27 September 1933, which formally acclaimed Ludwig Müller as Reich Bishop, no steps were taken to extend the decision of the Prussian 'Brown' Synod to the Church as a whole. Müller in providing a report of his stewardship made no reference to the hotly disputed Aryan Clause, nor would he permit any discussion of the whole vexed issue.[76] He was at that time very much under fire from Archbishop Eidem of Sweden who had written urging him to prevent the adoption of the Clause at Wittenberg, affirming that the introduction of such legislation would most seriously imperil the relations of the German Evangelical Church with other Protestant churches.[77] The German Foreign Office was scared of the possible political repercussions of the further and wider promulgation of the Aryan Clause and of a resultant increasing likelihood of an embarrassing attack upon Germany at the forthcoming session of the League of Nations for her handling of the Jews, and Müller was asked whether the Clause could not be quietly and effectively applied without actual legislation.[78] This

EOD

did not, however, prevent the Reich Bishop from declaring at the Synod that the Gospel had to be brought to the German people in their own language and style and that, therefore, those who administered the affairs of the Church and those who preached the Gospel on German soil had of necessity to be of German blood.[79]

Müller struggled during October to persuade the Swedish Archbishop that the Aryan legislation was both justifiable and necessary, since the office of pastor was a public office and could not be catered for by special and distinct ecclesiastical legislation.[80] He had also to contend with George Bell, the Bishop of Chichester, who, in his capacity as President of the Universal Christian Council of Life and Work, wrote to him on 23 October in polite and friendly but firm terms, expressing concern on behalf of himself and of many others at the shape of events in the German Evangelical Church. In particular he alluded to the projected robbing of non-Aryan pastors and officials of ecclesiastical offices and the branding of them as outcasts or lower grade Christians on account of their birth and descent. He asked whether it were not possible for Müller finally to declare, and by his action secure, that such discrimination against Church members of Jewish descent should no more take place as long as he were Reich Bishop.[81] But this letter which was given wide publicity did not stop Müller from four days later reassuring the 'German Christians' at their Reich Assembly in Berlin that he was inflexible in his determination to put the Clause into execution, undeterred by the misunderstandings that might be caused abroad. Only those, he declared, who knew the troubles that Germany had been through in the last fifteen years had a right to pass judgement upon the measure.[82]

On 13 November the 'German Christians', seemingly at the very height of their power (though the Nazi rulers already had serious doubts as to whether the self-declared 'storm-troopers of Jesus Christ' were not more of a cause of embarrassment than of real service to the cause) staged a mass demonstration in Party style in the Sports Palace in Berlin.[83] There was much dissension in the 'German Christian' Movement between the moderates and the extremists, and the latter planned to use this special occasion in order to take decisive command of the Movement. The principal speaker, Dr. Reinhold Krause, demanded that the Reformation should find its fulfilment in the Third Reich. This meant the bringing into being of a Volk Church, German to the very core, in which the whole stream of those returning to its fold could feel thoroughly at home. They should be enabled to draw their inspiration from truly German, and not Palestinian, sources. This called for the elimination of the Old Testament with its Jewish commercial morality and unedifying stories of cattle-dealers and pimps, and for the disavowal of the substitutionary and self-depreciating theology of the Rabbi Paul. 'The Jews are not God's People', declared Krause. 'If we National Socialists are ashamed to buy a necktie from the Jew, we should be utterly ashamed to accept the deepest things of religion from the Jew. This means that our Church ought not to be permitted to accept any more men of Jewish blood into her ranks. . . . Those of Jewish blood do not belong to the German Volk Church, either in the pulpit or in the pew. Jews occupying our pulpits must disappear as speedily as possible.' The resolution that was passed at the end of the meeting, with only one dissentient, called for the Aryan Clause to be implemented with the greatest of speed and without qualification, all evangelical Christians of alien blood being segregated into their own special congregations with the aim of founding a Jewish Christian Church.

So strong and so widespread was the outcry against the Sport Palace utterances and resolutions that the Reich Bishop was immediately obliged to disassociate himself completely from those responsible. Three days later he declared the Aryan Clause to be out of force.[84] Müller's temporary role of shocked and resolute defender of the evangelical heritage prompted him to reply at last on 8 December to Bishop Bell's letter, and in the course of this cordial message he confirmed that the 'so-called Aryan Clause is inhibited'. He also declared it to be his 'particular desire' that a future opportunity should be found to discuss with other Christian churches the racial problem.[85] This suspension lasted for only a few weeks. On 4 January 1934 Müller felt a revived sense of the strength of his position, and, therefore, pronounced the non-Aryan legislation to be again in force.[86]

Three months later as a peace move he announced the putting out of force of the Clause.[87] This concession endured till August of that year, when in the course of the second National Synod the ill-fated ban was once more imposed.[88]

It would be true to say that the Aryan Clause was never fully in force in the Church. The new constitution of the German Evangelical Church, which was made law on 11 July 1933 and was accepted as authoritative by all of the provincial churches and ratified by the government, contained no reference whatever to Aryans and non-Aryans. This fact was without any doubt of great encouragement and service to those who felt bound to oppose the subsequent non-Aryan legislation. It should be added that Article I of the Constitution,[89] which declared that the Gospel of Jesus Christ as testified in Holy Scripture and brought fresh to light in the Reformation Confessions, was the unassailable foundation of the German Evangelical Church, was regarded by the Confessing Church as a solemn substantiation of her stand and her claims, as were indeed its concluding words which asserted that the powers which the Church required for its mission were thereby both defined and limited.

Whether a particular non-Aryan parish pastor or Church official managed to continue in his position depended much upon local circumstances, how active the Gestapo happened to be, how acceptable he was to those to whom it was his duty to minister, and what was the attitude of his particular local church government.

Hans Ehrenberg, whose *75 Guiding Principles concerning the Jewish Christian Problem* attracted considerable attention in 1933 and in which he prophesied that 'in the ultimate stages of the Church Controversy the Jewish Christian issue will become its quintessence and its symbol',[90] was actively at work in his parish in Bochum in Westphalia until the summer of 1937, when a murderous attack upon him in an article in *Der Stürmer* persuaded him to resign. In his autobiography Ehrenberg remarks that the Confessing Church felt obliged to admit publicly that she was guilty of weakness in not giving him the necessary protection.[91] This was presumably a reference to the statement from his colleagues that was read from the pulpit; it described the struggle of the Confessing Church as being not that of maintaining a particular pastor in his post, but of assuring that the Sacrament of Baptism and the appointment to the ministry should be taken seriously, and admitted that 'the severence of Pastor Ehrenberg from his parochial ministry has happened, because the Church has no possibility of championing him and his parish in the requisite fashion'.[92] Wilhelm Niemöller describes how eager the fearless Ehrenberg was to serve actively in the cause of the Confessing Church, bringing his full intellectual weight to bear, but was firmly pushed into the background and regarded as an embarrassment, being urged to restrain himself as much as possible and not to publish any more writings.[93]

Ehrenberg lost his home and possessions in the anti-Jewish pogrom of 1938, was incarcerated in Sachsenhausen concentration camp, where he was given the grim job of corpse-carrier and was obviously himself a candidate for liquidation. The bold efforts of his wife secured his release and he found a fruitful continuance of his ministry during the war in England.[94]

Dietrich Bonhoeffer's close friend Franz Hildebrandt, whose mother was of Jewish origin, was very actively employed from 1934 on as Martin Niemöller's curate until the latter's arrest in 1937. He sought to take over from Niemöller, but was almost immediately arrested by the Gestapo, and after four weeks in prison was able to emigrate to England.[95]

In Hannover Bishop Marahrens, it has been claimed, was successful in preventing the Aryan Clause from being enforced, but he was inclined to allow an individual case to be considered and dealt with in terms of the effect upon harmonious relations in the community concerned. Paul Leo was obliged in 1934 to give up his chaplaincies in a State-controlled prison, convalescent-home and midwives' school. Instead he was placed on the staff of a parish, where his ministrations were greatly appreciated, and remained at work there till 1938, when he was forced to retire through pressure of State officials and the Party.[96] Bruno Benfey, member of a long-established Jewish Christian family in Göttingen, had served since 1927 as one of the clergy of the Marienkirche in that town. He had taken a prominent part in both social and ecumenical activities. While much loved and respected in his parish, he came under attack as an international and left wing Jew, and Nazi intrigues to have him displaced were soon in motion. Confident of loyal support from so many of his parishioners he stood his ground till 1936, refusing to be quietly removed to a distant country parish in which he would be expected to keep his non-Aryan descent secret. His enemies contrived to cause a disturbance when he was officiating at a special service in the autumn of 1936, and a 'German Christian' churchwarden led the chorus of 'Perish the Jews' which greeted him as he left the church. He was taken into protective arrest for a few days, then to be exiled from the district and retired. After a period in Buchenwald from 1938 to 1939, he accepted an invitation to work in Holland, where he was given during the war the pastoral care of the German-speaking non-Aryans.[97] Also in Hannover, Pastor Gurland, a half-Aryan, was able to remain in office until 1939 to the entire satisfaction of his congregation. Having then to resign from his parish, he found employment with the Hermannsburg Mission, occasionally taking services throughout the war.[98]

In Silesia Pastor Forell, the son of Jewish Christian parents, was retired as early as 1933, while Pastor Arnold, also of Jewish Christian parentage, survived in office till 1938, though in 1937 he was seized from his bed by S.S. men, was severely mauled, and was a long time off work.[99]

In Saxony Pastor Wach, whose grandfather, a distinguished ecclesiastical lawyer, had married a granddaughter of the composer Mendelssohn, was an early victim of 'German Christian' venom. He was in 1934 discharged from his cure of souls, and compelled to assume an insultingly subordinate position which carried no stipend.[100]

In Württemberg a young half-Jew was actually able to pursue his studies in Tübingen during the early part of the war, and having passed his examinations, was admitted into temporary church service.[101]

Very strange was the case of Pastor Auerbach in Schleswig-Holstein. Auerbach was a full Jew, and was in 1935 still pastor of the parish of Altenkrempe. There was an agitation for his removal from office, but he was reluctant to resign. Dr. Kinder, the former leader of the Reich Movement of 'German Christians', and at that time a head official in the Church administration in Kiel, arranged by devious means for Auerbach to quit his parish while still retaining the stipend in full. For five years he lived in Altona with full pay and no office. Then in 1941 the resourceful Kinder who had influential contacts, arranged for him to undertake, with the knowledge and permission of the Directorate of the Nazi Party in Munich, a roving ministry to a number of scattered Jews still left in that part of Germany.[102]

Once the flow during 1933 of statements on the subject of the Aryan Clause dried up, very little indeed was published about the

Jewish problem. It was certainly not on the agenda of the Synod of Barmen in May 1934. The purpose of Barmen was to provide decisive opposition to 'German Christian' heresy, and to do so without directly attacking the National Socialist political order. Manifestly powerful and effective were the anathematising of false doctrine, the confessing of the faith of a genuinely Evangelical Church subject to the divine Word of Scripture and the insistence upon the Church really and truly being the Church in acknowledgement of the Sovereignty of Christ. The emphasis was placed on purity of doctrine rather than on the taking of concrete Christian action. The predominant theological influence of Karl Barth gave expression to a transcendental, other-worldly christology rather than to one that was ethically and this-worldly orientated.[103]

At Barmen there was sharp and telling condemnation of 'German Christian' fanatical enthusiasm which claimed the Volk to be the new Chosen People, but this did not lead on to a theological statement of the promise and tribulation of Israel's election, let alone any expression of solidarity with the Jews in their suffering.[104] Right at the very end of his life Karl Barth wrote to Eberhard Bethge acknowledging that Dietrich Bonhoeffer was almost alone in his determination to give central, energetic, and practical consideration to the Jewish Question and make of it a point of attack. Barth freely admitted his guilt in not having himself publicly made a decisive issue of it, and, in particular, in the Barmen Declaration which was largely of his authorship. An outspoken inclusion of it would, he added, not have been acceptable to the Confessing way of thinking at that time. That, however, did not excuse his failure for, to put it bluntly, his interests lay in other directions.[105] Paramount among such interests was obviously the proclamation of the Word *pro domo*.

A cultured layman, who felt particularly disturbed by the passive and self-centred attitude that could overlook the plight of the Jews wrote: 'It seems to me to resemble a parson who, while reading piously in the Gospel, loses his way and, immersed in the text, walks on; or as if suffering was so near to his feet that he stumbles over it, and on seeing it retreats to a psalm of comfort to fortify himself.'[106] This quotation may be bracketed with Bonhoeffer's celebrated remark: 'Only he who cries out for the Jews may sing Gregorian chants.'[107]

The Synod of Dahlem, held five months after Barmen, took in one sense an altogether more practical turn, being concerned with the recognition and organisation of the Confessing Church based upon Barmen as the true Evangelical Church of Germany in contrast to the 'sham Church', the established Reich Church. It dealt with what was declared to be a situation of the greatest emergency, and earned criticism, by no means only from the 'German Christians' for being pharisaically exclusive and obsessed with the need for a 'chemically pure' Church, thereby demonstrating a want of outgoing love for those without.[108] The practical resolutions which this Synod passed were entirely concerned with the overcoming of the emergency within the Church. One searches in vain for expression of concern for those in any other kind of distress (*Not*), either within or without the Church. Such extreme preoccupation with the internal ecclesiastical crisis obviously left no room for any practical resolutions seeking to alleviate the continuing plight of the non-Aryans and other victims of Nazi cruelty and intolerance.

The contribution from the Marburg Theological Faculty had boldly and unequivocably defended the unlimited rights of baptised Jews within the Church. Such were admittedly its terms of reference, but it meant treating the Jewish Question as merely an ecclesiastical issue. The rights of both the Jews who were faithful in their attachment to the Synagogue and the Jews who were without confessional adherence were left out of consideration. Bultmann, for all his bold and vigorous countering of Wobbermin and the 'German Christians', did not allow himself even a passing reference to the inhumanity of the State legislation which surely also called for opposition on Christian grounds. Such exclusive preoccupation with the situation within the Church with the clear distinction being made between baptised and unbaptised Jews not only prevented the Church at this early stage of the Nazi regime when Hitler and company would still have had to show some circumspection from venturing upon a measure of general opposition, but played into the hands of the National Socialists. Subsequent events were to make apparent their skill in playing off the 'privileged'[109] against the 'non-privileged' non-Aryans, thus preventing the representatives of the Church from championing the cause of the persecuted Jews as a whole. This was assisted by the Church's preoccupation with the Confessional issue and her contention that the converted Jew was no longer a Jew but a Christian.

The Evangelical Church never spoke out officially against the Aryan legislation in general. Its effect upon the Jews as a whole did not seem to be a matter of direct Christian concern, but rather as something that just had to be accepted, or even as something that could be approved of in its secular setting. It took, in fact, many years before the Confessing Church came to recognise that it was not merely the Christian brethren of Jewish origin on whose behalf they had to take issue, but that the Jews who remained Jews and had not become Christians should not just be left to fend for themselves.[110]

There were still those whose protestantism remained fundamentally free and liberal and in the tradition of Harnack in subscribing to his insistence that practical recognition of God as Father involved real reverence for all that was human.[111] They belonged to the circle which clustered round and supported the periodical *Christliche Welt* which had sturdily championed freedom of conscience and maintained wide cultural interests ever since 1886 under the enterprising direction of Martin Rade.[112] Prominent among them was Professor Hermann Mulert of Kiel who had succeeded Rade as editor in 1932. In an article in June 1933 he felt moved to remark that, when highly respected churchmen apparently suggested that the Church should by all means take the part of baptised Jews, if they were suffering wrong, but need not be concerned about the non-baptised, this was far from the right Christian attitude. Surely Jesus had in the story of the Good Samaritan proclaimed it the duty of His disciples to render assistance altogether beyond the bounds of Volkstum and creed.[113]

In confessional circles great stress was laid upon 'brotherly love', and it was a common practice to refer to *Bruder* Schmidt rather than to *Pfarrer* or *Herr* Schmidt. Such love for the brethren was without doubt introverted. Its characteristics were, as Gerlach remarks, 'exclusiveness, special and personal limitation, accompanied by a certain self-protection from what lay outside'.[114] Such an attitude fell undeniably short of what Jesus meant by neighbourly love, as illustrated by the Good Samaritan. It militated against spontaneous, unrestricted humane reaction and activity. As Gerlach suggests, it was almost as if the Good Samaritan ought really, before performing his deed of compassion, to have sought scriptural clearing from his superiors.[115]

There were without doubt appreciable numbers of prominent churchmen who were troubled in their Christian consciences at the way in which the Jews as a whole were being treated, but who all too readily persuaded themselves that there was really nothing that could or should be done. Hugo Hahn, who was such a one, relates in his memoirs that, though he had hitherto been anything but friendly towards the Jews, he became in the course of 1933 increasingly indignant at the unfair and cruel way in which the Jews were being treated. 'I felt myself aware of my own complicity', he wrote, 'and also that of our whole Christian Church in this great injustice. I called upon the Jewish rabbi in Dresden, in order to assure him of my own sympathy and that of many Christians. He was grateful for the visit. Unfortunately, I had to admit to him that there was but little that we could do in practice, because we were ourselves also being attacked and on the defensive, and were altogether without influence upon the authorities. But I experienced then, as I do today, a real sense of guilt at our silence over the injustice committed against the Jews.'[116]

Dietrich Bonhoeffer was one of the very few who was really filled with passionate concern for the fate, not only of the baptised Jew, but also of the whole defenceless Jewish people. He repeatedly quoted from Proverbs 31:8, 'Open thy mouth for the dumb', and was deeply disappointed that the Synod of Augsburg in 1935 had concentrated upon the consolidation of the Confessional Movement rather than in boldly speaking out about the real vital issues, of pre-eminent importance among which was the whole Jewish Question and not just the spiritual welfare of baptised non-Aryans. It was Bonhoeffer's conviction that the time had come not merely to withstand the edicts of Reich Bishop Müller, but also to proclaim opposition to State legislation.[117]

Another who felt very strongly indeed about the Church's failure to espouse the cause of the afflicted was Freiherr von Pechmann. His protest took the form of secession from the 'German Evangelical Church'. In a forthright letter to Reich Bishop Müller written on 2 April 1934, he declared that the time had come to DO something in protest. What he had said and what he had written had been of no avail. He affirmed that he no longer desired to belong to a Church which ceased to deserve the name of Church, when she subjected herself to Nazi totalitarian claims. This was nothing more or less than a relapse into pre-Christian and anti-Christian absolutism. His extreme form of protest, he declared, was, among other things, an expression of his disgust that the Church had kept silent in the face of so much injustice and though confronted by all the misery and deep affliction that had to be endured in countless non-Aryan hearts and homes, both Christian and Jewish.[118]

One of the reasons without doubt that caused the Church to be so reluctant to protest officially against the utterly unchristian treatment of the Jews, Christian and non-Christian Jews alike, was the anxiety not to impair the purity and strength of witness to scriptural and doctrinal truth by running the risk of her becoming entangled in what could be regarded as secular opposed to specific religious issues. There was continuous concern to avoid being accused of hostility to the State, interference in politics, harbouring politically discontented elements within her religious organisation, and of furnishing increased material for criticism and condemnation from abroad of the Nazi regime. By and large the Confessing Church did not develop into an opposition front politically, and had no desire to do so.

In November 1933 in the thick of the controversy with the 'German Christians' and smarting under the accusation of being politically reactionary the leaders of the Pastors' Emergency League insisted that their members stood unreservedly on the side of Hitler as 'loyal members of our Volk, as true servants of the State and as Germans who gladly followed the Führer'.[119] Martin Niemöller had occasion in April 1934 to react indignantly against the report in the British *Morning Post* on a service in his church at Dahlem. The report carried the banner headline— 'Pastor defies Hitler' and characterised Niemöller as the 'former U-Boat Commander who is leading the revolt in the Evangelical Church against the unchristian ideas of the Nazi State' and 'one of the most intrepid fighters for freedom of thought in Germany today'. The report also described 'the growing opposition among Protestants . . . to the crude ideas of orthodox National Socialism' as 'one of the most urgent domestic problems engaging the attention of Herr Hitler'.[120] Niemöller lost no time in despatching the offending article to the Berlin Gestapo headquarters with a covering note requesting that it should be made clear to the foreign Press that 'the conflict within the Evangelical Church had no political purpose whatever'.[121] Karl Koch in his capacity as President of the Prussian Confessional Synod wrote to the Minister of Home Affairs, Frick, on 12 December 1934, asserting that the Confessional Synod of the German Evangelical Church had expressly stated time and again that it was not prepared to allow its ecclesiastical intentions and actions to be debased by political intrigue. There was no place in the Confessional Front for enemies of the State or traitors to the Fatherland.[122] Similar protestations of political reliability coupled with insistence that the Church's struggle was essentially a religious one continued to be made despite the increasing awareness of the unchristian methods and the anti-Christian policy of the Nazi State.

In March 1935 the *Reformierte Schweizer Zeitung* emphasised that personal inquiries from leaders of the Confessional Church had established time and again that there was not the slightest political intent in the resistance, and that the leaders of the Confessional Movement were, as German citizens, consistently loyal to their government. This assessment was reproduced in *Junge Kirche*, the Confessional fortnightly, with obvious appreciation.[123] In so bleak a year for the Church as 1937 a Munich pastor could avow that the Confessing Church had no politics of her own, but rather stood fully and completely behind the Führer, and that her pastors were as wholehearted in their support of National Socialism and the Third Reich as they had ever been. [124] It would be wrong to dismiss this apologia as just a tactical expression of loyalty. Many a pastor shared with other Germans in their judgement of National Socialism the obstinate and unrealistic differentiation between the Weltanschauung and the political system, between the welcomed advancement of Volk and Nation, and the unprincipled and oppressive means adopted. Kurt Gerstein was accurately representing the attitude of many members of the Confessing Church, who undoubtedly must have had reservations about the way in which Hitler's Germany had developed, when he wrote in 1938 to his uncle in the United States: 'Although there has been much to outrage our individual consciences, we have made every effort not to oppose National Socialism in purely political matters, since those are not our direct concern. We have sought only to defend the rights and responsibilities solemnly guaranteed to us by Herr Hitler and the Party, and which they still guarantee.'[125]

The Jewish issue in general had certainly to be regarded as a political issue. Openly and vigorously to take the part of the persecuted Jews, to speak in public in kindly and compassionate terms of them, and to criticise in any way the Nazi policy with regard to them was to invite an instant charge of political disloyalty, if not of actual treason, and meant playing into the hands of the anti-Church brigade and also the 'German Christian' foe.

This, however, did not prevent the Confessional Synod of the Prussian Church from publishing in March 1935 a sharp attack upon the 'deadly dangerous' new German Religion, in which Blood and Race and Volkstum were deified, and faith in the 'Eternal Germany' substituted for faith in the Eternal Kingdom of the Lord Jesus Christ. This idolatry had nothing to do with 'positive Christianity'. It was the religion of Antichrist. 'Those who substituted Blood, Race and Volkstum for God as the creative power of State authority were undermining the State.' The Church was determined to be true to her Lord's command to preach the Gospel of the Grace and Glory of Jesus Christ to all peoples, and was not prepared to allow herself to be thrust out of public life into a remote corner of private piety, where she would be disobedient to her commission.[126]

This bold statement had immediate effect. A large number of pastors were arrested or forcibly prevented from reading the statement from their pulpits. It also evoked a counter-statement from Müller and a number of 'German Christian' leaders insisting that they, the representatives of the legally authorised Prussian Church, were also pledged to raise their voices and vigorously resist a 'new religion' that sought to make 'an idol of earthly values and of human self-redemption', but would at the same time certainly not be prepared to deny the values of Blood and Race, but would look for every opportunity to interpret such values as 'God's Gift to our Volk'. The 'Lord of History' alone decided the question as to who was responsible for undermining the State. The Church opposition took the shape of an utterly un-Lutheran theocracy. To seek to enter into competition with the authority of the Total State, and to insist upon imposing a theological and christological interpretation upon it, was an unevangelical denial of the truth that the Kingdom of God was not of this world.[127]

Very sparse attention had been, and was being, given to the plight of the 300,000 or so evangelical non-Aryan layfolk, and there was almost complete silence regarding the application of the Aryan Clause in the case of the appreciable number of them, who had been deprived of their jobs on purely racial grounds, and were suffering other disabilities and humiliations.[128]

In 1934 a Reich Association of Christians of Non-Aryan and Impure Aryan Descent had been brought into being on an inter-church and self-help basis, but the State was unwilling to afford it the same recognition as the fully Jewish Reich Association, and it proved too weak an organisation to be able to give much practical assistance to those in need. The provision of some form of relief agency was urged by Superintendent Martin Albertz and his colleague Marga Meusel, a Christian welfare worker in Berlin. In 1935 Albertz had urged, but in vain, that the Augsburg Synod should consider that practical steps should be taken to assist the evangelical non-Aryans. In 1936 he was appointed a member of the provisional administration of the Confessing Church and given special responsibility for the care of the Christians of Jewish extraction. This facilitated negotiations, and enabled a certain amount of individual help to be given, but the situation of the Christian non-Aryans remained pitifully precarious.

A remarkable service was rendered by Marga Meusel in making so overwhelmingly clear to the Confessing Church how desperate was the plight of the non-Aryans and really how pitifully little was being ventured or undertaken on their behalf. She was the author of a couple of memoranda on the subject that not surprisingly had but a limited circulation.

Her first contribution, dated 10 May 1935, was entitled 'A Memorandum on the Tasks to be undertaken by the Confessing Church on behalf of the Evangelical Non-Aryans'.[129] It was presented by Martin Albertz to the Synod of Augsburg. In it she contrasted the tragic plight of the Evangelicals as compared to that of the Catholics and the non-Christian Jews. The Catholic Church, she contended, was proving altogether more effective in looking after her non-Aryan members who could take comfort in the knowledge of belonging to a powerful and well-organised world-wide communion. What mattered was that they were Catholics, and their Jewish ancestry was a matter of minor consideration. Those who were Jewish by confession had the support of an organised community within Germany and of World Jewry. It was suggested that the Evangelical non-Aryans should apply for help to the Reich Association of Non-Aryan Christians, but it could not be maintained that they thereby found their deepest needs met. The service offered by the Association was mainly that of compilation of statistics and of genealogical research accompanied by a programme of lectures, cultural entertainments, sporting activities, and youth work. The Evangelical non-Aryans had great need for something far more than that. Inner, spiritual help was essential, were they to be able to cope with their manifold difficulties and their feelings of hopelessness and despair. The assistance required was fellowship with other believers in Christ. The Confessing Church should be the place in which they could be assured that questions of race and descent were of no concern. Help from their fellow-Christians in finding employment should be governed solely by considerations of professional ability and the recognition of unity in Christ. There should be unrestricted admission of children and others into evangelical institutions. Attempted segregation into special non-Aryan communities was not acceptable as a Christian solution. A central organisation to arrange for professional and trade training and for emigration was also an urgent need. 'Many thousands of evangelical non-Aryans have been waiting a long time for a word from the Confessing Church that would prove to them that they completely belong to us as our brothers and sisters', were her concluding words.

There was silence from Augsburg, and in mid-September Marga Meusel produced a further and much more outspoken document. This time the memorandum was entitled simply 'The Situation of the German Non-Aryans'.[130] It was laid before the Prussian Synod due to be held at Berlin-Steglitz, a few days after the passing of the Nuremberg Laws, but again without any very marked result.

In the belief that the indescribable hardships caused by the persecution of the non-Aryans were not widely enough recognised, Marga Meusel supplied numerous and varied well-documented examples, particularly stressing the terrible effect upon children, marriage, and livelihood. Appalled by the sea of hatred, insult, and barbarity, she described the situation as altogether desperate, not only for those who had to endure it, but still more for the people who perpetrated such things or permitted such things to happen. The Confessing Church had solemnly admitted to its prophetic role of Watchman in the light of Ezekiel, chapter 3. The time had more than come when the Church should show compassion to her members, and send forth her clarion call to open eyes and stir and awaken consciences; a call not only to the Faithful but to the whole people to return to everything that went by the name of Christianity to the practical Christianity of the Good Samaritan, himself a despised cross-bred alien. It was no exaggeration to speak of the extermination of the Jews in Germany. It had been stated from the beginning that there was no need of Bartholomew's Eve. There were other methods. The fruit of such methods was already to be seen in the hundreds or more of suicides that had already taken place. Was the Christian answer to the question, 'Where is Abel thy brother ?' to be that once given by Cain ?

Reverting to a theme of her first memorandum, Marga Meusel proceeded to ask with passionate, and admittedly somewhat exaggerated bitterness, why so much cause was given for non-Aryan Christians to be continually having to complain that they felt neglected by the Church both at home and abroad, and that the help that they did receive came to them from Jews and Jewish relief organisations and not from their own Church. They observed their Catholic counterparts being cared for, but could only say of the attitude of the Evangelical Church, 'Lord, forgive them, for they know not what they do'. The Catholic Church found, whenever possible, posts for non-Aryan doctors and sisters. In contrast, Bodelschwingh (so enormously revered for his care of the helplessly infirm) had advertised for an Aryan medical practitioner. The Evangelical *Innere Mission* had its Aryan clause, and required a stenographer to produce proof of her Aryan descent. It was not surprising that there were non-Aryans, who had for long been baptised Christians, who in the face of what they had experienced from Christians and the Church, reverted to Judaism, and that others who sought for baptism looked to the Catholic rather than the Evangelical Church.

The Evangelical Church was looking on and doing nothing, as unspeakable injustices were being perpetrated, while at the same time repeatedly assuring the National Socialist State of her joyful support in political confessions which implied approval of measures directed against a part of her membership. All that was absolutely irreconcilable with present-day despised humanity appeared to be reconcilable with Christianity. If the Church could in many cases, from fear of her own destruction, do nothing, why was she not at least conscious of her guilt ? Why did she not pray for those who were afflicted by undeserved suffering and persecution ? Why were there no services of intercession being held for them, as were done for the imprisoned pastors ? The Church made it desperately hard for anyone to defend her. Her Commission was to preach obedience to *all* the commandments of God, if she was not to fall under the condemnation: 'His blood will I require at thy hand!'

The final paragraph expressed horror that there were actually within the Confessing Church those who dared to believe that they were entitled, even called, to proclaim the Gracious Judgement of God in what was at present happening to the Jews and in the sufferings that they themselves were guilty of assisting in afflicting upon them. This was a fact that filled the heart with icy fear. 'Since when', was her final inquiry, 'has the evildoer had the right to pass off his evil deeds as being the Will of God ?' It was nothing other than blasphemy to suggest that the doing of such injustice could be the Will of God.

In a postscript added in May 1935[131] after the Nuremberg legislation had been promulgated, Marga Meusel described the situation of the Christian non-Aryans, and especially those who were Evangelicals, as being still more grievous than that of the Jews. Energetic, large-scale efforts to help particularly in assistance to emigrate, had so far only been made from the Jewish side. This was a serious reproach to Christianity, both in Germany and ecumenically. Her verdict remained that the Evangelical Church had still not, 'late, much too late, but all the same better too late than never', found the right word to utter; she continued day after day unforgivably to leave her non-Aryan members in the lurch.

That the predicament of many non-Aryan Christians did not become less acute was made clear in a lecture given in Frankfurt in 1937 by Pastor Leo in which he spotlighted the peculiarly distressed circumstances of the baptised Jews. While outwardly in the same situation as the unbaptised, their predicament was, inwardly, vastly different. The unbaptised, denied their rightful place within the German community, could fall back upon their comparatively secure position within Jewry. The baptised, on the other hand, no longer accepted members of the Jewish community and equally deprived of their German citizenship, were in danger of being pathetically isolated. This was tolerable if through baptism they had entered into a living relationship to the Church, and were practising their Faith within a Christian Fellowship. A large majority of these baptised Jews, many of whom were baptised in infancy largely for social reasons, did not have more than a purely formal connection with the Church. They were, in fact, not to be regarded in the present circumstances as real Jews, Germans, or Christians. The Church had obviously a great and urgent evangelistic responsibility to befriend them, especially as in the past she had so frequently connived in the promiscuous administration of baptism. It was not pharisaical exclusiveness to contend that the baptised had the first call upon the Church's loving care. A mother naturally had the duty of providing first and foremost for her own children. Only after having conscientiously discharged that duty, could or should she give help to others outside her family. Leo recommended that missionary work to the uncommitted non-Aryan Christians should, whenever possible, be carried out by fellow non-Aryans, and that, if the State would permit, a full-time travelling representative of the Church could fulfil a valuable role.[132]

The 'German Christians' had come under new and much less truculent and boisterous management. The Reich Movement of 'German Christians' as it was now called, under the more moderate leadership of Dr. Christian Kinder, 'a man of good intentions and of genuine Lutheran convictions',[133] claimed to be loyal to the fundamentals of the established Faith. The dropping of the title 'Faith Movement' was designed to show that matters of faith should no longer be entangled with ecclesiastic power politics. The new aim was to unite all those who were equally concerned with affirming their Christianity and giving expression to their National Socialist convictions, especially having in mind the avowed Christians within the Party membership, and also to bring Volk and Church closer together by making the Gospel message more readily understandable. The 28 Theses of the Saxon Volk Church were adopted as theological guide. They affirmed the full acceptance of the National Socialist racial attitude. Office-bearers in the Church were to be made subject to the same racial legislation as the State officials. The non-Aryan could not be regarded as a

member of the Volk Church, though he would not be excluded
from attendance at church services or refused admission to the
sacraments and participation in the wider Christian fellowship of
faith. There was no recommendation of a separate Jewish Christian
Church. Justification for such a point of view was, it was claimed,
to be found in the earnest contention that the Christian Church
had not yet entered into the perfection of eternity, but was subject
to the ordinances which God had bestowed upon this present life.
As on other previous occasions it was endeavoured to make it all
sound more 'Christian' by admitting that the Christian of another
race was not a Christian of lower grade but one of a different
character (*art*).[134] The Rhenish Brotherhood of pastors in a
detailed criticism of the Theses had no hesitation in proclaiming
that a Church with such a racial outlook was no longer to be
accounted a true Church of Christ, but was in point of fact a
judaistic, volkish sect, a State-allied organisation for the cultivation of German *Volkreligion*, bearing the name of Christianity
but in point of fact a relapse into heathenism.[135]

Dr. Kinder in his book *Volk vor Gott* insisted that the Jewish
Question as a racial problem was distinct from the Jewish Question
as a religious problem, and should be kept so. Only once the racial
issue had been settled and its conclusions accepted and implemented by the Church, could the religious issue be dealt with.
The solving of the racial problem was clearly and unreservedly
the responsibility of the State. The German people were entitled
to take measures to ensure their own racial integrity, just as the
Jewish people had themselves done in the past. The German
Evangelical Church, if it desired to be a genuine Volk Church,
and thus serve its own people without hindrance, had to be prepared to allow the State regulations for racial control to operate
within the Church. Baptism, according to Kinder, did not cancel
the Divine Creative Ordinances. The Christian Jew remained
racially a Jew. Holy Scripture did not provide rules and regulations regarding the exercise of the ministry, just as it did not
legislate for the training needed for the ministry. Such were considerations of external order, and had to be worked out at various
different times and in various parts of the world according to the
non-religious circumstances that held good at a particular time.[136]

The 'German Christians' in Thuringia[137] having severed
themselves from the main 'German Christian Movement' after

the Sport Palace rumpus, embarked upon a 'National Church' line of their own. One of their leading spokesmen, Siegfried Leffler, recommended in unambiguous terms the formation of a quite independent Jewish Christian Church. Christ, as the Way and the Truth, Leffler declared, was to be found and experienced in varied fashion in each different Race and People. There was no objection to Jews being converted to Christianity, provided the object was the attainment of personal salvation, and not a convenient means of entering into European society. The Jew on conversion remained as much a Jew as ever. Jewish Christians should be encouraged to form their own Jewish Christian congregations with their own expressions of faith and worship and their own pastors and teachers. In recommending this, he claimed to be speaking as one of the sons of Luther, who after cruel and bitter disappointment, gave unwearying and prophetic warning of the Jews and their lies.[138]

A copy of a small pocket book used by the Thuringian 'German Christians' entitled *Unsere Kampflieder* (Our Battle-songs) has been preserved in the Wiener Library in London. One of the most bombastic of these hymns includes the startling and menacing line 'Germany, awake, death to Judah'!

As a tail-end to this chapter, it may come as somewhat of a shock to learn that in a book published in 1935 entitled *Hitlerism, Communism and the Christian Faith* an Anglican clergyman, by name Evan Thomas, who proudly claimed to be late of the universities of Berlin, Jena, Heidelberg, and Freiburg, and who had no hesitation in proclaiming that Hitler and his ideals had been the salvation of the German people and had removed for the moment a very great danger to the peace of Europe, made a bold bid to rival the 'German Christians' in vilification of the Jews. He wrote: 'They have always been, and still are, a parasitic people. . . . In respect of the stranger upon whose life they feed, they have only one principle, namely—"Thou shalt spoil the Egyptians". . . . They believe and act as though all the nations of the world are called into being merely to minister to their glory and to their wealth. Is it any wonder, therefore, that Germany, into whose vitals Jewry has dug its claws so deeply, should regard the Jews as a veritable cancer to be eradicated at all costs?'[139] As far as is known, this utterance did not cause any disturbance or provoke any definite protest.

NOTES TO CHAPTER 4

1. Meier, 65.
2. Peter Neumann: *Die Jungreformatorische Bewegung, Arbeiten zur Geschichte des Kirchenkampfes*, Band 25, Göttingen 1971, provides an excellent account of the origin and development of this short-lived movement and of the inevitable dissension within its membership.
3. Joachim Gauger: *Gotthardbriefe, Chronik der Kirchenwirren*, d. 77.
4. Kurt Dietrich Schmidt: *Die Bekenntnisse des Jahres 1933*, Göttingen, 1934, pp. 146–8.
5. Eberhard Bethge: *Dietrich Bonhoeffer. Eine Biographie*, München, 1967, p. 322. English edition, *Dietrich Bonhoeffer. A Biography*, Collins, 1970, p. 206.
6. Dietrich Bonhoeffer: *Gesammelte Schriften*, Band I, p. 37.
7. Dietrich Bonhoeffer: *Gesammelte Schriften*, Band II, pp. 44 ff.
8. *Volk und Kirche. Berichte der erster Reichstagung 1933 der Glaubensbewegung 'Deutsche Christen'*, ed. Joachim Hossenfelder, p. 13.
9. Ibid., 54.
10. Ibid., 47.
11. Ibid., 54.
12. Ibid., 45.
13. Gauger, 77.
14. For full accounts of the proceedings of the Synod see AELKZ, 1933, pp. 859–62, and JK, 1933, pp. 192ff. A vivid account by a Swedish journalist of an earlier 'Brown' Synod of the Brandenburg Provincial Church held in Berlin is to be found in Heinrich Schmid: *Apokalyptisches Wetterleuchten*, München, 1947, pp. 39–41. Pastor Gerhard Jacobi, leader of the 'Young Reformers' Group, had the courage to declare that the introduction within the Church of the attitude of the State towards the non-Aryans was contrary to the interests of the Church. This was received with salvoes of laughter. An English translation of the account is to be found in Conway, p. 47.
15. Gauger, 98, 100.
16. *Die Evangelische Kirche in Deutschland und die Judenfrage*, Geneva, 1945, p. 36. [Henceforth EKDJF.]
17. Johann Bielfeldt: *Der Kirchenkampf in Schleswig-Holstein, 1933–1945*, Göttingen, 1964, pp. 46–7. Ruth Rouse of the World Student Federation in a confidential report on her visit to Germany in October 1933 wrote that at the Synod a prominent non-'German Christian' who had merely said, 'We must consider what they would say abroad' was greeted with shouts of 'To the Concentration Camp!', 'Out with him!', 'Traitor!' (World Council of Churches, Geneva, *Kirchenkampf*, 284 (43).
18. JK., 1933, p. 178.
19. EKDJF, 37.

20. Eberhard Klügel: *Die Lutherische Landeskirche Hannovers und ihr Bischof, 1933–1945*, Berlin, 1964, pp. 84, 492.

21. Fischer, III, p. 74.

22. Ernst Kinder: *Neue Beiträge zur Geschichte der evangelischen Kirche in Schleswig-Holstein und im Reich*, Flensburg, 1968, pp. 82–3 This and other such revolutionary legislation was accepted light-heartedly, without a sense of responsibility and in unworthy haste. The great majority of those who took part scarcely knew what they were doing (Bielfeldt, 44).

23. Arndt Müller, 216.

24. Gauger, 104. It was also reckoned that there had only been ninety-eight pastors of Jewish extraction in the service of the German Evangelical Church since the Reformation. There is record of a naval officer writing to the Reich Bishop in October 1933, pleading that his son, Gerhard, whose mother was a baptised Jewess, should be allowed to continue his theological studies at Halle, and that his dismissal by the Theological Faculty there should be rescinded. Professor Hans-Michael Müller, theological consultant to the Reich Bishop, sent a pious and ambivalent reply to this plea, in which, patently disregarding the indeterminate application of the Aryan legislation within the Church, he expressed his regret that no exception could be made. 'As men of faith', he wrote, 'we can only beseech God, that He will by divine dispensation, such as He alone can provide, cause what for both your son and you yourself appears to be a quite incomprehensible and altogether hostile fatal blow to turn out for the best. . . . The Church is not in possession of the omnipotence of God, and can consequently not be held responsible for the hardships and sacrifices entailed by essential historical development, in face of which she feels herself powerless. (Wolfgang Gerlach: *Zwischen Kreuz und Davidstern, Bekennend Kirche in ihrer Stellung zum Judentum im Dritten Reich*. Unpublished Dissertation, Hamburg, 1970, pp. 132–3.) Not only was this sanctimonious reply manifestly inhuman, it was also not legally justified, for in point of fact it was not until early in 1936 that the Aryan legislation was officially applied to students of theology, but even then Gerhard with his Aryan father would appear to have been exempt.

25. Bonhoeffer: *Gesammelte Schriften*, II, pp. 70–1. Niemöller and Bonhoeffer hoped that this declaration would collect many signatures, but there was a set-back, when no less a person than Friedrich von Bodelschwingh expressed misgivings about the reference to the exclusion of those approving the new legislation from the fellowship of the Church (Jürgen Schmidt: *Martin Niemöller in Kirchenkampf*, Hamburg, 1971, p. 120). This was one of the first of the many objections that continued to be raised to the hard and narrow confessing line.

26. Jürgen Schmidt: *Martin Niemöller*, 119.

27. Bonhoeffer: *Gesammelte Schriften*, II, 71–3.

28. Ibid., 128–9. English translation in *No Rusty Swords*, ed. Edwin Robertson, Collins, 1965, pp. 231–2.

29. *Die Nation vor Gott* (2nd edition, 1934), p. 123.

30. Ibid., 126.

31. Ibid., 132.

32. Ibid., 137.

33. Heinrich Fausel who may be described as one of the most thorough-going and resolute of the Confessing pastors wrote in his parish magazine early in 1934—'When the National Socialist State adopts measures for the protection of Race and People, such in accordance with the realities of the situation is its duty. . . . That, nevertheless, does not infer that such State legislation that in its right place is necessary, legitimate and sensible, may without any further ado be applied within the Church. State and Church are not the same. The State legislates. The Church proclaims the Gospel. The State resorts to force, because man is sinful. The Church witnesses to the freedom to which the same sinful man is called through the Holy Spirit. If it be true that the Congregation is the Body of Christ, then in it in faith and in Christ the overcoming of volkish differences is realised. Membership of the Church cannot be dependent upon membership of a particular race, but is bestowed through baptism and faith. To legislate concerning such membership is tantamount to denial of the efficacy of the Holy Spirit and dissolution of the Church of Christ. If the Church does so, she repeats the Jewish Christian error of restricting the Divine Freedom and destroying it by means of an earthly ruling. A Church which introduces the Aryan Clause with legislative authority has already succumbed to the false spirit which it is meant to combat. The People of God, Israel after the flesh, that will not accept the Son of God incurs the judgement of the Wrath of God—that is for us the core of the Jewish issue' (Fischer, III, 99).

34. A group of pastors in Nuremberg expressed their objection in the following terms—'The Church has committed the preaching office to her pastors through ordination. She cannot withdraw it to meet an outside point of view. The Aryan Clause means that neither Peter nor Paul, not even the Lord Jesus Christ Himself would be permitted to preach' (Arndt Müller, 216).

35. Karl Kupisch: *Durch den Zaun der Geschichte*, Berlin, 1964, p. 421.

36. *Evangelischer Ruf*, Breslau, 14 October 1933. It is not surprising to learn that the *Evangelischer Ruf* was shortly afterwards banned until further notice. Ivan Welle, a Church historian from Oslo, concluded a report of a visit of his to Germany as follows: 'Many cries of distress ascend from Germany to God's Throne in Heaven. As a result, the Good God said to His Son: Will you not descend and come to the help of Germany? He answered: No, I have no right of entry any longer because of the Aryan Clause. Then God the Father said to the Holy Spirit: Will you not descend? He

answered: No, everything that goes by the name of Spirit is forbidden in Germany. The Second and Third persons of the Trinity asked God the Father Himself: Will you not go down? He answered: No, for if I vacate My Throne for only a moment, Adolf Hitler will come and occupy it. So Germany obtained no help in her distress' (Gerlach, Beiheft, 35).

37. The contrary 'German Christian' view was stated to Charles Macfarland, for many years senior Administrative Officer of the Federal Council of the Churches of Christ, U.S.A., on a visit to Germany in October–November 1933, by Professor Georg Wobbermin who declared that the so-called Aryan Clause did not violate the fundamentals of the Christian Faith, for it had to do only with the outward ordering of the Church, and was necessary to satisfy the concrete conditions of a particular historical situation. Nothing else than just that was its intention. The German Evangelical Church sought to see the Will of God in what Adolf Hitler and his Movement had done to save Germany from the abyss of bolshevism which in its turn had been so obviously furthered by Jewish influences. The German people cherished the ardent desire to guard against any repetition of that danger, and the Evangelical Church found herself obliged to work in the same direction and for the same purpose. The operation of the Aryan legislation within the Church might prove to be of only temporary necessity, but was at the present absolutely essential to maintain peace, unity and order (C. S. Macfarland: *The New Church and the New Germany*, New York, 1934, p. 82). It was obviously painful to this American Germanophil to have to take into account the merciless and ruthless treatment of the Jews 'that shocked the sensibilities of the entire Christian world' (p. 63). He could only hope that the Führer, whom he personally regarded as a 'likable fellow', would 'remove the dark page by acknowledging his injustice' (p. 68).

38. Niemöller: *Evangelische Kirche im Dritten Reich*, 112.

39. Jürgen Schmidt, 132.

40. In a letter to Pfarrer Holtz of Mecklenburg, 5 October 1933, *Bielefeld Archiv, Judenfrage*, I.

41. Schmidt: *Bekenntnisse*, 1933, pp. 96–8.

42. Jürgen Schmidt, 134. In a letter written in September 1933 to the Reich Bishop, Präses Koch of Westphalia admitted that, were there circumstances in which a congregation, stirred by the National Movement to consciousness of being German, could no longer accept the preaching of the Word of God, if or because it was being preached by a pastor of non-Aryan blood, the Church had no alternative but to request the pastor concerned to be charitable enough to discontinue his present ministry, and, in doing so, honour the working of God in so pronounced an instance of German volkish feeling (Gerlach, 66).

43. Ibid., 135.

44. See the collection of Martin Niemöller's sermons, 1933–1935,

published under the title of *First Commandment*, Hodge, 1937, p. 54.

45. Jürgen Schmidt, 135–6.

46. Ibid., 470, note 269.

47. Hans Buchheim ed.: *Ein NS-Funktionär zum Niemöller-Prozess* in *Vierteljahrshefte zur Zeitgeschichte*, 1956, p. 313. Cf. Niemöller's remark in a sermon preached on 24 April 1937—'It has pleased this Living God to let his Son become Man expressly in the Jewish People; we indeed know how great is "the stumbling-block and the offence"!' (*The Gestapo Defied, The last 28 Sermons of Martin Niemöller*, Hodge, 1942, p. 182.)

48. Gaus, 114.

49. Ibid., 114.

50. Martin Niemöller: *Alles in allen Christus*, Berlin, 1935, pp. 87–9. English translation in *First Commandment*, 246–7.

51. Dietrich Bonhoeffer: *Der Arierparagraph in der Kirche*, August 1933 in *Gesammelte Schriften*, II, pp. 62–9.

52. Karl Barth: *Theologische Existenz Heute*, München, 1933, p. 25. *Theological Existence Today*, Hodder, 1933, p. 52.

53. Schmidt: *Bekenntnisse*, 1933, p. 85.

54. Ibid., 178–82.

55. Ibid., 189–92.

56. Ibid., 182–6.

57. Hans Michael Müller: *Der innere Weg der deutschen Kirche*, Tübingen, 1933, pp. 46–58.

58. Rudolf Bultmann: *Der Arierparagraph in Raume der Kirche* in EKDJF, 78 ff.

59. EKDJF, 72–7.

60. J. R. Porter: *The Case of Gerhard Kittel* in *Theology*, 1947, pp. 401–2. This article is written in sympathetic terms and with the avowed purpose 'to rehabilitate at least to some degree the reputation of a great scholar and Christian' (402). Porter, however, does admit that Kittel did at some point 'surrender far too much ground to racial theories' and 'failed to hold together all the various emphases of Scripture', consequently proving guilty of raising up rather than breaking down the 'middle wall of partition' (405).

61. The *Neues Tübinger Tagblatt*, a local Nazi newspaper, issued on 2 June 1933, a highly critical review of Kittel's original lecture, terming it a 'scandal' and complaining that 'he did not merely advocate tolerance of believing Jewry, but went so far as to demand for its representatives the most extensive "guest" privileges. . . . The culmination of his anti-volkish argumentation was his description of missions to the Jews as one of the principal obligations of the German Christian Church.'

62. Review of *Die Judenfrage* in *Jewish Chronicle*, 11 August 1933. This indignant review complains that 'Kittel is anxious to cast out the Jews, lest they spoil the specific qualities of the Germans. What are these qualities ? Brute force, injustice, deception, meanness,

cruelty, glorification of murder. Kittel with his kindly soul writes "It was never the German way to mock at the suffering of another" One wonders at the temerity of the man as one recalls the treatment meted out to people who served their Fatherland. This Professor of Theology must be singularly satisfied with himself and his party His style is marked by religious and political conceit.... It is because he himself is filled with hate that he advocates the de-mancipation of Jews. Would Kittel be content to belong to a pariah class ? Would he be satisfied to be herded into a political ghetto ?' For a devastating and intemperate attack upon Gerhard Kittel which goes so far as to accuse him of 'selling himself to Satan' in the abandonment of the 'Judaeo-Christian tradition of the Fatherhood of God and the brotherhood of man' and having 'the grim distinction of making extermination of the Jews theologically respectable' and being 'clearly responsible for much of the guilt resting on the German Protestant Churches for their silence', see W. F. Albright: *History Archaeology and Christian Humanism*, Adam and Charles Black 1965, pp. 229–40.

63. Friedrich Heiler in a review of *Die Judenfrage* in *Eine Heilige Kirche* April 1934, p. 187, accuses Kittel, a New Testament specialist in the grips of the all-powerful new revolutionary movement, of being no longer capable of appreciating the essential requirements of the Christian commandment to love. 'Kittel maintains that it is a diseased form of sentimentality and not Christian love to be concerned for the fate of the individual Jew. He calls time and again and with the fullest emphasis for ruthless severity towards the individual, because everything depends upon the whole people fulfilling its determined role as stranger among the peoples. The answer to this is a reminder that the basic command to love is couched in purely individual terms. "Thou shalt love thy neighbour as thyself". In a certain parable the concern of Jesus the Good Shepherd was for the one lost sheep. In another Jesus said, "I was a stranger, and you took me in. ... What you have done for one of the least of these my brethren, you have done for Me".' Heiler concluded by remarking that 'the Jewish Problem is only to be solved from the New Testament, and that means the whole New Testament'

64. 'All those who have failed to reflect that the assimilation of Jewry is the denial of the clear and manifest Will of God for the Jewish people are to blame for the hard and terrible happenings of the present time.' Gerhard Kittel: *Neutestamentliche Gedanken zur Judenfrage* in AELKZ, 19 September 1933, p. 905; an important article which should be read in conjunction with *Die Judenfrage*. This article could scarcely have been appreciated in certain Nazi quarters with its reference to 'many noble and righteous Jews' and its sounding of a Christian warning that the Lord God would punish uncalled-for arbitrary actions and brutality perpetrated against the Jews (905).

65. *Die Judenfrage*, 3rd edition, Stuttgart, 1934, pp. 38–9.

56. Ibid., 73–4.
57. Gerhard Kittel, as the present writer, who was one of his pupils and greatly valued his friendship can testify, was a gentle and warm-hearted person. He appears to have done much to implement this recommendation. A Swiss colleague paid the following tribute shortly after the conclusion of the war—'As regards Kittel's personal relationship with those Jews, half-Jews and Jewish Christians with whom he had dealings, scarcely a single instance can be cited, in which he did not take pains, if at all possible, to mitigate hardships and heal wounds; regardless of the considerable dangers that could result for him from such activity.' Richard Fischer (II, 109) relates how Kittel gave proof of real brotherliness on Jewish Boycott Day, when in Tübingen he spent a long time going up and down in company with Hugo Löwenstein, a baptised Jew, in front of the latter's wall-paper shop in the Wilhelmstrasse, in order to protect him from acts of hooliganism. A half-Jewish actress in Vienna, where Kittel lived and worked during the war, testified in 1945 what his friendship and encouragement meant to her in her anxious and lonely existence. Another grateful tribute has been paid by the daughter of a Jew who was committed to a concentration camp in 1938, and who experienced Kittel's sympathetic and practical help in her distress. 'We Jews who belonged to the Church', she declared, 'knew that we could approach him confident of receiving help and advice.'
68. AELKZ, 1933, p. 906.
69. Professor Emanuel Hirsch of Göttingen, generally regarded as the leading 'German Christian' theologian, made a similar point in claiming that in a Volk Church it was the most natural and obvious thing in the world that the task of Christian preaching and teaching should be carried out by men who belonged themselves to the Volk. This had in the past been the almost universally recognised practice within the Christian Church as a whole. As far as the German Evangelical Church herself was concerned, the Swabians did not have North Germans as their pastors, nor would a Swabian be found ministering in Schleswig-Holstein. In fact, in the German provincial churches as a whole there had been to date an astonishing narrowmindedness in the exclusion of clergy of good German blood, because they were accounted as foreigners in not belonging to the particular locality. This was not violation of the Christian conscience. It was fully recognised that a clergyman, for instance, from the excitable cheery Pfalz would be at the greatest disadvantage, were he to seek to operate as a pastor in the Lüneburg Heath area. In the face of this, it was difficult to understand why the Christian conscience should become so incensed, when it was sought to make membership of the German Volk a condition of ministering within the German Volk Church. For most other Protestant Churches in Europe the pre-supposition for pastoral office was national citizenship. A German pastor could not become a minister in the Swedish

Church if the Swedish State refused to grant him Swedish citizen
ship. German-speaking Jews in Germany were no longer in pos
session of full rights of citizenship, and probably in a few years
time would have much less right to regard themselves as Germar
citizens. Christian opposition to the imposition of the Aryar
Paragraph within the Church was to be interpreted as a refusal t
recognise the Jews as a guest or alien people within Germany
And this was a political not a Christian challenge (Emanue
Hirsch: *Theologische Gutachen in der Nichtarienfrage, Deutsch
Theologie*, May, 1934, pp. 192–4).

70. *Die Judenfrage*, 109.
71. Ibid., 106.
72. Fischer, III, 84–7.
73. Fritz von der Heydt: *Die Ziele der Deutschen Christen*, Bonn, 1934
74. Fritz Engelke: *Christentum deutsch*, Hamburg, 1933, pp. 23–5.
75. Klügel: 491. The complete text of Leo's memorandum is to be foun
    in the companion book of documents, 189–96. See also Hein
    Brunotte: *Die Kirchenmitgliedschaft der nichtarischen Christen in
    Kirchenkampf, Zeitschrift für evangelische Kirchenrecht*, Septembe
    1967, p. 149.
76. Bethge, 373. English edition, 249. Bonhoeffer did his utmost t
    promote a discussion of the Aryan Clause, but, when this wa
    refused, he nailed to neighbouring trees a prepared statement or
    behalf of 2,000 pastors. It included the sentence: 'The Gospel i
    not to be circumscribed or altogether invalidated by human laws'
    (Bonhoeffer: *Gesammelte Aufsätze*, II, 74–6).
77. Eino Murtorinne: *Erzbischof Eidem zum deutschen Kirchenkampf
    1933–1940*, Helsinki, 1968, p. 29. Boyens, 67.
78. Murtorinne, 30. Boyens, 68.
79. Gauger, 104.
80. Murtorinne, 34. A few days previously at a 'German Christian
    rally in Hannover Ludwig Müller had had the following to say abou
    the Jewish issue. 'In every nation it has always happened that th
    man who tells the people the truth has been put to death. This was
    ultimately the fate of the Saviour Himself. Christianity is not ar
    offshoot of Judaism. It took shape in constant conflict with Jewry
    For the first time in the Christian era a people has dared to declare
    war upon the Jews. In this struggle we Christians must all stand
    together, even if for a time we have to feel the pinch.' (Wurm
    Nachlass, Stuttgart Archiv.)
    One would imagine that the Reich Bishop was pleased rather than
    embarrassed by the following tribute that appeared in the October
    issue of *Der Stürmer*: 'Reich Bishop Dr. Müller fought valiantly
    in the Great War, and has for a long time been a courageous con-
    fessor of National Socialism. He is tall in stature, and has a fair-
    skinned complexion and a noble forehead. A man that looks like
    him personified what we term the nordic race. A Reich Bishop who
    himself is such a fine racial specimen must of necessity desire

the good of the Church of which he has the care. That Reich Bishop Müller has the welfare of the Protestant Church at heart has already been proved by his introduction of the Aryan Paragraph' (Bielefeld Archiv., *Judenfrage*, I).

81. Published in *The Times*, 13 November 1933. German translation in *Kirchliches Jahrbuch für die Evangelische Kirche in Deutschland, 1945–1948*, ed. Joachim Beckmann, pp. 258–60, Gütersloh, 1950. [Henceforth KJB.]

The present writer recalls being summoned to the Palace at Chichester in 1938 to receive his curate's licence and being welcomed at the front door and ushered into the episcopal presence by Franz Hildebrandt who was temporarily acting as bishop's chaplain.

82. Gauger, 112.

83. Gauger, 109, 111.

84. Gauger, 112.

85. KJB, 1945–8, 260–1.

86. Gauger, 130.

87. Gauger, 170.

88. See JK, 1934, p. 334, for a concise summary of the see-saw fate of the Clause.

89. For the full text of the Constitution see KJB, 1933–45, 17 ff.

90. Schmidt: *Bekenntnisse*, 1933, p. 71.

91. Hans Ehrenberg: *Autobiography of a German Pastor*, SCM, 1943, p. 68.

92. Wilhelm Niemöller: *Bekennende Kirche in Westfalen*, Bielefeld, 1952, p. 261.

93. Wilhelm Niemöller: *Wort und Tat im Kirchenkampf*, München, 1969, p. 363.

94. The present writer remembers with great satisfaction how he was instrumental in arranging for Hans Ehrenberg to be the special preacher in a key Birmingham parish at a war-time National Day of prayer.

95. Mary Bosanquet: *The Life and Death of Dietrich Bonhoeffer*, Hodder, 1968, pp. 185–6.

96. Klügel, 493–4.

97. Gerlach, 258–63.

98. Klügel, 495.

99. Gerhard Ehrenforth: *Die Schlesische Kirche im Kirchenkampf, 1932–1945*, Göttingen, 1968, pp. 209–10.

100. Gauger, 303.

101. Gerhard Schäfer: *Landesbischof Wurm und der nationalsozialistische Staat, 1940–1945, Eine Dokumentation*, Stuttgart, 1968, p. 171.

102. Christian Kinder: *Neue Beiträge*, 119–26. Kinder remarks that it proved necessary in 1933 to introduce the Aryan Clause into the Schleswig-Holstein Church in order to avoid conflict with the State, the Party, and, as he claims, at least 90 per cent of ordinary church members. But, having done so, the putting into practice of the provisions of the new legislation was as far as possible avoided. It was

practical help that he and others managed in individual cases t give to non-Aryan pastors and lay people, and it proved far mor effective than the theological statements and written or spoke protests that were being published in other parts of the Evangelic Church, statements and protests often unaccompanied by an practical assistance.

103. See Gerlach, 148–9 and 488–9.

Eberhard Bethge has admitted that the *Solus Christus* of Barme encouraged the Church to adopt a ghetto-like existence and to mak a false separation of the 'Two Kingdoms' (*Geschichtliche Schul der Kirche* in *Christliche Freiheit im Dienst am Menschen, Zum 8 Geburtstag von Martin Niemöller*, Frankfurt, 1972, p. 136).

104. Heinz Schmidt: *Die Judenfrage und die Christliche Kirche in Deutscl land*, Stuttgart, 1947, p. 32.

105. *Evangelische Theologie*, 1968, p. 555.

106. Hans von Haeften, member of the Kreislau Resistance Circl quoted by Ger van Roon: *German Resistance to Hitler*, Londor 1969, p. 136.

107. Bethge, 685, English edition, 512. It does not appear to be know when Bonhoeffer produced this dictum. Bethge suggests it ma have been in 1938, directly after 'Crystal Night'.

108. One delegate to the Dahlem Synod declared that, if things went to far, he would 'rather be in a heretical church than in a pharisaic one' (Wilhelm Niemöller: *Die Zweite Bekenntnissynode zu Dahlen Arbeiten zur Geschichte des Kirchenkampfes*, Band 3, p. 94). I Confessional circles in Hannover there was apprehensive mi giving as to 'donatist inclinations and the endeavour to manufactu a "chemically pure church"' (Klügel, 174). Theodor Dipper fro Württemberg ventured to inquire whether it could not continue t be possible to 'sit at table with the Bible in the hand with "Germa Christian" leaders', to which Martin Niemöller replied that sever ance from what was of the Devil was essential, and that it wou be 'spiritual adultery' to read the Bible with a 'German Christia pastor, thereby making light of the persecution of the Church God for which such a pastor shared responsibility (Wilhelm Ni möller, op. cit., 148, 150). Friedrich von Bodelschwingh detecte in Dahlem rigidity, more of the Law than of the Gospel; a lac of elementary evangelical love (Wilhelm Brandt: *Friedrich v Bodelschwingh*, Bethel, 1967, p. 157).

109. See p. 263.

110. Georg Kretschmar in *Tutzinger Texte, Sonderband I, Kirche un Nationalsozialismus*, München, 1969, p. 136. See also Otto Elia *Der evangelische Kirchenkampf und die Judenfrage* in *Information blatt für die Gemeinden in den niederdeutschen lütherischen Lande kirchen*, July 1961, p. 214.

111. Karl Kupisch: *Zwischen Idealismus und Massendemokratie*, Berli 1963, p. 137. See his section on *Der Freie Protestantismus*, p 134–9.

12. Martin Rade wrote in *Christliche Welt* in 1890 'Anti-semitism is a reaction of the natural man in face of doubtless existing evils. For that very reason we must not, as Christians, just simply join in the hue and cry.' In 1891 he insisted that 'a solution of the Jewish issue is only possible in the context of the reform of our whole moral, political, and economic relationships'.

13. Johannes Rathje: *Die Welt des freien Protestantismus*, Stuttgart, 1952, p. 439. This work provides fascinating extracts from the *Christliche Welt*, 1886–1941. It is quite remarkable that this publication survived right into the war-days.

14. Gerlach, 477.

15. Gerlach, 188.

16. Prater: *Kämpfer wider Willen*, 31.

17. Bethge, 323, 499. English edition, 207, 356.

18. AELKZ, 1934, pp. 351–2 and Kantzenbach: *Widerstand und Solidarität*, 79–80. Pechmann did not declare *expressis verbis* his secession from the Bavarian Provincial Church, and maintained his connections with the local Evangelical Church until 1946, when he became a Roman Catholic. What is instructive to note is that, in severing his connections with the official Reich Church, he did not find his way into the Confessing Church—an indication of his lack of confidence that the Confessing Church could be relied upon to make vigorous protest against the wrongs of which he so bitterly complained and give practical help to the afflicted.

19. Jürgen Schmidt: *Martin Niemöller*, 142. See also Friedrich Baumgärtel: *Wider die Kirchenkampf-Legenden*, Neuendettelsau, 1959, p. 34.

20. *Morning Post*, 9 April, 1934.

21. Jürgen Schmidt, 182.

22. Heinrich Hermelink: *Kirche im Kampf. Dokumente des Widerstands und des Aufbaus in der evangelischen Kirche Deutschlands von 1933 bis 1945*, Tübingen, 1950, p. 231.

23. JK, 1935, p. 327.

24. Helmut Witetschek: *Die Kirchliche Lage in Bayern nach den Regierungsprasidentenberichten, 1933–1943*, Mainz, 1967, Vol. II, p. 215.

25. Pierre Joffroy: *A Spy for God. The Ordeal of Kurt Gerstein*, Collins, 1970, p. 70.

26. KJB, 85–6.

27. KJB, 87–9.

28. Johannes Kübel of Frankfurt had the experience, early in 1935, when he had been invited to address an anniversary meeting of the local group of the Reich Association of Non-Aryan Christians, of crossing swords with the Gestapo. The Gestapo, learning of his intention to address the Association on the subject of 'The Fight for Freedom by the Early Christians', insisted upon seeing his manuscript, complained that what he proposed to say about Paul's struggle for a form of Christianity that should not be bound up with

a particular Volkstum was objectionable as being concerned with Church politics rather than with Church history, and banned the lecture. Kübel then offered to read to his audience certain New Testament passages in place of the lecture. This, however, did not satisfy the Gestapo who insisted upon vetting the chosen extracts. To Kübel's protest that surely Holy Scripture had always and everywhere the right to find utterance the answer came that, as it was non-Aryans that were being addressed, it was necessary for the Gestapo to know what Bible passages would be used. Kübel then requested the local council of Brethren to intervene, in order to establish whether the Evangelical Church had freedom to proclaim the Scriptural Word only within the walls of the church, and whether the Gestapo really claimed to have sovereign control over the Word of God. It is not known what was the final outcome of this controversy (Gerlach, 157–8).

129. Bielefeld Archiv., *Judenfrage*, 3.
130. Wilhelm Niemöller: *Die Synode zu Steglitz, Arbeiten zur Geschichte des Kirchenkampfes*, Band 23, Göttingen, 1970, pp. 29–48.
131. Ibid., 48–58.
132. Bielefeld Archiv., *Judenfrage*, 3.
133. Hans Buchheim: *Glaubenskrise im Dritten Reich*, Stuttgart, 1935, p. 145. See Arthur Cochrane: *The Church's Confession under Hitler*, Philadelphia, 1962, p. 116. Cochrane characterises Kinder as 'a well meaning man of the middle wing of the "German Christians" who strove to neutralise the "German Christians" theologically, so that the Nazi Party would not be directly identified with any particular religious group . . . and encouraged the illusion that the Christian Faith and Nazism were reconcilable, or at least that they could be confined to separate compartments'.
134. Schmidt: *Bekenntnisse*, 1933, pp. 98–102. English translation Conway, 353–7.
135. JK, 1934, pp. 494–8.
136. Christian Kinder: *Volk vor Gott*, Hamburg, 1915, pp. 34–5.
137. The building up of a 'German Christian' Movement in Thuringia was the work of two young pastors, Siegfried Leffler and Julius Leutheuser. They started their ministry together in the Bavarian Church full of volkish enthusiasm and highly critical of what they regarded as the stiffness of the established Lutheran Orthodoxy. The Church seemed to them to be lacking in warmth of fellowship and in concern for the conditions in which men and women lived from day to day. Their embracing of National Socialism was in the nature of an ecstatic spiritual experience, and they were in particular enthralled by the comradeship which they enjoyed in the Movement, so utterly unlike what the Church as a rule had to offer. In 1927 they moved from Bavaria to Thuringia. The prevailing churchmanship in Thuringia was so liberal, that it could almost be described as a Church without any Confession. The two young pastors spent more time in propagating National Socialism than

in carrying out ecclesiastical duties, and their respective parishes became closely identified with the local Nazi groups. They sincerely held that the greater their success in spreading Nazism, the stronger would be the influence of the 'German Christianity' for which they stood. In November 1929, with strong official Nazi support, they brought into being the 'Church Movement of German Christians'.

Leffler and Leutheuser's method was not that of large-scale rallies or of powerful Church-political agitation, but rather of patient and sympathetic missionary activity among the many protestants who found the traditional Lutheran teaching and biblical exposition largely irrelevant, and wanted a religion they could understand and that would consecrate their awakened feelings. There was a ready response to the preaching of the Germans as the divinely chosen people and Hitler as the present saviour and the assurance that God was revealing Himself in contemporary events. Leffler and Leutheuser both knew how to speak and to write in an exciting and fanatical style that proved to be an acceptable spiritual accompaniment to Nazi political claims.

In 1932 the Thuringian Church Movement identified itself with the Faith Movement of 'German Christians', in order to widen its recognition and its influence, and to increase its financial resources, but shortly after the Sport Palace rumpus of November 1933, this alliance came to an end. The Thuringian 'German Christians' thenceforward pursued their independent and increasingly radical and fanatical course, proclaiming themselves to be the 'National Church Movement' with the battle cry 'One Volk, One God, One Reich, One Church!' and reiterating the slogan 'Germany—our Task, Christ—our strength!' While the Reich Movement of 'German Christians' continually lost ground from 1934 on, and was repeatedly in danger of breaking up into fragments, the National Church Movement of 'German Christians' not only kept itself intact throughout the whole Hitler period, but spread its tentacles throughout the greater part of Germany, eventually numbering the great majority of 'German Christians' among its adherents. See Hans Buchheim; *Glaubenskrise im Dritten Reich*, 48–59; Helmut Baier: *Die Deutschen Christen Bayerns*, pp. 17ff. and *passim*, Kurt Meier: *Die Deutschen Christen*, Göttingen, 1964; Siegfried Leffler: *Christus im Dritten Reich der Deutschen*, Weimar, 1935; and Julius Leutheuser: *Der Weg zur deutschen christlichen Nationalkirche*, Weimar, 1935.
138. Gauger, 563.
139. E. E. Thomas: *Hitlerism, Communism and the Christian Faith*, Unicorn Press, 1935, pp. 37–8.

5

The Nuremberg Laws and their effect upon the Evangelical Church, 1935–1938

On 15 September 1935 at the Nuremberg Party Rally the Reich Citizenship Law and the Law for the Protection of German Blood and German Honour were promulgated.[1] This new legislation, which constituted a decisive advance in both the political and the biological isolation of the Jews, laid down that only those of German or closely related blood could be granted citizenship in the Reich, and be allowed to possess full political rights. Marriages contracted between Jews and those of German blood were, in future, forbidden, as were also extra-marital relations between Jews and Germans. Jews were also not permitted to employ domestic servants of German blood under the age of forty-five or to fly the German flag. These curtly phrased laws were to be extended in the following years by a series of decrees designed progressively to outlaw the non-Aryan more and more completely. The first of these decrees defined who was to be reckoned a Jew and who was to be regarded as a *Mischling* or cross-breed. Anyone descended from three or four Jewish grandparents was accounted to be a Jew. A *Mischling* was the offspring of a mixed marriage in the racial not the confessional sense, and was to be graded as either a half or a quarter Aryan. Such persons had been previously in a privileged position over the Jews, but owing to this new legislation were in possible danger of suffering like the Jews the penalties of the Aryan Paragraph and other disabilities, as were also partners, both Jewish and Aryan, of a mixed marriage. Certain people who felt themselves to be as German as anything and were in some cases quite unaware of possessing any Jewish blood were affected by this, when the prescribed genealogical research was made. There was the likelihood of scornful contempt for those who had been involved in the befouling of pure Aryan stock as well as an expression of disapproval from the strict Jewish angle. Consequently the cross-breed, being neither one thing nor the other, could be in almost more parlous plight than the full-blooded Jew.

The Church was now faced with the necessity of taking up an attitude to the new racial programme. Generally speaking, there did not seem to be much conflict among churchmen in accepting the Nuremberg Laws, as they stood. With the aid of Church registers documentary evidence of Aryan descent was readily provided, thus helping appreciably in making possible the identification of those who were henceforth to be branded as of impure Aryan extraction. The Church by being so compliant scarcely knew what she was doing. It was indeed, as Heinz Schmidt has remarked, 'for many pastors almost a relief to be able at least at this point to be obedient in satisfying the requirements of the Nazi Government'.[2] As Bishop Wurm was to testify much later on in 1942, no Evangelical Church contested the right to introduce racial legislation with the object of preserving the purity of the German Volk.[3] The State had the right to do so, and had justification politically. The question was rather whether the racial attitude was to find real footing within the ecclesiastical sphere, now that the State had so plainly decreed that the status of 'Jew' was to be determined by race and blood and not by religion. Walter Künneth, in an amended version of his essay on the Jewish problem and the Church,[4] insisted that the State's solution to the Jewish Question and that of the Church had to be kept separate. He was seemingly content to accept the new State ruling without venturing upon the mildest criticism. In fact he was inclined to regard it as promising an equitable, effective, and permanent solution to the problem, and quoted from a commentary on the Nuremberg Laws that claimed that, according to the will of the Führer, the measures that had to be taken were not designed to breed and to perpetuate race hatred, but were calculated to bring about a peaceful solution of German-Jewish relations.[5] The enforced legal separation meant legal protection for the Jews in Germany, since the converting of assimilation into dissimilation would make it possible to achieve a tolerable relationship between the two peoples in the same territory. The National

State, in Künneth's view, had not merely the fundamental right to make its political revision of the treatment of the Jews, but the Church could welcome and affirm its racial applications. The racially and biologically determined regulations were to be accepted as being just as valid for the Jews who had adopted the Christian religion as for the Jews who remained in the Jewish faith. Nevertheless, when it came to a question of the Jew within the fellowship of the Church, one was moving in a quite other dimension, one not of this world but of the Kingdom of God. Here the Church had an unquestionable obligation to give equal rights to Jew and to Gentile, and there had to be freedom to decide which of her members should be given various offices and functions necessary for the fulfilment of her preaching commission. The Holy Spirit and personal qualifications were to decide this, not racial or political considerations.

Though not going so far as to attempt to place a ban upon the Christian Jews, it was the obvious hope of the Nazi authorities that Evangelical pastors would in keeping with the new legislation prove increasingly reluctant to baptise non-Aryans. In November 1935 Pastor Karl Niemann of Bielefeld was rebuked for having first baptised a non-Aryan and then officiated at his subsequent marriage to an Aryan. Niemann was attacked in *Der Stürmer* for having furthered the cause of racial disgrace, and defended by the local church authority for having fulfilled his duty as a minister of the Church in obeying the Lord's command to 'baptise all nations' and in blessing the marriage of two Christians. This was in no wise to be reckoned as a violation of the Nuremberg Laws.[6]

Twelve months later Günther Harder, an active Confessing pastor in Berlin incurred the displeasure of Hans Kerrl, the Minister for Church Affairs, by providing Christian baptism for a 'full' Jewess and then announcing from the pulpit that he had done so. If, the complaint ran, he felt it incumbent upon him to perform this baptism, he might at least have had sufficient political tact to carry it out as inconspicuously as possible. He had also made matters worse by welcoming the two children of this baptised Jewess into his parish church choir.[7]

It was to be expected that the 'German Christians' would now agitate for some form of ecclesiastical apartheid that would bring into being a separate Jewish Christian community either within or right outside the German Evangelical Church. Bishop Coch[8] of Saxony who in his inaugural sermon as bishop had distinguished himself by describing Hitler as the Good Shepherd; who required not only his pastors but their wives as well to give proof of their Aryan descent,[9] and whose chief Press officer had been warm in his appreciation of *Der Stürmer*, purporting to see in the Church conflict sinister and foul Jewish influences at work,[10] urged the newly appointed Reich Church Minister, Hans Kerrl, to take steps to arrange for the formation of a separate Jewish Christian Church.[11] So also did Professor Rauchhaupt of Heidelberg, who declared the time to be ripe for the creation of such a church, and expressed his naïve opinion that, were the Jews eliminated, an indirect step could well have been taken towards the settlement of the conflict between the Confessional Front and the 'German Christians'.[12] Wilhelm Rehm, who had succeeded Dr. Kinder as leader of the Reich Movement of 'German Christians', claimed that the Nazis with their new racial laws were fulfilling the ideals of Martin Luther, and that the steps that they had taken were basically Christian. He went on to assert that the Christian National Socialist public expected the Church to make a corresponding decision, and confine the membership of the German Volk Church to those of German blood, and let the Jews in Germany have their own independent church after the pattern of the mission field.[13]

Rehm returned to the attack a month later, when he declared that 'it is our task in the Third Reich to see to it that everything is removed from the Evangelical Church that reminds us of the Jews and that is alien to our German character. A completely clear line must be followed with no room for compromise. In particular, Jews and those of Jewish descent must disappear from the German Evangelical Church.' He added that, if only the Evangelical Church had consistently made the Nazi view of the Jews her own, she would have been preserved from much unpleasantness, and would have been able to have placed herself joyfully and gratefully and without reserve at the disposal of the Nazi State.[14]

The 'German Christians' in Berlin recommended that, in future, the baptism of the Jews should rest in the hands of Jewish Christian missionaries, and should not confer entry into membership of a German congregation, but merely signify Christian religious adherence.[15] Reichminister Kerrl, notwithstanding, proved reluctant to act upon such recommendations. His hope and ambition was to promote peace and reconciliation within the Evangelical Church. He had just appointed church committees to this end. He was, therefore, unwilling to do anything at this point that would be calculated to offend the Confessional Front and discourage acceptance of the committees. He was also apprehensive of the hostile reception that the formation of a Jewish Christian Church would receive abroad.

The question inevitably arose as to what reaction might be awaited from the Confessing Church in the light of the Nuremberg Laws and whether there would be any expectation of Christian solidarity with those who were so obviously adversely affected, and, in particular, the non-Aryan Christians. A paragraph in the resolutions of the First Synod of the Confessing Lutheran Church of Saxony which met at the end of September could be taken as evidence in principle of such Christian concern. It stressed the importance of neighbourly love such as Christ had bidden in the parable of the Good Samaritan being observable from man to man. 'Our neighbour', it was asserted, 'is everyone who is specially dependent upon us, not only our relative and friend, our employer or employee, but also the alien whose distress God confronts us with. We have as Christians without respect of persons and without concern for our own advantage or detriment to practise Love. For the Bible says, "Let us do good unto all men, especially unto them who are of the household of faith".'[16]

The Confessional Synod of the Old Prussian Church was due to meet in Berlin-Steglitz at the end of September, and there was considerable apprehension as to whether the subject of the Jews would receive bold treatment. Bishop Meiser of Bavaria, who had a few months previously published in the Lutheran Missionary Yearbook[17] a plea that the Jews should be greeted in friendly fashion and comforted with genuine love, and had been repeatedly attacked by his enemies for so 'doubtful' a pronouncement, was not alone in feeling anxious as to whether the radical wing of the Confessional Church was going to cause embarrassment. He is quoted as having said, 'I await with considerable trepidation the coming Prussian Synod, if such things as the Jewish Question are to be broached. I would like to raise my voice against a self-inflicted martyrdom.'[18] According to Wilhelm Niemöller, both

Bishop Meiser and Bishop Marahrens attempted to persuade Karl Koch, President of the Synod, to take the Jewish Question right off the agenda.[19]

There was much difference of opinion among the delegates to the Synod. Martin Niemöller, Martin Albertz, and Heinrich Vogel among others earnestly desired that a positive word should be said in defence of the Jews and in protest at the progressive outlawing and relentless persecution that they were having to endure. Karl Koch, who had considerable support in his anxious desire that a damaging collision with the Nazi leadership so immediately after the publication of the Nuremberg Laws should be avoided, would have greatly preferred the Jewish issue to have remained undiscussed.[20] It has been claimed that Koch in all seriousness desired thanks to be expressed to the Führer for the new legislation, but Wilhelm Niemöller insists that such a desire on the part of Koch and others cannot be substantiated.[21]

Dietrich Bonhoeffer was not a delegate to the Synod, but on being informed from a reliable source that a resolution was being drafted on the baptism of Jews which would apparently convey if not direct approval then implicit acceptance of the Nuremberg Laws,[22] hurried along to Berlin-Steglitz with some of his pupils in an attempt to operate as a pressure-group, and to encourage a clear statement on the general persecution of the Jews that would be 'a voice for the voiceless'. He felt that this was the occasion, immediately after Nuremberg, when an effective word could, and should, be said. But, having no illusions as to the attitude of so many of his fellow-confessionalists and their sense of priorities, he was none too hopeful.[23]

Heinrich Vogel had been mainly responsible for the preparation of a spirited statement affirming the Christian duty of showing love towards unbaptised as well as baptised Jews. This statement also declared that all peoples, and not merely the Jews, stood under the deadly curse of original sin, and that, since God's grace had the last word regarding Israel, Christ's saying, 'Judge not, and ye shall not be judged', held good. None of this appeared in the final draft which Vogel sadly described as the 'minimum of a minimum'.[24]

In the published message of the Synod bold declaration was made that there could be no neutrality in the fight against false teaching inside and outside of the Church, and that it was required that every Christian should make confession of his faith. The only reference to the Jews was contained in the paragraph that dealt with the importance and sanctity of baptism. All Christians, it was stated, irrespective of the race and nation to which they belonged, owed their salvation to the boundless Love of God Who of His infinite compassion forgave sins. It was consequently the Will of God and the command of the Lord Jesus Christ that all peoples, including the Jews, should be offered salvation in Christ. Grief and shame were expressed that there were congregations in which the baptism of Jews was being forbidden. Anyone who reckoned such baptisms to be betrayal of Christ was blaspheming that Holy Sacrament.[25] This pious utterance was not accompanied by any reference, favourable or otherwise, to the newly promulgated Nuremberg legislation. By majority decision a recommended exhortation to the parishes to stand by the persecuted Jews and a passage stressing the equality of status of non-Aryans with Aryans within the Church were expunged. Responsibility for a public statement on the Church's approach to the Jewish Question as a whole was passed on to the Reich Council of Brethren, calling for a speedy answer based upon the principles of Scripture and Confession.

Martin Niemöller in a characteristic contribution to the discussion made plain his misgivings. He complained that they were confining themselves to the cold axiom, 'Jews shall be baptised' without further expression of concern as to their circumstances after baptism. It would lay heavily upon his heart, and would, he trusted, remain a burning issue to them all, until the essential word of true Christian brotherliness had been openly spoken. That the question of the treatment of the Jews had been constantly before them for over two years without a plain word being spoken was painful to him. He wished to God that it would pain them all and give them no rest. The worst thing about the debate was that it once again and for the time being gave the impression that everything was fine and that more could not have been said. 'We shall be obliged to say more, and it will be that our mouths will only be really opened, when we have to undergo suffering ourselves.'[26]

In May 1936 the Confessing Church did speak out in the celebrated though ill-fated memorandum to Hitler[27] which has been described as 'a brave utterance . . . moderate in tone but yet unmistakably resolute and with a frankness that was insufferable for people such as Hitler and his ilk'.[28] There was no other critical document of equal clarity published during the Hitler period and boldly presented to the highest authority. It was stated therein that, when eternal values were attributed to Blood, Race and Volkstum, the evangelical Christian in loyalty to the First of the Ten Commandments was obliged to reject such a notion. The sinfulness of all mankind testified to by the Word of God was the answer to any attempt to glorify the Aryan. It was further declared that, when the Christian had forced upon him an anti-semitism that demanded hatred of the Jew, he had to counter it by the Christian command of love to one's neighbour.[29]

It would, however, be a mistake to read too much into this courageous proclamation. It was not a plain disavowal of anti-semitism as such but merely of the militant Nazi version of it. The emphasis was not primarily on the plight of the Jews and Jewish Christians who were directly affected by the anti-semitic policy, but rather upon the severe conflict of conscience experienced by devout German churchpeople.[30] Bethge had no hesitation in describing it as 'far too mildly worded'.[31] The opportunity was in no wise taken of giving clear and positive expression to the Church's affinity with Israel.[32]

The text of the memorandum, which was designed to be a strictly confidential document and not for publication, became widely known abroad, and evoked a considerable amount of indignant and highly critical anti-Nazi propaganda, coupled with praise for the gallant Confessional opposition. Friedrich Weissler, racially a 'full Jew', a lawyer who had been dismissed from the State service in 1933, and from 1934 on had been given employment in the administration of the Confessing Church as a legal adviser, took an active part in the drawing up of the memorandum. One of his responsibilities was the secret organisation of a Press Service for the confessing cause, a principal aim of which was to assist in keeping the outside world informed of the Church situation. Two theological students, Werner Koch and Ernst Tillich, assisted Weissler in this dangerous activity. The latter was responsible for the unauthorised supply to contacts outside Germany of the full text of the memorandum, being apparently prompted by impatient disappointment at the silence maintained by both Nazi authorities and the Confessing Church as to the facts of the submission of the memorandum and as to its contents.

The Provisional Government of the Confessing Church, reacting indignantly to the undesired publicity and fearful of the serious political implications, took the unprecedented step of contacting the Gestapo and asking for help in identifying the culprit. Weissler became not surprisingly the scapegoat. He was dismissed from his post in the Confessing Church, and soon after was arrested along with Koch and Tillich. During his captivity the Confessing Church avoided including his name on the general intercession list. Particularly in view of the fact that he was a Jew, he was shown no mercy by the Gestapo, and, having been handled in quite bestial fashion, he met his death on 19 February in Sachsenhausen concentration camp as the first martyr of the Confessing Church.[33]

The Provisional Government of the Confessing Church saw fit to issue a Pulpit Proclamation for 23 August.[34] The emphasis this time was altogether upon the tribulations of the Church, and no reference was made to anti-semitism and hatred of the Jews as well as to concentration camps and the dishonesty of the recent Reichstag election. Such topics of manifest political interest were obviously deemed to be perilously unsuited for the pulpit.[35]

Cases are recorded of individual pastors having in 1935 and 1936 expressed their discomfort or indignation at the prevailing attitude towards the Jews. Ernst Fuchs of Württemberg proclaimed from his pulpit, 'We are . . . in God's eyes worse sinners than the Jews'.[36] Ulrich Bunzel, pastor of Mary Magdalene Church, Breslau, was exiled from the city for a whole year for having stated in a lecture, 'There are decent characters among the Jews, and "pig dogs" among those of Aryan race.'[37] Friedrich Middendorf of the Reformed Church in Hannover found himself in prison for having in correspondence with the local authorities protested among other things at the intolerable smear campaign directed against the Jews that was full of hatred, in part quite untrue and unworthy of the German people. He concluded his letter with the remark, 'What would the Führer say, if he found out how his cause has been sullied and disgraced? Heil Hitler!'[38] These somewhat enigmatic and mischievous final words helped to make his speedy release appear opportune. Georg Althaus, a village pastor in Braunschweig, was sentenced in February 1936 to six months' imprisonment for having in a confirmation class exhorted the boys not to take part in the clamour against the Jews, and for having prayed, 'God, defend the poor persecuted Jewish People!'[39] A confirmation candidate reported his misdemeanours. It was pleaded, on religious grounds, in his defence, that he had no intention of giving a political implication to his remarks. He had said what he felt it was his duty to say as an evangelical pastor. The prosecution was not prepared to accept this. He was invited to remind himself that Christ Himself proceeded with energy against the Jews, adopting the roughest of means in do so, and that the Reformer Luther made it abundantly clear what was his attitude to the Jews. In suggesting that the Jews were worthy of pity he had criticised the National Socialist treatment of them. He had poured poison into the souls of the children.

These same children, it may be remarked, were very possibly being encouraged in the classroom and at Hitler Youth meetings to develop a poisonous hatred of the Jew and to gain perverted enjoyment from reading the obscenities of *Der Stürmer*. The attitude of their instructors can well have been similar to that of Dr. Walter Scharrer who wrote as follows in *Der Weltkampf*: 'How can a class which includes a possibly in itself harmless Jewish child be brought to a proper pitch of racial pride and racial consciousness? The young teacher, consumed with zeal, unsheathes his sword and calls a spade and spade. He quotes from the Talmud, he refers to the stories about the Bible patriarchs, seizes every opportunity for emphasising the criminal role played by the Jew in politics, he posts up pictures from the *Stürmer*, and combats the legends of the so-called "decent Jew". He misses no chance of instilling into the hearts of his children hatred and contempt for the foreign parasite.'[40]

The following extract from a letter sent from the inmates of a Children's Home to the *Stürmer* is most revealing. 'We read every week with great interest your report. The *Stürmer* is always a very welcome guest in our Home. Through it we learn to know the Jew as he is. . . . We cut the pictures out of the *Stürmer* and pin them on to a special board in our dayroom. Thereby the boys and girls learn to recognise the Jews accurately in their appearance. Each evening our Superintendent with his glove puppets entertains us with a play about the Jews. We have got a puppet which is truly Jewish. It has a nose like that of Satan. When Mr. Punch comes along, we call upon him to drive away the wicked Jew. We regularly act plays about the Jews based upon what our

Superintendent has read to us from the *Stürmer*. We greet you, dear *Stürmer*, with a mighty "Heil Hitler!"'[41]

It would be difficult to disagree with the judgement that for all the appalling things that happened to the Jews in Germany a good measure of the blame must rest upon the anti-semitic propaganda which individual teachers had been perpetually instilling into their pupils at variously highly impressionable ages.[42]

A notably critical reference to anti-semitism appears on page 98 of the widely circulated official Report of the Confessional Synod of Oeynhausen held in February 1936. It records the remark of Professor Friedrich Delekat of Dresden that 'the Church can never silently condone the preaching by schoolteachers of an anti-semitism that stimulates their pupils to emotions of hatred'. Fritz Fink, one of the editorial staff of the *Stürmer*, urged in a pamphlet written in 1937 that racial 'science' and the Jewish issue ought to run like a silver thread right through the school syllabus at every stage. Every single subject in the school curriculum lent itself in unsuspected fullness for valuable apprehension of the Jewish problem. It was indeed his complaint that there were in fact still teachers who failed, contrary to the wishes of the children themselves, to provide the necessary enlightenment, and who, following the bidding of the Church, sought to be accommodating to the deadly enemy in a spirit of compassion and neighbourly love, when they should be recognising that their own people were in danger of being done to death by this same enemy.[43]

There were without doubt a number of occasions upon which Christian parents really saw red, and complained bitterly and vigorously at the crudities and blasphemies of which their children were the victims. Such an occasion has been recorded, when in November 1936 a Detmold teacher indulged in a burst of pastor-baiting before an assembly which included a number of confirmation candidates. 'Comrades', he declaimed, 'be on your guard against chimney sweeps in their black outfit who have the temerity to present as example for German youth a Jewish boy!' Outraged parents demanded that their children be removed from the influence of such a teacher, and urgently requested the local authority to take proceedings against the offender with the object of removing him from his position.[44]

It was not surprising that the state-engineered Reich Church

Committee, which had declared at its inauguration its whole-hearted acceptance of the fundamental National Socialist doctrine of Race, Blood and Soil as well as the Church's full Gospel,[45] and which was struggling throughout its existence of not much over a year in endeavouring to bring together the warring elements within the Church, kept free from the highly inflammable subject of the Jews. In nearly 1,400 pages of Kurt-Dietrich Schmidt's Documents of the Committee-Period just about the only reference to the Reich Committee's concern about the Jewish issue is to be found in the report of a request to all provincial Church authorities for details of the number of non-Aryan pastors, not in order, it was stated, that the Aryan Clause should be applied to them, but solely with the purpose of compiling an accurate record so that certain prevailing opinions and suppositions might be rectified. The Provisional Governing Body of the Confessing Church replied that there was no ecclesiastical ground for such an inquiry as to the racial membership of those holding office in the Church, since baptism and appointment by the congregation were alone determinative.[46]

The 'German Christians' continued to give expression to their suspicion of, and distaste for, everything Jewish. A 'German Christian' pastor in Oberhausen warned that the Jews were so sharp that, having been excluded from other callings, they were perfectly capable of forcing their way into the Evangelical ministry, and, therefore, recommended that office in the Church should only be open to those who could submit a certificate of Aryan extraction.[47] At a Westphalian district meeting on 1 April 1936 the Jewish Question was considered in some detail from both the political and the religious angle. As far as the political aspect was concerned, Christian love of neighbour came into the picture but it involved not sympathy for the Jews who had been and still were so great a menace, danger, and contamination, but for the German people who had suffered at their hands. Therefore the State measures to combat such injuries and dangers were to be supported by Christians, even if they caused hardship to the Jews, with the recognition that such treatment was, after all, more merciful than that once meted out by the Jews themselves, according to Esra 10 and Nehemiah 13. The Volk State had a divinely appointed task to perform in the preservation of racial and moral purity which the Church had no cause or right in the name of God or Christ to oppose. Any interference in the political sphere was a transgression of the authority which Jesus had willingly accepted and an offence against the basic view of Luther. As for the religious side, the Old Testament was to be regarded as only of importance, in so far as it pointed and led to Christ, while the Jewish element in the Bible which prevented the German Volk from finding its way to the Gospel had to be discarded. The attempted evangelisation of the Jews was no special duty of a German Church. Allowance had to be made for the genuine conversion of individual Jews to Christianity. They could become members of the Catholic Church of Christ, but they did not thereby become fully qualified members of the German Christian Volk Church. This was in line with the Nuremberg decrees.[48]

Kommende Kirche, a periodical for the publication of which Heinz Weidemann, the notorious 'German Christian' Bishop of Bremen, was responsible, devoted its issue of 15 November 1936 to a consideration of the Church's attitude to the Jewish Question. The Evangelical Church was declared to have disappointed the high hopes that had been placed in its positive contribution to the solution of this life and death issue before the German people. The Church had failed to implement within its own society the separation of German blood from Jewish blood, and was guilty of the sin of still allowing Germans to be ministered to by those of Jewish or mixed blood. This was nothing less than disloyalty and disobedience not only to Adolf Hitler but to God who had sent Hitler to the German people. National Socialism, including the Jewish legislation, was nothing less than God's Law for the German people. God was at work through Adolf Hitler. To further his work was to serve God, to sabotage his work was to serve the Devil. 'Thou shalt love thy German Volk'; this was God's Call, and it involved the protection of the German people from its arch-enemies, the devilish Jews. It was questionable whether the Jews who preyed in parasitic fashion upon other peoples could be regarded as being in any real sense a Volk. It had to be asked whether the command in Matthew 28:19 to baptise was intended to cover the Jews, and was not expressly applied to the Gentiles alone. 'We', the article concluded, 'dare to make a break with the traditional practice of the Church in baptising Jews, in order that we may be obedient to God in respect of our German people.'

This could almost be described as a sober utterance compared to the wild and uncontrolled fulminations in October 1936 of Karl Holz, Deputy Gauleiter of Franconia and arch-enemy of Bishop Meiser. 'If', he declaimed, 'in one night all Jews in the whole world were in one stroke struck dead, that would be the most sacred red-letter day in the whole of world history. No Christian love may be shown to the Jews. Christ showed none towards them. We see this clearly, when He drove them out of the Temple. The father of the Jews is the Devil. They have been murderers from the beginning. Anyone advancing the opposite of what I say is a traitor to Christ. Christ and Luther are crown witnesses for us. If the Jews are children of God, then God must be a Jew also. For like father, like children. That would be blasphemy.'[49]

John 2:13–17 and 8:42–44 were highly prized Nazi quotes from the Fourth Gospel. The 'German Christians' aspired to produce a version of the Gospel that was free from the historical relativity of the Old Testament. St. John's Gospel was regarded as favourable for this despite utterances such as 'Salvation is of the Jews' and 'Behold an Israelite indeed in whom there is no guile'.[50]

Ludwig Müller, though still nominally Reich Bishop, had been obliged to give way to Reichminister Kerrl and the Reich Church Committee. He felt free now to propagate a radical version of Germanic Christianity. In a press interview in April 1936 he affirmed that he had no intention of giving up his office as Reich Bishop, and would devote himself to being the leader of a church which would in its preaching be free of doctrinal pressures.[51] He had just hit the headlines with the publication of his Aryanised version of the Sermon on the Mount. In the epilogue to his attempted retranslation he sought to counter the view that was being increasingly propagated in certain Nazi circles that Jesus being a Jew, and Christianity being through and through so patently Jewish, the Christian religion ought to be rejected. He declared emphatically that Christianity had not grown out of the Jewish religion as a tree grows from its roots, but that Christianity had come into being in conflict with Judaism, and that Christian and Jew were as foreign to one another as fire and water. The Jew was the oldest and bitterest enemy of Christian thought and civilisation, and such he would remain to all eternity. Thanks to the experience of National Socialism German eyes had been opened to the impossibility of the future use in Christian teaching and worship of words and expressions which were alien to their very nature. The re-creation of the German Volk demanded the disappearance from Church usage of all that was foreign and unGerman.[52]

Towards the end of 1936 the Reich Church Committee found itself in increasing difficulty. Its task was probably impossible of fulfilment right from the beginning. It was not given a free enough hand by Kerrl who had certainly undermined its authority by the further decrees which he had introduced for the control of the Church. A number of the speeches and public announcements of the Minister had caused great embarrassment, and the extent of the anti-Christian and anti-Church propaganda emanating from within the Nazi Party was discouraging to say the least. The Committee had failed to gain recognition from the radical wing of the Confessional Church, and was convinced that the radical 'German Christians' were heretical and not a genuine part of the Evangelical Church. It was, therefore, no great surprise when on 12 February 1937 the Committee resigned.[53] The very next day Reichminister Kerrl in a shockingly uncouth valedictory speech, dubbed recognition of Jesus as the Son of God as ridiculously inessential. He claimed that the Führer was the purveyor of a new revelation, referring to the twofold command to love: love of God being the setting of the divine institution of the nation above all else, and love to neighbour consisting in love to one's brother by blood. He proceeded to liken the Jew to a tubercular bacillus, the carrier of racial defilement, and to declare it to be intolerable that German children should be taught that Jesus and Paul were Jews, and that salvation came from the Jews. Such teaching was a calculated effort to make mockery of the Party. In the light of such remarks it was no surprise when he guaranteed that there would be no more Jewish pastors.[54]

The collapse of the Committees were followed immediately by the Führer's instructions for a Church Election which, it was officially stated, would allow the Church full freedom to decide its future. A General Synod was to follow the election. Grave suspicion was felt by the Confessing Church which, despite the protestations of State neutrality, saw in this new move a sinister plot to further the creation of a National Church. The radicals quickly decided that they would have no part in such a doubtful election, and would utterly decline to join with the 'German Christians' in its organisation and in the forming of a subsequent synod. The more moderate Lutherans were only prepared to co-operate, if there were real safeguards to prevent political influence and disregard for the biblical and confessional basis of the Church. The 'German Christians', on the other hand, were jubilant. The election, they believed, would decide once and for all whether the Church was really prepared to be a Volk community and part and parcel of the Nazi State. They were obviously looking towards a future Church that would be exclusively composed of reputable and dedicated Aryans and that would have been purged of every-thing offensive to the Nazi way of life. Bishop Sasse of Thuringia announced that life in Germany was only possible in union with the Führer,[55] and Pastor Friedrich Tausch, a leader of the Move-ment in Berlin, confidently asserted that, if there was not a 'German Christian' majority, the Führer would dissolve the General Synod the very next day.[56] 'A Church free of Jews' was a favoured election slogan. This Wilhelm Rehm defined as in-volving not merely the removal of those who were Jews by race or cross-breeds from the pulpit and out of the Church, but also the removal of all 'creatures' who in their attitude could only be regarded as being patently judaised (*verjudet*).[57] It was difficult to avoid assuming that the despised 'creatures' included the pastors and lay people of the Confessing Church. Rehm himself in answer to a request from the Confessional periodical *Junge Kirche* for enlightenment, remarked that those pastors who were not willing to co-operate in a definite move within the Church to segregate the Jews, should draw the correct conclusion and sign on com-pletely in the planned new Jewish Church.[58]

The National Church Movement of 'German Christians' in its turn, declared that it stood for the suppression and elimination of all Jewish and alien elements in Church doctrine and Church life, Christ being affirmed to be not the offspring and fulfilment of Jewry but its deadly enemy and vanquisher.[59] In a pamphlet published in Thuringia at this time and entitled *Against the Jewish Spirit in the Church*, it was lamented that, while politics, economics, education, the law, historical studies and the arts had all been afforded new life by Nazi racial enlightenment, the Church alone stood aloof. 'German Christians' apart, the cry was 'The Church must remain the Church'. That meant that the

Evangelical Church was demanding living-space independent o
the State, with Christ, so to speak, regarded as *Gegenkaiser* (Riva
Emperor) and was seeking to establish her political power in
opposition—a demonstration of Jewish messianism. This attitude
inspired by the Swiss Social Democrat, Karl Barth, who had
in 1933 given his order 'Look steadfastly towards Jerusalem!'
involved the betrayal of the whole past history of Evangelica
Christianity, and endangered the very existence of the Church
The accompanying blatant bibliolatry had the effect of excluding
from the reckoning the living and contemporarily active God
and converting Christ into a Prince of the Church demanding
from Christians in Germany a greater obedience than that given
to the Führer of the Third Reich. 'We desire', the pamphle
stated, 'that everything Jewish shall be eliminated both outwardly
and inwardly from the Liturgy, from religious instruction and
from Christian usage.'[60]

The election had been planned for June, but it never took place
Instead, there was an increase in the persecution of the Con
fessing Church, particularly in Prussia, where there was a wave o
arrests culminating in that of Martin Niemöller on 1 July. The
publishing of Church protests had become altogether more com
plicated and hazardous, while the issue of the Jew within the
Church remained vague and undetermined. Authorities such a
the Reich Church Ministry were reluctant to take the radical step
of forbidding Jewish baptisms or legislating for the exclusion o
non-Aryans from German parishes. It was realised what un
desirable ecumenical repercussions there would inevitably be, and
also what effect there could be in the further stiffening of con
fessional opposition and, indeed, in the repairing of the convenien
dissension between the two confessional wings. While in certain
local areas pastors found themselves in difficulties, when they
baptised non-Aryans, and, in particular, laid themselves open to
violent attack in the Nazi Press, no attempt as a whole was made
to compel the Church to fall into line with Nuremberg. There wa
actually no official ban upon the baptism of Jews or their member
ship of the German Evangelical Church until the outbreak of the
war.

The brutal and unabated process of making life more and more
intolerable and humiliating for those of non-Aryan extraction
continued in 1938. It was insisted that they should all possess, and

ake use of, a Jewish first name.[61] An approved list was published, hich in deference for the feelings of Dr. Goebbels did not include e name 'Josef'. Anyone who possessed a non-Jewish name had, ccording to his or her sex, to alter it to either Israel or Sarah. he injured feelings of non-Aryan Christians who had thus to rgo the use of the name that had been so solemnly given to them baptism, can well be imagined. It is shocking to have to record at a worried inquiry came from one Württemberg parish as to hether Christian names in the church registers ought to be tered, where necessary, to 'Israel' and 'Sarah'. The official ling was that there was no obligation.[62]

Those responsible for the *Innere Mission* found themselves in ifficulties. An increasing number of non-Aryan Christians who ould no longer stand the fearful strain, and were urgently in need f care, were seeking admission into one or other of their institu-ions. This was far from easy to arrange, since the State was eluctant to continue its financial assistance to those institutions hat were looking after non-Aryans in addition to Germans. Some f the inmates and their relatives did not take at all kindly to the dmission of people of Jewish blood as their fellow-patients. It was athetic that those who were the victims of persecution and ill-reatment and who desperately needed asylum, were finding they ere still unacceptable in certain quarters. The suggestion was, herefore, made in October 1938 that it would be of service to verybody concerned, including the government, if the *Innere Mission* could as an act of Christian charity provide a place of efuge exclusively for non-Aryan Christians, as it was pointed ut that there was little prospect of their being accommodated in ully Jewish institutions.[63]

A disturbing anonymous report dating from the latter part of 1938[64] highlighted the peculiar plight of the Christian non-Aryans. It declared that it was practically impossible at this stage for the Confessional Church to do anything substantial on their behalf. Representations to the State proved quite useless, and were indeed dangerous, if they incurred publicity. Sermons and information from the pulpit by some pastors reached only a quite small circle of Christians who for the most part already thought along the same lines. Church collections in aid of Christian non-Aryans were quite impossible. The Confessional Church was only able to give sparse and temporary relief, confined in the main to spiritual assistance. The problem of the baptised Jews or part-Jews wa much the most difficult. They had no attachments to Jewry Jewish schools, offices, and committees were not open to them The baptised suffered immeasurably more. Besides which, th whole great world of Christendom gave far less help than th Jewish world. The disgust of the sufferers was no longer exclu sively directed against the Nazis but also against England, Scan dinavia, and other parts of the world where there was a refusal t help or, worse still, apparent sympathy with their persecutors Foreign countries were showing marvellous ingenuity in every nev measure for making their entry impossible. Countries abroa sometimes gave the impression of getting somewhat weary abou the whole business.

It is instructive to read Chapter 8 of the biography of Bishop Bell as complement to this depressing document. Bell had t employ all his characteristically untiring persistence to stir hi fellow-Christians in Britain to any action. 'Christianity in Default was an apt description. 'It is humiliating but true. The plight o these so-called "non-Aryan" Christians is grievous in the extreme ... The Christian Churches in England and elsewhere have mad the minutest response. There have been individual Christians wh have been generous. But the Churches as a whole are silent, and it seems, unconcerned. There is no deeper distress in German than that of the "non-Aryan" Christians: and none which makes stronger appeal on Christian fellowship and on Christian charity.'[6]

NOTES TO CHAPTER 5

1. See Paul Hilberg: *The Destruction of the European Jews*, London 1961, pp. 43–53, and EKDJF, pp. 145–6.
2. Heinz Schmidt, 33.
3. Schäfer, 155.
4. *Die Nation vor Gott*, 5th edition, 1937, pp. 116–36.
5. The Persecution of the Jews in the years that followed did no become so gruesome a reality because of the Nuremberg Laws bu despite them. Apparently Bernhard Lösener and Wilhelm Stuckar who were responsible for their drafting sincerely believed that thei legislation would be successful in establishing a norm for reasonable treatment of the Jews, and would restrain irresponsible and arbitrary ill-treatment of them (Arndt Müller: *Geschichte der Juden in*

Nuremberg, Nuremberg, 1969, p. 219). The Jews themselves appeared at first to have been cautiously optimistic that the new Laws might actually improve the situation. The *Reichsvertretung der Juden* which had existed since 1933 to further the collective interests of all Jewish organisations expressed in late September its readiness to work for a 'tolerable arrangement' on the basis of the Nuremberg legislation (Karl Schleunes: *The Twisted Road to Auschwitz: Nazi Policy towards German Jews, 1933–39*, André Deutsch, 1972, p. 126).

6. Wilhelm Niemöller: *Aus dem Leben eines Bekenntnispfarrers*, Bielefeld 1961, p. 239.

7. Gerlach, 231–2.

8. Friedrich Coch who had assumed office as Bishop of Saxony in July 1933 revealed clearly his extreme attitude as a 'German Christian' leader in the fulsome oration that he produced at the funeral on 12 September 1933 of Theodor Fritsch, the rabid veteran anti-semite and author of the best-seller, *Handbuch der Judenfrage*, who certainly did as much as anybody else over a long period in keeping the anti-Jewish fire ablaze. Coch expressed his appreciation at being enabled in the House of God and in the framework of a Church service as bishop of the local Evangelical Church to say a word of thanks at the coffin of a man who had seen his fearless and battle-proven life here on earth crowned with success. It was precisely in conflict with the Jews, the bishop declared, that this man had come to realise the essential meaning of Christianity. The real significance of world history was such conflict between Christianity and Jewry. It was so ever since that hour at Golgotha, and it remained so. This expression of episcopal eloquence terminated with the prayer that this 'honest fighter' might enjoy not only eternal rest but such eternal peace as was not of this world but which God alone could bestow out of His pure Grace (quoted by Poliakow-Wolf: *Das Dritte Reich und seine Denker*, Berlin, 1959, p. 252).

9. Gauger, 202.

10. AELKZ, 1935, p. 980. A certain Pastor Reichelmann from Saxony wrote to *Der Stürmer* in October 1935: 'We are enthusiastic in support of your fight against the Jewish gravediggers of the German Nation and against the Jewish supporters among the Evangelical clergy. We shall be fighting on your side, and shall not rest, till the battle against everything Jewish and against the murderers of our Saviour has been brought to a victorious conclusion in the spirit of Christ and of Martin Luther.'

1. Brunotte, 150.

2. Meier, 100.

3. Meier, 101.

4. Fischer, VIII, 185.

5. Brunotte, 151.

6. Schmidt: *Bekenntnisse*, 1935, p. 224.

7. *Lutherisches Missionsjahrbuch*, 1935, p, 32.

8. Niemöller: *Evangelische Kirche im Dritten Reich*, 383.

19. Wilhelm Niemöller: *Ist die Judenfrage bewältigt? Junge Kirche* Beiheft, 2. May 1968, p. 14.

20. Niemöller: *Steglitz*, 84.

21. Karl Kupisch: *Im Bann des Zeitgeistes, Theologische Existenz heute* Neue Folge, 169, p. 40. Niemöller: *Steglitz*, 15.

22. The preliminary draft contained the words: 'Baptism does not sub stantiate anyone's social, economic or political claims. It confers n secular rights of citizenship (*Bürgerrecht*), but admits a person into th Fellowship of the Kingdom of God, and bestows eternal salvatio upon all who believe in it.' This could be interpreted as emphasi upon the categorical difference between belonging by faith to th Church and being accepted into the political community of the Volk and admission that Christian ethical standards proclaimed by th Church had no relevance in the political sphere and that it was nc the province of the Church to criticise measures taken by the State The inclusion of the above words in the final published message c the Synod could indeed have given the impression that the Con fessing Church condoned the implementation of Nazi anti-Jewis. policy within the political sphere (Jürgen Schmidt: *Martin Niemölle* 317).

23. Bethge, 555–9. English ed., 403–7.

24. Niemöller: *Wort und Tat*, 164. Vogel, true to his Lutheran in heritage, remarked in the course of the discussion that 'the Churc does not interfere with the State in the discharge of its office for whic it is responsible before God, but the Church exercises her office i that freedom which derives from the commission given to her b Jesus Christ' (Niemöller: *Steglitz*, 184).

25. *Kirchliches Jahrbuch*, 99.

26. Niemöller: *Steglitz*, 302, 308.

27. The text of the Memorandum is to be found in KJB, 130 ff. For th full story of the preparation of this remarkable document, the un happy circumstances attending its publication and various reactior both in Germany and abroad see Wilhelm Niemöller: *Die Bekenn ende Kirche sagt Hitler die Wahrheit*, Bielefeld, 1954.

28. Max Geiger: *Der deutsche Kirchenkampf, 1933–1945*, Zürich, 196 p. 56.

29. KJB, 133.

30. Gerlach, 204.

31. Bethge, 603. English edition, 441.

32. Renate Heydenreich in *Der ungekündigte Bund*, p. 231.

33. Bernhard Forck: *Und folget ihren Glauben nach Gedenkuch f* die Blutzeugen der Bekennenden Kirche, Stuttgart, 1949, pp. 11–2. Bethge, 604–7, English ed., 442–4, Boyens, 174–6, who makes highly critical appraisal of the attitude of the Provisional Churc Government towards Weissler, and Wilhelm Niemöller: *Die Beker nende Kirche sagt Hitler die Wahrheit*, 29 and 46–8. Niemöller (p. 4 quotes from an article by Wilhelm Rehm, in which the Leader of th Reich Movement of 'German Christians' insisted that sinister Jewis

agitators were obviously sheltering behind and taking advantage of the Provisional Church Government since no 'truth-loving German' who had his eyes open to what had been achieved for his people could possibly have been responsible for the accusations made in the Memorandum.

4. KJB, 135 ff.

5. See Boyens, 176.

6. Kurt Dietrich Schmidt: *Dokumente: Die Zeit der Reichskirchen aus-schusses, 1935–37, Arbeiten zur Geschichte des Kirchenkampfes,* Band. 13, Göttingen, 1965, p. 946.

7. Ehrenforth, 247.

8. Friedrich Middendorf: *Der Kirchenkampf in einer Reformierter Kirche. Arbeiten zur Geschichte des Kirchenkampfes,* Band 8, Göttingen, 1961, p. 32.

9. AELKZ, 1936, pp. 207 ff.

10. Micklem Collection, Bodleian Library, Oxford, Vol. VI, No. 1.

11. *Der Stürmer,* 1936, No. 16.

12. Arnot Müller, 259.

13. Fritz Fink: *Die Judenfrage in Unterricht,* Nuremberg, 1937, pp. 5 ff.

14. Bielefeld Archiv., *Judenfrage,* 3.

15. Schmidt, *Bekenntnisse,* 1935, p. 274.

16. Schmidt, *Dokumente,* II, 770–1.

17. Pfarrer Brokelschen: *Wir antworten, 118 Antworten der 'Deutschen Christen' auf Glaubensfragen der Gegenwart,* 1936, Micklem Collection, Bodleian, Oxford, *Unerwünschte Literatur,* Nr 50.

18. Schmidt, *Dokumente,* I, 565.

19. Speech at Hersbruck, 27.10.36, quoted Baier, p. 524. Compare with this an utterance of Friedrich Häcker, a village pastor in Württemberg on 9 March 1936, when he told a 'German Christian' audience that he found the anti-semitism of *Der Stürmer* mild, Luther's instruction to burn down the synagogues, plunder the Jews and chase them away eminently reasonable, and the degree of anti-semitism represented in the Bible by Jesus and the Prophets as the harshest and most outspoken—'You have the Devil for father, you are of infernal origin, you are the people of Sodom and Gomorrah, that means, you are so utterly depraved, that you deserve to be exterminated by fire and brimstone from the face of the earth' (*Deutsche Sonntag,* 22.3.36).

0. See AELKZ, 1937, pp. 161–2, for a criticism of the new 'Gospel of John in German' by Dr. Weidemann, 'German Christian' Bishop of Bremen. The reviewer maintains that it is Weidemann's Gospel, and not St. John's, and that a stout stomach is necessary to read the Gospel. 'The Führer has pleasure in the great fighter who cleansed the Temple. He has cleared out of the temple of the German Volk everything that does not belong therein, everything that goes by the name of Jewish, and, in doing so, he has acted like Christ.'—An extract from German Confirmation Instruction given in a Berlin church (quoted by *Schweiz-Evangelische Presse Dienst,* 24.5.39).

51. JK, 1936, p. 386.
52. Ludwig Müller: *Deutsche Gottesworte*, Weimar, 1936, p. 38.
53. KJB, 151–3.
54. Schmidt: *Dokumente*, II, 1347–55. Two different versions of the speech are provided. For English translation see A. S. Duncan-Jones: *The Struggle for Religious Freedom in Germany*, Gollancz, 1938, 299 ff., and Otto Dibelius's reply, 303 ff.
55. KJB, 163.
56. JK, 1937, p. 288.
57. JK, 1937, p. 242.
58. JK, p. 330.
59. Meier, 31.
60. *Gegen den jüdische Geist in der Kirche*, Heft 2—*Deutsche Christen im Kampf*, Weimar, 1937.
61. AELKZ, 1938, p. 708.
62. Fischer, XIII, 21.
63. Meier, 106–7.
64. *Some Aspects of the Christian Non-Aryan Problem* (November 1938). Micklem Collection, Bodleian Library, Oxford, Vol. XIII, No. 159.
65. Ronald Jasper: *George Bell. Bishop of Chichester*, Oxford, 1967, p. 140.

6

The Pogrom of November 1938, its aftermath, and succour for the afflicted, 1938–1941

The tragic murder on 7 November 1938 in Paris of Ernst vom Rath, Third Secretary in the Germany Embassy, by a seventeen-year-old Polish Jewish refugee, provided the radical Nazis with the opportunity they were seeking for launching a pogrom against the Jews.[1] Only a few days before there had appeared in the Gestapo journal, *Schwarze Korps*, an article that proclaimed that every Jew in Germany was to be regarded as a hostage for any act of violence committed by Jews abroad. There was irony indeed in Rath's assassination, for he had been shadowed by the Gestapo because of his anti-Nazi attitude.[2] The fearful 'Crystal Night' followed on 9 November with a fantastic amount of broken glass as accompaniment to the wholesale assault, arson and pillage. One hundred and nineteen synagogues were set on fire, 76 completely destroyed and 20,000 arrests made. The destruction in broken glass alone came to five million marks. The Jewish community was fined a billion marks, eliminated altogether from the economy, and driven towards the Ghetto—and worse. This was indeed the beginning of the end. William Shirer in his *Rise and Fall of the Third Reich* testifies from personal experience that many Germans were as horrified by the 9 November inferno as were Americans, Englishmen, and other foreigners. 'But neither the leaders of the Christian Churches nor the generals nor any other of the representatives of the "good" Germany spoke out at once in open protest. They bowed to what General von Fritsch called "the inevitable" or "Germany's destiny".'[3] Samuel W. Honaker, United States Consul-General in Stuttgart, reported as follows to Washington on 15 November. 'These so-called reprisals against the Jews are not a spontaneous movement originating from the people as a whole. In any event the movement clearly seems to have been well organised and planned, and carried out by persons having the confidence of the authorities. While the demolition of Jewish shops was in full swing in Stuttgart, a new twelve-cylinder Mercedes carrying high S.S. officials drove up in front of the shops under devastation. These men made an inspection of what was going on, and apparently after giving their approval drove pompously away, while the destruction continued. A few Aryan people have been arrested for giving too open expression to their disgust over the events of the last few days. Many persons secretly sympathising with the Jews or discountenancing such ruthless treatment of helpless people are becoming more and more afraid to give expression to their feelings.' Honaker also reported to the United States ambassador in Berlin, 'The vast majority of the non-Jewish German population, perhaps as much as 80 per cent has given evidence of complete disagreement with these violent demonstrations against the Jews. Many people, in fact, are hanging their heads with shame. On the other hand, possibly 20 per cent have shown satisfaction as a result of the application of radical measures.'[4]

One of the most vivid and moving descriptions of a Christian reaction to this fearful event is preserved in the perilously frank diary kept by Frau Annemarie Viebig, a member of the Confessing Church in Breslau. Under 9 November she wrote—'Are we still living in a State that can in any way be called righteous or civilised rational or humane? Have human beings, or those in authority the right to treat their fellow-men and -women worse than vermin Throughout the whole community (I decline to write the word "Fatherland") the Jewish people have been treated worse than vermin. They have been humiliated and dishonoured, and have suffered the senseless destruction of their property and of their places of worship. As if that was not altogether more than enough whole hosts of innocent people have been dragged away in adequately clad into concentration camps, and placed into bitterly cold and draughty barracks. Deprived of heating and covering their hands and feet became frozen, and they died like flies. Some who came back home close-cropped and shorn have hung themselves: distinguished men among them. . . . Herded together, men who had formerly held high and honourable office were paraded

rough the streets accompanied by storm-troopers and persecuted
bawling children. . . . Among them were doctors, most of them
cellently qualified and noted for their philanthropy, many of
em members, like their parents and grandparents, of the
hristian Church. This last fact, accompanied by the complete
owerlessness of the Church to help or protect them in any way,
as profoundly distressed and tormented me. Shocking is the fate
individual families. Dr. Korn, father's best assistant: no way
at for him in any direction, no more professional employment,
nable to receive any money from his only son in Zurich, unable
emigrate. I have seen in my life a great deal of suffering and
isery, hopelessness and distress, but no human despair to com-
are with that of Dr. Korn and his wife. He has decided . . . to let
s son come, and the three can then commit suicide together.
is the only way out. Ought one not to be profoundly ashamed
be a German ?'[5]

A theological student in Tübingen, by name Krügel, was so
ocked by the brutality and destruction that he announced on
November his resignation from the S.A. The reasons that he
ave for such a step and the comment of Nazi officials upon it are
orth recording. Krügel did not hesitate to affirm that he regarded
e Jews as 'the most dangerous enemies of our people', and felt
at all the legal proceedings against them were thoroughly
istified. On the other hand, he felt that all illegal measures against
em should be prevented. This had obviously not been the case
uring the past days. An ominous concession had been made to
opular frenzy (*Volkswut*). This the Nazi Party had declared to
e justified, but he as a Christian could not share in such an
iterpretation of what was right. He was not therefore able con-
cientiously and as a member of the Christian Church to remain
ny longer a storm-trooper. The comment of the S.A. officials was
s follows—'It should be realised that the wicked Nazis have
imply carried out the instruction of Luther. The synagogues
ave been burnt, just as the father of protestantism required. . . .
rügel's anti-semitism is a highly questionable affair. We know
ell that there are Christians who do not share his view. . . .
nstead of doing justice to his Volk and his Führer he treats it all
s a highly personal matter, and wants to satisfy his own conscience
nd that of the Christian Church which is after all only a section
f the people. . . . He may happen to be a good theologian, he

certainly is a bad protestant, and a still worse S.A. man. The S.A. can rejoice to have one man fewer of such convictions.' Krüg came out unscathed from this encounter, continued his studies Tübingen till the following summer, then saw service with the armed forces with the opportunity of studying during the winte term of 1941–1942.[6]

Heinrich Grüber, whose heroic and tireless efforts to help the persecuted non-Aryans will shortly be described in some detail writes in his memoirs of having been like many another Christian champion of the maltreated Jews, almost literally paralysed by the sheer horror of 'Crystal Night'. The behaviour of the Nazis, he remarks, was so incomprehensible that 'we actually did not know what to say or to do'. He relates that on 13 November, the day that Goebbels had proclaimed that what had been happening to the Jews was the spontaneous will of the German people, he was addressing a large gathering of the Confessing Church, and told them, 'I will have nothing to do with this German people', a confession wrung at very great cost from a troubled heart, which upset and alarmed many even in the Confessing Church. 'My friends trembled, but nothing happened. So I repeated the same remark the following evening at a parish gathering in Lichterfelde. Grüber, like many another, went out of his way and at real risk to try to comfort, help and counsel individual victims, and find accommodation for those who had either been rendered homeless or who were too scared to stay in their dwellings. Some lives were certainly saved, and a number of suicides prevented. But no one found the decisive word or performed the decisive deed that could stem the evil. In a speech ten years after the event Grüber referred to the demonic stream of racial hatred that had overflowed on 'Crystal Night', and acknowledged the grave sin of omission of the Christian Churches in not having, when it was more possible, sought to erect 'a defensive dyke'.[8]

Non-Aryan Christians in their desperation looked to the Church for help. And where else could they turn? A commendable amount of individual assistance was certainly given, and at considerable personal risk. To be observed receiving a Jewish visitor or paying a friendly call upon a non-Aryan meant being put upon the black list and subjected to alarming threats. A pastor's wife who called upon a local rabbi after his synagogue had been destroyed to express her sympathy and that of her husband, found

e next day in her letter-box a card on which had been drawn a
vered head and a long knife, and which bore the inscription,
`his is the fate of those who stick by the Jews.'[9] A village pastor
ho had prayed for the Jews, was not only rewarded by finding,
ke others who had showed concern, a red placard outside the
carage branding him as a Jewish lackey (*Judenknecht*), but was
so taunted by the local lads, who told him 'Your time is coming.
ou will be called for next' and proceeded to smash his study
indows.[10]

In certain districts, where to the disgust and disappointment of
azi gangs there were scarcely any Jews upon whom they could
:nt their anti-semitic emotions, clerical households provided a
elcome substitute. Reports from Hesse-Nassau, Bavaria and the
hineland[11] gave details of crude and sadistic attacks having taken
lace between 10 and 13 November upon pastors and their families
ho were apparently in no way acknowledged sympathisers with
ie Jews, and who were obviously bewildered by the brutal and
estructive onslaughts upon them and their homes. 'Now we have
rreted out the Jews, the turn of the Confessing Church is
oming' was a repeated threat in Hesse. A wild mob advanced upon
vicarage in Upper Bavaria with cries of 'Traitor', 'Jewish cur',
Blackguard'. A doughty Superintendent Pastor in the Rhineland,
nding that his front door had been smashed in, fetched out his
ld service revolver, fired over the crowd, and was rewarded by an
npleasant wound over his left eye from a stone. That his wife
ad been observed, speaking briefly, when out shopping, to a
ewess whose house had suffered damage was the only explanation
e could find for the violent attack. These episodes could be
egarded as fulfilment of Bonhoeffer's prophecy in 1933 that the
hurch would herself experience tomorrow what she was today
lowing the Jews to suffer.

The 16th of November happened to be the Church's Day of
rayer and Penitence, and it is certain that a fair number of
astors prayed openly for the Jews and inserted into their sermons
nmistakable references to the persecuted, a favoured one being
ie emphasis that the man who fell among thieves and was rescued
y the Good Samaritan was a Jew.

In the Church of St. Lorenz in the centre of Nuremberg Pastor
Vilhelm Geyer spoke plainly from the pulpit in condemnation of
ie wrong done to the Jews, and this was followed by a solemn

reading of the Ten Commandments from the altar, in which]
and his colleagues took part.[12]

Helmut Gollwitzer, standing in Martin Niemöller's pulpit
Berlin-Dahlem and taking as his text Luke 3:7–14, contriv
without actually calling things by their names to speak out wi
plain and unmistakable reference to the horrors of the past wee

'What do we expect from God', he began by asking, 'when v
now come before Him, singing, reading from the Bible, prayin
preaching, and confessing our sins. . . . Our audacity and o
presumption must be abhorrent to Him'. He proceeded to rema
that those who were no longer able to be penitent before God soo
found themselves also no longer able to admit their guilt, whe
their fellow-men and -women were concerned. This led to 'tl
mania to persecute, in which one individual makes another out
be of the Devil, in order to idolise himself'. It was not just a matt
of sheer evil but of 'evil in repulsive fashion wearing a mor
disguise and hatred and thirst for revenge parading as somethir
great and good'. Honest and decent individuals were 'all at on
transforming themselves into cruel beasts'. This was an indicatic
that 'something wrong lies hidden in all of us. We are all par
to it'. Christians had their share of blame through cowardic
accommodation, side-stepping, closing of their eyes, silence, :
accursed form of caution which considered one's own selfi:
advantage and naïve optimism that liked to believe that ever
thing in the end would turn out to have been for the best. Th
were manifestly implicated as was evident by their own liv
which left room for only a limited love of God and neighbo
such as could be shown without real effort or inconvenienc
There was need to realise the demands of genuine love towar
one's neighbour. 'He does not possess what you have. You ha
two coats, he has none. You have something to eat, he no long
has anything. You are safe, he is defenceless. You have still
certain amount of money, he has none left. You have a roof ov
your head, he is homeless. . . . "Open thy mouth for the duml
and on behalf of all who are destitute.' The sermon ended with tl
words: 'Our neighbour waits outside in distress, defenceles
dishonoured, hungry, pursued, haunted by anxiety for his ve
survival. He is watching to see whether the Christian Church h
really and truly observed a Day of Repentance. Jesus Christ
watching too. Amen.'[13]

Paul Veil, a Württemberg pastor, in his Penitence Day sermon made plain reference to the wave of hatred and indignation that had resulted in the setting on fire of Houses of God, and proceeded to declare, 'We do not want today to pass judgement upon those who are obviously unaware of God's Word and of his Commandments, and who consequently no longer know what is right in the sight of God. Rather, on this Day of Repentance we are going to ask ourselves whether we are among those who hearken on every occasion to God's Word and Commandments, and who are prepared for unconditional obedience'. Veil was, not surprisingly, made to answer for such remarks. His line of defence lay in reference to Goebbels' solemn public declaration that neither State nor Party had had the least to do with such outrages that had been committed. He was let off punishment by receiving the Führer's pardon.[14]

An effective witness called for altogether more than prayers[15] and pulpit remarks and a certain number of individuals acting the Good Samaritan. There were no doubt pastors and layfolk who would have been boldly prepared to take their part in organised public protest meetings. Such a one was Pastor Lesser of Elberfeld who told his weekly Bible Study Group that instead of the usual consideration of God's Word, they ought to be going to the market place and as Christians raising their voices loudly in protest at the atrocities that had been committed. But when he asked who would accompany him there was no response. This caused his further remark, 'I as well do not feel strong enough to do it alone in such an action'. Only later on, and too late, did he discover that his Confessing brethren in the neighbourhood were reacting in exactly the same way.[16]

There was no chance of the Evangelical Church as a whole voicing her horror and indignation, and the Catholic Church kept almost completely silent, and their hierarchy found no word to say.[17] As Grüber subsequently remarked, 'What were the few who protested in comparison with the millions who co-operated or kept silent, and at their best stuck their heads ostrich-like in the sand, or clenched their fists in their pockets?'[18]

That no public protest came in those November days from the Confessing Church is understandable, when one takes into consideration the extraordinarily critical situation that had resulted from certain events earlier on in 1938. There had been

great heart-searching and profound difference of opinion ove
the proposed special oath of loyalty and obedience to the Führer
which could be regarded as admitting identification with th
policy of the Third Reich.[19] Very many of the Confessiona
pastors had finally taken the oath, which obviously made ai
outspoken attack so soon after on just about the most vulnerabl
issue of all appear out of the question. In addition to this, th
highly controversial publication in September 1938 by the radical
of a proposed Service of Intercession in event of war had shocked
many of the Lutheran Confessionalists, and had caused an almos
complete rift in the Front. It had also brought down upon the
heads of its authors the charge of flagrant high treason, and the
opportunity was taken to suspend those held principally respon
sible.[20] Karl Barth from his observation post in Basle had made
the situation still more tense by his letter to the Czech theologian
Hromadka, in which he referred to the stream of lies and brutality
emanating from Hitler Germany, and averred that every Czech
soldier who resisted Hitler would be acting on behalf of the
Church of Jesus Christ.[21] The Dahlemites[22] seemed to be as
pained and upset as anyone at what was described as being so
intolerable an utterance. The voice to them was not that of
Barth the theological teacher but of Barth the politician. He was
considered to be demanding a complete reversal of the role of
the Church as he himself had taught it.[23] The objection appears
to have been not just directed against a wrong judgement of
Barth, but the whole way in which he took up an attitude at all
to political events was disputed. This point of view did not
promise any opposition to political mishandling of the Jews. The
members of the Confessing Church in Mecklenburg began their
statement of their attitude to the events of 'Crystal Night' with
the words—'As justified as the political measures against the
Jews may be. . . .'[24] It was also no doubt felt that, if the cause of
the Jews as a whole was championed, it might well mean a diminished opportunity to be of assistance to the Christian non-Aryans,
which was the particular responsibility of the Church. The
ensuing political anxiety was so great, that the Reich Council
of Brethren decided to omit Dietrich Bonhoeffer, who was
known to be embarking upon a politically conspirative course,
from the Intercession List, if he got himself arrested.[25]

It fell to the lot of a humble village pastor, Julius von Jan,

f Oberlenningen in Württemberg, to speak out fearlessly for
he whole Church in an inspired sermon on 16 November.[26] The
ext for the Day of Prayer and Penitence was Jeremiah 22:29—
O earth, earth, hear the word of the Lord'. Considering how
erilously appropriate its choice was in the light of the relevant
errible events, the Württemberg Church authorities saw fit to
varn all pastors against any attempt to fling open the church
vindows and address the world outside (*Nicht zum Fenster hinaus
eden*).[27] This did not, however, deter Jan who felt it to be a
matter of conscience that he should speak plainly and relevantly.
Where', he asked, 'in Germany is the prophet sent to the king's
iouse to utter the word of the Lord? Where is the man who in
he name of God and of justice, will cry like Jeremiah, "Maintain
ighteousness, rescue those deprived of their rights out of the
ands of the transgressor? Do not oppress the stranger, the
rphan and the widow. Do no one violence, shed not the innocent
ilood." God has sent us such men. They are today either in a
oncentration camp or reduced to silence. . . . Our bishops have
iot recognised it as their duty to stand shoulder to shoulder
vith those who have spoken the Lord's Word. Who would have
hought that a crime in Paris could have as its consequence so
nuch criminal activity in Germany? Wild passions have been
eleased, God's Commandments disregarded, Houses of God
vhich were sacred to others razed to the ground without punish-
nent, men who have served our German people loyally, and have
onscientiously fulfilled their duty, have been thrown into
oncentration camps, merely because they happened to be of
nother race. A dreadful seed of hatred has been sown. A frightful
arvest will grow out of it, unless God in his Grace allows us
nd our people to show sincere repentance.' The sermon ended
vith the moving words—'This confession of sin which one did
iot believe one could proclaim has been at any rate for me today
ke the casting off of a great burden. God be praised. Utterance
ias been made before God and in God's name; the world may do
rith us what it will. We are in the Lord's hands. God is true.
"hou, O earth, earth, earth, hear the word of the Lord. Amen.'
an had, not surprisingly, to pay the penalty of his boldness. A
ew days later a mob of about twenty Party members came to
ie vicarage. Jan was brought out from his Bible class, and
hoved on to the roof of a shed to be publicly whipped, and was

GOD

then taken off to prison. But he survived, fought during the wa
in the front line, and returned in 1945 to his former parish.

Von Jan recorded in moving fashion his feelings, while bein
so savagely mishandled. 'Despite all such physical strain anc
exhaustion I felt imbued with a deep peace and immense com
passion for my persecutors, harrassed as they were by demons
and I was able to pray for them from my very heart. I experience
in my own body how one can be genuinely glad, when one i
accounted worthy to suffer stripes for Christ's sake. I raised m
eyes, and beheld my church, in which I had preached God'
Word, and I thanked God that I was permitted to confirm hi
Word in suffering before my parish. The S.A. men spat upon m
with no understanding how I rejoiced to be brought so near t
the Lord in such shame and in such discipleship.' At his subse
quent trial his defence lawyer urged that the sermon should no
be regarded as a mischievous or malicious attack upon the Stat
and Party but rather as a testimony of the Word of God agains
the sins of the people and of the *Zeitgeist*, such as was the duty o
an Evangelical preacher. If the sermon had caused disturbance, i
was the disturbance of conscience that was the inevitable accom
paniment of the preaching of the Word of God.[28]

Report of the sermon caused great consternation throughou
the Württemberg Church. A minority of radical churchme
called for its publication and adoption by the Church as a whole
This suggestion shocked the majority. Bishop Wurm himself ha
distinct reservations about the sermon. The preacher, he held
should in his sermon avoid unwarranted criticism of concret
political events. Pulpit utterance and public prayer alike had t
serve a pastoral end, and should not have the character of a demon
stration.[29] This did not, however, prevent Bishop Wurm from
energetically defending Jan. He wrote on his behalf to D
Gürtner, the Reich Minister of Justice and to Reichministe
Kerrl who declared that the Führer himself did not approve o
what had happened to Jan. He also addressed an eloquent lette
to Himmler, in which he remarked that the events of 'Cryst
Night' had greatly upset the majority of the population, an
that church congregations did not expect those who preached t
them to pass over this event in silence. He himself had not don
so, though he had commented differently from Jan. Jan, h
declared, had already paid for his indiscretion that had bee

prompted by honourable if exaggerated religious fervour. There were many much worse offenders against Law and Order and good community relationships who had received much lighter treatment. On patriotic grounds he, the bishop, laid great store upon being able to tell the Württemberg clergy that there was full understanding high up in the Reich government for the plea that he was making. Himmler who, unlike most of his other Nazi colleagues, set store upon being punctiliously correct, politely acknowledged the letter, and promised to give it his careful consideration. Richard Fischer suggests that Jan's escape from being committed to a concentration camp and his eventual release from prison were partly due to anxiety lest he should become a 'second Niemöller'. [30]

As the head of an 'intact', influential and largely united, Lutheran Church Wurm was obviously most apprehensive of the effect that an extension of incautious and open criticism from the pulpit upon current events could have upon the liberty and the welfare of the Church within the Third Reich, and he felt impelled to give episcopal warning that forthright preaching of Christian ethics was always in danger of being maliciously misinterpreted and of gratuitously providing ammunition for those who were all the time seeking grounds upon which to attack the Church. This was certainly the case, if the Church could be plainly convicted of being hand in glove with the Jews. The preacher should take care in his sermons to avoid anything that was in the nature of inadmissible criticism of concrete political events. It had to be realised that there was a danger of anything, and even what was purely religious, being immediately misconstrued as political. Consequently in so perilous a situation disciplined care had to be taken to ensure that pronouncements and prayers had a purely pastoral, and not a demonstrative, character, and that they had in mind those who were actually present in church and not those outside. While, of course, a form of preaching was to be avoided, in which the Gospel was proclaimed, 'as if nothing had happened', and as though it had no present relevance, care had just as much to be taken that the opposite error was avoided by which the sermon was politically loaded or charged with ecclesiastical politics.

Bishop Wurm in his memoirs declares that he spoke a solemn word in Stuttgart concerning the excesses of 'Crystal Night', [31] but he declined to allow a public protest to be made from all Württemberg pulpits. A letter which he wrote on December 6th to Dr. Gürtner, the Reich Minister of Justice, certainly did not take the form of a direct and unqualified protest against the recent pogrom or a stalwart defence of its victims. It would not be unfair to say that its message was far more that of concern that, while a reasonable and restrained anti-semitic campaign was justifiable and acceptable, on this occasion things had gone altogether too far.

The bishop, who remarked that he had urged his pastors to avoid anything that was calculated to be inflammatory in the present disturbed atmosphere, wrote: 'This state of affairs has created a particularly difficult situation for the Evangelical Church and her clergy. I may say after long years of experience that there can scarcely be a profession that has kept itself so free from specific Jewish characteristics and that has made such proof of its readiness to champion the cause of Volk and Fatherland as that of the Evangelical clergy. The gratitude of the clergy that Germany has an attitude quite different from that of twenty years ago is as lively as that of other lovers of the Fatherland. They are aware that this would have been impossible without the Führer and National Socialism. They can, however, not forget the saying of Jesus: 'What shall it profit a man, if he gain the whole world, and lose his soul?' They cannot forget that according to the teaching of Holy Scripture and the experiences of history those who have by commission of the Lord of the World to execute judgement, are under obligation to render account to the Supreme Judge, and that transgressing the Divine Commandments must sooner or later incur retribution. Because we would wish to spare our people from eventually undergoing the same humiliations and sufferings to which others are now abandoned, we raise our hands, as we observe our people, in intercession, exhortation and warning, even though we know that by doing so we shall be abused as Jewish lackeys, and be threatened with the same proceedings that have been employed against the Jews.'[32]

It would be scarcely uncharitable to comment that Wurm's expressed concern appeared to be more for the Germans than for the Jews. This is confirmed by another extract from this same letter in which he affirmed that he did not for one moment 'contest the right of the state to combat the Jews as a dangerous element in the population'. 'I have', he wrote, 'from my youth onwards held as conclusive the judgement of men like Heinrich von Treitschke and Adolf Stoecker on the disintegrating effect of Jewry in the spheres of religion, morals, literature, economics and politics'. That did not, however, prevent him from pleading that not every word of grief for or sympathy with the Jews should be interpreted as treason.

In his memoirs Wurm admits that the necessary, unanimous and full-toned witness of the church was certainly not provided on that critical occasion. 'A spell', he wrote, 'was laid upon us, and it was as if our mouths were kept shut by an invisible power'.[33] In a sermon after the war he remarked that it would be on his conscience to his dying day that he had not really spoken out.[34]

Who is to say that a really courageous and straightforward condemnation voiced at once and spontaneously by representatives of the churches throughout Germany might not have had a profound effect upon the population as a whole, who, it is to be believed, were deeply disturbed at events. Remarks such as 'The Jews after all are human', and 'places of worship ought not to be set on fire; that is absolute blasphemy', were frequently passed, especially in Christian circles. Laura Livingstone, sister-in-law to Bishop Bell, who was in Berlin at the time doing invaluable relief work among Christian non-Aryans has remarked that she had the impression that after 'Crystal Night' the population was deeply ashamed over what had happened. 'I actually hoped then', she wrote, 'that the Germans would at least understand the sort of government that they had, and would seek to be rid of it. These naïve hopes were not fulfilled'.[35] Hans Asmussen has remarked that the inhabitants of Berlin showed frequently and in many different ways what they thought about the treatment of the Jews. But the masses did not stir themselves, because they had no one to direct them.[36] There is certainly truth in H. D. Leuner's comment that 'the history of the Third Reich seems to show that the Nazi Government at least at that stage hesitated to fly in the face of spontaneous non-political opposition when backed by popular sentiment'.[37] A really widespread and decisive outcry could well have convinced the Nazis that there were limits to what the people, the great majority of whom subscribed to the Christian religion, would tolerate. It might have averted the subsequent massacre of millions.

'Crystal Night' may be taken to have provided the Nazis with a useful check as to the effect of their five years of unremitted and scurrilous anti-Jewish propaganda upon the population, and may perhaps even be regarded as a sinister try out of extreme measures as a prelude to their intended policy of final extermination. The population as a whole were observed to have regarded what took place quietly and passively but certainly not enthusiastically. Paul Sauer goes so far as to describe 'Crystal Night' as having caused a rift between the Nazi activists and the majority of the people which was never henceforth to be healed. It therefore brought about a turning point in the Nazi method of dealing with the Jews. Hitherto the attack had been an open one relying upon the population being sufficiently influenced by unceasing propaganda to assent to the removal of the Jews from public life and the restriction of their influence in the economic, academic and cultural spheres and the encouragement of emigration. Realising that the people as a whole would not willingly identify themselves with a really radical policy of brutal terror, or be persuaded that such treatment was either necessary or justifiable, the measures to be taken in the final act had to be top secret, and only to be revealed to a limited inner circle of the initiated. [38]

The Church as a body kept silent. [39] It was not until more than a month had elapsed, that word at last came. A conference of the Confessing Church was held in Berlin from December 10th to the 12th, and issued a Message to the Congregations which cannot be claimed to have provided what really was required. The Message opened with the words, 'Many among you are deeply moved in your hearts by the fate of our Christian fellow-believers among the Jews", proceeded to quote certain verses of scripture including the reference in the First Epistle of John to Jesus being the 'propitiation for our sins', adding none too happily, 'Jesus Christ is also the propitiation for the sin of the Jewish People'. The Message went on as follows: 'We are bound together as brethren with all the believers in Christ of the Jewish race. We will not separate ourselves from them, and we ask them not to separate themselves from us. We exhort all members of our congregations to concern themselves with the material and spiritual distress of our Christian brothers and sisters of the Jewish race, and to intercede for them in their prayers to God.' No reference whatever was made to the plight of the great majority of the Jews who were not Christians, and indeed the only reference to the Jewish People as a whole was a mention of their sin. It would have been possible to assume from this statement that only those Jews who were converted to Christianity qualified for compassionate help. In affirming the inadequacy of this statement it should not be denied that there was real courage and compassion in publicly expressing solidarity at this particular time with the Christian non-Aryans, but what was thus openly said could not be construed as direct disassociation with, let alone plain criticism of, the Nazi-inspired cruelty and barbarity. The statement ended not surprisingly on an eschatological note—'We await the Second Coming of our Lord, and trust in God's promise that is given to the People of Israel and to all Peoples.'[40]

In another statement from the conference concerned with the tribulations of 'many servants of the Church', reference was made to the fact that there were those who 'had been suffering persecution as a result of their earnest preaching of the Ten Commandments in relation to the proceedings against the Jews'.[41] This was, we may imagine, intended as an indirect condemnation of the events of the previous month, but a patently indirect one. It is only fair to add that if in this extremely tense situation a plain statement had been issued affirming solidarity with Israel and condemnation of her persecutors, it could have meant the end of the organised Confessing Church. But there was certainly more to it than that.

Theodor Dipper, a leading light in the Württemberg Confessional Fellowship, who took part in this conference, relates that men such as Wilhelm Jannasch strove hard but in vain to persuade the gathering to prepare a public statement protesting against the persecution of the Jews that could be read in church and forwarded to the State. Dipper also admits that he himself queried whether there was not a limit to the mandate given to the Church to make her own declaration in public. The Bible contained its eschatological pronouncement, to which witness had to be made faithfully. Did not that rule out the possibility of the Church directly addressing the State on this issue?[42]

The *Allgemeine Evangelisch-Lutherische Kirchenzeitung*, the strict Lutheran Weekly, revealed unexpected boldness in an article on the Jewish Question and the Old Testament in allowing the following sentence to appear—'The misfortune of the Jews is their enmity to the Cross. It would be the misfortune of the Germans, were they to become like the Jews.'[43] It is not surprising that the *Kirchenzeitung* was banned for some months after this issue.

From a neutral pietistic source came the comment that the murder in Paris followed by the retaliation of 'Crystal Night' denoted a state of war between National Socialist Germany and World Jewry which was obviously bent upon persecuting Hitler with deadly hatred. Such warfare was necessary, and it could well lead to the liquidation of the Jews. It was inadmissible to judge or to condemn it by reference to the Word or to the spirit or thought of the New Testament, since New Testament standards were valid only for the regulating of relations between believing Christians.[44]

In Thuringia the 'German Christian' Church authority published what it considered to be patriotic and edifying guidance for the due commemoration of the Day of Repentance. What was required was demonstration of being loyally at the Führer's side and that meant recognition that the fight against the world-wide Jewish menace had entered into its decisive stage. What the present crisis demanded was 'the unstopping of the springs of eternal truth, so that they might flow freshly for the good of the German people? The inner revival of the Christian Church within the German Volk and the promotion of the true union 'twixt Volkstum and Gospel were what mattered. 'Our generation must make practical proof of "positive Christianity". Let us strive for the renewal of the inner man with the strength of faith and in the spirit of genuine love.'

This emotional battle-cry had obviously no more in common with Evangelical repentance than had 'Down with the Jews' with genuine Christian love.[45]

A frightful example of full-blooded 'German Christian' reaction to the pogrom was the publication at the end of November by Martin Sasse, Bishop of Thuringia, of a pamphlet containing extracts from Luther's diatribes against the Jews which with monstrous unfairness gave no indication whatever of Luther's continuing desire to receive them into the Christian fold. In his preface the bishop took pleasure in the coincidence that 10 November was Luther's birthday, and in being privileged to write from Luther's town of Eisenach. He declared that the burning of the synagogues

was the crowning moment of the Führer's divinely blessed fight
for the complete emancipation of the German people. Luther,
once a friend of the Jews, had been driven by his conscience,
his experience and reality to become the greatest anti-semite
of his time. Sasse regarded it as worth while to produce the
pamphlet in English with a different preface. This time Luther
was described as 'one of the most energetic adversaries' of the
Jews who through 'increase of Christian wisdom, national and
social experience and his generally broader outlook in life' was
compelled to recognise that the Jewish race is the fundamental
and supreme enemy of Christianity. 'Only ignorance of the true
facts', he went on, 'can induce Christians to tolerate Jews. Only
absolute misapprehension as to Luther's aims and ideas can
permit Christians to take the part of and intercede for Jews. . . .
This pamphlet . . . has been disseminated into all countries to
prevent the lack of knowledge regarding the situation as it really
presents itself from developing into the instrument by the means
of which Christ may be disavowed and the honour of the Church
blemished'.[46]

In the 'German Christian' camp the Reich Movement under
Rehm counted now for comparatively little, and Rehm resigned
from his position on 14 November, 1938. His successor, Dr.
Petersmann, chose the new title of 'Luther-Germans'.[47] The
National Church Movement of 'German Christians', on the other
hand, markedly increased its influence, spreading its tentacles
throughout the greater part of Germany. The obvious reaction
of the 'German Christians' to the pogrom was to press hard for
the elimination of non-Aryans from the German Evangelical
Church. This had all along been the logical conclusion of their
advocacy of a full-blooded German Volk Church. They had
become increasingly sensitive to the formidable anti-Christian
propaganda within the Party, and desired to counter it by proof
that a protestant Christian could be as dedicated as anyone to
the Nazi Weltanschauung. Siegfried Leffler in a typically strident
speech at the Sport Palace Rally in Berlin in April 1938 had gone
so far as to declare that 'We recognise no specifically Christian
values. Being a Christian means for us nothing else than possessing
the strength to contend for the National Socialist *Weltanschauung*'.[48]

In Thuringia, headquarters of the National Church Movement,

it was announced on 30 November 1938 that it was no longer considered binding upon a pastor to minister to non-Aryans. They could remain members of the Church, but the ministrations of Baptism, Confirmation, Holy Matrimony and Burial, were no longer theirs by right. Their sole privilege was to be allowed to be present at Public Worship. A week or two later the Thuringian pastors were told that they were to carry out the duties of their office in conformity to their obligations to the State and the Volk. A pastor committed an offence, if in ministering to the Jews, he gave the impression that the Church was prepared to obstruct the segregation of the Jews from German cultural life. The baptism, marriage and burial of non-Aryans could be justifiably declined if there was a danger of them causing offence.[49]

Moritz Mitzenheim, at that time ministering in Eisenach, and after the war to become Bishop of the Evangelical Church in Thuringia, was prominent among those who resolutely declined to have any part in this outlawing of the non-Aryans. He was fiercely attacked in the 'German Christian' press as an 'incorrigible friend of the Jews'. Every decent German, it was declared, was right in having nothing more to do with the Jews living in Germany. Only one or two insisted upon thinking and acting otherwise. Such a one was the Confessional pastor Moritz Mitzenheim who in so doing forfeited his right to continue to minister to the German people and to be further subsidised by means of Church taxes. It was high time that action was taken to exclude him and any other pro-Jewish pastors from the local German Church.[50]

On 2 February 1939 a Law was published asserting that, in future, no Jew could become a member of the Thuringian Evangelical Church. No pastor was to be obliged to minister to those non-Aryans who were already members of the Church. Church premises with their equipment were no longer to be made available for such ministrations. Jews would no longer be required to pay church taxes. This naturally left the existing non-Aryan church members with a very dubious foothold, and with the onus placed upon the local pastor, particularly where the ministration of the sacraments was concerned. Four other regional churches, Saxony, Mecklenburg, Anhalt and Lübeck followed suit.[51]

The central Church authorities in Berlin realised that they would have to contemplate issuing in due course a ruling for the whole Church on this extremely ticklish matter of non-Aryan church membership, and were displeased with the action of the five 'German Christian' Churches in thus jumping the gun. It was also felt that the position of Jewish members of the Church needed altogether more clarification. Should they be encouraged to form congregations of their own? Would the State approve of additional non-Aryan groups coming into being and requiring policing? Could a workable situation be arrived at by granting Jewish Christians status within the German Evangelical Church which would allow of their spiritual needs being provided for, but which would deprive them of their formal rights of membership such as voting at church elections and holding any kind of office? But would that be disapproved of by the State as serving to give them a fixed status? In July the Reich Church Ministry pronounced it to be impracticable to make any regulations at this stage at all, and the independent 'German Christian' solution remained in force for the five churches concerned.[52]

Bishop Marahrens, with his tendency towards what can be called either compromise or comprehension, definitely rejected the 'German Christian' proposal in affirming it to be out of the question to resort to any form of exclusion from public worship and the sacraments. He, however, raised the question for discussion within the Church of Hannover as to whether there was not some solution possible either in the form of guest-status or the creation of a definite Jewish Christian community that could simultaneously do justice to a conscientious regard for the Nuremberg Legislation and the equally conscientious fulfilment of the ecclesiastical commission to care for all baptised persons.[53] As was to be expected, there was solemn and indignant rejection of the 'German Christian' proposals on the part of the Confessing Church.

Pastor Karl Kleinschmidt, Provost of the Cathedral Church in Schwerin, was so appalled at the anti-Jewish legislation that had been introduced into the 'German Christian' controlled Church of Mecklenburg, that he wrote a singularly forthright letter to Bishop Schultz. In it he challenged the bishop to give scriptural and confessional authority, if any, for what had been passed. It was, Kleinschmidt declared, an impossible situation, when pastors were being instructed to act in obvious contradiction to New Testament teaching and to their ordination vows. Had the command to 'go and baptise all nations' been excised from the New

Testament? What had happened to the Good Tidings that God excluded no one from salvation in Jesus Christ? 'How is it that you', he inquired of the Bishop, 'can desire to displace the Gospel by a Law, and one that you have thought out for yourself? Do you really rely upon the Lutheran pastors in Mecklenburg to be disobedient to the Command of Our Lord to baptise, merely because you instruct them otherwise? I tell you frankly and publicly that I will not accept this legislation of yours, nor observe it, as long as you are unable to provide justification for it in Holy Scripture and the Confessional Writings.' An attempt was made to discipline Kleinschmidt on the grounds of his disobedience to lawful authority and his transmission of his letter to all Mecklenburg pastors. His attitude to the handling of the Jewish issue was declared to be 'unworthy of a German clergyman'.[54]

A group of Confessional pastors in Anhalt, one of the churches affected, declared that the new legislation was in clear contradiction to the ordination vows that every pastor had taken, and that it destroyed the unity of the Christian Church and violated the belief of all Christendom in the Holy Spirit, the One, Holy, Catholic Church and the Communion of Saints. This plain statement evoked a rejoinder from the local 'German Christians' who professed to 'have been striving day in, day out for a German, Jew-free Church.' They accused the opposition of being Jewish partisans and lackeys rather than German pastors and ministers. They had come out of their holes. The masks had been removed. They were now known for what they really were.[55] The Conference of the Councils of Brethren issued a plain and trenchant criticism of the move to exclude the non-Aryans from the official Church, declaring that the church governments concerned were seeking to hinder those who were redeemed by Christ from receiving in their parishes the comfort of the Word and the sacraments. Their object was to make of no effect what Christ by His bitter passion had procured. Christ had fashioned Jews and Gentiles into one sacred body, they had re-erected the wall of partition which Christ had broken down, and, in doing so, had turned the Christian Church into a pharisaical sect. They had proved themselves to be the enemies of the Cross of Christ, and had excluded themselves, and not the Jews from the Christian Family.[56]

In the Evangelical Church as a whole there was increasing

hesitation in permitting the christening of Jews. The charge was more than likely to be levelled that the candidate for Holy Baptism was regarding the sacrament as a form of insurance policy, even though the Nazi attitude was that change of religion did not make a Jew any more of an Aryan.[57] Pastor Böckheler in Württemberg had agreed in October 1938 to baptise Michael Singer, a 70 year old non-Aryan, after a full period of instruction. The candidate earnestly desired to become a Christian. All the members of his family belonged to the Church. The Württemberg Church authorities, however, required the postponement of the baptism on the grounds that the present time was inopportune, while allowing that Singer should be treated as a member of the Church and should be given Holy Communion, if in *periculo mortis*. Böckheler on grounds of loyalty to Scripture and from pastoral concern was most reluctant to agree. His Parochial Church Council recommended, as a compromise, that the ceremony should be held in private, so that unnecessary provocation might be avoided. Böckheler's determination to baptise was reinforced by a conviction that among other considerations it was called for as an act of witness against the 'German Christians'. In April 1939 he declared that he could no longer put it off. The Church authorities gave way the next month, and the old man received the sacrament, and without any accompanying objection from the Nazi Party.[58]

On 4 April an assorted company of German Christians' and uncommitted neutrals issued the Godesberg Declaration.[59] Rumour, possibly mischievous, had it that this notorious statement was drawn up in the small hours of the morning after considerable alcoholic indulgence.[60] It was almost immediately afterwards accepted by eleven Church Leaders which afforded it widespread recognition. It called for good order and tolerance within the Church, based upon loyal acceptance of the Nazi Weltanschauung and disavowal of international and ecumenical versions of Christianity. On the Jewish-Christian issue it was denied that Christianity was in any sense a fulfilment of Judaism. On the contrary, the Christian Faith was to be regarded as in irreconcilable religious opposition to all that was Jewish.

The Confessional Church wasted no time in providing its answer to the Declaration, but, as Renate Heydenreich has pointed out, the chosen means which consisted in the quotation of an assortment of scriptural passages torn out of their context and void of commentary, in order to establish certain desired doctrinal conclusions was far from happy.[61] The Godesberg contention that the Christian Faith was in irreconcilable religious opposition to all that was Jewish was countered, first, by the insistence that the Church as the true Israel had inherited the promise originally made to Israel but then forfeited through disloyalty, and further by the admission that the Christian Faith was indeed irreconcilably opposed to Judaism, such Judaism being also discernible in national church aspirations. Such Judaism was declared to be representative of the effort of natural man to make his religious and moral self-justification unassailable through blending it with volkish messianic pretensions and thereby rejecting Jesus as God's Christ.[62]

The 'German Christian' leadership welcomed the Godesberg Declaration, and recommended the establishment of an institute for research into and elimination of Jewish influence upon the German people. This suggestion was implemented on 6 May when the Institute was inaugurated on the Wartburg. Its foundation was declared to be the result of the conviction that Jewish influence in all departments of German life, including the religious and ecclesiastical, had to be unmasked and smashed. *Christentum* was to be regarded as having nothing in common with *Judentum*. It was a present imperative duty and a future necessity that both Church and Christianity should be rendered immune (*entjudet*) from all that was Jewish; thus opening the way for a form of Faith, consonant with the original uncorrupted message of Christ, to be of service to the German Volk in the fashioning of its religious community. Men of academic renown and men of proved experience in practical pastoral work would be encouraged to cooperate in achieving this essential aim.[63] Siegfried Leffler accepted the position as Head of the Institute, and Walter Grundmann, principal author of the celebrated 28 Theses of the Church of Saxony, who had subsequently been awarded the Chair of New Testament and volkish Theology at Jena University, was made academic director.

There was clearly an apologetic object behind the new project which had the enthusiastic backing of Reichminister Kerrl, the aim being to present what could be claimed to be an intellectually reputable Germanised, Jewish-free version of Christianity as an acceptable accompaniment to National Socialism, and thereby to do something solid to counter the current and widespread condemnation in certain influential Nazi circles of Christianity as hopelessly Jewish in origin and character.

Grundmann in his opening address, and following the 'Stapel' line of argument, disclaimed the *heilsgeschichtlich* monopoly of the Old Testament with its exclusive line from Abraham via Moses and the Prophets to Christ. He insisted that it was the Purpose of God to prepare every people, and preeminently the German Volk, to find its own characteristic and appropriate fulfilment in Christ. He also renounced the view that the Church was the true Israel, and sought to persuade his hearers that there was no monopoly of salvation within the Church as an historical organisation. The question of the relation of Jesus to Judaism called for scholarly reappraisal, as also did the development of primitive Christianity in the light of comparative religion, the extent of the influence of Paul upon Luther and the Reformation, the effect of Jewish assimilation upon Christianity and the sinister responsibility of certain Jews for the origin and the development of Dialectical Theology and the causing of it to be in such patent contradiction to the National Socialist Weltanschauung.[64]

Pains were taken that the publications of the Institute should not all be on the highbrow side. Earnest attention was to be given as well to the provision of popular literature designed to be of assistance in the remodelling of German piety. The main project to this end was the production of a German *Volkstestament* which saw publication early in 1941[65] and claimed to be 'a Germanised translation of the Eternal Truth of God as set out in the New Testament'. It renounced all connection between the Christian New Testament and the Jewish Old Testament. One of the collaborators in this expurgated work declared that it seemed right in the new version of the Christmas narrative to exclude reference to the 'City of David', as Jesus was to be considered as having been born in Bethlehem of Galilee, not Bethlehem of Judaea. The offensive references to the validity and sanctity of the Jewish Law that appeared in the First Gospel (e.g. 5:18, 7:12—cf. Luke 6:31) obviously stemmed from Matthew the Jew and not from Jesus Himself, and were eagerly expunged. 'It was our desire to write the narrative of Jesus on the basis of the best tradition for Germany, and not, as Matthew did, for Jews and Jewish Christians.'[66]

Part I of the Testament entitled 'Jesus the Saviour' was widely distributed in an edition of over 200,000. In an article entitled 'Our Work on the New Testament'[67] Walter Grundmann described how both the Christmas and the Easter narratives had been trimmed. As far as the former was concerned, the legend of the birth of John the Baptist in Luke was omitted, since it was obviously copied from an Old Testament prototype. Matthew 1:18–25, was rejected as an apologetic legend. There was no place to be found in a German Testament for the Massacre of the Innocents or the Flight into Egypt. The account of the birth of Christ in Luke 2, the visit of the Magi, the appearance of the boy Jesus in the Temple, the Nunc Dimittis and the Benedictus were all retained on the grounds that they were treasured elements of German Volk lore and German art and despite their Jewish background characteristically Christian. All the same, the birth of Jesus in Bethlehem was of 'secondary importance', since He was to be considered to be a Galilean. As far as the Easter narrative was concerned, only the Galilean tradition came into consideration, as set out in John 21 and Matthew 28, 16 ff., in contrast to the Jerusalem tradition as recorded, for instance, in Luke 24 which was to be accounted as a product of typical Jewish Christian dogmatics.

A new Hymn Book, with the title of 'Great God, we praise Thee' was produced in June 1941. Offensive Hebraisms such as Zion, Hosanna and Hallelujah were dispensed with, and expressions of falsely ascetic and world-renouncing piety, so marked a feature of existing hymn books, were rejected. In addition, in the pipe-line were a popular devotional manual to help in countering 'the poisonous growth of Jewish irreligiosity',[68] a Christian Catechism for the German people to be entitled 'Germans with God' which was coloured by the conviction that 'eternal Divine Truth cannot be allowed to be held captive in tightly formulated doctrines and confessions', and included the insistence that Germans were to be in no wise subject to the Ten Commandments of Moses.[69]

The reports of the work of the Institute published between 1939 and 1941 reveal a hankering after award of the accolade of distinguished spiritual service to the overall war effort.

In 1940 Grundmann ended the report of his stewardship with the avowal that 'our work has all in all one sole purpose, that of service in the renewal of German piety within the victorious Führer's Greater German Reich'.[70] At the close of 1941 he described the work of the Institute as being of assistance in the forging of the weapons for the great spiritual battle which had to accompany the fight with material weapons, thus contributing to the total victory of the Reich over Judah. Such service as the Institute offered to the German soul was vital, if victories won on the physical field of battle were not to be ultimately lost.[71]

Heinz Dungs, a fanatical contributor, wrote in similar vein, emphasising that in the removal of Jewish influence from the whole of religious life lay the immense present task of German theology and of the German Church; a decisive neo-Reformation, in fact, that would be of immediate significance in the war-situation. At a time when English bishops were providing religious camouflage for the monstrous Jewish-inspired confederacy between Anglo-American plutocracy and the bolshevik forces of disintegration, the clear understanding of the true relation of Christianity to *Judentum* had to be regarded as the key to the solution of the whole religious issue.[72]

Another collaborator, Wolf Meyer-Erlach, Professor of Pastoral Theology at Jena University, showed great zest in providing vulgar anti-British propaganda. His booklet *Ist Gott Engländer?* was calculated to delight Dr. Goebbels. His lecture given at the first conference of the Institute on the theme of Jewish influence upon English Christianity was subsequently published as a tract for the times, and 30,000 copies were sold.[73] He set out to demonstrate that the arch-enemy England was thoroughly perverted by Jewish influences, and that there was a long and sinister history to this phenomenon. A contrast was invited between the England of the thirteenth century when Edward the First, supported by nobility and clergy, was in the sight of God defender and leader of his people against the Jews, and the English Church was propagating anti-semitism, and contemporary England, in which the English aristocracy, corrupt in both spirit and blood, were the vassals of the Jews, and in which those who preached Christ, and in particular the Church of England bishops, constituted a Jewish colony, concerning themselves far more about

the welfare of Jewish immigrants than about the poor of their
own people.

The Reformation in England was to be characterised as fateful
not only for England but for the whole western world also.
Henry the Eighth emancipated himself, his people, and his
church from Rome, in order to give free course to the beast in
man, and English Christianity was refashioned according to
political and national considerations. This was in glaring contrast
to the Reformation in Germany, in which Luther wrestled to
set the German free to serve God and his own people in kingly
liberty. Luther was converted from being a friend of the Jews to
being the greatest anti-semite of the whole western world and
becoming protector and guardian of the Christian West against
the murderers of Christ, the bloodsuckers and the usurers,
against the Jews who for 1,400 years had been, and still were, 'our
plague and pestilence and source of all misfortune'.

It was, in Meyer-Erlach's judgement, Oliver Cromwell who was
the real villain of the piece. He and his fellow-Puritans had no
regard whatever for Luther's conflict with the Old Testament or
for his warnings about the Jews. For Cromwell and those who
followed him God was Jehovah, the God of the Old Testament.
Their faith was similar to that of the Jews before Christ, their
ethics simply those of Judaism imbued with Jewish messianic
fervour. The Old Testament was interpreted not as preparation for the Coming of Christ but as vindication of England's
national aspirations. The God of Israel and not the God of
Jesus was, in point of fact, their God. The English were the
Chosen People, England was the Holy Land. Thus it came about
that for Englishmen God's cause and the cause of their own
people were completely one and the same. In the years that
followed, England's expeditions of plunder across the oceans of
the world and into all parts of the earth had the object of increasing
England's mighty empire. Such characteristically Jewish fanaticism permeated the whole of English Christianity, ministered to
the feelings of superiority, intolerance and infallibility, and provided sanction for interference in the affairs of all other peoples.
Every war waged by England was a holy war. English Christianity
and English nationalism were so welded together that to the
devout they were one and the same. The people became Jewish
(*verjudet*) in body, soul and mind, with English Christianity the

extended arm of Judaism, and put forward the claim to be the lost tribe of Israel; the Royal Family were regarded as directly descended from King David. The stone within the Coronation Chair in Westminster Abbey was widely believed to be that upon which Jacob once laid his head and dreamed the dream of promise. The Germans proved themselves right in unmasking the World Church Conference at Oxford in 1937 as the attempt of England, via the English Church and hypnotised World Protestantism, to isolate Germany morally. Without any doubt behind the English bishops and English imperialism stood World Jewry inspiring the resolutions that were passed against anti-semitism. Only those who were deaf and blind to the fact that, despite the large measure of doctrinal and confessional freedom, English protestantism was inflexibly intolerant in proclaiming the divinely willed domination of England over all other peoples, could deem it possible to cooperate in freedom and friendship with the English Church. Tearing off the mask of Christianity assumed by those English statesmen who proudly rode the moral high horse, supported by their faithful lapdogs, the archbishops and bishops, one would discover England eaten up by Judaism giving lip service to Love, Religion, Humanity and Civilisation, and not being able to mention Christ often enough, but with hands dripping with blood and murder deep down within the heart.

While Meyer-Erlach made his undoubted contribution to the psychological conduct of the war, a surprisingly large number of eminent theologians who were not to be regarded as extreme 'German Christians' proved willing to associate themselves with the work of the Institute, and some of them furnished solid and serious academic studies on various aspects of the relationship of Christianity to Judaism, in the course of which they made concessions to Nazi racial doctrines. The Nazi party certainly proved only too ready to make capital out of such respectable contributions at the time when the 'Final Solution' was being plotted.[74]

It appears to have been Reichminister Kerrl's quite sincere belief that National Socialism would collapse if it were not fortified by the Christian Religion.[75] He also considered that he would be doing a great service to the Evangelical Church, if he could succeed in integrating it into the Nazi system. In his spare time he liked to busy himself with religious literature, and he had started writing a book on Religion and the State. Like many another semi-intellectual his little learning was a dangerous thing,[76] and he became convinced that he knew better than others, and had grown to fancy himself as an amateur theologian. Realising that the other Church Leaders would certainly not be prepared to accept the Godesberg Declaration, he produced in May 1939 his own milder version. This is what he had to say about Christianity and Judaism: 'The Nazi Welt-anschauung is completely and relentlessly opposed to the political and spiritual influence of the Jewish race upon our volkish life. In obedience to the Divine Creative Ordinances the Evangelical Church affirms the responsibility for the preservation of the purity of our Volkstum. Consequently in the sphere of faith there can be no sharper contradiction than that between the message of Jesus Christ and the Jewish religion of legalism and of political messianic aspiration.'[77]

Kerrl proceeded to try out his vaunted words of wisdom on the Church Leaders' Conference which included Bishops Marahrens, Meiser and Wurm. The Conference, in its turn, produced a version which was very far removed indeed from the Godesberg original.[78] It omitted Kerrl's references to the Nazi Weltanschauung, the Jewish Race and the Creative Ordinances, and, while agreeing that there was indeed a contradiction between the Gospel and the Jewish religion, legalism and political messianism, insisted that there was to be found already in the Old Testament emphatic resistance to such expressions of religion. The importance of the preservation of the purity of the Volkstum was owned, but it was not made out to be the responsibility of the Evangelical Church but of those engaged in racial politics. One of Kerrl's main objectives was to re-establish a measure of peace within the Evangelical Church with the limitation of knowing that it was out of the question that the radical Confessing Church would cooperate. Bishop Marahrens, to the delight of Kerrl and the consternation of his fellow-bishops and of the Dahlemites, accepted the former's theses as a means towards the promotion of an honourable and fruitful collaboration between Church and State, and, on the understanding that the Church would have complete freedom in its preaching, its administration of the sacraments and in Church Order.[79]

The Confessional Synod of the Prussian Church meeting in

Berlin in May concerned itself directly with the Godesberg Declaration, and had no hesitation in proclaiming that those who were identified with this latest move had renounced the one true foundation of the Christian Church and had also put themselves outside of its fellowship. 'We are not prepared', it was stated, 'to surrender our Church to an alien faith. We are determined to go on with the fight to make of it, in its whole structure, the Church of Jesus Christ.'[80] The Conference of the Council of the Brethren took issue with the Declaration point by point. In countering the assertion that the Christian Faith was 'the irreconcilable religious opposition to Jewry', quotations were given from the New Testament including the last verses of Galatians chapter 3, 'If ye be Christ's, then are ye Abraham's seed and heirs according to the promise.' 'It has pleased God', the statement went on, 'to make Israel the bearer and agent of the divine revelation, and the disloyalty of the Jews in not responding to this has not cancelled the divine appointment. The Church as the true Israel is heir to the promise which has been given to the people of Israel. It is true to say that the Christian Faith stands in irreconcilable religious opposition to Judaism. But such Judaism is to be found not only in Jewry but every bit as much in all national church endeavours; it is nothing other than the effort of natural man to make his religious and his moral self-justifications unassailable by amalgamating them with volkish consciousness of being of the Elect, and so being able to reject Jesus as God's Christ.'[81]

Ecumenical support for such opposition came from the standing committee of the World Council of Churches in a message to the Christian Churches which affirmed that the Gospel of Jesus Christ was the fulfilment of Jewish hope. The Christian Church had an obligation to preach to the Jewish people the fulfilment of the promises that had been given them, and had joy in maintaining followship with those of the Jewish race who accepted the Gospel.[82]

The Godesberg Declaration had the effect of bringing the Aryan Clause right to the fore again. Dr. Friedrich Werner in his capacity as managing director of the official German Evangelical Church issued on 12 May 1939 a ruling which had the following wording: 'We regard it as necessary that every theological student before admission as candidate in a theological examination for ordination or for permanent appointment to minister in the Church shall produce proof of his Aryan descent and in the case of marriage of similar evidence for his wife.'[83] This was followed immediately by a further insistence that the current State legislation restricting the eligibility of non-Aryans for office was to be applied to the Church, and that consequently second-degree cross-breeds descending from one fully Jewish grandparent could not be permitted to remain in the ministry.[84] Heinz Weidemann, 'German Christian' Bishop of Bremen, lost no time in taking action and demanding evidence of Aryan purity from all his pastors[85]—a signal that practical steps would be taken to make the Evangelical clergy once and for all and everywhere entirely 'Jew-free'. The Confessing Church in Prussia was equally prompt in making its attitude known, and stated that 'anyone filling in the questionnaire proposed by the 'German Christian' Church bureaucracy, or in any other way responding to it, will be assisting in realising the Godesberg Declaration, and will bear responsibility for the exclusion from the ministry of colleagues of incomplete Aryan descent or married to a non-Aryan wife'.[86] It was not long before certain pastors were officially told that they were to be sacked. Max Weber who had a parish in Hesse was, for instance, communicated with in icy cold fashion, and told that on account of his Jewish grandparent his appointment was terminated, and that he was given to the end of the month to quit his cure of souls. The difficulties caused in his parish by his impure descent had been taken specially into account.[87]

There was in confessional circles much discussion and heart-searching as to whether a flat refusal to obey official instructions was really necessary (after all the numbers of those adversely affected were not very great!), and, if so, whether the opposition was to be primarily grounded on regard for the sanctity of ordination or on concern for the fate of threatened fellow-ministers. The question was also raised as to whether those who did fill in their forms were to be regarded as having committed a heinous sin against the brotherhood, and were to be reckoned to have thereby excluded themselves from its fellowship. In February 1940, when representations were made anew to those who had not furnished the required information, Heinrich Grüber, after suggesting that the Church had more important things to do in wartime than to subject to defamation those who, it was the clear will of the State authorities, should continue their work without further distraction, gave answer: 'From love for the brethren who are affected and from responsibility for the Evangelical Church of Germany I am unable to fill in the questionnaire, and I urge all the brethren who consult me on the issue, likewise to refuse.'[88]

We have been considering something of what was said or resolved regarding the non-Aryan Christians and their place in the Church. We must now ask what was done to help them. Generally speaking, they did not receive very much assistance from the Jews themselves who had from the beginning possessed their own officially recognised Reich Association and had the support of a world-wide Jewish community. They were quite often despised and rejected. They had embraced the Christian religion, and it was, therefore, the responsibility of the Church to look after them. Roman Catholic non-Aryans had distinct advantages over their Protestant opposite numbers. Within the Catholic Church there was no equivalent to the 'German Christians'. Their charitable and welfare organisations were numerous and well organised. International contacts and links were abundant. It would not be untrue to say that the plight of the Evangelical non-Aryans was probably the most pathetic and uncertain of all. The Evangelical Church, with certain honourable exceptions including the *Innere Mission*, Superintendent Albertz and Marga Meusel, was apt to neglect them.

It took a little time for those who were baptised to realise that they were not going to escape the disabilities and persecution that were the fate of the Jewish community, but they soon realised that, in the Nazi reckoning, blood and descent and not religion was what counted, and the fact that they were Christians was not regarded as making them any the less Jewish. The Christian Church outside Germany was very slow in appreciating this, and in thus showing real concern and a warm desire to be of practical help. It has been reckoned that at least 30 per cent of those affected by the Nuremberg regulations did not belong to the Synagogue. In 1937 the Reich Association of non-Aryans was renamed the *Paulusbund* (Association of St. Paul).[89] It was not, however, an influential or effective organisation, and proved incapable of facilitating emigration. In January 1937 Bishop Bell headed an ecumenical delegation that visited Berlin, and made contact with leaders of the Confessing Church and representatives of the *Paulusbund*.[90] As a result the bishop's sister-in-law, Miss Laura Livingstone, volunteered to go and do liaison work in Berlin, with the aim of helping some of the sorely pressed, and particularly children and young people, to escape. Miss Livingstone was treated with surprising courtesy by a high representative of the Gestapo, and a small office was set up with three or four workers including Dr. Spiro of the *Paulusbund*, but, as Miss Livingstone had to admit, there was really very little chance of being able to arrange for the emigration of adults.[91] Still it meant a lot to many in trouble to know that interest was being taken in their problems.

That the Church did at last really wholeheartedly espouse the cause of the non-Aryan Christians and manage to give them the most practical kind of assistance was due to the initiative and determination of one man—Heinrich Grüber.[92] Grüber had in the early years of his ministry been pastor of a working class parish and had also engaged in specialised activities among juvenile delinquents and the unemployed. In 1934 he became pastor of the parish of Kaulsdorf in East Berlin. He also looked after the Dutch protestant congregation in Berlin, and, being known to possess close contacts with the Dutch Embassy and the Church in Holland, he had frequently been approached by those who were seeking means to emigrate. In 1936, as the extent and the pressure of the Nuremberg measures began to be realised, Grüber felt that there was urgent need for some organisation to render advice and help. There was obviously no prospect whatever of the official Evangelical Church providing any such service. There would also have been grave difficulties in the way of the Confessing Church, stretched to the very limit, and contending for her own existence taking on so perilous and exacting an extra commitment that could have political implications and that would certainly call for delicate international negotiations. Besides which, prompt action was called for that would not be subject to the deliberations and findings of synod, council or committee. Grüber, therefore, called together five of his friends, who, he knew, had the welfare of the non-Aryan Christians very much at heart. He won their agreement to a plan to establish an Evangelical welfare office for their benefit. The appointment of a full-time director was visualised, but the right man was difficult to find. So Grüber agreed to take charge for the time being without relinquishing his other duties: a position which he was to occupy until his arrest in 1940.[93]

An office was established in Berlin, in Oranienburgerstrasse 20, the premises of the recently banned British Society of Hebrew Christian Testimony to Israel being made available. After the pogrom of November 1938 the urgent need for help was manifoldly increased. As Oranienburgerstrasse 20 was too cramped, larger premises were rented as an act of faith in the shape of an ancient patrician mansion, on the Stechbahn, not far from Berlin Schloss that would provide accommodation for a staff of thirty-five.[94] The new organisation did not gain official recognition from the Nazi authorities, but it was tolerated. The first communication from the Gestapo was addressed to Büro Pfarrer Grüber, and this became, and remained, its name. And how appropriate an advertisement that here the unhappy victims of a devilishly impersonal maltreatment could be assured of receiving compassionate, personal service! The main activities in 1937 and 1938 were the planning of emigration for individuals and families and the giving of such assistance as was possible to those who had lost their jobs. After 1938 the work increased a hundredfold, and the premises were besieged by a ceaseless stream of bewildered and terrified victims of the Nazi savagery. A tribute to the work, from Geneva, states that many who could not be helped materially yet left the office cheered and comforted, because they had experienced real brotherliness.[95] Such brotherly feeling was further encouraged by the fact that nearly all those who assisted Heinrich Grüber were themselves victims of the Nazi persecution, and set a great example by their readiness to help actively in serving the needs of their distressed fellow-men and -women instead of waiting passively and miserably for the sword of Damocles to descend upon them. Grüber, himself by nature a cheerful Rhinelander, saw to it that there was laughter mingled with the tears.

Close liaison was established with the representative Jewish organisations and the office was never conceived of as for Christians only. Later on, when the Jewish Association was severely hampered in its approach to the State officials, Grüber and his team were prepared to act on behalf of the Jews as a whole. Determined efforts were made to secure some easing and relaxation of certain of the new measures including the stringent food-rationing. A notable achievement was the obtaining in 1940 of necessary ingredients for the proper observation of the Passover Meal.

Emigration became top-line priority after 'Crystal Night', when the Nazi policy was to get as many Jews as possible out of the country, and the Gestapo proved willing to release immediately from concentration camps those non-Aryans who were provided with visas for entry into another country. The spreading of this news abroad did stir the Christian world into action, with Bishop Bell, as to be expected, right to the fore, but, in Grüber's judgement, the Churches could have given considerably more help than they did, and could have been instrumental in saving the lives of many who perished later in the gas chambers. There was, tragically, not the measure of ecumenical solidarity which was so evident after the war in dealing with the refugee problem.[96] Maria Zelzer has described the difficulties of the situation. On the one hand, a demand was made that emigration should be speeded up. On the other hand, almost insurmountable obstacles frequently lay in the way of effecting such emigration. Though in theory there were many possibilities open, in practice most countries were largely sealed off by the prevailing regulations governing immigration.[97]

The move having been made early in 1939 into more spacious premises, it was now possible to cope with a daily average of around fifty callers. The Grüber Office became welfare service, consulate, legal aid bureau, school headquarters, health department, clothing store and spiritual power-house all rolled into one. Branch offices were established in as many provincial centres as possible. A substantial sum of money was required to make expansion possible and to allow some material help to be given where there was really desperate need. Grüber, like certain other Christian workers before him, was convinced that, if the work was in accordance with the Divine Will, the Lord would provide. Such faith proved to be justified. Despite all his other activities, including the care of his own parish, he managed to find time somehow to enter into detailed discussion about the possibility of large-scale emigration to such places as Abyssinia, Australia, New Zealand, the Philippines and Brazil, and to visit certain other European countries.

The outbreak of the war severely curtailed, even though it did not altogether prevent, emigration. But it vastly increased the desperate need to provide whatever assistance was still possible to those who had no chance at all of quitting Germany. Grüber in his memoirs reveals the difficulty that he had in persuading Church leaders who were concerned with so many other matters, of the prime urgency of his work. Having spoken at perhaps too great length at a conference of Lutheran Bishops, he was greeted, not with definite offers of support, with a proposition that the meeting should move on to the next point on the agenda. The chairman, Bishop Wurm, led him to the door, saying, 'I thank you in the name of the brethren, and pray for God's Blessing upon you and your work.' He describes this as quite one of the greatest disappointments of his life.[98]

Grüber records that he had remarkable success in Government departments, in nearly all of which he had at least one sympathetic and helpful contact, one of the most surprising of which was Herr vom Rath, father of the murdered Paris diplomat, who was a devout practising churchman with a truly Christian attitude to the tragic death of his son. He worked in the Jewish department of the Gestapo, posted there presumably with crafty intent, but to be dismissed later on as unreliable. With vom Rath's aid the illegitimate children of Jewesses were helpfully classified as cross-breeds on the curious ground that the fathers concerned must have been Aryans, as Jews would not seduce Jewesses but only Aryans!

Grüber provides a vivid description of one of several abortive approaches to the frigid and heartless Adolf Eichmann. Eichmann asked him why he was so active on behalf of the Jews, seeing that he had no Jewish relatives, and did not require to take their part. He would get no thanks for it. It was hard to understand why he was doing it. Grüber's reply was a reminder of what once took place on the road from Jerusalem to Jericho. 'On this road there lay one who had been pounced upon and plundered. A man alien to him by race and religion, a Samaritan, came and helped him. To us all has the summons been given, "Go thou and do likewise".' Eichmann, so Grüber declared, was obviously taken aback for the moment, but then paid him a curt farewell.[99]

A further notable service was provided by the founding and equipping of a school in Berlin for Christian non-Aryan children who were no longer permitted to attend German Schools and who would not fit in very well in a special Jewish school.[100] Grüber with characteristic generosity used precious family capital to finance this establishment.

Early in 1940 there were ominous signs of still more brutal measures being planned, and emigrations became very hard to arrange. It was rumoured in Berlin that barracks were about to be erected outside the city, and that the local Jews were going to be placed in a ghetto. Many of them made contact with the Büro, to ask if anything could be done, to which Grüber replied, 'I don't know what is to be done, but one thing I promise you. If you have to go into the ghetto, I shall accompany you.'[101] The first batch of Jews was transported to Poland, being treated more like cattle than human beings. Grüber as usual went fearlessly and vigorously to work, and sought to carry to the very top his protest at this turn in events and at the inhuman way in which the victims were being handled. He found his way into the Reich Chancery, and made indirect contact with Göring. This resulted in a rebuke from the Gestapo that he was in unwarrantable fashion attempting to interfere with measures taken by the Party and the Government, and that it was a final warning. Next time an end would be put to his activities. To this he replied, 'As long as I can speak, I will speak, and as long as I can work, I shall work'.[102] On hearing of the desperate plight of some 75,000 Jews from Baden, the Pfalz and the Saar who had been placed in internment in the concentration camp of Gurs at the foot of the Pyrenees, and not forgetting the undertaking that he had made a short while ago, he sought to make his way there, to give them such support and encouragement as would be possible. Instead he was arrested, and placed in Sachsenhausen concentration camp, to be transferred later to Dachau. While in such confinement, he was at least once on the verge of liquidation, but after a heart attack in Dachau and thanks to the persistent efforts of his wife, he was released in June 1943, soon to resume his parish work, make perilous liaison with the Resistance Movement, and to stir the faint and struggling local Confessional leaders into fresh activity and prepare for what might come in the future. He was, most typically, distressed to find that the Berlin Council of Brethren spent most of the time at their meetings discussing doctrinal issues rather than in making concrete plans for the future.[103]

Heinrich Grüber's second in command, Werner Sylten, sought to keep the work going. This he managed to do for another couple of months, but was then removed to Dachau, and the Office was finally closed. After his ordination Werner Sylten had worked for some years in a couple of Church institutions for girls, but, being of partial non-Aryan descent, he was obliged in 1934 to give up this activity. Having lost his first wife, he was desirous of getting married again, partly for the sake of his children. But, as his intended bride was a pure Aryan, the marriage was forbidden. After some period in the service of the Confessing Church he was invited by Grüber in 1938 to join the Office team, and was entrusted with the pastoral side of the work, for which, considering the troubles that he had himself been through, he was peculiarly well suited. The cruelties and privations of the concentration camp undermined his health, and in August 1942, as one of a batch of men who were no longer reckoned to be capable of work, he was placed on the death transport.[104]

After the Office had been shut down other of Heinrich Grüber's former colleagues sought to continue the work in clandestine fashion. As devout Christians they had to deceive the authorities, smother their consciences and learn the ugly techniques of trickery, lies and forgery, and be prepared to keep company with criminals and conspire with corruptible elements within the Gestapo. Few of them escaped with their lives. Two of those who did, Helene Jacobs and Gertrud Staewen, have described their experiences. The former confesses that 'on innumerable occasions, in which we were too scared to take action, we were guilty of letting down our brethren, in that we left them alone in their distress, and of failing our whole people in that we withheld from them the witness to the Love of God', but proceeds to relate how they found courage not only to run immense risks on behalf of the afflicted, but also, by putting out of mind the bourgeois standards of what was right and legal, to enter boldly into direct communication with the criminal world as the only and desperate means of discharging their responsibility before God. Gertrud Staewen declared that it was almost too obvious to need mentioning that 'we of course did not merely concern ourselves about the wearers of the Star whom we saw sitting in the church pew—the last real home that was left to them. The least of these (the most in need) of Christ's brethren was for us every person of Jewish extraction, whether Christian or Jew'. Most moving is her account of her farewell visit to a Jewish lady doctor, Lucie Adelsberger who was on the deportation list after having tirelessly and to the very end dedicated herself to her profession. Gertrud Staewer confesses that on this occasion she was so overcome by shame and despair that she broke into a loud and wild hymn of hate at the expense of the Nazi tormentors. The frail little lady doctor embraced her, and said, 'You must not treat me like that, so that the last that I see and hear from a real German is nothing but hate. Through you I want to preserve my belief that not destructive hatred but love has the last word.' This gallant lady was one of the few who miraculously survived Auschwitz.[105]

It would be wrong to give the impression that it was principally in Berlin that succour was given to the Evangelical non-Aryans A list provided in September 1939 by Pfarrer Grüber of other agencies throughout Germany linked with his office shows that in at least twenty other cities organised help and relief was available. One or two of these agencies were able to continue at work long after the Grüber Office had been shut down.[106] A report is available of what was attempted in Bavaria. During the period from 1933 to 1938 the *Innere Mission* recognised it as one of its responsibilities to care for the non-Aryans, though it was realised that this might well embarrass or endanger other activities of the mission. At the end of 1938 the need was recognised to be so great that it was felt that the responsibility should be accepted officially by the Bavarian Church. Bishop Meiser appointed two pastors for the purpose, one to function in Munich, the other in Nuremberg. The whole cost was to be met out of church funds. A number of emigrations were arranged, work was, when possible, found for the unemployed, those not capable of looking after themselves were aided in finding accommodation in some institution or other, the sick were regularly visited and individuals were deterred from suicide. Only a fraction of the distress could be countered, but evidence was given that the Church cared and wanted to help. The work was able to be continued in some measure to the very end, and here and there lives were saved.[107] Numerous were the efforts of individual pastors and layfolk who went out of their way, not counting the risk, to befriend, and do what they could for, their non-Aryan fellow-Christians. Honourable mention, among these, must be made of Pastor Adolf Kurtz

of the Church of the Apostles in Berlin. He had a congregation
of up to a thousand, a quarter of which consisted of non-
Aryans. The SS mockingly referred to his church as the 'Synagogue in Nollendorfplatz'. He held open house in his vicarage
to Jews, both baptised and unbaptised. Thanks to his widespread
ecumenical contacts he was able to help hundreds to safety. He
founded in 1939 a school in part of the vicarage. In Holy Week
1942 he defied the Nazi regulations by admitting about forty
Jews who were wearing the Star of David to Holy Communion.
On being invited by the Bishop of Chichester to move to England,
he declined, having no doubt where his first duty lay.[108]

Friedrich von Rabenau, pastor of St. Paul's Church, Schöne-
berg, in Berlin, was another who went out of his way to make
non-Aryans welcome at his church and particularly at the Holy
Communion. He had a special handshake for them at the door,
and was prepared to accompany nervous or lonely Jewish Christians on their way back home after the service. In his Bible
Study Group training was given to those who might have an
opportunity subsequently to perform religious ministrations to
fellow-deportees. In 1942 a Jewish Christian widow destitute
and in desperation turned to him for help, and was greeted
with the comforting words—'You have not yet really experienced
what it can mean to belong to a congregation. We shall all of us
be behind you.' She indeed found herself admitted into a fellowship of loving help.[109]

In the Gossner House in Berlin, a lively centre of Confessing
witness and mission, one war-time Sunday at the close of the
Morning Service a mass baptism of Jewish families took place
involving about sixty individuals, from infants to the aged—a
patent act of genuine faith, since by this time admission into the
Christian Church offered no direct prospect of escape from the
fate reserved for the 'racially damned'.[110]

Another gallant Christian was Franz Kaufmann, a non-Aryan
who enjoyed 'privileged' status through being married to an
Aryan. He had occupied a high position in the Civil Service,
until the Nazi legislation put an end to his career. He had a good
chance of surviving, and the temptation must have been great
to live quietly, cautiously and correctly in retirement, devoting
himself to academic pursuits, but his conscience and his Christian
convictions did not permit him to go on living, 'as if nothing had

happened'. The Christian way was meant to be one of self-sacrifice and not of attempted self-preservation. What did fellowship in faith signify, if it did not include sharing in the perils of the persecuted? He therefore resolved henceforth to do all that lay in his power to befriend the Jewish victims, and inspired certain of his fellow-members of Martin Niemöller's former congregation at Berlin-Dahlem to the same resolve. There was scarcely a government ministry that he did not contact in a vain effort to secure a veto on the deportations. He left no stone unturned to attain the exclusion of as many individuals as possible, stoutly arguing that Jewish labour had an important contribution to make to the war effort and seeking to persuade foreign diplomats to take individual non-Aryans under their wing and employ them in domestic service or office duties, and endeavouring to achieve the postponement or cancellation of deportation orders on medical grounds, and even by being prepared to enter into murky secret deals with the Gestapo, if lives could thereby be preserved. At the greatest risk to his own safety he established contact with those whom he knew to be on the run from the Gestapo, gave them desperately needed encouragement, when they were at the end of their resources, and took, whenever possible, ingenious practical steps to organise their continued secret and illegal existence to the extent of unsavoury dealings with the underworld, in order to obtain forged documents and stolen ration-cards. He could have had no doubt that the day of reckoning would come, but for two years he amazingly avoided arrest, finally to be taken into custody, and then without trial or sentence removed to Sachsenhausen concentration camp to be shot.[111]

To give one or two other examples: Dorothea Schulze who worked in the Johannesstift, an institution run by the *Innere Mission* in Berlin-Spandau, surrendered her own identity papers to a Jewish nurse, in order to help her to escape.[112] Herta Dietz, assistant at St. Barbara's Church, Breslau, contrived during the war to spend half of her ministry in pastoral visitation of Christian non-Aryans throughout the city, and in Red Cross sister's uniform managed to smuggle some of them out of the city disguised as patients.[113] Pastor Hermann Maas, of Heidelberg, close associate of Heinrich Grüber, who was outstanding in the way that he made no distinction between baptised and unbaptised, made a point of ostentatiously moving about among the victims of 'Crystal Night' and cheerfully risked arrest and possible death, in order to be able to say a last farewell and words of comfort to his old Jewish friends in full view of the SS guards.[114] This outstanding Christian was carrying out in practice what he had stated in August 1935, when he addressed a gathering of the World Association for Friendship among the Churches on the problem of the Christian non-Aryans, the Protestant total of whom he estimated then at well over a million:

> Let us acknowledge the authority of the Scriptural word— 'The Love of Christ constrains us'. This love of Christ is a real love. We are to love the other person not in spite of him being so and so, but because he is so and so, and must identify ourselves completely with him as a disciple of Christ in his need and in his guilt, owning that it touches us, and we have a share in the blame. Our first concern is, therefore, not that person's guilt but his need.

Paying tribute to the generous support given from Jewish sources to the Jewish non-Aryans, he inquired whether it was impossible for the Christian Church to be equally helpful to her non-Aryan members. 'Have we any right, when God challenges us, to reply with our craven "Impossible"? We have a great God and a faithful Saviour; so nothing is impossible.'[115]

In Essen by as late as 1944 between fifty and sixty inhabitants of Jewish extraction had somehow or other contrived to survive deportation by taking refuge in the cellars of certain bombed houses. Had it not been for the practical assistance of the local Confessing Christian community they would have been in dire peril of starvation. Superintendent Johannes Böttcher undertook the clandestine supply of essential foodstuffs, appealing to members of the local church to forgo a portion of their all too meagre rations for re-distribution to their Jewish neighbours, most of whom, helped by such generosity, succeeded in surviving the downfall of the Third Reich.[116]

In Württemberg quite remarkable enterprise and daring was shown in assisting the persecuted Jews from Berlin who were on the run to escape deportation and death and who had managed somehow to escape to the south. They were befriended and assisted

by a chain of devoted and fearless benefactors. First passed of
as refugee air-raid victims, they were then, if possible, assisted
to cross the near-by border into Switzerland. Stuttgart had been
for some time a centre of help to the persecuted, thanks, above
all, to the championship of Hans Walz, a convinced Christian
who was president of the very powerful Robert Bosch industrial
concern. He persisted in employing Jews and in accepting young
non-Aryan apprentices, and arranged for the firm to make large
sums available to alleviate Jewish distress. It is indeed remarkable
that he managed to escape being brought to book by the Nazis.
Kurt Müller, Pastor of the Reformed Church in Stuttgart, was
the leader of the Württemberg rescue brigade, outstanding
members of which were Pastors Hermann Diem of Ebersbach
and Richard Golz of Wankheim. The latter on welcoming into
his temporary care a Christian Jewess on the run from Berlin remarked, 'Next Sunday we must sing a Te Deum in church
because we have the honour of having as our guest a daughter
of the House of Israel.'[117] He was eventually arrested, and put into
a concentration camp in 1944 for sheltering Jews.

Kurt Müller's widow has testified that the members of her
husband's congregation assisted in the enterprise. 'The whole
congregation knew what was going on, and my husband once
remarked that the gifts of gold, frankincense and myrrh for Jesus
were repeated in the shape of ration cards for Jews in hiding.'[118]

Max Krakauer published in 1947 a vivid and deeply moving
account of how he and his wife survived for over two years after
having been listed for deportation.[119] For the first few months
they were hidden and sheltered in Berlin and Pomerania by
members of the Confessing Church, and had many hairbreadth
escapes in the process. They could no longer hope to evade
detection in the north, and were encouraged to make their way,
though not in possession of identity cards, to Stuttgart. Arriving
there on 7 August 1943, and only just avoiding immediate apprehension at the railway station, they were made welcome by the
local rescue team, and were quite miraculously preserved from
arrest and consequent deportation, till handed over safely to the
Americans on 23 April 1945. The American officer in charge was
at first unable to credit the fantastic story.

During this long period they were accepted as guests on no
less than forty-three different occasions. A large number of

places where they stayed were vicarages. For safety's sake they remained not longer than three weeks in any one place, and in the last stages they had to be prepared to move on elsewhere almost every other day. They were passed off as Aryan refugees from stricken Berlin, and their various hosts were not in ignorance of what their own fate was likely to be, if the authorities uncovered the Jewish identity of their guests.

The Krakauers were Jewish by religion, and in all their wanderings in Württemberg they had only one experience of being refused Christian asylum because they had not become converted to Christianity. Nobody else dropped even the slightest hint that this was expected of them. It could be regarded as proof that the sole motive for helping them was that they were in need and persecuted.[120]

On arrival at one vicarage in the suburbs of Stuttgart they were embarrassed by finding that the household consisted only of the pastor and his wife already existing upon wholly inadequate rations. They were, however, put at once at their ease by the words of welcome that they received—'We are grateful for this opportunity of being able to give practical demonstration of how much we deplore so many of the measures that are being adopted at this present time and which we are powerless to prevent. We are especially distressed at what is being perpetrated upon you and others like you. Here in our house you must relax and take advantage of a rest-cure.'[121]

Max Krakauer provides a memorable account of the Stöffler household in the Vicarage at Nöngen:[122] the tubby little pastor with his made-up white tie and his everlasting cigarette whose serenity nothing could shake, certainly not the prospect of ending up in a concentration camp for repeatedly sheltering Jews; his wife suffering from a weak heart but never out of sorts and increasing in kindness the more calls that were made upon her motherly care; the daughters and the 16-year-old son who served to restore faith in the youth of the day, proving that perpetual Nazi indoctrination at school had not torn from their souls the command 'Love thy neighbour as thyself'. On three separate occasions their hospitality was experienced, and once it was not possible to give prior notice of arrival, but the reception, nevertheless, suggested that they had been patiently waiting for another visit.

Beata Steckhan, another of those who owed her life to these same 'Good Samaritans', has paid this warm tribute—'What they did will remain remembered for ever; it needs to be given publicity, in order that others may know the full extent of the courage and the greatness revealed by German men and women in order that by loving championship of the persecuted and tormented, they might rescue them from the hatred to which they were condemned. Such modest acts of help that were given on a day-to-day basis provide the answer to the foolish mood of resignation of so many who say, "What can we small and unimportant people do?"'[123]

NOTES TO CHAPTER 6

1. See Schleunes, 235 ff.
2. Ernst vom Rath, despite his suspect attitude, was accorded a Nazi hero's funeral in Düsseldorf. Bishop Friedrich Peter, veteran 'German Christian' leader, was given the task of providing the funeral oration which proved to be a nauseating mixture of sentimentality, rhetoric and venom. In the course of it he remarked, 'It was not God who swung the hammer at Golgotha. God's heart bled, when that happened. God has not struck down this dear man. We know who is responsible. Standing today at his grave, we ask the peoples of the earth, we ask Christians throughout the world, "What steps do you intend to take against the people of Whom Christ says, 'Their God was a murderer from the beginning, and is not rooted in the Truth'". . . . In our grief and our pride we inquire of the Peoples of the world, "What attitude do you intend, in future, to adopt towards the Jewish People?" We await their answer.' (*Rheinische Zeitung*, 18 November 1938).
3. Shirer, p. 435.
4. Paul Sauer: *Dokumente über die Verfolgung der jüdischen Bürger in Baden-Württemberg*, Stuttgart, 1966, Band II, pp. 39 ff.
5. Ehrenforth, 213.
6. Sauer: *Dokumente*, II, 29–31.
7. Heinrich Grüber: *Erinnerungen aus sieben Jahrzehnten*, Berlin, 1968, p. 110.
8. Heinrich Grüber: *Dona Nobis Pacem*, Berlin, 1956, p. 88.
9. Ehrenforth, 213.
10. Fischer, XIII, 222.
11. Fritz Klingler ed: *Dokumente zur Abwehrkampf der deutschen Pfarrerschaft gegen Verfolgung und Bedruckung, 1933–1945*, Nürnberg, 1946, pp. 67–77.
12. Arndt Müller, 245.

13. The full text of Gollwitzer's sermon is to be found in *Evangelische Theologie, 1951–1952*, pp. 145–51.

14. Fischer, XIII, pp. 230–2. Pastor Veil was again in trouble in 1941 for having told his confirmation candidates that 'Christians have no reason and no right to scorn a fellow human being simply because he happens to belong to another race and is a Jew and there is nothing else that he can be accused of'. He again came off lightly at the hands of the local police (Fischer, XVII, 173).

15. The Brandenburg Council of Brethren recommended that intercession in Church should include a prayer for 'Israel according to the Flesh', and provided an appropriate text for the petition. (Günther Harder: *Die Kirchenleitende Tätigkeit des Brandenburgischen Brüderrates* in *Arbeiten zur Geschichte des Kirchenkampfes*, Band 15, p. 212.)

16. Herwart Voörländer: *Kirchenkampf in Elberfeld, 1933–1945*, Göttingen, 1968, p. 546.

17. Guenther Lewy: *The Catholic Church and Nazi Germany*, Weidenfeld and Nicolson, 1964, p. 284. 'Provost Lichtenberg in Berlin, on the morning after the pogrom, prayed for the persecuted non-Aryan Christians and Jews, and added, "What took place yesterday we know; what will be tomorrow, we do not know; but what happens today we have witnessed; outside the synagogue is burning, and that also is a house of God". Lichtenberg's protest remained a solitary act of witness. His bishops remained silent in the face of the burning temples and the first round-up of the Jews.'

18. Grüber: *Erinnerungen*, 109.

19. KJB, 250–2 and 256–258.

20. KJB, 263–73. Niemöller: *Wort und Tat*, 202–18.

21. Karl Barth: *Eine Schweizer Stimme*, Zürich, 1945, pp. 58–9. See Daniel Cornu: *Karl Barth et la Politique*, Geneva, 1967, pp. 82–90.

22. The 'Dahlemites'—frequently to be found used as a convenient description for the Radical Confessionalists who resolutely followed the way of Martin Niemöller, the Pastor of Dahlem, and who continued to stand wholeheartedly for the decisions of the Confessional Synod of Dahlem which brought into being the emergency Church Order and declared the Confessing Church and not the official Reichskirche, to be the true Evangelical Church of Germany. The Dahlemites regarded the Synod as the chief organ of Church government, the Synod being composed of representatives of Lutheran, Reformed and 'Union' congregations. The Dahlemite outlook was markedly different from that of the *Lutheraner*, the strict Lutherans who set great store upon episcopal leadership, reverence for the letter of the original Reformation Confessions and emphatic respect for the State as divinely ordered.

23. KJB, 265–6.

24. Quoted by Heinrich Fink in *Stärker als die Angst*, Berlin, 1968, p. 13.

25. Kupisch: *Durch den Zaun der Geschichte*, 395.

26. Theodor Dipper: *Die Evangelische Bekenntnisgemeinschaft in*

Württemberg, 1933–1945, Arbeiten zur Geschichte des Kirchenkampfes, Band 17, Göttingen, 1966, pp. 262 ff.

27. Hermann Diem in *Stärker als die Angst,* 132.
28. Fischer, XIII, 237.
29. Dipper: 266–7.
30. Fischer, XIII, 253–7.
31. Theophil Wurm: *Erinnerungen aus meinem Leben,* Stuttgart, 1953, p. 150.
32. The full text of this letter is reproduced in Fischer, XIII, 223–6, but is not available in any collection of documents. Extracts are to be found in Gerlach, 297–9. The whole tenor of this communication makes it clear that Bishop Wurm was resolutely determined to safeguard being accused of making a political attack upon the Nazi regime. No section of the community, he declared, was freer from specific Jewish influences or more ready to devote itself to the service of Volk and Fatherland than the clergy who were certainly not lacking in deep gratitude for the transformation wrought by National Socialism. Evangelical Christians were so perturbed by what had just taken place, because they had a love for Volk, Fatherland und Führer, and were zealous for the good name of Germany and for its standing as a Great Power. Then followed what we can only describe as the terribly naïve suggestion that others besides Wurm were so pathetically ready to make, that a word might be said to the Führer, who possibly was not sufficiently well informed, as to the full extent of what had happened or as to the actual feelings of the People whose 'oneness with him in spirit' was 'so dear to his heart'.

It is evident that Hitler was completely in the picture as to the principal measures adopted against the Church and their effects. 'Certain things took place in the Third Reich without his knowledge, but there was nothing really decisive about which he was not informed. The ever-repeated pious ejaculation "If only the Führer knew" was an expression of a complete ignorance of the situation' (Steinert: *Hitlers Krieg und die Deutschen.* Düsseldorf, 1970, p. 223).

'If only the Führer knew . . . !' This cry was still being uttered in the war. When Marga Wolf, a much loved paediatrician and a Christian non-Aryan, was in peril of being evacuated from Stuttgart, some of the grateful mothers of her patients were bold enough to write in her defence, 'If the Führer was aware of what was threatened, he would most certainly not approve.' Marga Wolf had spurned the opportunity of being classified as an 'honorary Aryan', and worked without remuneration in children's homes in Stuttgart, giving, especially to Jews in their desperate need, all that she did not absolutely require for herself. She was instructed to apply 'euthanasia' to Jewish mental patients who, it was feared, would prove troublesome during transport. This she firmly refused to do, and she was herself deported in 1943 (Zelzer, 228).

33. Wurm, 150.
34. Dipper, 268.
35. In *Durchkreuzter Hass* ed. Rudolf Weckerling, Berlin, 1961, p. 43.
36. Hans Asmussen: *Zur jüngsten Kirchengeschichte*, Stuttgart, 1961, p. 115.
37. Leuner, H.D.: *When Compassion was a Crime*, Wolff, 1966, p. 114.
38. Sauer: *Schicksäle der jüdischen Bürger*, Baden-Wurttembergs, Stuttgart, 1969, p. 334.
39. Julius Rieger, Pastor of St. George's Lutheran Church, London, wrote in 1944 a booklet entitled *The Silent Church: The Problem of the German Confessional Witness* (SCM Press) which is well worth studying. Rieger insisted that the Church had 'to work out and, by prayer, find for herself an answer founded on the Bible and the Creed. Any other organisation might have answered, if at all, more quickly, more directly and more politically. The Church could not, and cannot, do this. By her very nature, she cannot speak in her own right, but always in obedience to her Lord, who, when He wills, gives her the word to speak. There would be no Confessing Church today, if this same Church had not had the courage to be the silent Church' (p. 50). He went on to suggest (p. 52) that there could be 'grounds fundamental to the very nature of the Church, which makes her sceptical as to the value of the moral protest'.
40. KJB, 275.
41. KJB, 273.
42. Dipper, 270.
43. AELKZ, 1938, p. 1106.
44. E. G. Ruppel: *Die Gemeinschaftsbewegung im Dritten Reich, Arbeiten zur Geschichte des Kirchenkampfes*, Band 22, Göttingen, 1969, p. 219.
45. *National Kirche*, 15 November, 1938, which contained an advertisement recommending Wolf Meyer-Erlach's new book on Luther and the Jews, with the bold caption 'Luther demands the burning of Synagogues'.'
46. Martin Sasse: *Martin Luther über die Juden. Weg mit ihnen!* Freiburg, 1938, which in one year achieved a circulation of 150,000 copies.
47. For Petersmann see Kurt Meier: *Die Deutschen Christen*, 258 ff. and Ehrenforth, 184–99. Petersmann professed himself to be opposed to the power politics of the early 'German Christians' and the wild fanaticism of the Thuringians. Intensive theological activity was called for to make Luther and his message understandable to the men of the New Germany, taking seriously the the Nazi avowal of 'Positive Christianity' and seeking alliance with the uncommitted 'Neutrals'. The emphasis was to be placed upon 'Christian Germans' rather than upon 'German Christians'
48. Meier: *Die Deutschen Christen*, 257.
49. Brunotte, 154. Gerlach, 356.
50. *Stärker als die Angst*, 142–3.
51. Brunotte, 157.

52. Brunotte, 158–9.

53. EKDJF, 167.

54. *Stärker als die Angst*, 56 ff.

55. KJB, 298.

56. EKDJF, 178–9.

57. A typical example of the Nazi reaction is to be found in the *N.S. Kurier* (Stuttgart), 11 December, 1935. 'In present-day Germany is anyone so naïve as to believe that a Jew becomes a Christian by means of baptism? The baptismal water has no such effect. The effort to convert a baptised Jew into a Christian is as vain as the holding of a herring under the tap in the hope that it may turn into a trout' (Fischer, VIII, 290).

58. Fischer, XIII, 263–9.

59. KJB, 293.

60. Paul Fleisch: *Erlebte Kirchengeschichte*, Hannover, 1952, p. 244.

61. *Der Ungekündigte Bund*, 236.

62. EKDJF, 175–8.

63. KJB, 296–7.

64. Walter Grundmann: *Entjüdung des religiösen Lebens als Aufgabe der Theologie*, Weimar, 1939. Grundmann was active after the war in the Eastern Zone of Germany as a leading New Testament scholar, and published studies on the Gospels and the Epistle to the Romans.

65. *Die Botschaft Gottes*, Weimar, 1941.

66. Wilhelm Niemöller: *Gottes Wort is nicht gebunden*, Bielefeld, 1948, p. 155.

67. *Verbandsmitteilungen des Institutes zur Erforschung des jüdischen Einflusses auf das deutsche kirchliche Leben*, Eisenach, 1939, Nr 1, pp. 6–22.

68. Ibid., 1940, Nr 2/3, p. 61.

69. Ibid., 1941, Nr 4, pp. 87–9.

70. Ibid., 1940, Nr 2/3, p. 37.

71. Ibid., 1941, Nr 5/6, p. 108.

72. Ibid., 1941, Nr 5/6, pp. 128–9.

73. Wolf Meyer-Erlach: *Der Einfluss der Juden auf das englische Christentum*, Weimar, 1940. The University of Jena must have been proud of such professorial eloquence. From 1931 on Wolf Meyer-Erlach gained a considerable reputation as a regular radio preacher. He was a born demagogue with a flow of telling and picturesque language, and he was successful in winning many back to the Gospel. Always a fanatic nationalist, he remained an orthodox Evangelical, until he came under the influence of the Thuringian 'German Christians', whose leader, Siegfried Leffler, impressed by his lively eloquence, secured him the professorship at Jena. He was apparently up to the summer of 1933 friendly inclined to the Jews, taking their part on Boycott Day. He found no difficulty, however, in converting himself into one of the most rabid of all anti-semites in the Third Reich. As a pastor in the Bavarian Church he had been most generously treated by Bishop

Meiser. This did not prevent him from 1933 on, though no longer a pastor in the Bavarian Church, from attacking Meiser repeatedly in the most violent and slanderous fashion, and seeking to persuade the clergy to renounce their oath of loyalty to the bishop. In his inaugural dissertation at Jena he declared heathenism with fanatical love of Germany to be preferable to 'godless' Barthian Theology. 'Our hearts belong to Germany,' he exclaimed. 'Because we are Christians, we are National Socialists.' In 1937, now enthroned as Rector of the University, he once more invaded his former Church, and in a wildly hysterical speech of hate he characterised it as a Church of Satan in which ruled the Anti-Christ. It cried out to be destroyed. As an itinerant war-time orator he perpetrated remarks such as 'If there is a Devil, he is assuredly an Englishman!' and 'We "German Christians" no longer recognise Evangelicals and Catholics, but only Germans.' It is not altogether surprising to learn that in the later stages of the War, he was too much for the Nazis themselves, and got into their bad books. This allowed him, after the war was over, to present himself as a martyr of National Socialism. He sought to find his way back into the service of the Bavarian Church, but this was energetically resisted. Martin Niemöller, however, accepted him into the Hessian Church, and incredibly he received in 1962 the high award of the *Bundesdienstkreuz, erste Klasse*. His published self-tribute was, 'Unswerving, inflexible . . . I look back with complete satisfaction upon my life.'
See Baier: *Die Deutschen Christen Bayerns*, pp. 57–8, 94–6, 348 and 529–31 and J. K., 1934, 479–80.

74. See Kurt Meier: *Die Deutschen Christen*, 291–3. Gerhard Kittel rendered similar assistance by contributing a booklet on historical hypotheses for Jewish racial confusion to a series sponsored by the Reich Institute for the History of the New Germany. He addressed the Jewish Research Department of the same Institute on the subject of 'The Connubium with non-Jews in Ancient Jewry', and thereby assisted to bolster the ideological justification of Nazi racial policy. See W. F. Albright, *History, Archaeology and Christian Humanism*, pp. 229–40.

75. Heinz Brunotte: *Der kirchenpolitische Kurs der deutsche evangelischer Kirchenkanzlei* in *Arbeiten zur Geschichte des Kirchenkampfes*, Band 15, p. 107.

76. Nathaniel Micklem in his autobiography *The Box and the Puppets*, Bles, 1957, p. 91, relates that Kerrl at a meeting of Confessional leaders took upon himself to defend the anti-semitism of National Socialism. 'Was not anti-semitism a christian principle?', he asked. He invited his audience to consider the contribution of the great Church Fathers, Marcion and Syrsin. His hearers were quite baffled by the reference to the latter ancient worthy, till someone realised that Kerrl had elevated into a Church Father the abbreviation syr. sin. employed in reference to an ancient and important manuscript.

77. KJB, 299.
78. KJB, 300.
79. KJB, 301 ff.
80. KJB, 315.
81. KJB, 327–8.
82. KJB, 330–1.
83. JK, 1939, p. 638.
84. Niemöller: *Kampf und Zeugnis der Bekennenden Kirche*, Bielefeld, 1948, p. 461.
85. Gerlach, 374.
86. Niemöller: *Kampf und Zeugnis*, 460.
87. Niemöller: *Wort und Tat*, 226.
88. Gerlach, 384–5.
89. See Johann Neuhäusler: *Kreuz und Hakenkreuz*, München, 1946, Band 2, pp. 389 ff., and *Durchkreuzter Hass*, 49.
90. Jasper, 138–9.
91. Jasper, 141. Laura Livingstone in *Durchkreuzter Hass*, 49.
92. The following account of Heinrich Grüber's work for the non-Aryans is principally drawn from his autobiography, *Erinnerungen aus sieben Jahrzehnten*, Berlin, 1968. But see also Heinrich Grüber —*Zeuge pro Israel*, Berlin, 1963, and Rudolf Schade: *Pontifex nicht Partisan* in *Durchkreuzter Hass*, 47–55. Grüber's sermons and speeches have been collected together in a volume entitled *Dona Nobis Pacem*, Berlin, 1956.
93. Grüber: *Erinnerungen*, 104–5. We have chosen to follow the information supplied by Grüber himself. Wilhelm Niemöller (*Kampf und Zeugnis*, 457) states that it was in September 1938 that Grüber was made responsible by the Provisional Government of the Confessing Church for the development of relief work on behalf of the non-Aryan Christians. Grüber denied in 1968 that he received a commission or any substantial support from the Provisional Government, and insisted that the organisation of the relief work was entirely due to his own personal initiative (Gerlach, *Beiheft*, 87). Gerlach disputes this, and contends (pp. 314–15) that in the summer of 1938 as a result of a discussion following a lecture in Berlin by Hermann Maas on the Jewish Problem, the latter proposed Grüber as director of a central relief Bureau, and that this recommendation was endorsed by the Provisional Government.
94. *Zeuge pro Israel*, 11.
95. Letter from Dr. Freudenberg, quoted in Grüber: *Zeuge pro Israel*, 27.
96. Grüber: *Erinnerungen*, 113.
97. Zelzer, 204–5.
98. Grüber: *Erinnerungen*, 124.
99. Ibid., 128–9. Hannah Arendt in her controversial study *Eichmann in Jerusalem* (Faber and Faber, 1966) writes disparagingly of Grüber's testimony for the prosecution in the Eichmann Trial in pointed contrast to the series of complimentary press reports to

be found in *Zeuge pro Israel*, pp. 59 ff., in which he was described as a 'saint among the nations of the world and a friend to Israel'. One who was particularly competent to judge declared that Grüber had reminded the Jews of a certain type of German who possessed moral courage and a conscience, and who had helped to restore respect for Christianity in this connection, and had reawakened faith in humanity. Hannah Arendt, in complete contrast, describes Grüber's testimony as having been vague and unconvincing. When asked by the chief defence lawyer, if he had tried to appeal to Eichmann's feelings, preach to him and tell him that his conduct was contrary to morality, 'of course the very courageous Propst had done nothing of the sort, and his answers were highly embarrassing. He said that "deeds are more effective than words", and that "words would have been useless". He spoke in clichés that had nothing to do with the reality of the situation, where "mere words" would have been deeds, and where it had perhaps been his duty to test the "uselessness of words". Eichmann was quoted as having said, "Nobody came to me and reproached me for anything in the performance of my duties." Not even Pastor Grüber claims to have done so." He then added, "He came to me and sought alleviation of suffering, but did not actually object to the very performance of my duties as such" ' (Hannah Arendt: *Eichmann in Jerusalem*, 115).

100. Grüber, 136–7. The Reich Minister of Education had already in July 1937 inaugurated a programme for the purging of German State Schools of Jewish pupils. Martin Albertz wrote in November 1937 to the Minister stressing the need for children from Jewish Christian families to be given Christian religious instruction instead of being compelled to attend Jewish schools, where they would be submitted to Mosaic and Zionist instruction. From November 1938 on it was made impossible for non-Aryan children to attend a German State School. The Confessing Church in Berlin urged the provision of privately organised schools for Jewish Christian children, and from 1939 on such provision was made. Pastor Adolf Kurtz arranged for classes to be held in his vicarage, and this catered at one point for as many as 100 pupils. In July 1942 all Jewish Schools were ordered to be closed (Gerlach, 331–41 and *Durchkreuzter Hass*, 60).

101. Ibid., 141.
102. Ibid., 139.
103. Ibid., 201–2.
104. *Dona Nobis Pacem*, 237–43 and Forck: *Und folget ihrem Glauben nach*, 78–82.
105. Helene Jacobs: *Illegalität aus Verantwortung*, and Gertrud Staewen, *Bilder aus der illegalen Judenhilfe* in *Unterwegs*, 1947, No. 3.
106. Meier, 110–11.
107. Heinrich Schmid: *Apokalyptisches Wetterleuchten*, 380–93.
108. Martin Albertz: *Die Synagoge am Nollendorfplatz* in *Durchkreuzter Hass*, 59–60.

109. Beate Steckhan in *Stärker als die Angst*, 186.
110. Gerlach, Beiheft, 59.
111. Leuner, 123–4 and Helene Jacobs in *Durchkreuzter Hass*, 62–8.
112. Leuner, 121.
113. Ehrenforth, 215.
114. Leuner, 126 and *Durchkreuzter Hass*, 74.
115. Gerlach, 270 and Beiheft, 72, note 600.
116. Werner Koch: *Heinemann im Dritten Reich*, Wuppertal, 1972, 182.
117. Beate Steckhan in *Stärker als die Angst*, 195.
118. Gerlach, 327.
119. Max Krakauer: *Lichter im Dunkelin*, Stuttgart, 1947.
120. Ibid., 96.
121. Ibid., 109.
122. Ibid., 74–5.
123. Beate Steckhan in *Starker als die Angst*, 204.

7

'The Final Solution', 1941–1945

At the outbreak of the war it was obvious that the Jews still
remaining in Germany were in special peril. In November 1938
in the SS periodical *Schwarze Corps* two future keywords *Ausrotten*
(Exterminate) and *Vernichtung* (Annihilation) were made use of
for the first time clearly and unambiguously. In this article the
recommended policy was to compel all the Jews to become
destitute and then of necessity to fall into delinquency. 'Let no
one imagine that we shall stand idly by merely watching this
process. The German People are not in the least inclined to
tolerate in their country hundreds and thousands of criminals.
We would be faced with the stern necessity of exterminating
this Jewish underworld in the same way as under our government
of law and order we are wont to exterminate any other criminals,
namely by fire and sword. The result would be the factual and
final end of Jewry in Germany, its final annihilation.'[1]

On 21 January 1939 Hitler told the Czechoslovakian Foreign
Minister frankly: 'We are going to destroy the Jews. . . . The
day of reckoning has come.'[2] On 30 January the Führer prophesied to the Reichstag that 'if the Jewish international financiers
inside and outside of Europe succeed in involving the nations
in another war, the outcome will not be world bolshevism and
therefore another victory for Jewry; it will be the annihilation of
the Jewish race in Europe'.[3] Robert Ley, Labour boss and notorious for his habitual drunkenness, blurted out early in 1939 that
'the fight against the Jews. . . . will not have ended, until the
Jews throughout the world will have been exterminated'.[4] The
Nazi organ *Völkischer Beobachter* proclaimed on 7 July 1939 that
the Jewish Question could only be regarded as entirely solved
when there were no Jews left in Germany. The important consideration was to be rid of them as soon as possible and as completely as possible.

These grim threats began to be really drastically implemented in 1941 directly after the beginning of the war against the Soviet Union. It would appear that 'Hitler had already made up his mind, early in the spring of 1941 that the "final solution" was to be the biological annihilation of the Jews'.[5] On 31 July 'Butcher' Heydrich was charged by Göring with the task of 'making all necessary preparations. . . . for a total solution of the Jewish problem in all territories under German control and submitting as soon as possible a draft setting out details of the preliminary measures. . . . for the achievement of the final solution to which we aspire'.[6]

On 1 September 1941 all non-Aryans were ordered to wear the star of David. This consisted of a black six-pointed star on yellow material, as big as the palm of a hand with the inscription 'JEW'. Martha Haarburger, a Jewess, described the wearing of the star as a form of torture, branding one as a malefactor. 'I had', she wrote, 'each day, when I ventured out on to the street, to struggle for repose and serenity'.[7] The star had to be worn in every place where there was a possibility of contact with Aryans. If it was either intentionally or unintentionally covered over only perhaps for a mere matter of seconds, and a zealous Gestapo official spotted such a breach of regulations, it would mean removal to a concentration camp. Maybe three months later an official death certificate would be issued from Ravensbruck or Auschwitz giving as cause of death heart failure or 'shot while attempting to escape'. But the real cause of death would be the concealed star.[8] The compulsory wearing of the star made any sort of contact between Aryan and non-Aryan Christians very much more difficult and highly dangerous. It also greatly hampered any assistance that it was desired to give. Many Christian wearers of the star were shy and self-conscious about attending church thus adorned, while they knew that to leave it off could mean immediate deportation. The Jewish wife of a Hamburg church organist who was spotted without her star, was promptly deported, and lost her life, the Church being powerless to save her.[9] In Berlin and elsewhere there were good Christians who were resolved, cost what might, to make those wearing the star especially welcome. The latter are reported to have attended in good numbers the service at the Gossner Mission on Sunday, 21 September 1941. It was altogether a matter of course for the congregation to be colour-blind as far as the black and yellow insignia was concerned, and to make them all the more heartily welcome. Any members of the congregation who were acquainted with Jewish Christians were urged to visit or write to them, begging them not to stay away through motives of false consideration or exaggerated and unjustified delicacy of feeling. It is interesting to learn that the official Reich Church apparently endorsed such an attitude, and a representative of Reichminister Kerrl affirmed that in the Christian Church there were neither Jews nor Greeks but only Christian brothers and sisters, and that it was expected that no distinction should be made between those wearing the star and those without it. The former were to have the liberty to attend church and participate in church meetings.[10]

Pastor Nay of Breslau described in moving terms the experience of administering the Holy Communion to star-bearers. 'Weeping men and women knelt down at the altar and experienced that in the presence of God it made no difference whether one was Jew or Aryan, and that all such demarcations only signified a difference in our earthly existence.'[11]

In Bremen three non-Aryan members of the congregation of Old St. Stephen's Church attended the Reformation Day service in October 1941 followed by Holy Communion. Their attendance was observed by the local 'German Christians' and reported to the Gestapo who accused the pastor of St. Stephen's and his congregation of having permitted the presence of non-Aryans in their midst. A lady-worker and eight members of the congregation were promptly arrested, being accused of having, additionally, supplied with certain necessaries a poor non-Aryan family that was booked for evacuation. The pastor and the Parochial Church Council protested boldly to the Reich Church Ministry that the three non-Aryans in question had been members of the congregation for the past ten years, and had been regularly and devoutly both hearing the Word and receiving the sacraments. They had complied with the state regulations in wearing their stars. It was deeply resented that both they and those who had befriended them, should be punished, and the demand was made that those arrested should be set free, and that the ban on non-Aryans taking part in the services of the Church—the first known case in the whole of Germany—should at once be lifted.[12]

Katharina Staritz who was engaged in church work in Breslau, with a special responsibility for missionary work among the Jews, and was also honorary director of the Silesian branch of the Grüber Office, published in September 1941 a circular letter on behalf of the star-wearers.[13] The letter urged that the obligatory wearing of the star should not make adult or child (it was required from six years upwards) in any way unwelcome in the congregation. They should be made to feel as much at home as any other worshipper. They stood in especial need of the comfort of God's Word. There was a danger of congregations being led astray in this matter by considerations that were not really Christian. Luke 10:25–37 and Matthew 25:40 should be constantly borne in mind. As a practical measure sidesmen and vergers might well be instructed to show special interest in the 'starred' members, and, if necessary, conduct them to honoured seats and not charity-benches. They should not be segregated, but be accompanied in the pew by those who knew what 'Church' really meant. A service could also be rendered in certain cases by calling for the non-Aryans and taking them along to church. The comment of the *Schwarze Korps* upon the above was that the Church which this female theologian claimed to represent could scarcely be regarded as a German Church. It was surely an international 'catholic' Church under the patronage of the Archbishop of Canterbury. Katharina Staritz's bold recommendation won the disapproval of the official church authorities, and she was dismissed from her post as 'city curate' in October.[14] Six months later she was sent to Ravensbruck concentration camp, where she was kept for over a year. She was then allowed to return to Breslau to perform certain limited duties subject to twice weekly reporting to the Gestapo.

The 'German Christians' in Thuringia bursting with pride and patriotic fervour at the Führer's preliminary successes in his Russian campaign composed a pulpit manifesto for Sunday, 10 August, declaring that the fight which was now being waged was in the most profound sense a conflict between the divine and the satanic forces of the world, between Christ and Antichrist, between light and darkness, between love and hate, between order and chaos, between the eternal German and the eternal Jew. In this battle the English and the American clergy, the representatives of international World-Christianity, had entered into fraternity with Satan. They had with the brotherly kiss which they had given to the bolshevik Judas, once more betrayed Christ and crucified Him afresh. This international world church organisation kept on referring to the Jews as a 'Chosen People', and that at the moment in which God was stretching out His hand to annihilate this people. 'We are opposed', the manifesto continued, 'to a form of Christianity which leagues itself with Bolshevism, which regards the Jews as the Chosen People, and which denies that our Volk and our Race are God-given'.[15]

This was not a bad effort at keeping up with Dr. Goebbels who surpassed himself in an article dated 16 November entitled, 'The Jews are to blame'. In it he had the monstrous impertinence to make the helpless, persecuted Jewish element responsible for the whole war. He declared that every Jew was a sworn enemy of the German people. Every German soldier who fell in battle was on the Jewish conscience, and his death had to be paid for. Anyone wearing a Jewish star was branded as an enemy of the people, and anyone cultivating private relations with a Jew was to be reckoned a Jew himself and to be treated as such. The Jews were suffering no injustice in what was being meted out to them. They had more than earned it.[16]

Another article followed a few months later under the heading of 'The War and the Jews', in which he hammered home once again the Jewish responsibility for the outbreak of the war, and warned that in response to the demands of State security grave and momentous decisions regarding the Jews might have to be taken. The war was fundamentally a racial conflict with its sinister aim that of annihilation and extermination of the German people.[17]

On 17 December 1941 the Churches of Thuringia, Saxony, Nassau-Hesse, Schleswig-Holstein, Anstalt and Lübeck gave publicity to their belief that the Jews were responsible for the war, and asserted that they themselves stood in the van of the historic defensive action against the Jews. The earmarking of the Jews as the born enemies of both the Reich and the World they claimed to be in line with the conclusions of Martin Luther. From the Crucifixion till the present day the Jews had for their own self-interests combated, abused and adulterated Christianity. Christian baptism did not alter the racial characteristics of a Jew, his adherence to the Jewish people or his biological entity. It was the task of a German Evangelical Church to cultivate and to promote the religious life of the Germans. In such a Church

Christians who were Jews by race had no place and no right. The proclamation ended with the words: 'The undersigned German Evangelical Churches and their leaders have on such grounds abolished all fellowship with Jewish Christians. They are determined to tolerate no sort of influence of the Jewish spirit upon German religious and church life.'[18]

One of the signatories of the manifesto, Klotsche, notorious for having in August 1937 taken control of the Church in Saxony at revolver-point,[19] had previously recommended that notices should be put outside parish churches saying, 'No entry for Jews.'[20] He had also created a fuss on learning that a woman wearing the Star of David had had the temerity to attend a Mothers' Meeting in St. Luke's Parish, Dresden.[21]

Heinz Eisenhuth, Professor of Theology at Jena, was the author of a notorious article which attempted to justify the exclusion of Jewish Christians from Church worship. He claimed that the German fight against the Jews was conducted in defence of the Volk, its culture and religion. The Church was bound to join in the fight not merely on grounds of her obvious duty to the Volk but also as a necessary consequence of her loyal discipleship of Jesus and Luther. Reception of the sacraments of Holy Baptism and Holy Communion had no power to effect a biological, historical or religious transformation. Birth, not baptism, was the qualification to belong to the German Christian Church. An individual after baptism continued just as before in the historical and volkish association which was his by birth. The arch-enemy in the present war was the Jew, and there could be no place within the fellowship of the German Church for a Jewish Christian, an enemy of the Reich even if he were an earnest and convinced follower of Christ. He was still a representative of the people which for all time according to the judgement of Christ were murderers and liars. The Church's preaching in time of war of necessity presupposed a volkish solidarity in which a Jew could not possibly share. The German Evangelical Church could not be expected to provide places of worship or Jewish Christian pastors for those who had to be excluded. Luther's definite requirement that the Jews should be banished had to be vigorously upheld by the German Evangelical Church.

Eisenhuth had the temerity to insist that the Church in taking her part in the self defence of the Volk was preserving intact he values of Christianity not only for European civilisation but, beyond that, for the peoples of the whole world.[22]

Both the Reich Church Ministry and the Reich Church Chancery were perplexed as to the best way of treating this radical move by a section of the Church. There were those in both bodies like Heinz Brunotte who had definite ideas of what was meant by Christianity and church membership but they were possessed with a profound sense of helplessness in face of the brutal attitude within the party and the SS. They were persuaded that to make any sort of a protest or to champion the cause of the non-Aryan Christians could well make the position of the latter still more precarious and also endanger the existence of the Evangelical Church itself.[23] This attitude was in all likelihood shared by quite a few of the leaders of the Confessional Church who had for some period been avoiding making any public protest.

Feeling, however, that in the light of the 'German Christian' manifesto some official guidance ought to be given to the Church as a whole and fearing that civil servants and members of Nazi organisations would not be allowed to attend a service at which men and women wearing the star were taking part, Dr. Furle, the Deputy Director of the Church Chancery, wrote to the provincial Churches. He wrote that the display of racial consciousness in the Volk, intensified by the experiences of the war, the increased exclusion of the Jews from the German community, had become an indisputable fact which the German Evangelical Churches could not ignore. The Churches should thus take appropriate steps to see that the baptised non-Aryans kept away from church life. The non-Aryans would have to seek ways and means of making their own arrangements for separate worship and pastoral ministrations. Efforts would be made to gain the approval of the appropriate authorities for these arrangements.[24]

While there is no reason to doubt that the last sentence was sincerely meant, it was pure illusion to imagine that the non-Aryans could in any way contrive to set up Jewish Christian churches of their own; besides which, there were scarcely any non-Aryan pastors available for the necessary ministrations. The circular chose deliberately to counsel the keeping at a distance, rather than the actual exclusion of, the non-Aryans.

This communication evoked a spirited rejoinder from Pastors

Böhm and Kloppenburg on behalf of the Confessing Church.
The Confessing Church was indeed capable of a flaming protest,
when scriptural truth and confessional integrity were plainly
being set at nought. The very essence of the faith and the existence
of the Church were at stake. The Church was committed to the
command of her Lord to go into all the world and preach the
Gospel to every creature, an instruction that allowed for no
limitation of race. Luther's final sermon in 1546 expressly acknowledged the duty of preaching the Message of Jesus Christ to the
Jews and of treating converted Jews as brethren. On racial grounds
there would be no hesitation in welcoming Japanese and Chinese
to the Church's services. With what right then were the non-
Aryans to be excluded? There was no desire to be like the Phari-
sees and earn the condemnation of Christ. 'If', they said, 'we
were to exclude the non-Aryans, it would also be necessary to
expel the Apostles, and indeed Jesus Christ Himself, on grounds
of the race to which they belonged'.[25] Spirited words indeed,
but yet this sharp protest included no reference to the drastic
and inhuman measures that the State had seen fit to adopt towards the Jews or any condemnation of such.

Bishop Wurm also made his disapproval known, and expressed
his objection that the church officials should apparently consider
it right to ground their outlawry of the non-Aryan Christians from
the Church on the fact of their exclusion by the State from the
Christian community and upon the prevailing racial consciousness
of the German people. The Church's first obligation was not to
the German people but to the eternal Gospel given to all men.
To exclude the unhappy Jewish Christians from the worship to
which they were accustomed would but increase their misery.
The experiences of the last nine years had proved that compromise
in matters of faith did not eliminate the prevailing hostility against
Christianity and the Church, but had the result, instead, of
undermining the solidarity of the Church.[26]

The *Geistliche Vertrauensrat*, a new body set up at the outbreak
of the war for liaison purposes between Church and State, and
consisting of Bishop Marahrens, the 'German Christian' Bishop
Schulz, and Dr. Hymmen, a neutral, took issue with Bishop
Wurm and insisted that the Church Chancery was not recommending the exclusion of the non-Aryans but their keeping of
their distance, suggesting that that would be a Christian attitude

n thus saving their German fellow-church-members from difficulties and embarrassment. The *Una Sancta* as the Body of
Christ was not in dispute, nor the validity of Baptism. But the
empirical form of the Church had to be distinguished from the
ideal of the *Una Sancta*. The concrete Church, whether one liked
it or not, was conditioned by temporal circumstances. It was not
in Germany alone that racial consciousness affected church life.
The same held good for the United States and South Africa, for
example. In time of war temporal factors had inevitably a sharp-
ened influence. The Jews were widely regarded as an enemy
people. Even Christian Jews would scarcely be on the side of the
Führer, the Army and the Volk. They almost certainly would
not be found praying for a German victory.[27] A representative
of the Church Chancery did actually make two unavailing efforts
to obtain official consideration from the State for the spiritual
needs of the Christian non-Aryans. The Reich Church Ministry
was unhelpful, observing that there would be no interest in
Gestapo quarters because the racial question had been settled
once and for all. It was now merely a matter of segregation and
gradual deportation. The same representative penetrated into the
very lion's den, and spoke with Eichmann who declared that for
him the Jewish Question was purely a political affair, and that he
was not concerned about matters of religious faith. He realised
from his acquaintance with the New Testament how difficult
the matter was for the Church, but that was none of his business.
In fact, the Jewish problem in Germany itself was now merely
one of transport. Nothing was to be gained from Eichmann,
either, regarding ministrations for Evangelical non-Aryans during
transport or when having arrived in eastern territory. When at
their destination they would be much too busy for that.[28]

There has been a great deal of discussion as to the extent to
which the German population was really aware of what was happening to the Jews. A recent English writer has claimed that 'there
appears to be no reason, except unthinking blanket condemnation
or hatred of all Germans, to doubt the plentiful evidence that
few Germans knew of the atrocious camp conditions or that a
policy of extermination was being practised.'[29] Apparent support
for this view is to be found in a message from a leader of the
opposition in Germany that reached Bishop Bell in August
1943, in which it was reported that 'the average civilian is not

aware of the extent of the persecution of the Jews. He is led to believe that, when a Jew is sent to the east, he goes there not only to be protected but to live a more "secluded" life.'[30] Powerful support is also contained in the message sent to the 5th Plenary Assembly of the Jewish World Congress meeting in Brussels in 1966, by the renowned German philosopher, Karl Jaspers, in which he maintained: 'The apparatus of murder was kept as secret as possible. The broad mass of the people knew nothing about it. Even I who lived in Heidelberg at the time did not learn the facts till 1945.'[31] There is, of course, the question here as to what is meant by 'facts'. If it be a matter of the details as to how the Jews were being liquidated, then it may be believed that there was a general lack of knowledge. But if it be a matter of knowledge that horrific special action was being taken to destroy the Jews, then it is hard to credit that there was really so widespread an ignorance, as has been subsequently claimed. Only a modicum of intelligence must surely have been required in order to be pretty certain that the Jews who had been treated with ever-increasing barbarity in Germany prior to the outbreak of war were being subjected to something yet worse following deportation. Wholesale and brutal massacre was after all just about the only method for the solution of the Jewish problem left untried. In the context of war, when killing was the order of the day, it was only too logical that those people whom Goebbels had in full publicity described as those really responsible for the war, and as emissaries at home of the enemy in battle,[32] and who had for the past decade in numberless speeches, articles, posters, films, jingles and even children's rhymes been castigated as vermin, should be candidates for total obliteration. Those who had learnt of the ruthless experiment of the so-called 'mercy killings' of their own kith and kin could scarcely have given the Jews, to whom no mercy at all could be shown, much chance of survival. Jaspers in his message had to admit that there was '"half knowledge". Everyone saw the Jews being taken away. They never returned. Nothing more was heard of them. . . . It was known that being taken away was synonymous with danger to life.'[33]

As in the case of the 'euthanasia' campaign it was intended by the Nazis that the process of annihilating the Jews should remain as far as possible hermetically sealed and kept away from the knowledge of the German people as a whole. The strict secrecy insisted upon from the very top resulted in the use of euphemistic language such as 'final solution' (which was surely open to a highly sinister interpretation), 'evacuation', 'labour in the east', 'resettlement' which was with remarkable readiness accepted not only by many Germans but also by other Europeans and indeed by the Jews themselves at its face value.[34] Psychologically, very many Germans had so fully accustomed themselves to the fortissimo of the unflagging propaganda campaign of hostility against the Jew, that their sensitivity to its enormity and inhumanity was to a great extent deadened. Jew-baiting, though never generally popular and frequently felt to be an unpleasant blot on an otherwise rosy picture, had after all been accepted by the great majority of the Germans from the very beginning of the Third Reich and 'without undue perturbation as an integral part of a system beneficial to themselves'.[35] If it was painful and distasteful to dwell upon the persecution of the Jews, it was best with the manifold worries and preoccupations of war-time to keep as far as possible switched off the whole subject. The less one found out about what was going on, the greater one's peace of mind and security. It was altogether safer and more comfortable not to be inquisitive about the purpose and outcome of the deportations. It was altogether better not to be told, nor to have definite knowledge. An attitude of ignorance and of genuine or simulated disinterest was the soundest way of keeping on the right side of the Gestapo.[36]

It must not be forgotten that, when the organised gassings were at their height and reports about what was happening were to a certain extent filtering through, many of those at home in Germany were experiencing to the full the terrors of enemy air attack. It would have been surprising if their receptivity for reports of happenings almost too ghastly to grasp and altogether destructive of German honour and decency taking place outside their own sphere of life had not been blunted. It may be believed that 'the lot of the Jews interested only that section of the population who either had personal and friendly relationships with Jews or were unfailingly prepared to exalt the cause of humanity above that of the nation. The mass of the people, engulfed in daily misery of their own, hardly took in what was said to be happening outside of their narrow professional and familiar atmosphere.'[37]

By the end of 1941, with fifty large-scale transports between November and December there must have been widespread knowledge of the deportations. In December 1941 in a letter to Reichminister Kerrl Bishop Wurm referred to 'rumours of mass-killings in the East'.[38] Such atrocity tales were certainly constantly in circulation from 1942 onwards. The entry in Ruth Andreas-Friedrich's Berlin diary for 2 December 1942 begins with the words: 'The Jews are disappearing in throngs. Ghastly rumours are current about the fate of the evacuees—mass shootings and death by starvation, tortures and gassing.'[39]

'A wave of rumours drifted back to Germany. . . . and, as the flow seeped into every town and every social quarter, the Gestapo felt itself surrounded by whispers.'[40] There were, of course, very strict instructions to secrecy, and particularly so at the actual killing centres. Soldiers home from the East on leave could not, however, be prevented from telling privately something of their grim duties in 'mobile killing operations', and despite the ban some photographs were certainly taken of the atrocities.[41] As Stewart Herman, Minister of the American Church in Berlin until December 1941, testified in 1943, 'it became definitely known through the soldiers returning from the front that in occupied Russia, especially at Kiev, Jewish civilians—men, women and babies—were being lined up and machine-gunned by the thousands'.[42] If only a handful or two of Germans were actually eye witnesses of the last agony in the gas chambers, literally hundreds of thousands had their appointed role to perform at one stage or another somewhere in the operation—civil servants, bureaucrats, engineers and construction workers, railway staff, for instance. The great extent of industrial activity in Auschwitz resulted in a constant stream of incoming and outgoing corporation officials, engineers, construction men, and other temporary personnel, all excellent carriers of gossip to the furthest corners of the Reich.[43] Every once in a while a 'careless man made a careless remark to the wrong person', as, for example, Louis Birk of Wiesbaden, a house painter, who was executed early in 1943 for his indiscretion in remarking at work to some ladies that 'all the remaining Jews in Germany would soon be destroyed by gas'.[44] But for each rumour bearer that was apprehended there must have been countless others who carried on unchecked in their whisperings. In January 1943 a local branch of the Winter

Help organisation of the Party complained that the clothing of
Jews received from a certain camp was perforated with bullet
holes, bloodstained, and bore the yellow star, and that the gar-
ments certainly could not be distributed to the needy in such a
condition, for those who received them would spread the knowledge of the origin of these things.[45] In the early part of 1943
Heinrich Baab, a Gestapo official in Frankfurt, did not hesitate
to threaten some of the Jews still in the city that they would
be 'going up the chimney' and 'making compost'.[46] Bishop Wurm
in his letter to Hitler in July 1943 having referred to the fact
that the German non-Aryans had to a large extent been liquidated,
added that such actions were known and much discussed in the
homeland.[47] Despite the ban and severe penalties for disobedience
we may be certain that a considerable number of people anxious
and curious for wider information than Nazi propaganda censorship allowed did listen in secret to foreign broadcasts, which
frequently gave details of Nazi atrocities, and that they passed
on what they heard to those whom they felt they could trust. It
is unlikely that such horrifying revelations were immediately
and indignantly dismissed as nothing other than fantastic products
of lying enemy propaganda. In the summer of 1943 the Royal
Air Force dropped leaflets over North Germany which contained
an extract from a sermon of Archbishop Temple, in which he
referred to the ghastly slaughter of the Jews, and expressed
concern at the apparent failure of Christian Germany to protest.[48]
By 1944 the German press and radio were informing the public
more and more openly, as, for instance, when it was stated that
'The Jewish population of Poland has been neutralised, and the
same thing is happening at the moment in Hungary. By this
action five million Jews have been eliminated in these two countries
alone'.[49] Gerald Reitlinger's verdict at the end of his detailed
study of the 'Final Solution' is that 'it is difficult to believe that
there existed any fully conscious beings in Germany. . . . in the
last two years of the war who did not know that most of the Jews
had disappeared, and who had not heard some story that they
had been shot or gassed'.[50] 'The systematic extinction of millions
of human beings over a period of five years', it was claimed by an
American military court at Nuremberg, 'could not possibly
remain unknown because of its very extent.'[51]

Whether the general population had by 1943 a fairly good

idea of the atrocities that were being committed or not, those in influential positions in the Churches were certainly well in the know. According to Günther Lewy, the German Catholic Episcopate by the end of the year 1942 at the latest was possessed of quite accurate knowledge.[52] Wurm, Meiser, Marahrens, Dibelius, and those who were most prominent in the struggle to keep the Confessing Church afloat were almost certainly equally well in the picture.

In January 1943 Bishop Marahrens wrote a personal letter to Reichminister Frick. Though the immediate purpose was to express his grave disquiet at the way in which certain Christian non-Aryans were being treated, resulting in the cruelly enforced separation of married persons, the deportation of the non-Aryan partner and the grief and bewilderment of their offspring, he could not keep silent regarding certain recent events that had caused severe disquiet to the Christian conscience of a considerable element in the population. 'God's unbreakable commandments', he wrote, 'remain valid in all circumstances. When the sanctity of life is not respected, and wrong and violence are done to the innocent, the most elementary laws of God have been broken. It is neither possible, nor is it the prerogative of our sacred office, to establish to what extent the rumours regarding such wrongs that are so widely circulated correspond with the facts. We earnestly beg you to do everything you can to ensure that necessary political measures are not saddled through irresponsible individuals with grave injustices, thereby imposing upon the conscience of our people a heavier burden than they can bear.'[53]

The bishop, however, anxious and wary, and ever a staunch upholder of the traditional Lutheran doctrine of the 'Two Kingdoms' hedged round his protest with so much care that it almost invited disregard. The letter was so private that no one else was permitted to know of its actual contents. It was addressed to a leading political figure who was a friend of his. No publicity was to be given to it, so that there should be no public impression of discord. As a strict Lutheran he admitted that it was not his business to criticise the political decisions of the government. The racial question was a volkish and political one, only to be solved by responsible political leadership which possessed the sole right to take the necessary measures for maintaining the purity of the German blood, and alone bore the responsibility before God and before history for so doing. As representative of the Evangelical Church he definitely declined to interfere in his responsibility.

Bishop Wurm relates in his memoirs that at a session of the Lutheran Church Leaders' Conference in Berlin in July 1943 it was decided, because of the increasing extent of the campaign against the Jews, to launch a powerful and concentrated assault upon the Reich Government.[54] He was himself commissioned to compose the document. Marahrens withheld his co-signature. Meiser was willing to sign, but it was finally decided that it would be best if it went out from a single person. Thus it was that Wurm's celebrated letter to Hitler, dated 16 July 1943,[55] came to be issued, a communication which found its way abroad and was later broadcast from London in Norwegian. Wurm claimed that this message to the Führer was proof for all times that the Evangelical Church did not remain dumb in face of the atrocities committed upon the Jews and the inhabitants of the occupied territories.[56]

That the Evangelical Church did not keep silent, but made known to the authorities what lay upon the Christian conscience and caused righteous indignation was due, after all, to the courageous and tireless efforts of Bishop Wurm.[57] Though far past normal retirement age and having nearly succumbed to a critical illness which put him out of action for nearly six months in 1941, and being very fully extended in his endeavour to be a real and effective Father-in-God to his large and by no means united 'diocese', he somehow managed to find time and energy to keep in touch with his fellow-Lutheran Church leaders and, as far as possible, with the Confessing Church in Prussia and the Roman Catholic hierarchy, and sought to promote church unity on a wide confessional basis. He succeeded in this, though constantly subjected to all the dangers, privations and limitations of an increasingly grave war-situation and having to endure a perpetual barrage of aggressive anti-church propaganda. And, as if that were not more than enough to tax even a perfectly fit man in the prime of life, he contrived to pour out a continous stream of letters to those most prominent in government circles. In the course of 1943 he wrote on no less than seven occasions to express his horror and concern at the treatment of the non-Aryans. This was only one of the subjects upon which he put pen to paper: he

had equally pungent words to say regarding the almost total
suppression of the Church press, the attempt at the elimination
of Christian teaching from the schools, the suppression of Church
seminaries, the threat to arrangements for confirmation, the
violation of religious freedom and of the legal rights of the Church,
the encouragement of paganism and the war against Christianity
in a country with a Christian population of 95 per cent, and
earlier on, the 'euthanasia' programme. The letters showed no
sign whatever of hasty or nervous composition. They were never
verbose, unreasonable or exaggerated. Wurm was the master of
the telling phrase that with an economy of words hit the nail
squarely on the head. The majority of these letters received no
answer, but this did not mean that their contents were ignored,
or that the carefully aimed shafts never went home. That his
representations were not without effect was proved by the warning
letter sent to him in March 1944 by Reichminister Lammers,
Director of the Reich Chancery, demanding that he should limit
himself to the ecclesiastical sphere, and cease to pronounce upon
questions of general politics, and telling him that he had been
treated with extreme indulgence, but warning him that this could
not continue, if he carried on as he was doing.[58] Evidence has
come to light that the radical element in the party would have
been only too glad to have seen him either imprisoned or executed, but, as in the case of Graf von Galen, Roman Catholic
Bishop of Münster, the Führer would not give his approval.
This was one of the scores that would be settled, once the war
was victoriously over. The continued freedom of both Wurm
and Meiser was ensured by the high regard in which they were
held in South Germany, and the real danger of serious disaffection
among the population, were they to be proceeded against.

The recipients of the various letters included Hitler, Goebbels,
Frick, Bormann, Himmler, Kerrl, Lammers and Murr, Governor
of Württemberg. Wurm selected this means of protest rather than
a general public declaration for several reasons. His deeply
ingrained patriotism forbad him to do anything that was obviously
calculated to impair his country's war effort. Indeed he frequently
emphasised the pre-eminence of the Evangelical clergy in their
devotion to and sacrifice on behalf of the Fatherland. He was
genuinely upset, when, despite his precautions, the contents of
his letters to Hitler and to Goebbels became known abroad, and

vere made use of for purposes of enemy propaganda.[59] Wurm had still in 1943 the sincere though naïve hope that his repeated expression of Christian anxiety and indignation could have a taming influence upon Nazi brutality. He had, furthermore, great concern for the welfare of the Church over which he presided, and urgently desired, if possible, to avoid a charge being brought against her of subversion and treason.[60]

Assuming that Wurm was before the end of 1942 no longer in doubt as to what was proving to be the fate of the majority of the deported Jews, one feels compelled to ask why he waited until the middle of 1943 before producing the first of his series of letters that contained condemnation of anti-Jewish atrocities. The probable answer is that his strong patriotic sentiments, combined with absorption in his primary task of caring for the interests of his Württemberg Church and his subscription to the traditional Lutheran doctrine of the 'Two Kingdoms', caused him to forbear from pronouncing upon what would be regarded as manifest political concerns, until the threat to the remaining and so far 'privileged' Christian non-Aryans had become acute, and it was evident, after the devastating reverses on the Russian front at the beginning of 1943, that Germany would not win the war.

While Wurm's immediate cause for writing was the championing of the cause of the 'privileged' non-Aryans and the partners of mixed marriages,[61] he was not afraid of extending his complaint to the inhuman treatment of the Jews as a whole, or of introducing the two words *Vernichtung* (Annihilation) and *Ausmerzung* (Extermination). The condemnation to death, without any trial, of non-Aryans was declared to be an offence against the clear commandments of God, and the reverse at Stalingrad, the destructive attacks by enemy aircraft and other national misfortunes in 1943 were asserted to be closely wedded to the flagrant injustices that had been committed.

Hitler was addressed in the name of God and for the sake of the German people, and told that the measures taken to annihilate non-Aryans were in the plainest contradiction to the Laws of God, and were an outrage against the very foundation of western civilisation, and, indeed, altogether against the divinely given right of human existence and of human dignity. At the end of the letter came the stirring words—'Nobody and nothing in the world shall prevent us from being Christians, and, as Christians from standing up for what is right before God.'

Lammers was addressed regarding the plight of the crossbreeds of the first degree, the majority of whom belonged to one or other of the Christian Churches. Despite the repeated reassurances that had been given right up to the outbreak of the war, they were now obviously to be condemned to the same fate as the full Jews, that of extermination. Such extermination, which was a manifest transgression of the divine commandments could but sooner or later result in retribution. The present sufferings that the German people had to bear were to be regarded as requital for what had been done to the Jews. The burning of houses and churches, the flight from destroyed homes with a few personal possessions, the perplexed search for a place of refuge reminded the population in the most agonising fashion of what the Jews had on previous occasions to endure. There could be no doubt whatever of the extraordinarily powerful influence that the measures against the non-Aryans had been having, and would continue to have, upon the way in which the enemy waged his war.

Bishop Wurm wrote two letters early in 1943, whose destination was local. A day or two before the announcement of the capitulation at Stalingrad he addressed a leading civil servant in Stuttgart by name Dill.[62] The letter claimed that in wide circles, not merely definite Christian ones, there was deep disturbance over the way in which the fight against other races and peoples was being pursued. Those on leave were telling of the systematic slaughter of Jews and Poles. Those who once held that the imposition of the Jews within various departments of public life was a severe misfortune, could not now accept that a people was justified in liquidating another people by measures which embraced every single individual irrespective of his personal guilt or innocence. To have brought men to their death without any trial before a judge solely because they belonged to another people was in contradiction to the clear commandment of God, and therewith to the conception of what was right and lawful and that was indispensable to a civilised people. It was a matter for reflection that, since the time that such measures were resorted to, German weapons had not gained the decisive successes that were won at the beginning of the war. There were many among the German people who felt not just distress at what had taken place, but who also had a sense of guilt, and would utter a sigh of relief, if through a courageous and magnanimous decision the State authorities would abandon all that besmirched the German escutcheon.

The overwhelming catastrophe at Stalingrad certainly had a profound influence upon Wurm. Directly after the news had been received, he wrote to Murr[63] as Reich Governor of Württemberg to express the feelings of the local population. In face of the grievous disappointments and the terrible losses that had been sustained the hard hit and dispirited people urgently needed a revived impetus. This could only be provided by the party declaring that it would adopt a different course by calling off the agitation against Christianity and the Church and in the cancellation of patently illegal measures such as caused the death of men simply because they happened to belong to a particular race or nation. The constant call to fresh external sacrifices was not sufficient in itself, if not accompanied by relief to the spirit and conscience of the German people.

Bishop Wurm also made use of the pulpit to express his concern. He declared in August 1943 that racial distinction had no significance in the Kingdom of Jesus Christ. No people as such and no race as such was as a matter of course excluded from salvation. Paul, a Jew by birth, had contended that the Greeks should have the same rights in the Church as the Jews. Because, he added, according to the New Testament, the Jewish people had been brought to such severe judgement for having rejected Christ, the Germans should not draw the conclusion that they would go unpunished, if they likewise rejected Christ.[64] Three months later he remarked in a sermon at Reutlingen that 'having seen the places of worship of others go up in flames, it is no surprise that our own churches are now being burnt to the ground'.[65]

Despite the limitations of the methods which the bishop adopted to give expression to what he conscientiously felt, and the understandable reaction that his protests would have counted for so much more if they had come months earlier or before the great majority of the German Jews had met their fate, his perseveringly repeated manifestoes, which were copied and duplicated and given wide though secret circulation, were and remain as Otto Elias has declared, 'a lasting memorial of courageous confession and of profound faith exalted right above fear of man or anxiety for his own person'.[66] The known fact that the Church had a bold and determined spokesman did without any doubt encourage and relieve the feelings of very many people. The Roman Catholic Archbishop of Freiburg, on receiving a copy of the letter to Hitler, thanked Wurm with the words, 'At one in Christ',[67] and Ulrich von Hassel, the Resistance Leader, wrote in his diary in July 1943 of Wurm's 'highly courageous action' and of its importance in showing that the Evangelical Church openly and clearly disapproves of 'the whole filthy business'.[68]

The recently published and laconic comment that 'the tug of war between him and the authorities was waged on paper and in private'[69] is as inadequate as it is derogatory to the memory of so brave a Church leader, whose indomitable persistence provoked the remark in the Brown House in Munich that the Third Reich would not really come into being until Wurm had been hung upon the gallows.[70]

It would be misplaced exaggeration to present Wurm, even in 1943, as an out-and-out champion of the Jews. He had certainly not shed his anti-semitic prejudices. The Nazi offence, in his judgement, did not lie in having proceeded with severity against the Jews, but was manifest in the inhuman and destructive manner in which the warfare was being conducted. Wurm did not appear in any marked way to have discarded his latent anti-semitism which could appreciate the case for eliminating the Jews from influence in public life. It was not the anti-semitic attitude as such but the unjustifiably barbarous wrong done to the Jewish people against which he felt bound to protest. In writing to Frick in March 1943 he gave an express assurance that he was not prompted by 'partiality for the Jews whose past overbearing influence upon cultural, economic and political life' had been recognised by Christians above all as disastrous.[71] In his letter in December 1943 to Lammers he denied having 'any philo-semitic leanings at all', and declared himself to be influenced 'solely by religious and ethical feelings'.[72]

Hermann Diem was the originator of what was subsequently known as the Munich Laymen's Epistle. Diem presented his text of a memorandum on the Church's attitude to the persecution of the Jews to a small group of pastors and laymen who had been meeting together in Munich since 1935, and until 1938 were under the leadership of a non-Aryan pastor, Superintendent Carl Schweitzer.

This particular circle represented the Barthian-Dahlem point of view in opposition to the more moderate official Bavarian Lutheran approach. Prominent among the members were Albert Lempp, proprietor of the well-known Kaiser publishing-house, Professor Hengstenberg, an orientalist and Emil Höchstädter, a judge of the Munich District Court. At Eastertide 1943 the two last-named personally presented a revised version of Diem's memorandum to Bishop Meiser with the urgent request that he would adopt it as the basis of an authoritative protest to the State giving plain expression to a truly Christian reaction to the treatment of the Jews. Meiser, it would seem, did not disassociate himself in principle from the substance of what was contained in the statement, but nevertheless expressed himself unable to take the required direct action in lending his name and authority to the document. He appears to have maintained that if he were to do so, he would himself in all probability be arrested, and the Jews would not be helped but would, rather, be threatened with even more severe persecution. Besides which he, Meiser, recognised his responsibility for the welfare of his Bavarian Church since official publication could well imperil thousands of her members. He sought to console his dejected visitors with an assurance of his wholehearted support of secret illegal aid to the Jews.[73] Diem himself has subsequently suggested that concern for the safety of the precariously placed 'privileged' Christian non-Aryans did much to influence Meiser, and has also revealed that the memorandum was, while under consideration by Meiser, being anonymously circulated and fell both into the hands of the Gestapo and into the possession of the foreign press.[74]

The 'Munich Laymen's Epistle' began with the assertion that they as Christians could no longer tolerate the Church in Germany keeping silent regarding the persecution of the Jews. The straightforward command to love one's neighbours, as set out in the parable of the Good Samaritan, demanded action. Every non-Aryan, whether Jewish or Christian, had fallen among thieves and murderers, and Christians had to ask themselves whether they would fulfil the role of priest, levite or Samaritan. The Church's witness should be that the Jewish issue was not primarily a political but an evangelistic one: the testifying to the People of

IOD

Israel through the Word of Scripture simultaneously with the
espousing of their cause. In the light of Romans chapter 11 there
was no place for 'Christian' anti-semitism which invited a passive
toleration of non-Christian measures against an 'accursed' people.
The Church should be testifying to the State as to the significance
of Israel in God's plan of salvation and protesting against every
attempt to solve the Jewish problem according to a political
gospel which included the annihilation of Jewry in defiance of
the God of the First Commandment. The Church as the true
Israel was, both in guilt and in promise, inextricably bound up
with Jewry, and the fight against the Jews was also warfare upon
Christ and His Church. Political arguments were not required in
admonishing the State but rather the testimony to its duty before
God to rule righteously. Such witness should be given publicly
in sermons or in the reading of a special episcopal letter. The
Church by its silence appeared to be concerned to maintain its
security at the price of its authority to bind and to loose.[75]

Pastor Walter Höchstädter, son of the Munich judge and
serving in France as a hospital chaplain, was shown the memorandum while on leave in November 1943. This inspired him to
have printed in France in the summer of 1944 his own uniquely
outspoken protest in an edition of a thousand copies suitable
for delivery by fieldpost to front-line soldiers. It seems worthy
of quotation at considerable length:

> In place of the mediaeval craze of witch-hunting our so-called
> 'enlightened' generation is revelling in an orgy of Jew-baiting.
> The anti-Jewish madness which in the Middle Ages raged in
> all its fury has now entered into its acute stage. The Church,
> the Congregation of Jesus Christ, has to make confession. If
> she does not do so, then she has failed in her trust, just as she
> failed when she encouraged the persecution of witches. The
> blood of millions of slaughtered Jews, men, women and children,
> cries aloud to heaven. The Church must not remain silent.
> She is not permitted to maintain that the Jewish issue is just
> a matter for the State, with Romans 13 conferring upon it the
> right of decision. The Church has no warrant to declare that
> the present terrible happenings are a justifiable punishment for
> the sins of the Jews. The attitude of those who belong to Jesus
> regarding the appalling fate of the Jews can be no other than

one of humility, compassionate identification and holy horror.
... There is no such thing as an indifferent Christian approach,
any more than it is possible to be a moderate, Christian anti-
semite, even if there would appear to be reasonable national
grounds or scientific (let's say pseudo-scientific) arguments for
such a position. The warfare against the Jews derives from the
same murky source as the witch-hunts, and witch-hunts were
in bygone days based upon the specialist faculties of Theology,
Law and Medicine. Contemporary man has not learnt to resist
looking for a scapegoat. What right have we to put the blame
exclusively upon the Jew? A Christian is forbidden to do just
that. A Christian cannot be an anti-semite. The objection that
without the counter-balance of a 'healthy' form of anti-semitism
there would be a terrible danger of pernicious Jewish influence
upon the life of our people derives from an unbelieving and
purely secular outlook which Christians ought to have overcome. . . . The Church's existence has to be one of Love.
Alas for that Church which fails to be activated by Love!
Alas for her, if by silence or through any other kind of questionable subterfuge she participates in the world's outbreak of
hatred! Alas for her if she adopts words and slogans which
emanate from the sphere of hatred! There are no limits to
Love proceeding from true Faith![76]

The Confessional Synod of the Prussian Church, meeting in
Breslau in October 1943, produced a manifesto on the exposition
of the Sixth Commandment, boldly affirming the responsibility
of those who rule to employ the sword only for the restraint of
evildoers, and not in order to destroy those who were peaceable
and defenceless. The divine order did not recognise expressions
such as 'extermination' and 'liquidation' and 'worthless life'.
The life of all mankind belonged to God alone. It was sacred to
Him. And that included the life of the people of Israel. 'To be
sure, Israel has rejected God's Christ, but neither as men nor as
Christians are we called upon to punish Israel's unbelief. The
Christian's neighbour is always he who is helpless and in especial
need of assistance, irrespective of race, nationality and religion.'[77]
    The only organised public protest at the extermination of the
Jews was contained in the message of the same Synod to be read
from the pulpit on Repentance Day. Though the Jews were not

actually named, the reference was unmistakable in the following extract: 'Woe to us and to our people, if life that is bestowed by God is treated with contempt, if man created in the image of God is judged merely in terms of his utility, if the killing of human beings is justified on the ground that they are considered unworthy of living, or because they belong to another race, and if hate and lack of mercy are widespread. For God says: Thou shalt not kill!'[78]

Occupying an unique place in the roll of honour of those who fearlessly registered their protest against Nazi crimes are two Evangelical students at Munich University, Hans Scholl and his sister Sophie who together with three of their fellow-students and a Roman Catholic professor were responsible for the production and dissemination between the autumn of 1942 and February 1943 of many thousands of hectographed 'White Rose' leaflets which they not only secretly passed round within the university but also conveyed personally by train to other large cities in South Germany for wider distribution. In the second of these leaflets they made reference to the Jewish Question, remarking that, 'since the conquest of Poland 300,000 Jews have been murdered in the most bestial fashion. This is the most frightful crime ever committed against human dignity, a crime without parallel in all history'. 'Why', they proceeded to ask, 'does the German people show such apathy towards all these frightful and inhuman crimes? Hardly anyone seems to trouble about them. They are accepted as facts and put aside, and the German people falls again into its dull obtuse sleep, giving these Fascist criminals the courage and the opportunity to continue their havoc—and they take it. Can this be a sign that the Germans have been blunted in their deepest human feelings, that no chord in them vibrates when they hear of such deeds, that they have sunk into a deadly sleep from which there can never, never be an awakening? It seems so, and it certainly will be so, unless the Germans awake at last from their stupor, unless they seize every opportunity to protest against this criminal gang, unless they suffer with the hundreds of thousands of victims'. Inge Scholl, their sister, has produced a short and most moving account of their daring and of the inevitable price which they had so soon to pay with their very lives.[79]

When considering and paying tribute to those who faithfully

and boldly made their testimony, Helmut Hesse and his father ought not to be overlooked. [80] Helmut was born in 1916, the son of Hermann Hesse, a Reformed pastor who was closely involved in the negotiations for the new Reich Church in 1933. Helmut was brought up in Elberfeld in the Ruhr, and pursued his theological studies at the Confessional Theological High School in Berlin. It was a struggle, because he was not naturally suited for such hard intellectual studies, and his health was indifferent, but he was finally ordained, and became his father's curate. It was a parish in the catacombs. Driven from the official church buildings, services had to be held in hired rooms. The war came, and Helmut who had declared that he would in no circumstances serve as one of Hitler's soldiers, was saved by ill health from becoming an actual conscientious objector. In June 1943 father and son to-gether held a service immediately after the terrible bombing attack upon Barmen and Elberfeld. At this service they testified that the air raids just experienced were a divine judgement upon the town for the way in which the Jews had been treated. [81] Hermann Hesse was accused by the Gestapo of having declared, 'As Christians we can no longer tolerate the silence of the Church in Germany over the persecution of the Jews. The Jewish Question is an evangelical, not a political issue. The Church, over against the State, has to testify to the saving (*heilsgeschichtlich*) significance of Israel, and promote resistance to any effort to liquidate Jewry. Every non-Aryan, whether Jewish or Christian by faith, is today in Germany the one who has fallen among thieves. The Church has to confess that as the true Israel in Guilt and in Promise she is inextricably bound up with Jewry. . . . She may no longer en-deavour to promote her own security in face of the attacks directed against Israel. She has on the contrary to testify that, when Israel is assailed, she and her Lord Jesus Christ Himself are also attacked'. Hermann Hesse was accused also by the Gestapo of having read out Diem's recent protest and of having prayed a few days earlier—'O, Lord, be with the Jews, bring together the outcasts of Israel! May Thy unmerited Grace be seen in the removal from our people of the anti-Christian forces!' [82] Both father and son were put into prison, where they continued witnessing to the scriptural promises made to the Jews. By personal command of Himmler they were removed to Dachau, and Helmut declared his joy that their witness for the Jews had penetrated to the very top. Ill-fed and deprived of essential medical treatment, Helmut's health rapidly declined, and he died on 24 November. His father survived the defeat of Hitler, and in 1948 wrote a forceful pamphlet on the subject of the Jewish Question and Contemporary Preaching in which he complained that the Church as a whole failed to utter from out of Scripture a decisive word on the Jewish issue. [83]

Honourable mention deserves also to be made of the witness of three Christian teachers who, feeling it their duty to take seriously the command to love their neighbours as themselves, made a point of visiting certain local Jews and offering them assistance. For this they were in due course brought to book, and dismissed from their posts and sentenced to a reduced pension. The president of the Court in which they were tried enquired of them how they would behave, if the Führer required them to do something that they felt could not be squared with the Laws of God. A reply being insisted upon, the answer came to the effect that, if Christian conduct, such as theirs was designed to be, was misinterpreted as being of political intent, they would be bound in that eventuality to restrain themselves. But in general terms this did not mean that they would be able to regard themselves as dispensed from the command to love their neighbours. That instruction would in given circumstances include helping a Jew, if there was no other possible assistance available. Ultimately they had to be prepared to obey God rather than man. What was notable in this brave statement was the reference to helping a Jew not just a Jewish fellow-Christian. [84]

This survey would be incomplete without some mention and consideration of the remarkable case of Kurt Gerstein, celebrated through Rolf Hochhuth's use of him as a leading character in his controversial play 'The Representative'. [85] Gerstein was a convinced and earnest Christian who had been influenced by Karl Barth, was closely associated with Martin Niemöller and an adherent of the Confessing Church, and yet in 1941 he applied to be admitted into the service of the Health and Hygiene Department of the SS. His character and his general religious outlook help to explain the apparent enigma. There was a great deal of the nonconformist, the individualist and the idealist in his make-up, and there was wedded to this a conviction that God would be requiring him at a certain point to undertake a very special role.

At first in 1933 like many another he had felt enthusiastic about the New Order, but this soon turned into distrust and hatred of the Nazi regime. A born activist, his idea of resistance to the enemy was a wellnigh impish resort to practical means of sabotage. He found himself to be increasingly impatient with the manner in which the Confessing Church entered into the fray and carried out its opposition. In his view, the so-called confessing pastor very frequently took refuge in an abstract and sterile preaching of pure, traditional doctrine, and only in a few individual cases did the preacher cast off his shyness of being found 'in the world' and 'for the world' and make really concrete application of the message or issue an explosive demand for Christian decision.[86] He remarked on one occasion: 'You can't beat Hitler in a frock-coat'.[87] He had great contempt for what he would describe as cheap piety that was concerned with the cultivation of personal holiness or of liturgical fulfilment with other pious souls. To him Christian loyalty was not a matter of preserving undefiled articles of the faith and moral rules but in direct and concrete realisation of compassion and help for one's neighbours. All this led to a firm conviction of the preeminent importance of the lay apostolate with the individual pursuing his job out in the world acutely aware of his responsibility to every brother in need.[88]

His startling decision in 1941 to enter the SS was immediately occasioned by his shock and concern at learning that his sister-in-law had been one of a number of victims of the Nazi 'euthanasia' campaign, but was also prompted by the adventurous desire to find out for himself from right within what was the truth of the rumours of the massacre of the mentally afflicted, the Jews and other persons. His aim he described at a later date as that of 'casting a close look into Hitler's kitchen, in order to see clearly what he and his gang were concocting'.[89] But it went deeper than that. It was the challenge to enter into the lions' den, into the Nazi hell, and to fulfil a unique role in doing so as Christ's representative 'putting on as God's spy the uniform of the Devil'[90] and in working in any way that might prove feasible to sabotage the Nazi system and to relieve the lot of the persecuted. 'Christian in his love of his fellow-men, he was Faust the experimenter as well.'[91] It involved the quitting of the ark of the visible Church with its security and its respectability, and becoming vicariously a sinner, representing other sinners before God, and indeed representing God in Hell. 'I had but one desire', he declared after the war was over, 'to see clearly into this whole mechanism and then cry it aloud to the whole nation! Even if it meant that my life would be threatened, I had no compunction. I myself had twice been fooled by agents of the Security Service who had infiltrated into the innermost circles of the Protestant Church and had prayed at my side. I thought to myself: If you can do it, so can I'.[92]

It may seem quite inexplicable that at a period when definite church allegiance on the part of the Nazi elite was discouraged or forbidden, this particular individual who was known to have been an ardent protagonist of the Protestant opposition, and who had twice undergone imprisonment on grounds of anti-Nazi propaganda should have been admitted so readily to a highly responsible position within the SS, and that he should have been allowed to witness at first hand the unspeakable horrors of mass-extermination in Poland. This can be partly explained by the fact that Gerstein gave an assurance that he was finished with the Confessing Church, and that the department which he was to join was, as Reitlinger has described it, 'a pool of murderously inclined medical men, where, as in the Foreign Legion, few questions were asked'.[93] Gerstein himself recounts how an SS man said to him: 'An idealist like you should be a fanatical member of our Party.'[94] The Nazi system was based upon making full use of all talent available. Gerstein's potentialities were so obvious and so considerable; and there was the added satisfaction of having captured so obdurate and so determined an opponent.[95]

It may also seem incredible that, back in Berlin after his ghastly experience, he should have escaped being apprehended and brought to book for his double dealing, and have survived as an SS man till the very end, particularly as he went about, according to those whom he secretly contacted, looking wild and ravaged with fear and anguish, and that he did not exercise any exceptional care in the contacts that he made or in the telling of his fearful tale. If it be asked why Gerstein, having witnessed such inhuman Nazi devilry, and knowing full well that he would be expected to assist in the expedition of future exterminations, did not contrive to get out of the SS as soon as possible, the obvious answer is that, having seen what he had, he would not have been allowed to do so, or else he would have been himself speedily eliminated. Besides which, he felt that it was an essential part of his peculiar divine commission, and of his deliberate self-sacrifice, that he should remain within the SS to do anything he could to hold up such executions. And there is full evidence that some of his efforts at sabotage proved effective.

Gerstein felt impelled to try to let the world know of what he had experienced.[96] He claimed, in his own words, to have informed 'hundreds of people of the horrible massacres', including a Swedish diplomat, who passed on a report to his own Government, a Swiss press attaché in Berlin who informed Berne, a Dutch engineer who was prepared to transmit his report to London, and also the Papal Nuncio and the co-adjutor Catholic Bishop in Berlin for information to Rome. But it did not result in any dramatic espousal of the cause of the Jews by allied or neutral powers or by the papacy and he was left 'peering vainly into the sky for the great shower of leaflets that was to arouse the conscience of the German people'.[97] Individual Germans whom he was instrumental in informing reacted in differing ways, but it is no surprise to learn that one regarded him as mad, another as a liar, while a third dismissed his fearful story as 'allied propaganda' and a fourth stoutly declared that 'Germans would be incapable of anything so atrocious'.[98]

As far as the German Evangelical Church was concerned, he told his story to Otto Dibelius, the Niemöller family, Pastor Mochalsky, Pastor of Niemöller's old church in Dahlem, and an old friend of his, Pastor Rehling. A conversation that he had with the latter is of the greatest possible interest. They discussed what they could do to prevent the continued atrocities. Pastor Rehling raised the question whether they should shout the facts from the top of the City Hall steps, or tell the story the following Sunday from the pulpit. Gerstein shook his head at such suggestions, declaring that no newspaper would print the story, and that people who might have listened to the report in church would be told the next day that their beloved pastor had become unbalanced, and had to be rushed to a mental hospital. 'Once there', he exclaimed to Rehling, 'you would betray me and all my friends, and action that we might take to help would be impossible.' To Rehling's further enquiry whether the moral necessity to utter was possibly not to be subject to any consideration of success, Gerstein replied that they should do nothing that was senseless or that would endanger others.[99] It would seem that apart from Rehling no one who was taken into Gerstein's confidence suggested any form of public protest. Bishop Dibelius commenting in 1963, confessed: 'I was shaken. Until then no one had ever told me of such things. Whatever I could do was very little. After all we ourselves were prisoners under constant surveillance by the State police.'[100]

All the same if it had been possible at the end of 1942 or early in 1943 on the basis of the Gerstein report for the heads of both Catholic and Protestant Churches in Germany to have made a simultaneous public protest against the extermination of the Jews, and what had been told had sickened and outraged a large number of ordinary decent Germans, the great majority of whom were registered members of one or other of the Churches, it would have been difficult to have taken action against them. There was indeed a precedent in the case of the enforced 'euthanasia' being called off, when, following determined protests from von Galen, Wurm and others, the killings were obviously causing dangerous unrest among so many people.[101] If the evidence given after the war by one who was heavily involved in the euthanasia campaign is to be trusted, Hitler's train was held up outside Nuremberg on account of some mental patients being loaded into a truck. The crowd watching were so enraged that they actually jeered the Führer.[102] But it should be added—and it is to be trusted not unfairly—this was a matter of the murder of one's own kith and kin, a different matter from the fate of men, women and children of alien and suspect race. Gerald Reitlinger's comment is that, 'When it was a matter of the deaths of Germans, the public conscience could assert itself, even in 1941. Himmler was stirred and, finally, Hitler. Decency and good sense prevailed. If they failed to do so regarding another matter, it was because decency and good sense were lacking.'[103]

For a detailed account of what Gerstein contrived to do, as purveyor of appallingly lethal prussic acid to the extermination camps, to prevent supplies reaching their goal and being available, and also for a discussion of all aspects of the Gerstein case including the mystery of his death (apparently suicide) in a French military prison on 25 July 1945, Saul Friedländer's book *Counterfeit Nazi* and Pierre Joffroy's record of his exhaustive researches in *A Spy for God* should be studied. The following concluding words of Friedländer invite quotation: 'What lends Gerstein's tragic fate its unique character and its full magnitude is the complete passivity of the others. Had there been in Germany thousands or even hundreds of Gersteins, had some of them tried to divert shipments of toxic gases, while others caused files to go astray or instigated delays in the construction of gas chambers and crematoria; had still others warned the Jews in the occupied countries and, above all, laboured untiringly to keep the Germans and the world informed, then hundreds of thousands of victims would undoubtedly have been saved.'[104]

That a desperately determined demonstration could work wonders is proved by the following extract from Ruth Andreas-Friedrich's Berlin Underground Diary dated 7 March 1943: 'The so-called privileged ones, the Jewish partners in racially mixed marriages . . . were taken to a collecting point last Sunday for examination and final determination. That same day the men's wives set out to find their arrested spouses. Six thousand non-Jewish women crowded around the portals of the building in the Rosenstrasse where the Aryan-connected ones were being held. Six thousand women called for their husbands, screamed for their husbands, howled for their husbands, and stood like a wall hour after hour, night and day. . . . This incident was extremely disagreeable to those in the SS Headquarters in the Burgstrasse. It was not considered an opportune moment to open up with machine-guns upon six thousand women. Conference of SS leaders. Debates back and forth. . . . Privileged persons are to be incorporated in the national community, SS decides at noon Monday. Anyone who chances to have been lucky enough to marry a non-Jewish wife can pack up his things and go home.'[105] It is probably true to say that there was no other demonstration like this in the whole of the Hitler period. It certainly has its permanent place in history as the only public anti-Nazi revolt during the war.[106]

The success of this unique demonstration certainly does raise the question whether, when Christian people felt impelled to unite together in expressing their feelings at the treatment of the Jews, they were right to do so largely by written or spoken word rather than by some dramatic form of action in public. Events in Holland in July 1942 furnish a case in point. After the Jews had been systematically rounded up in Amsterdam, it was proposed to the Council of Churches that a church in the centre of the city should be turned into a house of refuge for persecuted Jews, and that the clergy of the various churches should, fully vested, take up their positions at the entrances to the church, and stand or fall with the Jews inside. This proposal was rejected by a majority who regarded it as a 'sublime but useless gesture which might well cause a bloodbath and at the very least an acceleration of deportations'. Instead, it was resolved that various telegrams of protest should be sent. The Nazi authorities had no difficulty in dealing with this move, and effectively broke through the dangerous united opposition front by persuading the Dutch Reformed Church that they should not make public in their services their message of protest in return for the concession not to deport non-Aryan Church members. The Synod of the Reformed Church made the extraordinary admission that 'among decent people one party does not publish any documents, if the other party objects'.[107]

Georges Casalis, one of the devoted band of Frenchmen and Frenchwomen who showed such remarkable enterprise in giving practical assistance to Jewish victims in their locality and in enabling a few of them to escape to safety in Switzerland, has suggested in retrospect that during the period of the extermination of the Jews the one and only Christian attitude would have been a solemn declaration by all Churches accompanied by the summons to all Christians to wear the yellow star as token of the shame and the glory of the Son of David. 'I still believe today', he has written, 'that such an obedient act of witness by Christians would have sufficed to have obliged the Nazis to give way'.[108]

NOTES TO CHAPTER 7

1. *Schwarze Korps*, 24 November, 1938.
2. Helmut Krausnick: *The Persecution of the Jews* in *Anatomy of the SS State*, p. 44.
3. Meier, 86.
4. Andrew Sharf: *The British Press and the Jews under Nazi Rule*, Oxford, 1964, p. 98.
5. Krausnick, 68.
6. Krausnick, 68.
   Hitler apparently decided on the actual form of the final solution while planning the Russian war (Karl Dietrich Bracher; *The German Dictatorship*, Weidenfeld and Nicolson, 1971, p. 424).

Uwe Dietrich Adam in his recently published study *Judenpolitik im Dritten Reich*, Düsseldorf, 1972, pp. 305–16, convincingly challenges this generally accepted conclusion, and claims that Hitler's final and irrevocable decision to resort to full-scale planned massacre of European Jewry was not made until the autumn of 1941, when it was becoming obvious that within the foreseeable future there was no prospect of engineering a mass deportation of Jews into Russian territory, where at any rate as a temporary expedient the fullest and most ruthless employment of them in forced labour could be effected.

7. Zelzer, 231.
8. Victor Klemperer: *Die unbewältige Sprache*, 3rd edition, Darmstadt, 1966, p. 188.
9. Heinrich Wilhelmi—*Die Hamburger Kirche in der national-sozialistischen Zeit, 1933–1945*, Göttingen, 1968, p. 279.
10. Bielefeld Archiv., *Judenfrage*, IV.
11. Ehrenforth, 212.
12. Meier, 114–15.
13. EKDJF, 184–6.
14. Ehrenforth, 214.
15. KJB, 498–500.
16. Niemöller: *Wort und Tat*, 274.
17. Steinert: *Hitler's Krieg und die Deutschen*, p. 256.
18. Meier, 115–16.
19. Schmid: *Apokalyptisches Wetterleuchten* 161 and Prater: *Kämpfer wider Willen*, 153–5.
20. Brunotte, 164.
21. Brunotte, 165.
22. *Zur Frage der Beteiligung der Judenchristen am Christlichen Gottesdienst, Verbandsmitteilungen des Institutes für Erforschung des jüdischen Einflusses auf das deutsche kirchliche Leben*, December 1941, pp. 125–7.
23. Brunotte, 165.
24. Brunotte, 166–8.
25. KJB, 484–5.
26. Schäfer, 153–6.
27. Brunotte, 170. This Council of Three distinguished itself by expressing in 1941 in a telegram to the Führer the devout hope that under his inspiring leadership and with God's Blessing the 'deadly bolshevik foe of all good order and of western Christian Civilisation' and his British accomplice would be thoroughly routed, and that 'in the whole of Europe a new order would emerge, in which an end would be made to internal corruption, defilement of that which was most sacred and all violation of freedom of conscience' (KJB, 478). The same three gentlemen, one of whom, Bishop Marahrens, had been once a revered leader of the Confessional Church, produced in July 1944, a further telegram after the attempt on Hitler's life assuring him that in all evangelical churches in Germany a prayer of thanksgiving would be offered for God's gracious protection and patent preservation of the Führer (Klügel, 409).

28. Brunotte, 170–72.

29. Peter Phillips: *The Tragedy of Nazi Germany*, Kegan and Paul, 1969, p. 179.

30. van Roon: *German Resistance to Hitler*, 365.

31. *The German Path to Israel*: Documentation ed. Rolf Vogel, Dufour, Chester Springs, Pennsylvania, 1967, p. 244.

32. Niemöller: *Wort und Tat*, 274.

33. *The German Path to Israel*, 244.

34. The very idea of such cold-blooded and deliberate mass-butchery proved to be incomprehensible and beyond imagination. An impressively documented recent article by a Dutchman, Louis de Jong (*Die Niederlände und Auschwitz in Vierteljahrshefte für Zeitgeschichte*, 1969) substantiates this. de Jong writes about the inability of Dutchmen, not Germans, to accept reports of the mass-extermination even when they were provided personally by witnesses who had been upon the spot. There were many in Holland who despite their sufferings under German occupation refused to credit the BBC announcement in June 1942 of the murder of more than 700,000 Jews, and chose to dismiss it as anti-German war-propaganda. A Dutch Jewish leader maintained that there were limits to what one could accuse the Germans of. An SS man and a political prisoner who came directly from Auschwitz in January 1943 to assist in establishing a concentration camp in Holland, were either not believed or not taken seriously after having described in detail some of their dreadful experiences. Two young Dutch Roman Catholics who had been sent in 1941 to Auschwitz and were amazingly permitted to return to Holland in 1942 had their tales to tell, and were disconsolate, when Church officials showed a lack of interest in their experiences, and their own personal friends refused to believe them. A small group of Dutch Jehovah's Witnesses who had been quartered close to the gas chambers and daily subjected to the smoke from the crematoria returned to Holland in 1943 to find that the great majority of those to whom they gave their first-hand reports were unprepared to credit them. de Jong's concluding judgment that paradoxically 'it is an historical and also psychologically explainable fact that the Nazi extermination camps were for the majority of people only a psychical reality—and a qualified one at that—when they had and because they had ceased to exist' (p. 16) has to be taken into serious consideration. The whole atrocious affair, it has to be admitted, was at the time, unless directly observed, unthinkable and unimaginable. Human beings just could not behave like that!

So shrewd and sensitive an observer as Dr. Visser 't Hooft has recently written as follows about the reaction of many, both inside and outside Germany, to reports of the massacre of the Jews. 'People could find no place in their consciousness for such an unimaginable horror. . . . They did not have the imagination together with the courage to face it. It is possible to live in a twilight between knowing and not knowing. It is possible to refuse full realisation of facts because one feels unable to face the implications of these facts.' Visser 'tHooft admits that in his own case it took several months for the ghastly information to sink in, for it concerned 'a dimension of man's inhumanity to man which did not fit in with any previous experience' (W. A. Visser 't Hooft: *Memoirs*, S.C.M., 1973, pp. 165, 166).

35. Richard Grunberger: *A Social History of the Third Reich*, Weidenfeld and Nicolson, 1971, p. 460.

36. Norman Cohn in his book *Warrant for Genocide* (Pelican Books, 1970, pp. 232–3) refers to the highly interesting private investigations carried out by Michael Müller-Claudius in November 1938, and then again in 1942. Sixty-three per cent of those whom he casually asked in 1938 expressed indignation at the treatment that was being meted out at that time to the Jews, 32 per cent showed indifference and only 5 per cent expressed approval. In 1942 26 per cent showed concern, 69 per cent indifference and 5 per cent, as before, fanatical approval. On the basis of these figures Cohn claims that by 1942 most people in Germany at least suspected that something dreadful was happening to the deported Jews, an appreciable number must have known just what was happening, but that few cared much, and that the whole population had been highly conditioned to utter indifference.

This severe and sweeping indictment of the whole population may be challenged on several counts. Müller-Claudius's investigation was confined to members of the Nazi Party; it involved asking no more than a few dozen persons. Allowance must be made for those who in 1942 out of understandable anxiety at such an enquiry disguised their real feelings and feigned indifference. Is it really to be credited that those who had genuine Christian convictions, and that must have been quite a large number, did not care much whether the Jews were being liquidated ? There is reason to believe that uneasy, deep-seated guilt was fairly widespread, notwithstanding the failure to give open expression to it. The population was surely conditioned to fearful suppression of their feelings and to uncomfortable silence rather than to cold indifference. The present writer has on recent visits to Germany found that most of those to whom he has revealed his subject of research have proved unwilling to talk, and have obviously been relieved when the subject has been changed. This was not due to indifference but to a still remaining numbed feeling of unhappy guilt. The Jews are the albatross that the Germans are still wearing. The question that persists, and that is so hard and so necessary to try to answer, is how could all this have happened in a highly civilised country so rightly proud of its splendid past cultural achievements and inhabited by a population over 90 per cent Christian on paper, including a very fair number of men and women, either Catholics or Protestants, who took their religion really seriously. See Leo Katcher: *Post Mortem—*

The Jews in Germany Now, pp. 65, 88, 134–5, 186, 189, 214–16, where there is support for Cohn's contention.

Regarding those Germans who insist that they did not know what was going on, and that they are just unable to credit the extent of the massacre, some words of Arthur Koestler in an article in the New York Times, January 1944, are worth quoting—'I have been lecturing now for three years to the troops, and their attitude is the same. They don't believe in concentration camps, they don't believe in the starving children of Greece, in the shot hostages of France, in the mass-graves of Poland; they have never heard of Lidice, Treblinka or Belsen. You can convince them for an hour, then they shake themselves, their mental self-defence begins to work, and in a week the shrug of incredulity has returned like a reflex temporarily weakened by a shock' (quoted in Arthur Koestler: The Invisible Writing, Hamish Hamilton, 1944, p. 192).

37. Steinert, 594.
38. Schäfer, 158.
39. Ruth Andreas-Friedrich: Berlin Underground, Latimer House, 1948, p. 76.
40. Hilberg, 299.
41. Hilberg, 212. Saul Friedländer: Counterfeit Nazi, Weidenfeld and Nicolson, 1969, pp. 140, 142.
42. Stewart Herman: It's your Souls we want, Hodder and Stoughton, 1943, p. 208.
43. Hilberg, 623.
44. Hilberg, 300.
45. Friedländer, 143.
46. Gerald Reitlinger, The Final Solution, London, 1968, p. 175.
47. Schäfer, 306.
48. Fritz Raddatz, ed.: Durfte der Papst schweigen? Hochhuths 'Stellvertreter' in der öffentlichen Kritik Rowohlt, 1963.
49. Friedländer, 138, quoting from a Danzig newspaper of May 1944.
50. Reitlinger, 527.
51. Quoted by Pierre Joffroy: A Spy for God. The Ordeal of Kurt Gerstein, Collins, 1971, p. 179.
52. Lewy, 288.
53. Klügel: Dokumente, 202–3.
54. Wurm, 170.
55. Schäfer, 305–7. See Appendix V for a translation of the letter.
56. Wurm, 170.
57. See Reinhold Sautter's letter to Reichminister Lammers: Schäfer, 316. 'Before me stands a man who despite his age of seventy-five is still unbowed, and with a freshness of spirit, a liveliness of disposition and a clarity of judgment at which we younger men can only marvel.' There is a present lack of a biography of Bishop Wurm, nor is there a published account of the Church Struggle written around Wurm as there is in the case of Marahrens. The slender volume by Reinhold Sautter, Theophil Wurm, sein Leben

und sein Kampf, Stuttgart, 1960, is little more than an appreciation by one of his closest associates. Richard Fischer, of course, writes in great detail of Wurm's years as Bishop of Württemberg, and Gerhard Schäfer is engaged in the preparation of six volumes of documents dealing with the Evangelical Church in Württemberg, 1932–45, the first three of which have already been published— *Dokumentation zum Kirchenkampf; Die evangelische Landeskirche in Württemberg und der Nationalsozialismus*, Band 1—*Um das politisches Engagement der Kirche, 1932–1933*, Stuttgart, 1971, Band 2—*Um eine deutsche Reichskirche, 1933*, Stuttgart, 1972, Band 3—*Der Einbruch des Reichsbischof in die Württembergesche Landeskirche, 1934*, 1974.

58. Schäfer, 313–15.
59. Hermelink, 556. Wurm's letter to Goebbels, dated 1 April 1942, was published in a Swedish weekly, and broadcast from London, Morocco, and Cincinnati, and distributed in German, Italian, English, and French.
60. Martin Niemöller in a speech in December 1945, while complimenting Wurm upon his manifest courage, voiced his regret that he did not expressly speak in the name of his Church but just personally as a devout confessing Christian. Wilhelm Niemöller: *Neuanfang 1945, Zur Biographie Martin Niemöllers*, Frankfurt, 1967, p. 102.
61. See Hilberg, 115 and 268–77. The cross-breeds were the 'recurring problem children of German bureaucracy'. The Party would have liked to have made them subject to the 'Final Solution'. The Civil Service was opposed to this, and would have preferred to have seen them die out. It was suggested in June 1941 that crossbreeds of the first degree, those with two Jewish grandparents, should be equated with the Jews and deported, unless they were married to Germans with children, or have given recognised service to the German people. The cross-breed of the second degree, with only one Jewish grandparent, was at the same time in danger of being regarded as a Jew, if not married to a German, and if he looked or behaved like a Jew. Those who on paper were very safe were readily put on the extermination line, if they broke the regulations or incurred the displeasure of the authorities. As regards mixed marriages, the decisive consideration was the religious status of the children of the marriage. 'Privileged' status was not awarded, if there was an intention to bring up the children as Jews. The partners of mixed marriages were 'privileged' with the exception of the Jewish male partner in a childless marriage. 'Privileged' couples outnumbered unprivileged by three to one. In 1942 the suggestion was made that all Jews in mixed marriages should be deported, and that this should be accompanied by divorce. In 1943 the Gestapo did deport a handful of 'privileged' Jews. But the divorce and deportation of the 'Privileged' obviously could not be kept secret, and this was regarded as jeopardising the operation as a whole. The cross-breeds largely escaped, because they were mostly regarded as being more German than Jewish.

The Nazis found, as Hermann Diem has pointed out, that it was very useful, in dealing with the Church, to have a 'privileged' category of Jews. If the Church was threatening to make public attack upon their anti-Jewish measures and atrocities, a counter-threat to take steps to include the 'privileged', a considerable number of whom were Christians, as well, could prove most effective (*Stärker als die Angst*, 136). 'What was so morally disastrous in the acceptance of "privileged" categories was that everyone who demanded to have an exception made in his case implicitly recognised the rule, but this point, apparently, was never grasped by those 'good men', Jew and Gentile, who busied themselves about all those special cases for which preferential treatment could be asked (Hannah Arendt: *Eichmann in Jerusalem*, 117).

62. Schäfer, 378–81.
63. Ibid., 159–60.
64. Ibid., 168.
65. Ibid., 169.
66. Elias, 219.
67. Fischer, XIV, 190.
68. *The Von Hassell Diaries, 1938–1944*, Hamish Hamilton, 1948, p. 278.
69. Grunberger, 441.
70. Karl Schumacher: *Theophil Wurm in den Krisen und Entscheidungen seiner Zeit*, Stuttgart, 1948, p. 20.
71. Schäfer, 162.
72. Ibid., 312.
73. Gerlach, 437–8 and 441–2. Gerlach has obtained his information about the Munich circle from an account given to him by Emil Höchstädter's son and from the archives of the Bavarian Church in Nuremberg. His description of what happened is to be regarded as altogether more accurate than the brief notice provided by Hermelink (*Kirche im Kampf*, 653) who suggests that Meiser was unable to persuade the laymen who presented the Epistle to append their signatures to it, and therefore took no further action. Elias (219) declares that the laymen had not the courage to sign. He also states quite correctly that the Letter was passed on from Meiser to Wurm, and adds that it must have made a deep impression upon him. Kurt Meier (*Kirche und Judentum*, p. 40) is certain that the Epistle did much to strengthen Wurm in his attitude of protest. Schäfer (p. 165) declares, however, that, when it reached Stuttgart, it was filed away and disregarded. Hermann Diem in an interview informed the present writer that, as far as he is aware, his composition did not have any direct influence upon Wurm. See also Uvo Andrea Wolf in Hermann Diem: *Sine Vi et Verbo*, München 1964, p. 273.
74. Diem in *Stärker als die Angst*, 133, 136.
75. A translation of the majority of the Epistle is to be found in Appendix 5, pp. 350ff. For the full text see EKDJF, 196–9 and Hermelink, 650–3.
76. Gerlach, 443–5.
77. KJB, 401.

78. KJB, 403.
79. Inge Scholl: *Six against Tyranny*, Murray, 1955.
80. Forck: *Und folget ihrem Glauben nach*, pp. 90–4. See also Hermann Hesse's moving account of his period of captivity in *Sieger in Fesseln*, Freiburg, 1947, pp. 64–71.
81. Bishop Wurm wrote to Himmler, petitioning for the release of Hermann Hesse, and argued that his reference in a sermon to the destruction of Barmen by air-attack as a 'Judgement' ought not to be regarded as a political attack. It had taken the form of a religious judgement forced from the lips of one who saw in all happenings a divine activity at work (Schäfer, 441).
82. Vorländer: *Elberfeld*, 544–5.
83. Hermann Hesse: *Die Judenfrage in der Verkündigung heute*, Stuttgart, 1948, p. 8.
84. Fischer: XVII, 204 ff.
85. See Rolf Hochhuth: *The Representative*. Penguin Books, 1969, Historical Sidelights, pp. 315–20. For Gerstein see Helmut Franz: *Kurt Gerstein. Aussenseiter des Widerstandes der Kirchen gegen Hitler*, Zürich, 1964; Saul Friedländer: *Counterfeit Nazi*, Weidenfeld and Nicolson, 1969; and Pierre Joffroy, *A Spy for God. The Ordeal of Kurt Gerstein*, Collins, 1970.
86. Franz, 20.
87. Joffroy, 60.
88. Franz, 20.
89. de Jong in *Vierteljahrshefte für Zeitgeschichte*, 1969, p. 8.
90. Franz, 30.
91. Joffroy, 98.
92. Friedländer, 73.
93. Reitlinger, 162.
94. Friedländer, 73.
95. Joffroy, 91.
96. Friedländer, 128.
97. Joffroy, 187.
98. Joffroy, 178.
99. Friedländer, 135.
100. Otto Dibelius: *Obrigkeit*, Stuttgart, 1963, p. 141.
101. For von Galen's Protest see Patrick Smith: *The Bishop of Münster and the Nazis*, Burns Oates, 1942, pp. 40–7 and Lewy, 263–7. For Wurm's Protests see Schäfer, 115–46. See also Niemöller: *Wort und Tat*, 276–9, and Hans Christoph von Hase: *Evangelische Dokumente zur Ermordnung der 'unheilbar Kranken' unter der national-sozialistichen Herrschaft in den Jahren, 1939–1945*, Stuttgart, 1964.
102. Reitlinger, 139.
103. Reitlinger, 139.
104. Friedländer, 227–8.
105. Andreas-Friedrich, 82–3.
106. *Stärker als die Angst*, 208, 217.
107. Johan Snoek: *The Grey Book*, Assen, 1969, pp. 128–9.

108. Adolf Freudenberg, ed.: *Rettet sie doch! Franzosen und die Genfer Oekumene im Dienste der Verfolgten des Dritten Reiches*, Zürich, 1969, p. 200. Being happy to live in days when relations and co-operation between Catholics and Protestants are by and large so encouragingly harmonious and 'Christian', we may feel inclined to query why determined resort could not have been made in the Hitler period to joint protest and common action. It has, of course, to be remembered that, despite isolated instances of Roman Catholics and Evangelicals praying for one another, and offering sympathetic mutual support under persecution, and both becoming increasingly aware of being involved in a life or death struggle with the State, the Catholic and Protestant Churches still kept rigidly apart.

In September 1941 Bishop Meiser placed before a meeting of Evangelical Church leaders in Berlin the draft of a proposed joint statement from Evangelical and Catholic bishops addressed to the Nazi Government setting out the disabilities and forms of persecution from the effects of which the Churches were suffering, and which could be interpreted as a planned elimination of Christian influence. The meeting could not decide whether to support such joint action. A month later Bishop Wurm strongly recommended joint action with the Roman Catholics, and after misgivings had been expressed by some of the Lutheran and Reformed representatives present, unanimous agreement was reached. Bishop Wurm was able the very next day to meet the Roman Catholic Bishops of Berlin and Osnabruck. It was then decided to draw up two independent statements and present them simultaneously at the Reich Chancery. This was done. Assurance was given that they had been placed before the Führer, but, though this may indeed have been the case, no reply came, and no action followed (Schäfer, 269–71). At the beginning of 1943, when the threat of State legislation to compel the divorce of Aryan and non-Aryan partners in marriage was causing the greatest anxiety to both Catholics and Protestants, the suggestion of a joint protest was then mooted. The Confessing Church leader Wilhelm Jannasch went secretly to Breslau to discuss this with Cardinal Bertram, the presiding Roman Catholic prelate. The plan this time was to read simultaneously from all Roman Catholic and Evangelical Confessional pulpits an identical message of protest. It has been claimed that the threat to do so was effective in hindering the intended legislation, though it must be doubted whether it had anything approaching the effect of the unique revolt of the Aryan wives in the Berlin Rosenstrasse (see p. 257). We have regrettably no information as to the text of the proposed pulpit declaration. Perhaps it was never fully drafted. It would be of great interest to learn whether the chief emphasis was placed upon the agonised plight of the married couples concerned or upon the shocking violation of the sanctity of the marriage bond (Gerlach, 407–8 and *Konrad, Kardinal von Preysing, Bischof von Berlin*, Berlin, 1950, p. 103).

8

Conclusion

Karl Barth in a lecture delivered very soon after the end of the war expressed his belief that, where the Confessing Church was concerned, during the whole period of the Church Struggle as much as was humanly possible was done for the persecuted Jews.[1] This tribute is certainly not borne out by the evidence that this present study has sought to furnish. The pessimistic judgement of Wilhelm Niemöller, an assiduous apologist in nearly all respects for the Confessing Church, would seem to be far nearer the truth. He writes with reference to the Church and the Jews, 'What did the Evangelical Church say and do in those years? Only a small part of the Church, the so-called Confessing Church, endeavoured to do a little, and frequently with hesitation, in fear and dread and with distinct reservations. . . . The picture as a whole is dismal. One of the most glorious opportunities to make proof of Christian profession through Christian action was, taken as a whole, missed and unexercised.'[2] Julius von Jan, one of the few who really spoke out, felt bound to admit—'We were all of us scared of crossing the Nazi regime at its most sensitive point.'[3] To which it may not unfairly be added that it was undeniably one of the most sensitive points where the Church herself was concerned. The repeated verdict of post-war commentators has been—'Too little, too late!' An attempt must be made to provide some explanation of the Church's undeniable failure to do and to say what could be expected of the representatives of Christ, and it will of necessity call for one or two digressions involving the consideration of particular theological and ecclesiastical attitudes.

There was no possibility whatever of the Evangelical Church as a whole protesting or taking action. Not only did the 'German Christians' and also the official central Church government prove to be accommodating to the National Socialist programme, but from 1936 on, and, in particular, during 1938 and 1939 within the Confessional Church itself there was so much tension between the extreme and the moderate wings that joint pronouncements upon so burning an issue were out of the question. It should also not be forgotten that a very considerable number of pastors and lay people adopted a neutral position in the Church conflict with the avowed intention of steering clear of church politics and keeping generally out of trouble, and that would certainly have included getting involved in controversy over the Jews.

The Church as Church did not find a decisive word from Scripture as a whole to embrace the issue as a whole. The Confessional Synods, as Hermann Hesse expressed it, 'appointed commissions only to come to the conclusion: we are not theologically developed enough to pronounce upon the Jewish question'.[4] Many earnest confessing Christians remained instinctively anti-semitic in outlook, nursed in nationalistic traditions, and not altogether immune from the ceaseless Nazi propaganda. Discouraged by Luther from making a real break-through; deprived by recent theological criticism from accepting the old orthodox eschatological view of the fate of Israel, they were uncertain how to interpret St. Paul.[5] Maybe I Thessalonians 2: 15 with its reference to the Jews as having 'killed the Lord Jesus' and 'persecuted us' and as having failed to 'please God' and being 'contrary to all men' proved more palatable than Romans 11: 28, 29 with its emphasis on God's irrevocable choice of Israel as His People. It was not surprising that, instead of wrestling with the Jewish question in its whole theological breadth and depth, they chose to concentrate so largely upon issues such as missions to the Jews, church membership of non-Aryans and the welfare of the so-called 'privileged'. Throughout the Conflict nobody in a position of authority made a full and plain denunciation of anti-semitism as such. Only a very few Church leaders such as Heinrich Grüber were prepared to take up the cudgels decisively on behalf of the pious orthodox Jew or those persecuted simply on account of race. 'Nothing', Leuner remarks, 'paralysed the Church's fight for the oppressed from the beginning so much as the distinction between baptised and unbaptised Jews'. 'This' he contends, 'encouraged the average churchgoer in thinking that the unbaptised Jew, i.e. the Jew as such, was to be left to the Devil'.[6]

There was no one to be found making a protest like that of the Roman Catholic Archbishop of Toulouse: 'It has been reserved to our time to witness the sad spectacle of children, of women, of fathers and mothers, being treated like a herd of beasts. . . . Jews are men, Jewesses are women. . . . They cannot be maltreated at will. They are part of the human race. They are our brethren as much as are so many others. Christians cannot forget that.'[7]

When it came to a question of practical assistance to the Jews in their desperate need, there were not lacking, as has been shown, individuals who were ready to help at very great personal risk. The Krakauer odyssey is a testimony to the effectiveness in operation of a local network of Good Samaritans. It has been asked why it could not have been arranged within the Confessional Church as a whole for the simultaneous and open reception of threatened Jewish fellow-citizens into Christian households.[8] It is to be doubted whether the Nazi regime would have dared to liquidate along with each Jew Christians of recognised German citizenship who had in such a determined and practical fashion witnessed to their solidarity with the persecuted. The story of the Church Struggle reveals that in the Confessional movement when there was any question of taking resolute action, which could or would be interpreted as political opposition to the policy of the State, there were inevitably always those who would decline to go so far.

Otto Dibelius in an article criticising Rolf Hochhuth's *Representative* refers to the contribution of the Confessing Church. As well as personal underground assistance given by individuals, the Church, he claims, had made public utterance, but with the greatest possible care that it was ecclesiastically legitimate. 'Otherwise,' he writes, 'we would have been silenced at the outset. Among the non-Aryans were countless Christians. They had the first call upon our endeavours. This was the one and the only standpoint that was at all possible for a Church in a totalitarian State'. Dibelius went on sadly to admit that the post-war world had scarcely any understanding for such an inevitable limitation, and professed to detect a cleavage between institutional and ecclesiastical thinking on the one hand and elementary Christian humanity on the other, with the Churches thinking only of themselves and without proper feeling for others who had to suffer. 'This is unfair', he declared, 'since under totalitarian dictatorship anyone who stands up in the market-place in order to indict the State is immediately reduced to dead silence. His cause is a lost one. In order to have any success, it is essential to have a base, valid in law, from which to speak and to act'.[9]

It was Otto Dibelius who in 1926 had so eagerly published a book entitled *Das Jahrhundert der Kirche* ('The Century of the Church').[10] It attracted considerable attention particularly among his fellow-pastors, and by 1928 it had passed into six editions. 'My purpose', wrote Dibelius in 1961 in retrospect, 'was to show that in the space of three hundred years Protestantism in Germany had not become a Church in the proper sense of the term, but had remained a department of ecclesiastical affairs within the secular government. Only since the middle of the nineteenth century had something like a Church developed on evangelical foundations. This new state of affairs had to be accepted with joy at a time when the era of individualism was drawing to a close and social thinking was making mighty strides forward. A genuine Church required freedom from the State, it required episcopal office, a definite social purpose and many other things'.[11] In describing the situation after the 1914–1918 war he declared that the mood of the Church was quite overwhelmingly hostile to the Republic and very reserved where the new State was concerned. Nevertheless, the independence of the Church had been achieved. 'The period of dreamings and of utopias is over', he declaimed, 'the work of the Church is now on a secure foundation. Ecclesiam habemus! We have a Church! The goal is achieved!'[12] It was to be a Church which would comprehend the life of her members in its totality, a home for the whole of man and for every department of life and subject only to her own laws. The Evangelical Church could now be established upon a firm, assured and immovable foundation with its course no longer prescribed by individual men or by the contingencies of the time. A Church which adapted herself to circumstances, definitely compromised herself with the prevailing *Kultur*, and was a different Church under the Republic from under the Monarchy, in the sunshine of peace from the storms of revolution, would have ceased to be a true Church.[13] As such she would not adapt herself to men, but would expect them to adapt themselves to her. She would not allow herself to be influenced internally through being either recognised or ignored by the State. In any conflict between Church and State the Church would always emerge victorious, so long as she concerned herself with issues that affected her very essence. The Church had inherited a so-called Christian order of society whose guardian had of late been the State. The tasks before the Church were more vast than they had been for 500 years, but the growth of the Church was commensurate with the immensity of such tasks. Her influence upon the State, upon economics and politics, upon the spiritual and eventually also upon the material life of the nation would expand from year to year. This exciting growth in the effective role of the Church was in no wise confined to Germany. The same situation was manifest through the whole of the world. 'Christian Churches', he affirmed, 'are on the threshold of a new epoch. They are gathering their strength. They are venturing upon new tasks. Their horizons are broadened, their hopes and their responsibilities are enormous'.[14]

This all sounded very fine, and Dibelius was certainly influential in encouraging many of his fellow-churchmen to feel an invigorating confidence in the Church as Church and in her mission and ability to be an influence in public life. This may be accounted to have been of value in preparing the Evangelical Church for her coming conflict. But there were none the less serious miscalculations and deficiencies in such an appraisal of the ecclesiastical situation. The existence of a genuine and vocal Church was declared to be required as a bulwark in the defence of western Christian civilisation against anti-Christian Soviet Russia.[15] There was, however, no accompanying suggestion whatever of a parallel need to curb the spread of alarming and exaggerated volkish pretensions and yearnings both within and without the Church. In fact, a restrained but none the less patent acceptance of the volkish outlook was discernible throughout the book. The need was expressed for an 'orientation according to the guiding principles which God has provided for the German people in their particular history. . . . The tree can only grow and yield fruit when it has its roots deeply buried in mother-soil'.[16] According to God's creative will all healthy human life was to be found reposing in the Volkstum. The contribution that German Evangelicals could make œcumenically was to provide a Church that not only revolved round Martin Luther, but one in which

Jesus Christ was 'seen with German eyes' and 'believed in with German hearts'.[17] The Church might be regarded as full of assurance as to its newly found independence and self-determination, yet if there should be a threat of conflict with the State it was very far from clear what line should be adopted. Dibelius could boldly declare on one page that 'the Church cannot recognise an omnipotent State',[18] only on the very next page to affirm that, while historical events could drive the Church into opposition against a certain form of State, there could be no fundamental conflict between State and Church. On principle an Evangelical Church could acknowledge any form of State and render service in every such administration. It was in no way in the interests of the Church to be pushed into opposition against the State.[19]

So enthusiastic a build-up for what could be described as the status and the prestige of the Church was by no means confined to Otto Dibelius. Of great influence through the 'twenties was Johannes Schneider as editor of the Official Annuals of the German Evangelical Church. He was at his most eloquent in the 1928 edition, applauding the empirical Church for both its staying-power and its elasticity. 'The Church leadership of the last decade', he wrote, 'has been masterly. Even her critics are more and more conscious of this. The truth of this will be seen more clearly in times to come than at this present. Capital has been made of her freshly gained freedom and strength in order to make her existence secure for coming generations and to develop and expand her latent powers for the welfare of the 'Soul of the People' (*Volksseele*), making out of her a genuine *Volkskirche*.'[20] 'We are far from having climbed over the mountain', he averred, 'but we have made our way through the narrow pass, and we see before us an open field'.[21]

No one exercised more powerful influence than Paul Althaus upon the idea of a Volk Church fitted to meet the needs and opportunities of the hour. From 1917 on he was tireless in insisting that Germany's revival depended upon the German people finding its way back to the Church, and the Evangelical Church showing positive sympathy to volkish aspirations through giving them a sound Christian interpretation. In 1919 he declared that the time was favourable for the rediscovery of a 'lost' Church. 'Now', he wrote, 'the great hour of the Church is at hand'. . . . If we do not learn today what Church really is, when

hall we ever learn it?'[22] In 1927 Althaus had his great oppor-
unity as principal speaker at the German Evangelical *Kirchentag*
t Königsberg. The Churches and the Volk movement, he
eclared, were beginning to come together. Both had at heart
he interests of the whole people. The Volk Movement was
nocking at the door of the Church. The Church had to make
lear that the promotion of the Volk was the Will of God and to
e prepared to serve in God's name to prevent the 'noble glow
f Love for Volk' from developing into a wrong and fundamentally
nchristian direction. In order to do so, the Church had to become
genuine *Volkskirche*, not concerned with ministering to individual
ouls or just gathered congregations but to the people as a whole
nd providing a really relevant preaching of the Gospel, testifying
o the special commission from the God of history and pointing
o the true source of communal existence.[23]

It is no surprise to find Althaus in 1933 eagerly contributing
n article with the title *Das Ja der Kirche zur deutsche Wende*
'The Yes of the Church to the German Turn of Events'). In
rder to guard himself against the kind of fanatical enthusiasm
hat was being shown by the more exuberent of the 'German
Christians', he soberly admitted that thankfulness for an historical
urning-point needed to be different in tone and in character
rom gratitude to God for what He had done once for all men
n Christ. No historical revolution was without stain and shadows.
t was wrong to cast a veil over what was human, all too human,
nd what was amiss, in the recent happenings. But all the same a
rateful 'Yes' was in order in view of the observable transforma-
ion from disintegration to renewal and from indisposition to
estoration of health. The German people had come to its senses!
The new State was daring to 'bear the sword'. The shocking
rresponsibility of Parliament had been smashed to pieces. Filth
nd corruption was being swept away. The people were being
ummoned to give expression to a powerful new community-will
nd to practical socialism by virtue of which the strong would
e prepared to carry the burdens of the weak.[24]

It is no surprise, either, to discover Althaus taking a prominent
part in 1934 in the formulation of the *Ansbacher Ratschlag* (Ans-
bach Counsel)[25] which took issue with the Theological Declaration of the Confessional Synod of Barmen. It rejected as false
the doctrine that the Church could acknowledge as a source of

her proclamation, beside and in addition to the One Word of
God testified to in Scripture, other events, powers, forms and
truths as the Revelation of God, and regard herself as permitted
to frame her message according to the prevailing Weltanschauung
and political conviction. It was claimed in the *Ansbacher Ratschlag*
that the Will of God was constantly taking effect in the here and
now, and at definite moments in a People's History bound them
to a particular ordering of People and Race (i.e. Blood relationship). 'We as believing Christians', it was declared, 'thank the
Lord God that He has in our need presented us with the Führer
as pious and faithful overlord, and that in the National Socialist
political system he will provide us with good government, a
government with discipline and honour. We therefore acknowledge
before God our responsibility in our profession and calling to
assist the work of the Führer'.[26] This same Führer had piously
proclaimed in *Mein Kampf* that he would be doing the work of
the Lord in taking stern measures against the Jews. This statement emanating as it did from two such respected and erudite
orthodox theologians as Werner Elert and Paul Althaus was
indeed welcome grist to both the Nazi and the 'German Christian'
mill.

In the same year Althaus coined the highly dubious phrase
'gratia historica' in an article, in the course of which he wrote
'The Church lives from the Grace of Jesus Christ. But as the
Christian community within her Volk she also lives from *gratia
historica* by virtue of which God calls Peoples, leads them on
to higher things and summons heroic personalities to help them
out of their distress'.[27]

Althaus may himself have considered that throughout the
years he had remained true to his Lutheran inheritance, and had
not fallen prey to romantic idealism or surrendered Gospel Truth
and sound doctrine to national enthusiasm. This is open to serious
doubt, but what is certain is that he enormously encouraged
others altogether less well trained in theological sense and altogether more ardent and uncontrolled in pro-Nazi enthusiasm to
attempt to justify from a volkish outlook, such as his, religious
support and vindication of the Nazi racial programme.

The dramatic and enthusiastic recovery of the Church, in so
far as it was not a matter of the Church for the Church's sake and
was outward-looking, was severely restricted by Volk-obsession.

Comparatively little direct attention was paid to social and economic want and moral disorder, and the regard that was shown
for such issues tended to be more volkish than evangelical or
humanitarian, the Church offering herself, as Ernst Wolf has
described, as makeshift for defunct national solidarity and a
'top-gap for slumbering devotion to Fatherland'.[28] This meant
that, when the National Socialist momentum quickened in
1931 and 1932, and in 1933 brought to its triumphant conclusion, the Evangelical Church was to a considerable degree
concerned either with her own aggrandisement or with oppor-
unities of establishing herself more fully as the Church of the
Volk, both in the popular and the mystical sense. This largely
precluded consideration of her likely fate under a professedly
totalitarian and racial regime, and of her responsibility to hold a
watching brief in the name of Christ and for righteousness sake,
and be really concerned about any future victims of the New
Order, among whom there was no doubt that the Jews would be
prominent.

The youthful Dietrich Bonhoeffer had chosen for his doctoral
thesis an enquiry into the nature and working of the Church.
Written between 1926 and 1927 it was published in 1930 under
the title of *Sanctorum Communio*.[29] His approach proved to be
very different from that of the 'Century of the Church' brigade.
Bonhoeffer saw the Church as being at one and the same time an
historical fellowship and a God-established reality by virtue of
the fact of Christ. The reality of the Church he claimed to be
a 'revelational reality'—'Christ existing as Community'. In the
actualising of the Church at a given point of time the significance
of Christ occupied of necessity the central point. Active work
for one's neighbour was one of the essential expressions of the
Christian Church. The connecting thread of the whole book was
the thought of the Church being the place in which the vicarious
representation of Christ for mankind is fulfilled in the representation of believers both in mutual relationship and in contact with
the world. Here was a basic point of departure in forming a right
attitude to the forthcoming Church struggle. It was not enough
for the Church just to preach the Word purely; vicarious representation such as was the Church's calling found its fulfilment in
concrete application to men and women, and the Church which
fought shy of suffering on behalf of the brethren who were being

deprived of their rights, and especially the Jews, could not b accounted an obedient Church.[30]

Karl Barth in two of his most eloquent and blistering article *Quousque Tandem . . .* (1930)[31] and *Die Not der Evangelisch Kirche* (1931)[32] sought to prick the bubble of the 'Century of th Church'. Johannes Schneider's paean of praise for the empirica Church was castigated as a scandal that cried to heaven, a reall dangerous conspiracy against the substance of the Evangelica Church. It was Barth's conviction that Schneider was the spokes man for 'dozens and dozens of our leading ecclesiastics and c hundreds and thousands of our pastors'.[33] The proud claim tha 'God is for us because we are so unflinchingly for ourselves' an that 'nothing can be done against us, as we ourselves are s successfully all set to do so energetically and so clear-sightedl what is necessary in our defence' was nothing more or less than denial of the Divine Promises and of genuine faith. The preachin of the Gospel was being neglected in favour of an unwarrante trust in what the Church could do of herself. Barth was at hi most cruel in suggesting that, when the 'resurrected Church which boasted that she had won her way 'through the narrov pass' spoke of Jesus Christ, it was in point of fact her own reple tion and security that was being emphasised, and that with a the talk about 'Jesus Christ' she was deaf to the actual needs c real men and women.[34]

Barth accused Dibelius of unpardonably superficial optimisr and self-satisfaction over the sure standing of the Church an could not forbear characterising him as the obdurate Laodicea 'rich, increased with goods and having need of nothing' (Revela tion 3:17).[35] In failing to take into account the essential an inalienable tribulation (*Not*) of the Church he and others like minded were actually working for her destruction and not he glorification. The Evangelical Church was in essence a Churc under the Cross. She was required humbly and in a spirit c true penitence to share in the humiliation of Christ instead c wanting to elevate man into the sphere of the divine. The Churc had only one fundamental task, that of serving God. She coul thereby indeed be of service to man, but it was in no way he task to be serving mankind, still less to be wanting to manipulat God in man's service. She had no abstract right to be fulfillin human interests. Concern for the existence and influence of th

Church was matched by indifference to her essential character. There was also a complete lack of eschatological horizon, an ominous desire to blame the world outside rather than the Church herself for what was wrong and lacking, a sinister desire to make the Church really powerful, secure in her relationship with the State and full of influence upon society, impressive to the masses; and a still more sinister tendency to harp upon and to exalt the hyphenated 'German-Christian' element, making that the real criterion of ecclesiastical orthodoxy, delighting to quote Luther's dictum—'For my German people have I been born, them will I serve!'

This eloquent protest was, according to Ernst Wolf, scarcely heeded at the time.[36] The Church was altogether too much concerned about herself to pay attention. Otto Dibelius subsequently admitted that twenty five years later Martin Niemöller had reproached him with never having been a man of the Confessing Church but only a man of the Church, and he added the comment 'What else should I be than a man of the Church?'[37] Dibelius, it must be readily conceded, had during the Church Struggle his moments of most courageous and telling witness, but it was very much ecclesiastically orientated. Without doubt the 'Century of the Church' had a definite influence upon many Lutherans who came to regard the conflict with the Nazis in terms of Church defence more than as a Christian fight against evil and on behalf of its helpless victims.

Dialectical Theology, of which Karl Barth was the most prominent exponent, was also instrumental in encouraging the Church to be primarily concerned with her own affairs. The Church at all costs had to remain the Church, pledged to proclaim and to defend an intolerantly one-sided and transcendental faith laden with paradox. This certainly discouraged any kind of all-embracing or liberal idealism. Barth said a fierce and pugnacious 'No' to Natural Theology in whatever guise.[38] His steadfast refusal, and that of his numerous disciples who took so predominant a part in shaping the Confessing approach, to make room for a *revelatio generalis* prevented the requisite development and assertion of a theology of the natural. The Confessing Church at Barmen was set on a rigidly determined dogmatic course which resulted in what has been described as the *Thematik des Humanum* being treated as suspect, and to be rejected along with theological liberalism.[39] It is not surprising that the conflict was by and large conceived of in doctrinal rather than ethical terms. Barthian theology with its ethical *Weltresignation* played into the hands of the Nazis with their demand for undisputed control of secular life. John Bowden has written recently of the price that an approach like that of Barth has to pay: 'One longs for him to say, just once "In the name of mankind, this is wicked", for him to show insight into what other men, women and children think and feel and suffer as fellow human beings. But this he cannot do. Is the concentration on the Word, on Jesus Christ and him alone, worth this neglect? Whatever benefits Barth's championing of the Confessing Church brought, it was bound up with some terrible connotations from which he never managed to escape.'[40]

Dietrich Bonhoeffer was largely the odd man out in developing an ethical christology, and this made him constantly an uneasy and disappointed collaborator in the Church Struggle. He came to the final conclusion that the 'decisive factor' with the Confessing Church was 'being on the defensive' with 'unwillingness to take risks in the service of humanity'.[41] He wrote from prison in 1944 to a friend: 'The place of religion is taken by the Church—that is, in itself, as the Bible teaches it should be—but the world is made to depend upon itself and left to its own devices, and that is all wrong.'[42]

It was, to Barth, the substance of the Faith (*Die Sache*) that was the paramount concern not the situation in which men and women happened to be placed (*Die Lage*). In *Theological Existence Today*, his first great battle-cry, issued in June 1943, he affirmed the supreme importance, in contrast to the excited determination of so many Churchmen to be thoroughly 'with it', of carrying on with this theology, 'as if nothing had happened' (*als wäre nichts geschehen*).[43] This phrase *als wäre nichts geschehen* became celebrated, and, lifted out of its context, was in future repeatedly to be quoted in the Church Conflict. Another extract from this famous pamphlet, 'The Church has in no way whatever to serve mankind nor the German people. She has alone to serve the Word of God', ('*Die Kirche hat überhaupt nicht den Menschen und auch nicht dem deutschen Volk zu dienen. Sie dient aber allein dem Worte Gottes*')[44] was all too liable to be misquoted and misapplied. While recognising that he changed his tune very considerably as

the Church Struggle developed, it is instructive to note that Barth
saw fit to emphasise at the end of 1933 that he was in opposition
not to the National Socialist ordering of State and Society but to
a theology which at that present time was seeking refuge with
National Socialism. It was not for the Church to be endeavouring
to govern or to shape State and Society, her aim in the midst of
State and Society was, rather, to function soberly and essentially
as Church. This one object had to be pursued 'with passionate
onesidedness for its own sake and therefore unassociated with any
scheme or programme directed towards State and Society'.[45] To
combine this determination to let the Church be the Church with
political opposition would be an indication in reverse that one
was doing exactly the same as that for which one was reproaching
the 'German Christians.'

Barth, and indeed all those who wholeheartedly subscribed
to the Barmen Declaration, did not see eye to eye with the great
majority of British and American supporters of their cause who
were moved enthusiastically from the touchline to cheer on the
gallant Confessional pastors in what they believed to be a fight
for freedom against absolutism and for democracy against dictatorship.[46] They either could not, or would not, understand that
the opposition of Christians in Germany to National Socialism in
both its theory and its practice was basically neither political
nor idealistic. Actually, it was grounded upon a narrow, intense
and intolerant form of biblical outlook which firmly rejected
natural theology and regarded with deep suspicion any attempt,
however conscientious and well meaning, to trim the Faith in
order to make it more readily conform with so-called modern
thought. Transferred to Britain, Barth and those associated with
him would without doubt have entered into conflict with the
prevailing liberal evangelism and modernism that they found
there. As Barth wrote in December 1933, 'Christians in other
countries ought not to consider themselves as being righteous
over against the unrighteous in Germany. Is the Gospel for
instance in Switzerland, England, France or America being
purely preached uncontaminated by current ideologies ? Are you
sure that religious heresy as manifest as that of the 'German
Christians' would not break forth in your Churches ? I very much
fear that many of those from abroad who are at present deriving
a certain pleasure in following the course of the Church

KOD

Opposition in Germany are now in another perhaps milder form in point of fact exactly akin to our 'German Christians' in their ideas. I am very much afraid that, if I lived anywhere abroad, I would be finding myself very soon indeed in opposition within the Church just as I am here in Germany'.[47]

The Anglo-American writers, as John Conway has remarked, were 'unanimous though onesided in regarding the Conflict as a fight between Church and State, between good and evil, between the Confessional Church and the 'Brown Terror'. For them the political aspects of the Church Struggle were more important than the theological. . . . Taken as a whole, those who belonged to the Confessional Church never had the will to become the crystal-lisation point of political resistance against the National Socialist State or to perform the role in which they were seen by the aforementioned foreign observers'.[48] Indeed, the same men who were unflinching and intrepid when it was a matter of confessional resistance were so often dismayed and consumed with anxiety when the issue became directly political, which it all too readily did, especially where the Jewish Question was concerned, for as Kupisch has expressed it, 'the Jewish Question was laden with political actuality'.[49] Both Dietrich Bonhoeffer and Kurt Ger-stein felt impelled to enter into total opposition against total evil, and in their different ways to go right out into the world to do so with the burden of being misunderstood and shunned by many of their fellow-Christians. We find with both of them impatient despair of those addicted to church-bound piety and strict orthodoxy.

The contrast is evident between the manifest resolution shown by those who valiantly defended their church territory from state invasion, the open and eloquent countering of Rosen-berg's Myth and criticism of various manifestations of Nazi *Ersatz* Religion, on the one hand, and equally manifest hesitation, reluctance and failure, on the other hand, to wage warfare upon the political as well as the religious front, and to speak and to act openly in the name of Christ and for righteousness sake in that sphere. It would be both foolish and unfair to minimise the high order of faith and courage that was required by subjects of a ruthless totalitarian police-state in challenging the enemy on his own ground; the Confessional leaders were by and large— neither lacking in faith nor in courage. Had they been utterly convinced that God required of them open criticism of and disassociation from what was prevailing in the world outside the Church, they would have sought to respond. The great majority of them, however, regarded as sacred Luther's doctrine of the 'Two Kingdoms',[50] and were conscientious heirs of the commonly held Lutheran view that social and political events lie outside the Christian sphere of responsibility, and are fundamentally the affairs of the State authorities, political issues being meant to be regulated according to different laws from those provided for individual morality.[51] The Church appeared to them to be the only realm in which in the present dispensation Christ's Kingdom was truly operative and relevant, no explicit foundation existing for a consistent witness by the Church concerning Christ's Lordship in and over the world.[52]

It had become obvious that the great majority of Lutherans were not in tune with the type of democractic and parliamentary government provided by the Weimar Constitution. In contrast, they came to believe for a time at any rate that the victory of National Socialism had established a genuine political authority that expressed itself in terms of *Obrigkeit*[53] (Supreme Authority) and *Untertanen* (Subjects), and offered an era of strong and disciplined control. And with such they could feel at home. They were, therefore, only too ready to adhere to a relationship of Church and State in which the two spheres were held rigorously separate. This meant that the State authority, in its direct and independent derivation from God, could no longer be called in question from the Gospel standpoint, and that the Church would need to limit itself to what may be termed the 'inner line', and confine itself to defence against State-interference in the reserved territory of the Church's Faith and Order.[54] Consequently, in the all-important first and formative stages of the Church Struggle sharp protests concerning what was happening within the ecclesiastical sphere went hand in hand with earnest protestations of political loyalty involving submission to the new style of State control. The offence of having presumed from a Christian standpoint to pass a political judgement upon National Socialism would have been as seriously regarded by prevailing opinion within the Church as by the Gestapo.[55] As late as the summer of 1939, and despite all that had transpired in the past six years, the Conference of Lutheran Church Leaders, including Bishops

Wurm, Meiser and Marahrens, felt able to reassure Reichminister Kerrl that 'the Evangelical Church has learnt from Martin Luther to distinguish clearly between the spheres of Reason and of Faith, of Politics and Religion and of the State and the Church. The Evangelical Church holds the State in reverence as an Order set up by God, and requires from its members loyal service within that Order, and instructs them to apply themselves with full devotion to the furthering of what volkishly and politically is the constructive work of the Führer'.[56] This was followed by an admission of the necessity of an earnest and responsible racial political programme for the preservation of the purity of the Volk. Karl Barth felt moved to comment in 1944 that 'the whole disaster in Germany would perhaps never have been possible, had the Christian Church not for centuries accustomed itself to keep silent, when it should have witnessed and spoken up, when issues of genuine earthly power and Government and of Right and Freedom were at stake'.[57] Nevertheless Barth himself is quoted as having in June 1934 advanced the view that the Church had no warrant to elevate herself as judge over the State.[58] 'As a Christian Church we have not to exercise a political censorship',[59] was how Paul Althaus expressed it in a lecture delivered to a Lutheran Congress in 1935, in the course of which he emphasised that, while the Church has to bear witness to everyone including the politicians regarding the Sovereign Judgement of God, she does not administer the divine Judgement or exercise on God's behalf supervision of the State. There was, according to the Lutheran interpretations, a direct relationship between the conscience of the statesman and God and His holy Word, and the mediation of the Church was not required.[60]

The Lutheran was expected to establish his attitude to the Government on the basis of the first verses of Romans 13 fortified by 1 Peter 2: 13–14, but was scarcely encouraged to give similar attention to what was to be found in other passages of Scripture. Karl Barth wrote in June 1935 in the following terms in criticism of the protestations of loyalty to the Nazi State published by the Confessional Synod of Augsburg, questioning whether they were honest and sincere. 'How singularly naïve and unsuspecting or slumbering must German Christianity have been in assessing the developments of the last years! . . . I do not understand how one can in honest fashion time and again behave as if the Christian understanding of the present concrete relation of Gospel and State has to be regulated in accordance with Romans 13 alone and not by consideration also of the Apocalypse and of the attitude of the Old Testament Prophets. . . . The Confessional Church has as yet no heart for the millions who are suffering because of injustice, and has not a single word to say about the most elementary questions of integrity in public affairs. She speaks—when she does speak at all—invariably only in her own interests. She insists upon maintaining the fiction that in dealings with the present State she has to do with a *Rechtsstaat* in the sense of Romans 13.' At Augsburg reference was made to the sincere and heartfelt prayer for People and Führer. Barth asked whether a more genuine form of prayer would not be a cry for deliverance from what has become 'an accursed tyranny in which falsehood and injustice were elevated into a principle'.[61]

Martin Luther certainly affirmed that there were occasions when obedience had to be given to God rather than to man, but he did not provide clear or concrete guidance as to what those circumstances would be. Those in the Lutheran tradition were prone to regard them as occasions when freedom to preach the Word was at stake rather than circumstances in which the State was legislating or acting in a manner irreconcilable with the Christian ethic. One of the very few statements published by the Confessional Church on the subject of obedience to the *Obrigkeit* appears in the Message of the Augsburg Synod of 1935 to the Congregations, their Pastors and Elders. 'The *Obrigkeit* derives its power from God. By divine command the Christian is subject to it. Obedience to the *Obrigkeit* finds its limitations at that point at which the Christian by his obedience would be compelled to sin against God's Commandments. When the witness that is of necessity laid upon Christians is hindered or forbidden, the point is reached at which it is their duty to God without fear of man to testify in action and in suffering to the grace and glory of Jesus Christ. Despite oppression and persecution you must not fail to submit to the *Obrigkeit* with deference. Remain obedient to those who are set in authority over you, and do not become embittered! Be steadfast in true love to your Volk! Honour the Gift of God which you have received in belonging to our people! Be tireless in service. Pray for Volk and *Obrigkeit*![62]

Luther in his reformulation of the Christian faith and ethic

and his determination at all costs to differentiate between the
functions of the Law and the Gospel and to avoid the errors
of both Roman Catholics and fanatical Protestants (*Schwärmer*)
saw fit to differentiate sharply betwixt the spiritual and the
temporal spheres.[63] It was of course true that he declared God to
be in sovereign command of both realms, but it has not really
been surprising that very often such differentiation came to be
conceived of in terms of separation, and that the autonomy of
the State within its own sphere became a customary Lutheran
tenet. Further, Luther's teaching that the existence and the
operation of the State was a necessary outcome of human sin and
his undoubtedly pessimistic assessment of the quality of secular
government were scarcely calculated to encourage subsequent
Lutherans to insist that the secular realm should be subject to
Christ's rule and to Christian ethical standards or that the Church
should regard herself as holding a joint responsibility with the
State and expect to be permitted to co-operate directly in the
provision of sound and effective government. Luther, as Helmut
Gollwitzer has observed, was intent upon discouraging the
utopia of world improvement, apt to be resigned to compromise
with the world as it is, and prone to write off too quickly and
too easily revolt against existing unrighteousness as *Schwärmerei*,
thus neglecting to take into proper account the rule of Christ
in the realm of the political as well as of the spiritual.[64]

The need to 'let God be God' is central to the whole Lutheran
approach, and does not overmuch encourage the Christian to
take it upon himself to interfere actively with the aim of putting
abuses right in the sinful outside world or in promoting political
righteousness. The Lutheran is counselled to beware of zealously
wanting to do God's work for Him, and is taught to believe that,
'when God looks on silently at the activity of an evil government,
this happens because He wills to use this particular government
as an instrument to punish sin by means of the sinner. God in
the bringing into fulfilment of His plan for Salvation makes use
of both the right exercise of the sword and its abuse. In the case
of a tyrannical government misusing the office of the sword with
which it has been invested, there is all the greater cause for him
to turn to God. For God alone is the Lord who provides the
Government, and can avert the evil'.[65] Bishop Wurm, writing in
1950, described his fellow-bishop August Marahrens as having

been consumed with an exaggerated loyalty towards the State, 'understanding, as perhaps most Lutherans, Romans Chapter 13 in the sense of an unconditional subordination to the supreme power of the State and showing a respect for the leading men of the Third Reich when in authority that they did not deserve. He and many others did not come to see that a government which not only permitted but also directed the *Putsch* of 30 June 1934, the anti-Jewish pogrom of 1938 and the murder of the mentally afflicted did not belong within the category of governments commissioned to punish those who do evil'.[66]

Bishop Marahrens had three years earlier in a lengthy apologia to his Hannoverian Church reaffirmed his conviction that it had been consistent with Holy Scripture and Luther's teaching to have regarded the organs of the Nazi State as a genuine form of government and to have behaved towards them as such. 'True we had not failed to perceive that this government had revealed itself in increasing measure as unchristian, and indeed as anti-Christian. Nevertheless we rendered to it in outward things due obedience. For even an unchristian or anti-Christian State authority such as that of the Roman Emperor in the New Testament context or the Turks according to Luther's theology is *Obrigkeit* which in *rebus politicis* can command obedience.'[67]

It is Hermann Diem's contention that Bishop Wurm in his turn, though he showed a high order of personal faith and courage, all the same did not give a really inspired or adequate lead in the Church's attack. Diem regards him as having in his celebrated letters—salved his own conscience and stated his own personal convictions rather than having presented a challenging Church pronouncement.[68] Wurm, according to Diem, never broke free from the shackles of the traditional 'Two Kingdoms' theory. He was never to be persuaded that the real course lay in open prophetic utterance, laying bare the enormities of the Nazi regime. He was, for instance, not prepared to adopt Diem's suggestion that on the Third Sunday in Advent 1941, an unambiguous word should be simultaneously spoken from all Württemberg pulpits upon the subject of the treatment of the Jews.[69]

In Württemberg, as in other intact Lutheran Churches, again according to Diem, the Church Conflict took the form principally of an 'Investiture Struggle', the main object being to bring the

Nazi world to halt before the doors of the Church, and, in pursuance of this aim, being content to leave the State largely to its own devices, assuming no responsibility for it.[70] This 'inner line'[71] called for a considerable measure of tactful accommodation and of caution in deciding the limits to which it was advisable to go. It ruled out the exercise of an office such as that performed by the Old Testament Prophets both over and for the world, and in fact on certain occasions also by Luther himself, who in the Peasants' Revolt, and the war against the Turks, and in criticism of usury and taxation, did not hesitate to resort to outspoken public political preaching rather than moralising.[72] This course could be bolstered up by strange arguments such as that advanced in 1939 by a well-known Tübingen theologian who declared that the authorities with which the Church had to do had become so callous and hard-hearted that the Church had, therefore, no longer the obligation to provide them with the Gospel witness.[73] This desire to keep the Church's established position inviolate was in point of fact a sure way of excluding it increasingly from public life and in converting it into a private association of the pious. In 1944, when there was much underground conspiracy afoot, Eugen Gerstenmaier sought to persuade Bishops Wurm and Meiser to speak out for once emphatically and exclusively on the subject of political offences instead of confining their remarks to what they chose to regard as 'legitimate ecclesiastical concerns'. The only result, to his disappointment, was the issuing of yet another of the familiar series of worthy messages featuring the interests of the Church to which friend and foe alike had grown so accustomed.[74]

In radical or 'Dahlemite' circles which acknowledged the powerful influence of Karl Barth and in which the Lutheran position was tempered by Calvinist-inspired activism, there was also at times considerable disagreement and uncertainty as to what ought to be rendered to the Nazi Caesar. The supreme moment of testing came in the summer of 1938, when all pastors were ordered to take a special oath of loyalty to Hitler. This proved to be a cause of great heart-searching and bewilderment within the Confessing Church. With comparatively few exceptions the pastors concerned showed that they were still wedded to an idealistic view of the State, and sought to separate its political intentions from the National Socialist ideology. Thanks to the long existence of the Church under the patronage of a so-called Christian *Obrigkeit* they were unaccustomed to political judgement or action. They therefore did not conceive of the oath-situation as an opportunity for analysing and criticising the political activity of the State to which they belonged.[75] Instead of this they allowed themselves to identify the Nazi State with the *Obrigkeit* of Reformation thought, and avoided facing the issue as to whether a twentieth century totalitarian regime hostile to God could possibly be included in the terms of reference of either St. Paul or Luther. Bethge describes the shame that Bonhoeffer felt for the Confessing Synod which had decided in favour of the oath to the Führer, since he already knew that a regulation was coming by which the non-Aryans would be compelled to have a large 'J' stamped on their identity cards—an omen of worse things to come.[76]

The following sentences from his *Ethics* written between 1940 and 1943 reveal Bonhoeffer's struggle to emancipate himself from the traditional Lutheran conception of submission to the 'Powers that be'. In the exercise of the divine commission to govern 'the demand for obedience' he wrote, 'is unconditional and qualitatively total; it extends both to conscience and to bodily life. The Christian's duty of obedience is binding on him until government directly compels him to offend against the divine commandment'. 'In cases of doubt obedience is required, for the Christian does not bear the responsibility of government.' 'Even an anti-Christian government is still in a certain sense government.' 'In all political decisions the historical entanglement in the guilt of the past is too great to be assessed, and it is therefore generally impossible to pass judgement on the justice of a single particular decision. . . . Even in cases where the guilt of the government is extremely obvious, due consideration must still be given to the guilt which has given rise to the guilt.' Notwithstanding such provisos he felt bound to assert that 'an apocalyptic view of a particular government would necessarily have total disobedience as its consequence, for in that case every single act of obedience obviously involves a denial of Christ'.[77]

The stalwart and manly bearing of Martin Niemöller, the intrepid Pastor of Dahlem, fired the imagination of countless Christians both in Germany and in many other countries, and he certainly became for many the symbol of fearless and outspoken resistance to the Nazi tyranny. Numerous tributes have been paid to him as political adversary as well as defender of the Church and her Faith. If anyone endeavoured to make a thorough break-through in refusal of submission to corrupt authority, and really sought to champion those in bondage, surely it was he. Hans Bernd Gisevius, Civil Servant, for a period a devoted member of the Dahlem inner circle, and later wartime conspirator, makes the claim that Niemöller 'saw that the true path of the Protestant Church led straight into an area that had been a kind of *zone interdite* for German Protestants since 1933. That straight and narrow path led directly to politics, and his stern rejection of National Socialism was in essence pure politics'. Gisevius believed that Hitler and Himmler had no doubt whatever that they were fighting Niemöller on their exclusively political plane.[78] Thomas Mann in his foreword to the 1942 English edition of Niemöller's Last Twenty Eight Dahlem Sermons suggested that the Pastor of Dahlem in his obligation to contradict the megalomaniac pretensions of the Führer 'soon found himself a political agitator with the border-line between religion and politics . . . wiped out and his church . . . a centre of political opposition'.[79]

This, however, has to be accounted a false though understandable emphasis. Wilhelm Niemöller—and who has better claim to pass judgement?—has described his brother's warfare as 'a fight for the Confession of his Church'.[80] George Bell in paying public tribute in 1937 to Niemöller, wrote, 'The announcement of the grounds for his arrest suggests that he is an agitator against the State. What is his crime? The truth is that he is a preacher of the Gospel of God, and that he preaches the Gospel without flinching'.[81] Martin Niemöller himself in a lecture given in 1936 took care to affirm that it was not the province of the Church to exercise herself over secular matters or to pass judgement upon them. The Church was required to utter the Word of God, and that included reminding the German people of the Sovereignty of God involving a recognition of His Will and of the validity of His Commandments.[82] At about the same time he informed a correspondent that it was his purpose 'to wage warfare never against the State but at all times solely on behalf of the Church'.[83] Defence of the Word and the confession entrusted to the Church of course involved ceaseless controversy with the

Nazi ideology that did in point of fact result in criticism of the very foundations of Nazism and its method of government, but, as Jürgen Schmidt has pointed out in his recent full study of Niemöller's contribution, it 'was not his concern to figure as "opponent of the System" but as preacher of the Word,' and that he 'continuously took pains to preserve the distinction between the expounding of the Gospel and the expression of a political opinion'.[84] In his televised conversation with Günter Gaus in 1963 he was asked by the latter why he had insisted upon regarding and defining his conflict with the Nazi State as a purely ecclesiastical issue of freedom of preaching (*Verkündigung*). He replied that he had little or no conception of politics. His activities lay in a quite other direction. The emphasis of his opposition to National Socialism had no political accent; the issue was for him how the Gospel could be protected from corruption by the so-called Nazi Weltanschauung.[85] In his later utterances from the pulpit which simultaneously gave such encouragement and so great offence he was most careful in his choice of language to speak theologically not politically. His disparaging references to Nazi leaders were manifestly of religious inspiration.

At his trial his counsel defended him as 'a completely unpolitical man whose activity has been exclusively determined by the Word of God',[86] and as one who had never contested what were pure and simply measures taken by the State.[87] Niemöller himself, according to a National Socialist official present at the trial and whose report is to be accepted as reliable, declared in his self-defence that his exclusive concern was Christianity in accordance with Scripture and Confession, and that he had no desire to interfere in any way with day to day politics.[88] Full allowance must, of course, be made for the tactics of such defence, but it became obvious as the trial progressed that there was no compelling evidence that the defendant had misused the pulpit for political ends or that he had been guilty of political opposition to the authority of the State. The result was the verdict of the Court that there was nothing in the least treasonable about the personality of the accused. The report of the National Socialist official to which reference has been made included the remark that 'it was interesting that Niemöller represented the Lutheran, not the Reformed, interpretation of Romans 13, according to which obedience is to be rendered in all circumstances to the

Obrigkeit. In conformity with this, the sermon alone can provide a vehicle of expressing disagreement with certain measures taken by the Government, and what is said from the pulpit may not be translated into action'.[89] Niemöller's concluding words of self-defence consisted in a description of his resistance in terms of defence of the Christian Faith from various forms of attack and secular infiltration and the preservation of the integrity of the Church as guaranteed by the State. To such he was bound by his ordination vows. He had, so he protested, in his sermons never converted such Christian loyalty into an attack upon the State institutions, and he gave his assurance that he was resolved to maintain his loyalty to the Führer to the last breath, saving only his obedience to God's Word. 'At that point', he solemnly declared, 'all totalitarianism ceases, whether it be the totality of the State or of man or of the world. The true destiny and the ultimate goal of the State, of mankind and of the whole world are ruined, if there is a failure to recognise the frontier here drawn'.[90]

It has to be acknowledged that Niemöller's conflict with Nazism had from beginning to end a predominant religious interest; defence of ecclesiastical integrity and independence from unwarranted state control, repulse of heresies wedded to the Nazi Weltanschauung that had been infiltrated into the Evangelical Church, vigorous assault upon the spread of anti-Christian influences and ideas in public life in the confidence that the pure Gospel possessed its own unmistakable ethical and moral challenge. In contrast to all this there was, as Jürgen Schmidt has pointed out, 'avoidance of the adoption in public of a standpoint opposed to the political, legal and social situation in the Third Reich'.[91] Close perusal of his published sermons confirms this judgement. It was possible, as indeed many people did both in Germany and abroad, to read between the lines and draw conclusions, but Niemöller took care not to cross the line that led to political opposition. Immediately after the war he admitted his personal guilt in having kept silence over the merciless treatment of the Jews, Communists and other victims of the Third Reich.

Whether he would have broken that silence or become involved in political conspiracy, had he been set free from his captivity, is very much open to question. It may, however, be argued that his progressive emancipation from the strict interpretation of the doctrine of the Two Kingdoms would, if he had remained free, have reached a point at which he would have openly attacked National Socialism and all its works.

Jürgen Schmidt, by making full use of Niemöller's correspondence and of his lectures and talks as well as his sermons, throws much valuable light upon the development of his attitude to the Government. In May 1933, already in the thick of inner church conflict and vigorously opposing the Church politics of the 'German Christians' whereby Nazi ideas and methods were so patently being brought into operation, he proclaimed that the Church had the task of answering questions raised by contemporary political and social development solely from out of the Gospel and with reference to the Eternal Word.[92] The Church had her particular share in the inner renewal of the German people and, when spiritual decisions had to be made, the Church had the obligation in the light of current events to say fearlessly what it was her commission to declare. His disillusionment with the professed 'positive Christianity' of the Nazis was manifest by the beginning of 1934, and he recognised that ecclesiastical resistance would be suppressed with the same brutal means as any seeds of political opposition. His original hope that the Third Reich would bring about national moral and religious renewal was shattered, and he grew increasingly sceptical of Nazi politics. The Blood Bath of June 1934, so obviously the Führer's responsibility, confirmed his worst misgivings, and on the Sunday following he recited from the altar, instead of the Creed, the Ten Commandments with special stress upon the Sixth—'Thou shalt not kill!'[93] His recommendations of a Service of Penitence for the crime and of a public statement of protest by the Confessing Church found little or no support.[94] This did not, however, prevent him from making profession but a short time afterwards of devoted and loyal obedience to the authority of the State in secular matters as contrasted to unqualified resistance to State compulsion in the ecclesiastical sphere.[95]

His sermon in February 1935 on Romans 13: 1–10, revealed a conservative interpretation of Christian submission to authority. 'The conflict between enthusiastic national feeling and passionate desire for the true welfare of the Church', Niemöller declared, made submission to the 'dispassionate objectivity of the Word of God'[96] essential. According to the Word the powers that be received their authority directly from God, and it was impermissible to ascribe a higher value to a power which is in harmony with our desires and ideas than to a Government which is opposed to our demands.[97] It had to be remembered that, when Paul wrote, Nero was emperor (scarcely a compliment to the Führer!). The authority peculiar to the State as a divine ordinance was subject to no human conditions whatever, and those who ruled were answerable and responsible alone to God. Those who suffered injustice had no right to be disobedient. Their sole weapon was a continuance in doing good. The right and the duty of the Christian to disobey only occurred when he was required to do wrong; at that point God had to be obeyed rather than Man, but even in such circumstances there was still the obligation to render to Caesar what was his. A Protestant Church in enmity to the State was a contradiction in itself.[98] A lecture which Niemöller gave in August 1935 defending the legitimacy of German rearmament and a Christian's unconditional duty to bear arms in event of war revealed that his pronounced nationalistic bias had not diminished in company with his reservations regarding National Socialism, and that he subscribed to the Lutheran differentiation between Law and Gospel whereby the Christian as citizen of the State was obliged to comply with the demands of the political ruler, and could only within the citadel of the Church take seriously the injunctions of the Sermon on the Mount.[99]

It is possible to detect in 1936 a change of emphasis in Niemöller's approach to the State that is exemplified by the remark in a private letter that the Church being *Volkskirche* has the right to tell Caesar 'It is not lawful!'[100] He was one of the prime movers in the composition and delivery to Hitler in May 1936 of the Memorandum in which outspoken representations were made in protest against the unlawful and immoral practices of the Nazi regime. Though the Church did not presume to give concrete directions for the reshaping of political conditions, criticism was directed against concentration camps, Gestapo methods, virulent anti-semitism and blatant utilitarianism in the interpretation of Justice. Of particular significance was his lecture delivered in June 1936 under the title of 'God the Lord of Church and People',[101] in which the responsibility of the Church for the moral and political as well as the spiritual development of the people was emphasised. The Church's doctrine of the absolute sovereignty of God was a challenge to the claim of the State to political autonomy, and necessitated the Christian witness that the Lord reigned, that His Will was dominant and His Laws inviolate, and that a Christian should be determined in cases of conflict to obey God rather than Man. This meant passive resistance, not active interference, in worldly matters, but it ruled out a clear and peaceful dividing-line betwixt the Two Kingdoms with the Church confined to operation within a limited sacred realm of her own. In the Dahlem Sermons of 1936-7 are to be found repeated expressions of this modified doctrine of the Kingdoms. Niemöller's exegesis of Matthew 22:15-22 (The Tribute Money) strikes a very different note from that of his earlier exposition of Romans 13. The emphasis was this time upon the absence of a clear-cut boundary when facing the vexatious question of the relationship of politics and religion and of a Christian's bad conscience in the disassociation of earthly calling from divine vocation.[102] The twin injunctions 'Render unto Caesar the things that are Caesar's' and 'Render unto God the things that are God's' were not on the same plane. 'We cannot act as though Caesar has power on earth and God the power in heaven. . . . If the world demands what is God's, then we must manfully resist.'[103] Another sermon delivered in January 1937 challenged still more clearly the traditional line of demarcation. The work of Jesus was 'from the very beginning an attack upon the wicked world; His message proclaims the sovereignty of God over the whole domain of our human existence. . . . If we seek to help ourselves by deciding that there is in our life a sacred region over which God rules and side by side with it a human region in which we ourselves are in control, Jesus does not recognise such a demarcation. From the very beginning He carries God's claim into the temporal sphere and the secular world'.[104]

In his speeches and sermons shortly after the war Martin Niemöller made repeated confession of his personal guilt and that of his fellow-Christians. He acknowledged that in public life he and others had either just simply left out of reckoning the peculiar responsibility of their standing as Christians or else had shunned such responsibility, because the whole political field was to be regarded as something unchristian.[105] When it really came to the point, they had failed both to represent Christ and to recognise Him, when He impinged upon their lives in the form of a suffering brother.[106] Christian guilt could actually be accounted worse than Nazi guilt. 'The Church was uniquely aware that the course that was being pursued led to perdition, and she had not warned the people, nor exposed the wrong that was taking place; at any rate not until it was too late. Confessing Churchmen had seen more plainly than any one else what was going on and how things were developing. They had even found tongue, but had grown weary and proved that they feared Man more than the Living God.'[107]

In retrospect, it must be said that, once the extermination programme had been revealed in all its horror, there was but one counter-solution possible, the complete overthrow of the Nazi regime. To have worked secretly towards that end before the outbreak of the war would have been formidable enough, but once the nation was at war, it was quite out of the question except for a very few. It was not just National Socialist Germany that was at war, but the beloved Fatherland, and the representatives of the Church were as desirous to prove patriotic as anyone else. Many Confessional pastors were called up, and served valiantly in the German forces, most of them as combatants, and a few as chaplains.[108] There is little evidence that any of them felt profound misgivings at lending their aid to the German war effort. In many of Bishop Wurm's repeated messages to those in authority he took pride in pointing out that the loyal sacrifices made by Christians to the cause of the Fatherland were second to none. In his letter to Goebbels in October 1941 he described himself as one 'who from his youth on had been devoted, with ardent love, to his Fatherland'.[109] In one of his protests in which he referred plainly to the murder of Jews and Poles, as well as complaining about the campaign directed against Christianity and the Churches, he seriously argued that it would be greatly to the political interests of the Nazi rulers themselves to call a halt to such enormities, and to permit the Christian population to devote themselves gladly and in good conscience to the war effort. It would do so much to promote the unity and the powers of resistance of the whole people.[110] There was indeed a long history to the persistent hope that it should be possible to restrain the brutality of the Nazi regime and humanise it. The Christian conscience had ample cause long before Hitler came to power to be shocked by the many expressions of Nazi racial venom and at the brutal and callous proceedings against the Jews that were so manifest an accompaniment of the reawakening of the nation, and that were so patently irreconcilable with the much advertised public profession of 'Positive Christianity'. When there was so much that was desirable in the National Socialist programme, it was fatally easy to agree that any revolution must bring with it excesses and injustices, and to hope that the rough edges would be smoothed out. In retrospect it has to be acknowledged that 1932 and 1933 were the key years for vigorous Christian protest out of love and concern for fellow-man.

A similar case of shortsighted blindness is to be detected in the failure of the vast majority of Churchmen to recognise that the extermination programme of the Nazis was not limited to the elimination of the Jews. In the long run their totalitarian ambitions would inevitably include the supression of the Christian Churches. Hermann Diem in a lecture on the Church and anti-semitism makes the point that long before the still unsuspecting Church perceived it, the Nazis had as their target, and desired to give battle to, the God of the Christians as much as the God of the Jews, and were set upon suppressing the Church along with the Synagogue. 'In their hatred they knew better than most theologians that in the God of Abraham, Isaac and Jacob and the Father of Jesus Christ they were dealing with one and the same God.'[111]

Very little research is required to unearth the plainest of statements regarding Nazi determination to bracket together Jews and Christians as joint enemies standing in their way and requiring to be suppressed. The following three examples have been picked almost at random out of many that might have been quoted.

Wilhelm Kube, Gauleiter of the Kurmark, who was responsible during 1935 in Party gatherings and publications for a spate of venomous attacks upon the Confessional Front, made it abundantly clear that in the Nazi view the Jews and the reactionary Church were to be seen as joint enemies to be destroyed. The Confessional Church he declared on one occasion to be 'accomplices of the Jews'. 'They have the impudence to represent them to us as the Chosen People. They are plainly to be seen as auxiliaries of the Jews in their fight against the National Socialist State and the Führer.' On another occasion he claimed that there was no doubt whatever that the Jews possessed in the Confessional Front 'a camouflaged bodyguard'.[112]

In the canteen of a railway repair works in Munich could be read in large letters for all to see the words—'When will all mankind be in a state of salvation? When will the world be enlightened? When the last Jew is strangled with the intestines of the last parson.'[113]

Those being coached in 1937 by the pagan 'German Faith Movement' in leadership and speech-making were taught that 'the Jews are the prime cause of all that is evil. We are not able to eradicate such evil, because its product, Christianity, is rampant in our midst. We must eradicate Christianity in order to gain the victory over the Jews'.[114]

These were in no wise statements that were not meant to be published. The young in school, in Hitler troops and in labour camps were continuously being submitted to cheap and vulgar propaganda in which Church and Jews were jointly execrated.

Such identification of Christian and Jew was not by and large seen anything like as clearly by the Church. There were many Christians, and not only so-called 'German Christians' who were reluctant despite the mounting evidence to the contrary to write off completely the 'positive Christianity' still avowed by the State and in which they had initially put so much trust. The persecution that many of them had to endure had not submerged their feelings as patriotic Germans. Indeed, such disillusionment as they had experienced under the New Order had in many cases the effect of increasing their devotion to the Fatherland and to traditional national values. Their consciousness of being pure and loyal Germans must have made it very difficult for them to grasp that those who were set in authority politically over them could really plan eventually to eliminate them as well as the Jews. The distinction remained in their thinking between the converted Jew, who by Faith in Christ had become 'a new man' and had thereby shed Jewish characteristics which they found suspect and distasteful, and the unconverted Jew who continued to reject the Christ and remained, therefore, under the enduring wrath and Judgement of God. In the later years of Nazi rule they would no longer have been prepared to endorse the view expressed by Friedrich Heiler in 1934[115] that the innocent suffering of many Jews lay in God's Will and served the best interests

f the Jewish people and the Christian Church, but they would
a all probability not have entirely disassociated themselves from
is further remark that it was not the task of the Christian Church
o contest evidence of the Divine Purpose that lay behind certain
f the measures taken against the Jews. Their function was to
rotest, if they could and they dared, against the human arro-
ance and unrighteousness involved, to provide some relief to
hose in desperate need, and to save, help, comfort and mitigate,
here it was feasible. Such a feeling of Christian duty to show
ity and provide succour for individual Jews was far removed
rom what Karl Kupisch has subsequently described as the
ecognition of 'the mystery of Jews and Christians in their
xistence side by side, together and for the sake of each other
nder the one and the same God'.[116] 'God's determination to
lect', declared Kupisch, 'is irrevocable. The Christian ought to
oe fully aware of this. All hatred of the Jews is sooner or later
urned against believing Christians. The anti-semite has seen
right. The elect belong together. He therefore persecuted them
ogether in his hatred. For both Jews and Christians find their
rue existence in loyalty to the one and the same God who has
:hosen them by Grace.'[117]

In retrospect, it does seem strange that so few of those who were
undeniably good and orthodox Christians and well versed in the
Scriptures proved able to grasp, if not from the beginning yet
:arly on, that their acceptance of the Old Testament along with
:he New Testament as the Word of God, and their belief in a scheme
of salvation centred in Jesus, the Christ foretold in Jewish prophecy, born of a Jewish maiden, and proclaimed to be the King
of the Jews, could be anything else than offensive and unacceptable to the Nazis. Their trust in the promises made to Abraham,
Isaac and Jacob, their loyal obedience to moral laws derived
from Mount Sinai, their emphasis upon the cardinal doctrine of
Justification by Faith, presented originally by one who took such
pride in being a Hebrew of the Hebrews, inevitably meant a life
and death struggle between their Faith and the Nazi Myth.

'If the synagogues burn today, the churches will be on fire
tomorrow' was Dietrich Bonhoeffer's terse comment upon the
atrocities of 'Crystal Night'.[118] Karl Barth, outraged by the same

monstrous barbarities, told a Swiss audience on 5 Decembe 1938, but with an altogether wider public in view, 'when tha takes place which has in Germany now been manifestly deter mined—the physical extermination of the People of Israel, the burning of their Synagogues and the Rolls of the Torah, the outright rejection of the God and the Bible of the Jews as the very epitome of all that has to be regarded as an abominatio to the German—an attack is being made upon the Christia Church at its very roots. What would we be and what are we without Israel? He who is on principle an enemy of the Jews even if he were in other respects an angel of light, is to be recog nised as on principle an enemy of Jesus Christ. Anti-semitism is the sin against the Holy Ghost. It signifies rejection of the Grace of God.'[119]

The positive significance of simultaneous persecution of Jew and Christian can be appreciated in retrospect. For 'in the days of the Third Reich something happened which at any rate has never taken place in the western civilised world—namely tha Jews and Christians were subject to persecution together and to a certain measure even if in differing degree by the same token'.[120] This is a fact that has assisted enormously in preparing the ground for all genuine and positive post-war confrontation between Evangelical Christians and Jews.

Several of those who have written in retrospect about the Church and the Jews have got a certain distance in attempting to explain, if not to justify, the Church's record, only to have in the end to confess that a spell lay upon those who knew in the depths of their hearts that they should be doing altogether more. Hans Asmussen declares that it was not because of cowardice, for many an individual ran the risk of the scaffold in identifying himself with the Jews. 'But a carefully cast noose was around our throats before we were aware of it.'[121] Kurt Meier suggests that there was something terrifyingly irrational about the Nazi enmity to the Jews that made it proof against rational arguments.[122] Heinrich Grüber has commented as follows, "We confess not only that during the twelve years of the Nazis we have been found wanting, but that we had not in the past developed sufficient resources to counter the demonic forces which burst forth and led to this infernissimo'.[123] This is in line with what Maurice Samuel wrote in 1940—'We have left the normal field of human

ntity, and have entered into the realm of the primitive demono-
ogical'. Samuel characterised Nazi anti-semitism as 'a proliferating
iabolism which testifies to a kind of insanity', and thereby
ranscends the so-called Jewish Question, even as it transcends in
unction all the familiar hatred of our time'.[124] H. D. Leuner
omments in similar vein, when he remarks, that the fact that
Iitler 'succeeded in persuading a whole nation to watch in
orrified or passive submission, but at any rate in silence, as
is plans were carried out, will make little sense to many who
o not believe in the existence of a personal devil', and quotes the
ndings of the Provincial Court of Appeal in Cologne in 1961
hat 'it seems appropriate to point out that the trains of thought
nd the decisions apparent in the national socialist policy against
he Jews were totally nonsensical and defy all rational compre-
ension'.[125]

The spell was not lifted immediately the war had come to
n end. In the Stuttgart Declaration of October 1945 Leaders of
he Evangelical Church in Germany headed by Bishop Wurm and
Martin Niemöller sought to express to ecumenical representatives
nd to the world at large their feelings of responsibility and
uilt for the infinite suffering which Germany had inflicted
pon many peoples and countries. This brief and solemn con-
ession of guilt included words which have been quoted and
equoted, and have passed down into history—'We have for a long
eriod of years fought in the Name of Jesus Christ against the
pirit that found its terrible expression in the National Socialist
ule of tyranny, but it is our self-indictment that we have not
nade a more courageous confession, that we have not been
nore faithful in prayer, that we were not more cheerful believers,
nd that we did not love more ardently.'[126] But no direct reference
t all was made to the widespread failure to espouse the cause of
he Jews or to withstand the propagation of anti-semitism.

However, in the altogether less frequently quoted 'Message
o the Christian People Abroad' which, under the signature of
Bishop Wurm, accompanied the Declaration, the following
bviously inadequate words appear, though they were possibly
he most that could have been awaited at this particular moment
o soon after the suspension of hostilities, 'We condemn in
articular the killing of hostages and the mass murder of German
nd Polish Jews. It has been a very great cause of grief to us

Christians in Germany that such things have brought disgrac
upon the German name and have been so great a stain upo
German honour. We left those in positions of responsibility i
no doubt as to how we felt, although this was very much resentec
When from the fact that there was no loud public protest th
representatives of Christendom from abroad have drawn th
conclusion that we had kept silent, it has been an obvious sig
that they have been incapable of conceiving of the extent of th
suppression of freedom of speech under the National Sociali
regime. Many of those who did speak out in public had to pa
the penalty for it in a concentration camp.'[127] How one woulc
in retrospect, have preferred a simple, honest statement c
failure with no attempt whatever at excuse or self-justificatio
accompanied by a plain disavowal of anti-semitism!

The small group of radical Confessing Christians in Württem
berg, one of whose leaders was Hermann Diem, were it woul
appear, the first to apply the confession of guilt in the Stuttga
Declaration plainly and specifically to the treatment of the Jew
A statement of theirs, dated 9 April 1946, included the admissior
'We shrank back in cowardly fashion and in avoidance of takin
any action, when members of the People of Israel dwelling amon
us were dishonoured, pillaged, tortured and put to death. W
allowed fellow-Christians who originated according to the fles
from Israel to suffer exclusion from office and ministry in th
Church. We also countenanced the refusal to allow baptism t
the Jews. We did not speak up against the ban on missions t
the Jews. . . . By the supply of innumerable certificates provin
aryan descent we indirectly afforded impetus to racial arroganc
and therewith prejudiced the ministry of the Word of goo
tidings to all mankind.'[128] This had a very different ring about
from the remark addressed by Bishop Marahrens to his flock i
Hannover a few months earlier: 'In matters of belief we ma
have been far removed from the Jews, a succession of Jews ma
have caused grievous harm to our people, but they ought not t
have been attacked in inhuman fashion.'[129] This was indeed
statement from which it would be difficult to have avoided draw
ing the conclusion that despite all that had happened, the bisho
had not shed all of his instinctive anti-semitism, and still felt in h
heart, despite undoubted emotions of guilt, that the Jew was a
alien and a potential menace, to be dealt with in 'human fashion'

From Oldenburg, one of the smallest of the provincial Churches, came in October 1947 the acknowledgment that 'in the past years Christians have allowed themselves to be governed more by State regulations and demands and by general anti-semitic feelings than by Christian obligations', but it was accompanied by the same old stricture that 'the people of Israel through rejection of the Messiah sent by God has become for all peoples a warning instance of divine judgement'; which seemed to come very near to suggesting that the indescribable horrors suffered so recently by the Jews had been part and parcel of the divine censure. Emphasis was placed, as traditionally, upon the need for conversion and baptism which would bring the renegade Jews within the fellowship of the Christian Church; but with the not at all happy proviso that this must not be taken to mean that differences of descent and of volkish characteristics would thereby be done away with, as far as public and cultural life was concerned.[130]

In April 1948 the Council of Brethren of the Evangelical Church in Germany issued a much fuller statement that sought to pronounce upon the theological significance of the People of Israel.[131] 'We feel', so ran the preamble, 'that we should no longer keep silent about this question which lies as so great a burden upon our hearts. We are disturbed about what took place in the past, and that we failed to utter a united word. Now that we in our turn are being made to pay the penalty for what we inflicted upon the Jews, there is a grave danger that we may take refuge from the Judgement of God in a fresh burst of anti-semitism. We earnestly beseech pastors and congregations to join with us in making a deep study of this question in the light of Holy Scripture. . . . and we pray that the right understanding may be granted, and a right way of approach be opened out.'

In the ensuing theological consideration it was stressed that Jesus was according to Scripture a Jew and a member of the People of Israel as created by God's Election, and that this was not a matter of indifference, and that it did not permit the assignment of Jesus to another race or people. In the Birth of God's Son as a Jew, the election and the destiny of Israel found its consummation. The Church could not, therefore, accept any purely humanitarian idea as to the role of Jewry. The Jews were not to be branded as solely guilty for the crucifixion of Jesus. The election of Israel

had been transferred through Christ, and after Christ, to the
Church consisting of all peoples, thus making Jewish and Gentile
Christians joint and inseparable members of the Body of Christ
and brothers one of another. God in his faithfulness had not
abandoned Israel despite its disloyalty and consequent rejection
by Divine Judgement, and the Church was guilty, if she did
not take seriously God's long-suffering and patience towards
Israel. The Church was forbidden to regard the Jewish problem as
an a priori racial volkish issue, and had to witness to the world
that the problem could not be realised or settled from such an
angle. It had been a fateful error that in past decades churches
and congregations had chosen to view the Jewish question from
secular points of view, such as the purely humanitarian and that
of either emancipation or of anti-semitism. The voices of Christians had been heard, in particular, in the anti-semitic choir.
Consequently when radical racial anti-semitism swept with its
brutal force through the German people and German parishes
there was not to hand the strength to resist, because true understanding of and love towards Israel had been supplanted and
extinguished within the congregations. In consequence, a hand
was lent to all the injustice and suffering that was meted out to
Israel. It would not, however, be of assistance to make light of the
continuing separation between Christians and those Jews who
went on rejecting Christ. That situation called for unceasing
prayer, constant humility and love and hopeful expectation of the
day in which Jews and Gentiles would be truly brothers in
Christ.

While there was much that could be applauded in this statement,
nevertheless the repetition of the traditional charge that, in
crucifying the Messiah, Israel had renounced her Election, the
reference to the Judgement of God manifest in Israel's rejection
continuing to this very day and the denial of the continuity
between pre-Christian and post-Christian Israel caused great
offence to the Orthodox Synagogue Jews. The reiteration of the
traditional recrimination was declared to be blasphemous with its
implication that God had bloodthirstedly required the gruesome
and degrading death of six million men, women and children.[132]

As an example of persisting anti-semitic prejudice Ernst
Wolf relates how one of the delegates, himself a leading light in a
local Confessing community, expressed his honest astonishment

hat the marriage of a Christian to a Jew could be countenanced.
It would be a clear transgression of the Order of Creation![133]

The Synod of the Evangelical Church in Germany met in
Berlin-Weissensee on 23 April 1950. It had been decided that
the Synod should issue a statement on the Church's contribution
to the promotion of peace. There was, however, an unexpected and
quite spontaneous conviction that, before any utterance was made
about peace, a public statement ought to be issued regarding the
Jewish Question. Of fundamental significance in this statement
was the affirmation that 'we believe that God's Promise concerning
His Chosen People Israel still remained in force after the Crucifixion of Jesus Christ'. This was followed by the solemn admission that 'we through neglect and silence have been accomplices
in the outrages that have been perpetrated by representatives of
our people upon the Jews', and it continued—'We warn all
Christians to be prepared to take into reckoning that that which
as the Judgement of God has come upon us Germans is a recom-
pense for what we have done to the Jews; for in Judgement
God's Grace seeks the penitent. We beseech all Christians to
renounce every kind of anti-semitism, and earnestly to oppose it,
if it be stirred up anew, and to encounter both Jews and Jewish
Christians in a brotherly spirit. . . . We beseech the God of Mercy
to bring about the Day of Fulfilment, in which we along with
redeemed Israel may extol the victory of Jesus Christ.'[134] The
sense of German Christian guilt found its most heart-searching
expression, when one of the delegates to the Synod, Präses
Kreyssig, declared: 'In every train which carried Jews to their
death-camp in the East, at least one Christian should have been
a voluntary passenger.'[135]

Martin Niemöller who in 1933 had denied possessing warmth
of feeling for the Jews declared in a sermon in 1945—'There were
in 1933 and in the following years here in Germany 14,000
Evangelical pastors and nearly as many parishes. . . . If at the
beginning of the Jewish persecutions we had seen that it was
the Lord Jesus Christ Who was being persecuted, struck down
and slain in 'the least of these our brethren', if we had been loyal
to Him and confessed Him, for all I know God would have stood
by us, and then the whole sequence of events would have taken a
different course. And if we had been ready to go with Him to
death, the number of victims might well have been only some ten

thousand.'[136] He also suggested in a lecture given in Switzerland the following year that it could well be that 'Christianity in Germany bears a greater responsibility before God than the National Socialists, the SS and the Gestapo. We ought to have recognised the Lord Jesus in the brother who suffered and was persecuted despite him being a communist or a Jew. . . . Are not we Christians much more to blame, am I not much more guilty, than many who bathed their hands in blood ?'[137]

The ultimate failure of the Church lay not in the inability of bishops and synods to make plain and outspoken pronouncements in public, though what was most regrettably never attempted was a really united clarion call from responsible Christian leaders transcending all denominational and confessional barriers, issued on principle and irrespective as to whether it had a chance of proving acceptable or not, calling upon all, Evangelicals and Catholics alike, who took their Christianity really seriously, to raise their voices together in joint protest against what every true Christian must have known to be elementary violation of the most fundamental and manifest Divine Laws. Most tragically of all, what was missing was a spontaneous outburst at any point by ordinary decent Christian folk, who certainly existed in considerable numbers. A really widespread, public visible expression of righteous indignation would have had to have been taken very seriously indeed by the Nazi leaders, and would assuredly have had a profound effect in curbing the most inquitous excesses and brutalities, if not in bringing about the downfall of so monstrous and unprincipled a tyranny. But it never once came to that, and Adolf Hitler, despite his inability to bend the Church completely to his will, never really feared that it would. The ghastly thing was just the fact that it was not gangsters and roughnecks, but decent, intelligent and moral people who allowed themselves to be induced to acquiesce in something deeply evil, and to serve it.[138]

Criticism or condemnation on our part, living as we did then, and do now, in a remarkably free and democratic society, need to be tempered by the sober and honest self-enquiry as to whether we are certain that we could have done better, if as well, in the same circumstances. As Hitler fell, C. E. M. Joad, writing in the *New Statesman*, asked, 'I wonder how many of those who criticise the Germans for ignorance or docility or condemn them for

ositive complicity would have raised their voices against the
overnment in their own country, had they known that death or
orture were the penalties of criticism?'[139] Another correspondent
n the same issue wrote, 'The indifference of the average decent
erson to the misery of his fellow human beings is appalling.
nd that without an ever-present Gestapo to discourage undue
uriosity as to what was going on behind official walls. Let us
ot take refuge from unpleasant facts by glibly accepting the
onvenient theory that this is not human nature we are witnessing
ut *German* human nature'.[140]

Our last word must be one of wonder and appreciation that
here were indeed those who despite everything did by the Grace
f God 'open their mouths for the dumb' and at the risk of their
wn future prospects and lives and the well-being of their own
amilies, did come to the succour of the helplessly afflicted.

NOTES TO CHAPTER 8

1. Karl Barth: *Die Evangelische Kirche in Deutschland nach dem Zusammenbruch des Dritten Reiches*, Stuttgart, 1946, p. 15.

2. Niemöller: *Wort und Tat*, 275, 276.

3. Elias, 217.

4. H. A. Hesse: *Die Judenfrage in der Verkündigung Heute*, Stuttgart, 1948, p. 8.

5. See Kupisch; *Durch den Zaun*, 388–90.

6. Leuner, 100.

7. Saul Friedländer: *Pius XII and the Third Reich*, Chatto and Windus, 1966, p. 115. It is not in any way suggested by this quotation of such a courageous Roman Catholic outcry that the Catholic Church outshone the Evangelical Church in expressing concern for the Jewish people. Pope Pius XI kept silent when the Aryan legislation was first introduced, when the Nuremberg Laws were promulgated and when the pogrom of November 1938 took place. His famous encyclical *Mit brennender Sorge* of 1937 did not mention the crimes against the Jews. Hans Müller writing with reference to 1933 describes how the plight of the Jews, who were already then being to a great extent deprived of their civil rights and persecuted, was as far as the Catholic Church was concerned a matter of secondary consideration. As far as any interest at all was shown for the non-Aryans, he remarks, it was limited to those who had been converted to the Catholic faith. A lone voice was to be heard here and there on behalf of the Jews in general over against the utterances of those Catholics who were either condoning or

justifying the prevailing anti-semitism. *Katholische Kirche un Nationalsozialismus, Deutscher Taschenbuch*, München, 1965, p. 70

Dr. Alois Wurm, editor of *Die Seele* complained to Cardina Faulhaber of Munich in April 1933 that not one single Catholi journal was proving courageous enough to proclaim that no on should be hated or persecuted on grounds of his race, and tha in many Jewish and Christian circles it was not understood wh the Christian leaders were keeping silent. Faulhaber's excus proved to be that there were far more important contemporary questions demanding representation by the Church authoritie such as the schools issue and sterilisation. He did not feel incline at that time to take up even the cause of the Jews who were baptise Catholics, since the purpose of baptism was to promote eterna life, and no one ought to expect to derive earthly advantage from it. Ludwig Volk: *Der Bayerische Episkopat und der National sozialismus, 1938–1934*, Mainz, 1965, pp. 78–80.

As late as March 1941 Archbishop Gröber of Freiburg in pastoral letter abounding in anti-Jewish utterances had blamed th Jews for the death of Christ, and added that 'the self-impose curse of the Jews "His blood be upon us and upon our children" has come true terribly until the present time, until today.' (Lewy 294.)

Lewy's verdict upon the Catholic bishops in Germany is that the found themselves prisoners of their own anti-semitic teaching, whe they might perhaps have wanted to protest against the inhuman treatment of the Jews. He maintains that with a few exceptions th overall picture was one of indifference and apathy (294–5).

8. Gerhard Bassarak: *Bekennende Kirche einst und jetzt* in *Stimmer aus der Kirche der DDR.* Ed. Be Ruys, Zürich, 1967, p. 52.

9. In *Berliner Sonntagsblatt*, 7 April 1963, reproduced in *Durfte der Papst schweigen?*, p. 192. It is interesting to compare the contribution of Dibelius with one from a stalwart pioneer of the Confessing Church, Gerhard Jacobi, which also appears in *Dürfte der Papst schweigen?* (p. 189). 'We in Germany' Jacobi wrote, 'ought in our thousands to have preached out, called and shouted from the housetops "Righteousness exalteth a nation: but sin is a reproach to any people." This would certainly not have been of any avail and all who had cried out in such fashion would have disappeared into a concentration camp. Nevertheless we have as Christians not to ask ourselves what promise there may be of success, but we have to say the truth. Dietrich Bonhoeffer quoted repeatedly at our meetings in Berlin the proverb: "One person asks what will result from it, the other what is right, and thereby the freeman is distinguished from the slave." The truth was assuredly expressed with such clarity from many a pulpit, that the hearers were left in no doubt. But it did not thereby reach either the public or the State. Consequently we must take our share of the corporate guilt.'

10. Otto Dibelius: *Das Jahrhundert der Kirche*, Berlin, 1928. In a further publication of his, *Nachspiel: Eine Aussprache mit den Freunden und Kritikern des 'Jahrhunderts der Kirche'*, Dibelius continued and enlarged his commentary upon the contemporary Church situation and his optimistic version of the emerging Church.

11. Otto Dibelius: *In the Service of the Lord*, Faber, 1965, p. 111.

12. *Das Jahrhundert der Kirche*, 77.

13. Ibid., 89.

14. Ibid., 192–3.

15. *Nachspiel*, 24–5. See Wolf: *Barmen*, 22–3.

16. *Jahrhundert der Kirche*, 205–6.

17. Ibid., 256.

18. Ibid., 236.

19. Ibid., 237.

20. *Kirchliches Jahrbuch für die evangelischen Landeskirchen in Deutschland*, 1928, p. 314.

21. Ibid., 316.

22. Paul Althaus: *Das Erlebnis der Kirche*, pp. 3–4, quoted by Wolf: *Barmen*, 20.

23. Paul Althaus: *Kirche und Volkstum*, Gütersloh, 1928, *passim*.

24. Paul Althaus: *Die deutsche Stunde der Kirche*, 5–8.

25. Schmidt: *Bekenntnisse*, 1934, pp. 102–4.

26. Ibid., 103.

27. Paul Althaus: *Theologische Verantwortung*, in *Luthertum*, 1934, p. 22.

28. Wolf: *Barmen*, 21.

29. Dietrich Bonhoeffer: *Sanctorum Communio: Eine dogmatische Untersuchung zur Soziologie der Kirche*, Theologische Bücherei, Band 3, München, 1925. English translation, Collins, 1963. See John Godsey: *The Theology of Dietrich Bonhoeffer*, S.C.M., 1960, pp. 27 ff.

30. Martin Pertiet: *Das Ringen um Wesen und Auftrag der Kirche in nationalsozialistischen Zeit*, Arbeiten zur Geschichte des Kirchen-Kampfes, Band 19, Göttingen, 1968, p. 47.

31. Karl Barth: *Der Götze wackelt*, ed. Karl Kupisch, Berlin, 1964, pp. 27–32.

32. Ibid., 33–62.

33. Ibid., 28.

34. Ibid., 31.

35. Ibid., 61.

36. Wolf: *Barmen*, 27.

37. Dibelius: *In the Service of the Lord*, 112.

38. See Emil Brunner: *Natur und Gnade—Zum Gespräch mit Karl Barth*, and Karl Barth; *Nein! Antwort an Emil Brunner* in *Dialektische Theologie in Scheidung und Bewährung*, ed. Walter Furst, München, 1966, pp. 169–258.

39. Manfred Jacobs, quoted by Gerlach, Beiheft, p. 1, note 4.

40. John Bowden: *Karl Barth*, S.C.M., 1971, pp. 74–5.

41. Dietrich Bonhoeffer: *Letters and Papers from Prison*, Collin Fontana Books, 1962, p. 164.
42. Ibid., 95.
43. Karl Barth: *Theologische Existenz Heute*, p. 3.
44. Ibid., 24.
45. Karl Barth: *Die Kirche Jesu Christi, Theologische Existenz Heut* No. 5, pp. 8–9.
46. It is significant that Dr. Duncan-Jones, the Dean of Chicheste chose in 1938 for the title of his account of the Church Conflict- *The Struggle for Religious Freedom in Germany*, and that Marti Niemöller's last sermons, published in Germany under the titl of *Jesus Christ is Lord* were, when translated into English, give the title of *The Gestapo Defied*.
47. Karl Barth: *Die Kirche Jesu Christi*, 9–10.
48. J. S. Conway in *Vierteljahrshefte für Zeitgeschichte*, 1969, pp. 454–!
49. Kupisch: *Durch den Zaun der Geschichte*, 396.
50. The translation 'Two Kingdoms' is liable to misunderstandin The reference is 'rather to two ways in which God governs mankin or two orders of government, Word and Sword' (W. D. J. Cargi Thompson: *The Two Kingdoms and the Two Regiments—Son Problems of Luther's Zwei Reiche Lehre, Journal of Theologic Studies*, 1969, p. 165). In consideration of Christian acceptanc of Hitler and subsequent failure to resist, care should be taken n to lay too much blame upon Luther and his doctrine of the Tw Kingdoms in view of the fact that the Lutheran Churches c Scandinavia distinguished themselves in spirited and outspoke opposition, and that the German Catholics proved to be just abou as submissive as the Protestants. Konrad Gröber, Archbishop c Freiburg, for instance, wrote in 1935— 'The *Obrigkeit* is, accordin to Catholic interpretation, the embodiment of an eternal ide established by God Himself. The *Obrigkeit* which misuses it rights does not thereby forthwith lose its legitimacy' (Gröber *Kirche, Vaterland und Vaterlandsliebe*, Freiburg, 1935, p. 98). I must, further, not be forgotten how deep-rooted and obdurat were the nationalistic political convictions of so many leadin Evangelical churchmen when Hitler assumed power, and ho appreciative many of them continued to remain, as German increasingly became a power to be reckoned with. For evidence c the Scandinavian attitude see *The Grey Book*, ed Johan M Snoel
   It is not easy for a German Protestant, and is altogether mor difficult for an English Christian, to attain to a clear understandin of Luther's teaching on Church and State and of the duty to obe and the right to rebel. Luther, as Heinrich Bornkamm (*Luther World of Thought*, Concordia, 1965, p. 237) has remarked 'wa neither a statesman nor a political philosopher but a preache of the Gospel, and for this reason it is not easy to fit him int political history and to label him and his views. Luther's pronounce ments on questions of political and national life are all spiritua

counsel. They do not lend themselves to being pieced together as a systematic whole'. 'His was not a systematic mind that creates a logical harmony of thought and action. Had he possessed the gift of systematic thought, he would not have been the prophet that he was. He thought and worked as the spirit moved him, and gave utterance to the rush of his ideas, as the occasion and the subject demanded' (James Mackinnon: *Luther and the Reformation*, Longman, 1930, Vol. 4, p. 248). What he taught has to be pieced together from a number of different short writings, some of which were hastily composed for ad hoc purposes. Inexact in his use of words, he is liable to contradict himself and be inconsistent, and it must be remembered all the time that his method of thought was dialectical.

51. Reinhold von Thadden: *Auf verlorenem Posten?* Tübingen, 1948, pp. 40–41.

52. W. A. Visser 't Hooft: *The Kingship of Christ*, S.C.M., 1948, p. 15.

53. The German word *Obrigkeit* is difficult to render into English. It therefore seems best to leave it untranslated. Otto Dibelius (*Obrigkeit*, Stuttgart, 1963, p. 53) has pointed out that in German Bibles that appeared before Luther's the *potestatibus sublimioribus* of the Vulgate was straightforwardly translated and made equivalent to the 'Supreme Authorities' of our New English Bible. Luther had other ideas, and produced as his version *Die Obrigkeit die Gewalt über ihn hat*. *Obrigkeit* being in the singular suggests that Luther was thinking definitely in German national terms of the local ruler of his time, be he bad or good, and of that ruler being responsible for his subjects and their whole welfare, a point not made in Romans 13. It was a patriarchal responsibility such as a father bears for his children, and it called for a pious, respectful and obedient response from his 'subjects'. Increasingly from the seventeenth century on what we today call democracy with its political parties and elections developed, and the supreme authority was no longer to be accounted *Obrigkeit* in Luther's original sense. Instead of the *Obrigkeit* being responsible for the people, the people had become responsible for the sort of governors that they had. This did not, however, prevent orthodox Lutheranism from still thinking in terms of the original patriarchal authority which in the twentieth century would appear to be realisable in a national totalitarian dictatorship.

54. Hermann Diem: *Karl Barths Kritik am deutschen Luthertum*, Zürich, 1947, p. 5.

55. Hermann Diem: *Kann die Kirche Busse tun?* in *Evangelischer Korrespondenz*, October 1970, p. 580.

56. KJB, 300. It is interesting, in contrast with this statement, to read the following in a private letter from Wurm to Zöllner, dated December 1935: 'We have not to deal with what appears to us people of the older generation to be the divinely prescribed organ for Law and Order, to which we owe obedience, even if it is painful to us, but we have to do with a new religion which avails itself of

the power of the State, in order to establish itself in place of the Christian Faith' (Fischer, VIII, 262).

57. Karl Barth: *Verheissung und Verantwortung der christlicher Gemeinde im heutigen Zeitgeschehen* in *Eine schweizer Stimme*, p. 328.
58. Jürgen Schmidt: *Martin Niemöller im Kirchenkampf*, p. 254.
59. Paul Althaus: *Kirche und Staat nach lutherische Lehre*, Leipzig 1935, p. 29.
60. Ibid., 18.
61. Quoted in Heinz Hürten: *Deutsche Briefe*, Mainz, 1969, Band 1 pp. 124–5.
62. Schmidt: *Bekenntnisse*, 1935, pp. 124–5.
63. Much has been written since the war on the subject of the doctrine of the Two Kingdoms. Reference should be made to the article by Cargill Thompson in the Journal of Theological Studies (note 45). Among the chief contributions in German to the discussion may be mentioned in addition to Diem's important lecture (note 49). Paul Althaus: *Luthers Lehre von den beiden Reichen im Feuer der Kritik* in *Luther Jahrbuch*, Berlin, 1957, Karl Barth: *Christengemeinde und Burgergemeinde*, Zürich, 1946 (English translation in *Against the Stream*, S.C.M., 1954); Otto Dibelius: *Obrigkeit*, Stuttgart, 1963: Helmut Gollwitzer: *Die christliche Gemeinde in der politischer Welt*, Tübingen, 1954; Gunnar Hillerdall: *Gehorsam gegen Gott und Menschen—Luthers Lehre von der Obrigkeit und die moderne Staatsethik*, Göttingen, 1955; Franz Lau: *Luthers Lehre von den beiden Reichen*, Berlin, 1952; Johannes Heckel: *Im Irrgarten der Zwei Reiche Lehre*, *Theologische Existenz Heute*, Neue Folge 55, München, 1957: Walter Künneth: *Der grosse Abfall*, Hamburg 1948, pp. 166–95; Peter Meinhold: *Römer 13*, Stuttgart, 1960; and Ernst Wolf: *Kirche im Widerstand?* München, 1965, *Die lutherische Lehre von den Zwei Reichen in der gegenwärtige Forschung*, Zeitschrift *für evangelischen Kirchenrecht*, 1957–58, pp. 255 ff., *Die Königsherrschaft Christi und der Staat*, *Theologische Existenz Heute*, 64, München, 1958. Despite the bitter and overwhelming experience of inhuman and godless Nazi tyranny and almost unavoidable misgivings as to the role played by the Church, conservative theologians are to be discovered after the war still stating the traditional doctrine of the Two Kingdoms in uncompromising fashion. Franz Lau wrote in 1952, 'The Christian, in so far as he is subordinate to the Emperor has not to pay heed to Christ's Law. Christ's Law concerns only the sphere of the inward . . . It is not permissible to speak of the amelioration of the world through the power of the Gospel' (quoted by Wolf in *Zeitschrift für evangelischen Kirchenrecht*, 1957–8, pp. 264–6). Hans von Soden who was in the thick of the Confessional fight wrote in 1956: 'The duty to obey the *Obrigkeit* is in its obligation altogether independent of whether its rule is a liberal or a total one. . . . The *Obrigkeit* can do anything that is in its power to do, and must do what it seems to be necessary for the State. The Church has to contest for her own office (*Amt*) and only for that.'

64. Gollwitzer: *Die christliche Gemeinde in der politischer Welt*, 16–18.
65. Gunnar Hillerdall: *Gehorsam gegen Gott*, 42.
66. Ernst Wolf: *Kirche im Widerstand?* 9–10.
67. Eberhard Klügel: *Die lutherische Landeskirche Hannovers und ihr Bischof*, Dokumente, 221.
68. Hermann Diem: *Kirche und staatliche Autorität in Württemberg*, in *Schwäbische Heimat*, December 1969, pp. 329–30. Bishop Wurm had concluded his letter of July 1940 to Frick regarding the Nazi 'Euthanasia' campaign with the words—'*Dixi et salvavi animam meam*' (Schäfer 124). Diem took steps to inform Wurm that this ending was 'impossible'. As bishop he had to do more than just salve his own conscience.
69. Schäfer, 157.
70. Diem: *Karl Barths Kritik*, 11.
71. The 'Inner Line' was also pursued by prominent Roman Catholic leaders. Konrad Gröber, certainly one of the most forceful and outspoken of them, writing in November 1941 in reply to the Baden Minister of Education who had accused him of high treason, emphasised that in reality he had neither openly nor in any underhand fashion attacked National Socialism or the National Socialist State as a political institution, but had solely out of feelings of Christian honour and duty offered resistance against attacks upon Christianity (*Hirtenrufe des Erzbischofs Gröber in die Zeit*, ed. Konrad Hofmann, Freiburg, 1947, p. 121).
72. Diem: *Kirche und staatliche Autorität*, in *Schwäbische Heimat*, 328.
73. Hermann Diem: *Restauration oder Neuanfang in der evangelischer Kirche?*, Stuttgart, 1946, p. 47.
74. Mentioned by Eugen Gerstenmaier in an article in *Vierteljahrshefte für Zeitgeschichte*, 1967, p. 243.
75. Angelika Gerlach Praetorius: *Die Kirche vor der Eidesfrage*, Arbeiten zur Geschichte des Kirchenkampfes, Band 18, Göttingen, 1967, p. 218.
76. Bethge, 680, English edition, 507, where there is an apparent mistranslation declaring that the Confessional Synod knew of the forthcoming regulation, not Bonhoeffer.
77. Dietrich Bonhoeffer: *Ethics*, S.C.M., 1955, pp. 307–8.
78. Hans Bernd Gisevius: *To the Bitter End*, Cape, 1948, p. 220.
79. *The Gestapo Defied*.
80. In *Bekennende Kirche*, Martin Niemöller zum 60 Geburtstag, 318.
81. In a letter to *The Times*, 3 July 1937.
82. Jürgen Schmidt: *Martin Niemöller*, 405.
83. In a letter to Professor Julius Richter, 29 May 1936, quoted in Schmidt, 410.
84. Ibid., 409–10.
85. Gaus: *Zur Person*, 113.
86. Schmidt, 441.
87. Ibid., 442.
88. *Ein NS-Funktionär zum Niemöller-Prozess*, in *Vierteljahrshefte für Zeitgeschichte*, 1956, p. 313.

89. Ibid., 313–14.
90. Jürgen Schmidt, 440.
91. Ibid., 446.
92. Ibid., 67.
93. Ibid., 254.
94. Wilhelm Niemöller: *Die Geschichte des Kirchenkampfes*, lecture given in Detroit, 17 March 1970, 1 Beiheft, *Junge Kirche*, 1971. 'There was not one single voice to be heard affirming in public that murder is murder.'
95. Jürgen Schmidt, 256.
96. *First Commandment*, 150.
97. Ibid., 151.
98. Ibid., 155.
99. Jürgen Schmidt, 278–9.
100. Ibid., 395–6.
101. Ibid., 404–5. The title of the lecture was *Gott der Herr über Kirche und Volk*.
102. *Gestapo Defied*, 25.
103. Ibid., 31.
104. Ibid., 96.
105. Martin Niemöller: *Die politische Verantwortung des Christen im akademischen Stand*, Giessen, 1946, p. 16.
106. Ibid., 14.
107. Martin Niemöller's speech to the Conference of Evangelical Church Leaders at Treysa, August 1945 in *Treysa, 1945*, Lüneburg, 1946, pp. 23–4.
108. Bishop Wurm and others repeatedly quoted statistics to prove that the Evangelical clergy were second to none in their valiant service to the Fatherland.
109. Schäfer, 275.
110. Schäfer, 378–81. See also Wurm's letter to Kerrl, December 1941, in which he emphasised the value that the State would undoubtedly derive from making it possible for the Church to re-establish herself in real strength and in being of service all down the line (Schäfer 286).
111. Hermann Diem: *Kirche und Antisemitismus*, in *Deutsches Geistesleben und Nationalsozialismus*, ed. Andreas Flitner, Tübingen, 1965, p. 20.
112. Gauger, 522.
113. Neuhäusler, I, 330.
114. Ibid. Published in *Die Reichspost*, 18 March 1937.
115. Friedrich Heiler in *Eine Heilige Kirche*, April–June 1934, p. 173.
116. Karl Kupisch in *Der ungekündigte Bund*, p. 85.
117. Ibid., 125.
118. Dieter–Wolf Zimmerman ed.: *I knew Dietrich Bonhoeffer*, Collins, 1966, p. 50.
119. Karl Barth: *Die Kirche und die politische Frage von heute* in *Eine Schweizer Stimme*, p. 80.

120. Günther Harder: *Christen vor dem Problem der Judenfrage* in *Christen und Juden*, p. 252.

121. Asmussen, 115.

122. Kurt Meier: *Der Kirchenkampf im Dritten Reich und seine Erforschung* in *Theologische Rundschau*, 1968, p. 137.

123. *Durfte der Papst schweigen?*, 201.

124. Maurice Samuel: *The Great Hatred*, Gollancz, 1940, pp. 12 and 32.

125. Leuner 17. Martin Niemöller in a lecture delivered in December 1945 suggested that reference to the demonic could be perilous in helping to excuse men and women from facing up to their past responsibility and from making present confession of their guilt. 'I appreciate it', he said, 'when a Christian has today a more sensitive impression than he previously had of the fact that the Devil is at work. For we have seen and experienced things that bear an emphatic and previously undreamed of witness to the power of Evil at work in the world. Nevertheless, we should not be preaching the Devil, but Him who has robbed the Devil of his power. I have both read and received a whole collection of letters in which the responsibility for what has happened has been shoved on to the Devil or on to demons. This is a dangerous sign. Our speech is to be of sin and of guilt, but of the Devil only peripherally and of demons with great caution' (Wilhelm Niemöller: *Neu Anfang 1945*, Frankfurt, 1967, p. 103). Karl Barth made a similar point, when he declared in 1945, that in Confessing circles there was suspiciously fervent talk about the acquaintance made in the past twelve years in Germany with seductive demonic powers. 'Would not', he added, 'a sober confession of sin have proved better than so profound an avowal of the reality of demons?' (*Die Evangelische Kirche in Deutschland nach dem Zusammenbruch*, p. 38.)

126. KJB, 1945–8, 26–7.

127. KJB, 1945–8, 28.

128. Quoted in Heinz Schmidt: *Die Judenfrage und die Christliche Kirche in Deutschland*, Stuttgart, 1947.

129. Klügel, Dokumente, 204.

130. KJB, 1945–8, 223.

131. KJB, 1945–8, 224–7.

132. Renate Heydenreich in *Der ungekündigte Bund*, 250.

133. *Volk, Nation, Vaterland*, 194.

134. KJB, 1950, pp. 5–6.

135. Erica Küppers: *Kirche und Israel*, supplement to *Bekennende Kirche—Martin Niemöller, zum 60 Geburtstag*, 1952, p. 16.

136. KJB, 1945–8, 34.

137. *Not und Aufgabe der Kirche in Deutschland*, lecture given in Zürich, 7 March 1946.

138. See Melita Maschmann: *Account Rendered*, London, 1964, p. 221.

139. C. E. M. Joad in *New Statesman*, 28 April, 1945, p. 269.

140. Eric Warman in *New Statesman*, 28 April 1945, p. 272.

Luther and the Jews

Peter Wiener in his savage war-time attack upon Martin Luther as 'Hitler's spiritual ancestor' declared, 'I do not believe that even the notorious *Der Stürmer* of Dr. Streicher surpassed the sayings of Brother Martin.'[1] Streicher himself told the Nuremberg Tribunal that Luther ought to be in the dock in his place, for Luther had long before said what he himself had to say about the Jews, and much more sharply.[2] A year or two ago a play by a Finn, entitled *The Other Luther*, which suggested that he had furnished a moral alibi for the gassing of the Jews, had two public performances in Helsinki before it was banned by the authorities.[3] Wolf Meyer-Erlach, one of the most rabid of all Nazi Christians, claimed Luther to have been the most passionate anti-semite in the past history of the western world.[4] A case can be made out that Luther centuries ago in a programme for the suppression of the Jews foreshadowed the burning of Synagogues, forced labour and deportation, and even that a collection of his more violent denunciations of the Jews, removed from their context, encouraged the eventual 'Final Solution' by extermination. An American Jew in a recent embittered indictment of the Christian Churches for their leading part in the creation and the encouragement of anti-semitism holds Luther responsible for having given Hitler his basic programme. 'There was', he maintains, 'no anti-semitic crime prescribed by Luther that the Germans failed to carry out, and there was no crime perpetrated by the Nazis that Luther had not ordered'.[5] The Nazis were certainly only too delighted to be able to quote for their evil purposes the words of the Great Reformer, and eagerly promoted the publication of new and popular editions of his most scurrilous outpourings. Here was a veritable arsenal of vulgar anti-semitism!

This is admittedly a terrible indictment. What can be said, if not in excuse, yet in explanation and defence?

It may appear a mere platitude to remark that Luther was a man of his time. But it does serve to remind us that a certain crudity in expression and singular lack of tolerance was common in his day. We have no right to expect him to have reacted in accordance with our enlightened standards of what is liberal, fair and humanitarian. His fellow-Christians, both papists and fanatical protestants, were also objects of his venom. 'Luther harboured an immense capacity for hatred which could be directed variously at Jews, Papists, *Schwärmer* or other adversaries, and which in each case quite obscured the human countenance of the opponent.'[6]

At the beginning of the sixteenth century the situation of the Jews was scarcely more favourable than it was during the Hitler period. Luther was schooled in the traditional, mediaeval attitude of defamation and suppression of the unconverted Jew. He appears to have been prepared to give some credence, like most other people, to the current stories of Jewish contamination of wells, kidnapping, torturing, ritual murder of children, and the practice of witchcraft and conjuring tricks.

In his earliest utterance upon the Jewish issue in 1514–1515 Luther affirmed the wholesale rejection of the Jews by God. It was a token of the Divine Wrath that they were so widely scattered and with no secure standing, a judgement upon their attitude to Jesus Christ. Such divine punishment in no wise provoked a sense of guilt followed by the desire to be converted to Christianity. As borne out by Old Testament prophecy, only a small remnant would be saved. By such obduracy the Jews revealed themselves to be active foes of Christianity, eager to lead others astray. The issue was one between lies and the Truth, which allowed of no tolerance on the part of faithful Christians, though it was salutary for professed Christians to reflect how readily they too could incur the same condemnation. This early attitude of Luther remained bascially unaltered throughout his life, and caution should be observed in any attempt at playing off the young Luther against the embittered and disillusioned old Reformer.

Having triumphed in his challenge of the Papacy, and standing as the champion of the preaching of the pure Word, Luther came to feel that, despite his continued conviction that the Jewish People were rejected of God, there was yet a missionary opportunity of converting individual Jews, who, instead of being confronted by what Luther relished calling 'popishness', 'monkery' and 'sophistry', and subjected to forced conversion, might now respond to the Gospel approach of love and compassion. This more optimistic attitude is to be found expressed in his christological study, *That Jesus was Born a Jew*, published in 1523. It soon ran into nine editions, and penetrated as far as Jerusalem. 'I hope', wrote Luther, 'that, if one deals in a kindly way with the Jews and instructs them carefully from Holy Scripture, many of them will become genuine Christians, and turn again to the faith of their fathers, the Prophets and Patriarchs. They will only be frightened further away from it, if their Judaism is so utterly rejected, that nothing is allowed to remain, and they are treated only with arrogance and scorn. If the apostles, who also were Jews, had dealt with us Gentiles as we Gentiles deal with the Jews, there would never have been a Christian among the Gentiles. Since they have dealt with us Gentiles in such brotherly fashion, we in our turn ought to treat the Jews in a brotherly manner, in order that we might convert some of them. For even we ourselves are not yet very far along, not to speak of having arrived.'[7]

'So long as we treat them like dogs', he concluded, 'how can we expect to work any good among them? Again, when we forbid them to labour and do business and have any human fellowship with us, thereby forcing them into usury, how is that supposed to do them any good? If we really want to help them, we must be guided in our dealings with them not by papal law, but by the law of Christian love. We must receive them cordially and permit them to trade and work with us, that they may have occasion and opportunity to associate with us, hear our Christian teaching, and witness our Christian life. If some of them should prove stiff-necked, what of it? After all, we ourselves are not all good Christians.'[8] Luther was also perfectly willing to admit that the Jews were more closely related to Christ than 'we Gentiles'. 'We are aliens and in-laws; they are the blood relatives, cousins and brothers of Our Lord.'[9] This courageous and friendly tone was something that the Jews had not heard in a thousand years, and it gained for him from his enemies and his critics the titles of 'Half-Jew' and 'Patron of the Jews'. It would be a mistake, however, to imagine that Luther had changed into a humane philosemite. His concern was radical conversion.

The hoped for flow of conversions was not realised. Some of those who had been won over to Christianity did not, to his manifest grief and disappointment, retain their new faith. In the next twelve or so years Luther suffered from increasing disillusion, and complained of resistance to conversion due to stubborn and irredeemable trust in righteousness by works, obstinate clinging to the dream of a Messiah or a new prophet still to come, and offence at the Church making exclusive claim to the title of God's Elect People. In an exposition of the 109th Psalm Luther referred in the following terms to the incorrigibility of the Jews: 'Where they are, and where their schools stand, they must stick to their old poison. My God, in how many lands have they set up their little game against Christ which is why they have been hunted and burned and killed.' On another occasion he remarked: 'Because they and their children will not accept Christ, there is no mercy left for this hardened people, and so they suffer.'[10] He was upset and offended by unfortunate encounters with individual Jews and apparent threats to his own personal safety. To his great consternation efforts were being made to reverse the process, and make Jews out of his fellow-Christians. He learnt of Jewish propaganda among the Moravians which had some success in persuading them to observe the Jewish sabbath and adopt the rite of circumcision. In his bitter conflict with the Anabaptists and other Protestant fanatics he detected unmistakable evidence of judaistic messianic and legalistic influences. He was incensed at every instance of Jewish blasphemy of Christ, and complained of 'truly satanic envy and hatred of Christ and the Christians'. The friendly note vanished, and the Jews began to overtake the Turks and the Papists as his bitterest enemies. Apart from the individual here and there whom God would, maybe, of His mercy bring to the Truth, the Jews were to be regarded as unconvertible.

From 1537 on it became obvious that he was no longer concerned with addressing himself to the Jews. His mission was to warn the Christians against them. 1543 saw the explosion of his pent-up *furor teutonicus* in the publication of *Concerning the Jews and their Lies* which has been not unfairly described as 'a perfect hurricane of invective, a blazing volcano of hatred and fury'.[11] The Jews were castigated as vampires, blasphemers, thieves, usurers and devils incarnate, and the Christians were declared to be guilty of not having avenged the shedding of the sacred and innocent blood of their Lord, and also of countless subsequent victims of the Jews, and of having allowed them to continue dwelling among them, protecting their schools and houses, persons and property. The practical measures suggested by Luther for dealing with the pernicious Jews including the destruction by fire of their synagogues and schools, pulling down and destroying their houses, burning their sacred books, a teaching ban upon their rabbis, drastic curtailment of their movements, depriving them of moneys obtained through usury, and, following the example set by Spain, France and Bohemia, permanent expulsion from the country. Luther must have more than doubted whether the authorities would be prepared to implement such drastic recommendations, and in point of fact no one took his programme seriously. He, therefore, included an exhortation to 'his dear gentlemen and friends who are pastors and preachers to warn their parishioners to be on guard against the Jews and avoid them as far as possible, not encouraging them in their wanton lying, slandering, cursing and defaming by giving food, drink and shelter, and by other neighbourly acts, but rather recalling that the Jew whom they might be inclined to befriend was a regular blasphemer of the Lord Jesus Christ and one who prayed to God that all Christians might be stabbed to death and perish miserably'.[12] Luther's vindictive programme was with ironical inconsistency prefaced by the words, 'with prayer and the gift of God we must practice a sharp mercy to see whether we might save at least a few from the glowing flames. Avenge ourselves we dare not. Vengeance a thousand times worse that what we could wish them already has them by the throat'.[13] The lengthy tirade concluded with the prayer—'Christ, our loving Lord, convert them in thy Compassion!'

To be fair to Luther, it should be pointed out that a very large part of this particular writing was theological in character, though of course alarmingly polemical throughout, and devoted to an attempted Christian interpretation of the Old Testament as opposed to a Jewish one, intended to fortify the faith of his fellow-Christians. Though Luther was undoubtedly given at times to gross exaggeration, there certainly were Jews who did not hesitate to refer to Jesus as a sorcerer, to the Virgin Mary as a whore and to the New Testament as a pack of lies. He was very much in earnest, when he declared that nothing less than 'God's honour and the salvation of us all including that of the Jews are at stake'.[14]

If the blasphemies were not combated with full vigour, there was, so he believed, a danger of the same divine wrath that fell upon the Jews descending upon Christians as well. Not in excuse but in attempted explanation of his savage practical recommendations, it should be accepted that the destroying of the synagogues, the suppression of Jewish books of prayer and copies of the Talmud, the ban on rabbinic teaching and the holding of Jewish religious services were drastic measures aimed at preventing the Name of Christ from being profaned. That no proclamation in public of anti-Christian doctrines would be tolerated would be proof of an evangelical territory being truly Christian.

The vitriolic fury was unabated in *Schem Hamphoras*, which appeared in the same year. The Swiss Reformer Bucer in condemning it as 'piggish' and 'mucky' declared that, even if it had been written by a swineherd and not by a famous Shepherd of souls, it would be indefensible. Luther described the Jewish heart as being devilishly hard and immovable as a block of wood and as stone and iron. Hope of conversion was at an end. Even if Moses and the Prophets were to appear and work wonders before their very eyes, as Christ and the Apostles once did, it would be in vain. Cruel punishment of them with the streets flowing with blood and hundreds of thousands slain would not turn their hearts. They would still regard themselves as in the right and God as a liar. They were children of the Devil, condemned to Hell. Their awaited Messiah would not allow himself to be crucified, but would strike the Gentiles dead, and give the Jews mastery in the world. The purpose was, again, to counter libellous Jewish perversions of the Truth, and to assist in preventing any belief by Christians in them. Very regrettably the promotion of such an aim had the effect of perverting the gloriously liberating preaching of the Gospel into the anxious and cantankerous defence of doctrine, resulting in a perilously exclusive orthodoxy which left no room for really constructive discussion of the Truth.

In a sermon delivered at Eisleben a day or two before his death Luther made his final reference to the Jews. He spoke of their many blasphemies including the calling of the Virgin Mary a whore and Christ a bastard, and averred that 'if they could kill us all they would gladly do so'. But he also expressed the desirability of treating them in a Christian fashion, provided there was a chance of making Christians of them. If only they would become converted, and cease from their blasphemies and other misdeeds, he would be only too glad to forgive them. If not, they could no longer be tolerated. The alternative was baptism or expulsion.

While we can of course do nought else but deplore Luther's violent and uncharitable utterances, and may feel bound to regard him as a Jew-hater, it does not seem right to designate him as an anti-semite in the modern sense. His 'anti-semitism' was patently religious and theological in character. Attitude to Christ was for him the beginning and end of the Jewish issue. The basic offence of the Jews was their disobedience to God in their wilful rejection of His offer of salvation promised in the Old Testament and then fulfilled in the New, thereby subjecting themselves to the inextinguishable fire of the Divine Wrath which no amount of sentimental human tolerance would dampen. They withstood the Word of God, as Luther understood it, and failed to acknowledge Jesus Christ as Messiah and accept the one and only true form of justification. Such decision against Jesus had settled the fate of individuals and people alike. They had sold themselves to the Devil, and were as assuredly destined to eternal damnation as were Evangelical Christian believers to eternal salvation. Luther, followed later by numerous other interpreters of the eighth chapter of St. John's Gospel, claimed Christ's own authority for so wholesale a condemnation and hatred of the Jewish people, citing verse 24, 'If ye believe not that I am He, ye shall die in your sins', verse 37, 'My word hath no place in you', verse 43, 'Ye cannot hear my word', verse 44, 'Ye are of your father the Devil, and the lusts of your father ye will do', unable to discern that for the 'Fourth Gospel as a whole the Jews are the representatives of the world as such.'[15] Because the Jews did not accept the New Testament, Luther insisted that they had forfeited their right to the possession of the Old Testament. They were no longer the People of the Covenant. The true Church of Christ was the sole inheritor of the original Divine Election. The Jews were to be accounted godless outcasts, an alien body with no place in German Christian society on religious, not racial, grounds. Haunted by the fear that they might corrupt the purity of faith in his fellow Evangelical Christians, he proclaimed that a Christian had no more dangerous enemy than a Jew determined to be one in earnest.

It is absurd and unjust to present and to condemn Luther as a racial anti-semite. He had no concern whatever about the issue from the racial angle. It is equally ridiculous and unfair to insist upon making him directly responsible for the misdeeds and atrocities of the Nazis. Luther with his choleric temperament wrote brutally about the Jews, but there is no evidence that any Jew was executed at his behest or murdered with his approval. He is never to be found expressing his aversion to the Jews in biological terms. Indeed, when on one occasion he upbraided the Jews for their watering down and defiling of Israelite blood through intermingling with the Gentiles, he did not express a similar concern that German blood might have been contaminated by Jewish infiltration.[16] Karl Kupisch has rightly remarked that 'it is pure cynicism, when modern anti-semites whose standpoint is nihilism, appeal to Luther, the man of faith'.[17] Nevertheless one can only concur with the final judgement of Rabbi Lewin in his classic study of the subject, that 'the seed of hatred of the Jews which Luther disseminated has had continuous effect through the centuries, and that anyone whoever and from whatever motive writes against the Jews, believes that he possesses the right to refer triumphantly to Luther.'[18]

The following attempts to evaluate the attitude of Luther towards the Jews have been consulted in the preparation of this appendix:

Friedrich Gruenagel: *Die Judenfrage*, Stuttgart, 1970, pp. 25–39.

Herbert Hug: *Das Volk Gottes. Der Kirche Bekenntnis zur Judenfrage*, Zurich, 1942.

Reinhold Lewin: *Luthers Stellung zu den Juden*, Berlin, 1911.

James Mackinnon: *Luther and the Reformation*, Longman, 1930, Vol. 4, pp. 192–204.

Wilhelm Maurer: in *Kirche und Synagoge*, ed. Karl Heinrich Rengstorf and Siegfried von Kortzfleisch, Vol. 1, Stuttgart, 1968.

Kurt Meier: *Zur Interpretation von Luthers jüdischen Schriften*, in *Kirche und Judentum*, Göttingen, 1968.

Wolf Meyer-Erlach: *Juden, Mönche und Luther*, Weimar, 1937.

Rudolf Pfisterer: *Im Schatten des Kreuzes*, Hamburg, 1966, pp. 64 ff.

Gordon Rupp: *Martin Luther and the Jews*, Robert Waley Cohen Memorial Lecture, 1972, Council of Christians and Jews, London.

Hansgeorg Schroth: *Luthers christlicher Antisemitismus heute*, Witte, 1937.

Martin Stohr: *Luther und die Juden* in *Evangelische Theologie*, 1960.

Martin Stohr: *Martin Luther und die Juden* in *Christen und Juden*, ed. W. D. Marsch and K. Thieme, Mainz, 1961.

Erik Vogelsang: *Luthers Kampf gegen die Juden*, Tübingen, 1933.

NOTES

1. Peter F. Wiener: *Martin Luther. Hitler's Spiritual Ancestor*, Hutchinson, 1944, p. 60. Reference should also be made to the brilliant refutation by Gordon Rupp in *Martin Luther. Hitler's Cause or Cure?* Lutterworth, 1945.
2. The city of Nuremberg presented Streicher in 1937, as a birthday present, a copy of the rare first edition of Luther's *Von den Juden und ihren Lügen* (JK, 1937, p. 198), which was described in *Der Stürmer* in March of that year as the most radical anti-semitic tract that had ever been published.
3. Friedrich Gruenagel: *Die Judenfrage*, Stuttgart, 1970, pp. 38–9.
4. Wolf Meyer-Erlach: *Juden, Mönche und Luther*, Weimar, 1937, p. 1.
5. Dagobert Runes: *The War against the Jews*, New York, 1968, pp. 80–1.
6. Martin H. Bertram in vol. 47 of American edition of Luther's Works, ed. Franklin Sherman, Philadelphia, 1971, p. 132.
7. Vol. 45 of American edition of Luther's Works, ed. by Walter Brandt, Philadelphia, 1962, p. 200.
8. Ibid., pp. 201, 229.
9. Ibid., p. 201.
10. Quoted by Gordon Rupp: *Martin Luther and the Jews*, Robert Waley Cohen Memorial Lecture 1972, pp. 12, 13.
11. James Mackinnon: *Luther and the Reformation*, Longman, 1930, vol. 4, p. 199.
12. Luther's Works, American edition, vol. 47, p. 274.
13. Ibid., 268.
14. Ibid., 287.
15. See Rudolf Bultmann: *The Gospel of St. John*, Blackwell, Oxford, 1971, p. 21.
16. Herbert Hug: *Das Volk Gottes*, Zürich, 1942, p. 131.
17. Karl Kupisch in *Der ungekündigte Bund*, 84.
18. Reinhold Lewin: *Luthers Stellung zu den Juden*, Berlin, 1911, p. 110.

Special Note

Since the writing of this Appendix there has come into the hands of the author Johannes Brosseder's exhaustive study of the many conflicting interpretations of Luther's attitude to the Jews. The work, published in 1972, is entitled *Luthers Stellung zu den Juden im Spiegel seiner Interpreten* (Band 8, Beiträge zur ökumenischen Theologie, ed. Heinrich Fries, München). With its summary of practically all known contributions in the nineteenth and twentieth centuries, it is quite indispensable for any detailed study of the subject.

Brosseder's own conclusion is that Luther was governed throughout by overriding theological and christological interest. In his judgement Luther's observations 'can be understood and rightly evaluated only in the light of his doctrine of Justification' (p. 386), with its fundamental emphasis upon the Wrath of God. Brosseder altogether rejects the commonly held view that a distinct transformation took place in Luther's attitude to the Jews. He maintains that the main purpose of what is interpreted as Luther's kindly writing in 1523 was to defend his christology from a grave charge of heresy. Only of secondary import is his apparent change of front in controversy with the Jews. His recommendation of friendlier treatment of the Jews had not converted him temporarily into a *Judenfreund*. His exposition of Scripture could scarcely be described as benevolent to the Jews. There was no diminishing of his theological judgement of the gravity of the divine rejection of Israel and Jewish obduracy and enmity towards the Church of Christ. There was no expression whatever of hope for the conversion of the Jewish people as a whole.

Brosseder insists that *Concerning the Jews and their Lies* and *Shem Hamphoras* are to be regarded by and large as an endeavour to furnish a Christian interpretation of the Old Testament. Luther's recommended 'sharp mercy' was relatively mild compared with the death penalty prescribed for heretics, and his practical counsel for suppression of the Jews was animated by his abhorrence of the Jewish religiosity of Works, a blasphemy identical with the denial of the Divine Godhead. As Luther's apologist, Brosseder goes so far as to claim that Luther, addressing exclusively his fellow-Christians, had no real desire to wage warfare against the Jews but was governed rather by concern for preserving and strengthening the faith of his fellow-Christians.

While concurring with Brosseder's emphasis upon Luther's theological and doctrinal earnestness and appreciating his refusal to accept psychological, sociological, or volkish explanations of Luther's vehement outbursts, it cannot but be felt that he sweeps all too conveniently to one side the Reformer's intemperate and scurrilous invective which by any reckoning must be accounted as dubiously Christian. He is effectively answered in a most impressive lecture summarised in his book which was delivered on the thirtieth anniversary of Crystal Night by a Berlin theologian, Joachim Rogge. Rogge so rightly emphasizes that Luther unfortunately in 1543 allowed his particular christological interpretation of the Old Testament to divert his attention from the New Testament emphasis upon the brotherhood of all men as consequence of Christ's Death upon the Cross and His Resurrection. The suffering of the Apostle Paul at the hands of his People and for his People, as Rogge points out, found no echo with Luther who was patently at fault in deciding that the Jews were to be regarded as having worn out the divine patience. Luther was one among many who have ominously failed to take into reckoning what stands written in Romans 11:32—'God hath concluded them all in unbelief, that He might have mercy upon all.' 'The Jewish brethren', as Rogge expresses it, 'have their share in God's Mercy through Jesus Christ' (p. 330).

APPENDIX 2

Judenmission

There was but little incentive in seventeenth-century Lutheran Orthodoxy to seek for the conversion of the Jews to Christianity. God's judgement upon his former Chosen People was held to be so absolute and condemnatory that individual conversions were almost out of the question. The situation changed with the advent of Pietism, and the Jew came to be regarded in pietistic circles as the brother to whom love was to be shown, and who should be brought to salvation for his own sake. Philip Jacob Spener[1] called for an exercise of genuine Christian love which should feel bound to seek the spiritual well-being of one's every neighbour. He regarded the Dispersal of the Jews among Christians as being not merely an example of the divine judgement but also an opportunity for the practice of evangelical love. 'We have to love all Jews', he wrote, 'for our dearest Jesus's sake, whose kinsfolk they are according to the flesh'.[2] Spener drew particular inspiration from both Isaiah chapter 53 and Romans chapter 11. The homecoming of the Jews to God through Jesus was for him not a far-distant apocalyptic event but a possible happening in the near future, and he rejoiced to contemplate the stimulus that the zeal of newly converted Israel could bring to the existing Church. Missionary endeavour among the Jews, he recommended, should show understanding for their obedience to the Law and the peculiarity of their traditions, avoid all compulsion and respect their freedom of conscience. Harsh and insensitive treatment of them was contrary to the instructions of Jesus. Christians were required to give evidence of an ethical concern for the legal rights of their Jewish neighbours, for their social amelioration and for the provision of generous opportunities for fair and useful employment corresponding to their talents. Evidence of the effects of the propagation of such kindly sentiments is to be found in a Decree of 1703 of King Frederick of

Prussia, which admonished the clergy to exercise gentle persuasion
upon Jewish unbelievers, and called upon each and every person
who confessed the name of Christ to take earnest pains not to
cause offence to his Jewish neighbours.

August Hermann Francke who had become celebrated for his
missionary zeal and for his charitable activity in Halle had established a college for oriental studies in the newly founded university.
It was a pupil of Francke, Johann Heinrich Callenberg, who called
into being the first German Protestant *Judenmission*. He also
brought the famous *Institutum Judaicum* into being in 1728.
Callenberg[3] inspired and trained a number of enterprising and
devoted missionaries, pre-eminent among whom was Stephan
Schultz[4] who had a quite phenomenal gift for languages. This was
accompanied by an altogether fearless and indefatigable desire
for travel which took him right through Europe and into the
Middle East in search of Jews whom he could befriend and
influence. He regarded as a primary task the persuasion of the
Jews to take the message of the Old Testament really seriously.
It was the achievement of Schultz and other stalwart missionaries
of this period to impress upon many of the Jews with whom they
made contact that there was upon the basis of the Old Testament,
which they possessed and revered in common, a real spiritual
kinship between Jews and Christians.

The *Judenmission* scarcely flourished in the period of Enlightenment and Emancipation. The latter half of the nineteenth century,
however, witnessed an impressive revival. This was due above
all to the efforts of Franz Delitzsch.[5] His reputation as a pre-
eminent Old Testament scholar became increasingly recognised.
His interests were not just academic, for he gave evidence of a
deeply rooted love and concern for the original Chosen People.
His warm desire to bring as many Jews as possible to an acceptance
of Jesus Christ as Messiah caused him, like St. Paul, to become
'unto the Jews as a Jew', and to produce a splendid Hebrew
translation of the New Testament which made a profound impression in Jewish circles. In 1870 he revived the *Institutum Judaicum*
in Leipzig with branches in other German universities. Leipzig
that same year became the headquarters of a co-ordinated *Judenmission*. In the course of a stirring speech in Berlin in 1870 he
described Germany as being 'so poor in love for the Jews, with so
tragically little concern evidenced for the people from whence

our salvation sprang forth'. He called for 'devoted love to Israel, since those who do not show love to the People which gave birth to Him have no true love for Jesus Himself'.[6] The whole Christian Church, he believed, needed to draw practical conclusions from Romans 9–11 which he regarded as the heart of the Epistle, and to recognise that without the conversion of the Jews the Church would not find her fulfilment. The object of missionary activity was as much to encourage warmth of Christian feeling towards the Jews as to promote Jewish faith in Christ. The charity which 'hopeth all things' needed to replace the current despondent antipathy. In a speech in Halle in 1886 he pronounced 'the *Zeitgeist* to be against us, but the spirit of the Prophets and Apostles with us'.[7] Shortly before his death in 1890 he asserted that it was a disgrace for Christians to call themselves anti-semites or to allow themselves to be termed such, thereby subscribing to 'the orthodox anti-semitic view that the Election of Israel, though a fact of past history, has become no longer tenable, and is without present relevance or future promise'.[8]

The good work was carried on, above all, by Hermann Strack and Gustav Dalman. Hermann Strack, internationally renowned as co-author of the massive Commentary to the New Testament from the Talmud and Midrash, was instrumental in establishing an *Institutum Judaicum* in Berlin in 1883, which took the form of a theological seminar at which students were assisted in making sound and unprejudiced assessment of Jewish religion and culture with, in Strack's own words, 'as objective as possible a judgement based upon Christianity and scholarly research unclouded by class, racial and mob hatred'.[9] His widely read 'Introduction to the Talmud' served to promote a more sympathetic understanding of the Jewish religion. Under his editorship the Institute published no less than 42 booklets, the most celebrated of which authoritatively countered the notoriously false and damaging accusations of Jewish ritual murder.[10] He wrote in 1900: 'I recognised it as my sacred duty as a Christian theologian to contribute everything that lay in my all too weak power, to the end that Israel might gain firm assurance that what Jesus desires is not lies but truth, not hate but love.'[11] In 1893 he went so far as to seek a legal injunction against the publishers of an anti-semitic pamphlet containing extracts from the Talmud, of which more than 300,000 copies had been circulated, and which he

egarded as a quite unprincipled and poisonous libelling of the
Jewish religion.[12] In 1920 he took determined issue over the
spurious 'protocols of the Elders of Zion'.

A warm tribute was paid to Strack, on the thirtieth anniversary
of the founding of the Institute, for his indefatigable labours in
opening the eyes of a small but thoroughly equipped succession of
students to the positive values of Judaism, who could then be
trusted to go out into public life eager and competent to contradict
anti-semitic prejudice and ignorance. It was the anguished cry
of this same correspondent: 'When will the *Judenmission* at last
cease to be the "Cinderella of the Evangelical Church" and the
preserve of a tiny circle of pious Christians? When will the Jews
no longer be the only people to whom the German people denies
the benefit of its continually boasted virtue of fairmindedness?'[13]

Gustav Dalman succeeded to Delitzsch's chair at Leipzig in
1902. He acclaimed his predecessor as 'the most significant
adversary of anti-semitic pseudo-scholarship through his demonstration that Christianity has nothing in common with unfair and
unsubstantiated censure of Judaism'.[14] In a paper delivered in
Cologne in 1900 on the themes of Anti-semitism and Missionary
work among the Jews Dalman remarked that 'worse than the
anti-semitic movement itself is the general disposition in circles
far removed from it to speak in disdainful tones of the Jews and to
regard any one not yet affected by the prevailing epidemic as
lacking in discrimination or as camouflaged Jews'.[15] The *Judenmission*, he contended, could never aspire to be popular. To
persuade the ordinary member of the Church that the Jewish
race was capable of reform, and that consequently the reception
of Jews into the Church was desirable, was a daunting task. 'There
is', he declared, 'for the anti-semitic malady a sole effective
remedy, and that is recourse to our evangelical faith. . . . It is
all too possible to be a nominal Christian, and indeed a committed
churchman as well, and at the same time to indulge in anti-
semitism. But for a Christian really animated by and nourished
upon the New and the Old Testaments that should be impossible.
Such a man learns to think differently of the Jew, not more
charitably or more indulgently but more earnestly and more
profoundly'.[16] In the light of Holy Scripture, the German people,
he believed, stood in need of recognising that what had befallen
the Jews could be their fate as well, and that, if they proved to be

unjust, unloving and spiteful, they had then every reason to stand in awe of the divine judgement. If they really appreciated what God had done for them, they would yearn for the Jews to share in the same saving Grace.

The work of the *Judenmission* and of the *Institutum Judaicum* continued to bear fruit, as is witnessed by the modest number of sincere conversions to the Christian Faith. The largely lukewarm and reserved approach from within the parishes was, however, far from encouraging. Interest in what was being endeavoured was scarcely more pronounced in academic circles. A noted scholar writing in 1913 described it as an ecclesiastical enterprise of which one hears but little. 'The circle of those who show a special interest appears to be very restricted'.[17] The Berlin Institute was still going strong in the late 'twenties with Professor Jeremias, the distinguished New Testament scholar, as its Director. Its sole missionary aim at that time was described as being *wissenschaftlich*, that of providing as objective, fair and unprejudiced an assessment as possible of post-biblical Judaism, and being to this end prepared to invite Jewish scholars as guest-lecturers.[18]

Otto von Harling, Director of the Leipzig Mission, expressed in the *Kirchliches Jahrbuch* of 1929 his satisfaction that earnest and fruitful conversations had been taking place between Christian and Jewish scholars, and rejoiced to be able to quote Hans von Ehrenberg's optimistic statement that there were signs that the Evangelical Church was approaching the situation of the Primitive Church in which a genuine dialogue between disciples of Christ and believing Jews was feasible.

Harling was, nevertheless, obliged to stress the gravity of the prevailing and mounting national and racial fanaticism that was not merely crippling the work of evangelisation among the Jews but was also frequently having its terrorising effect at the parish level. In such circumstances support for the *Judenmission* was more than ever an act of confession that demanded great courage and a touchstone of faith.[19]

Reporting again in 1932 he referred to the numerous barbarities committed against the Jews, and commented that this was regarded by the general public scarcely as shameful and unjust, and was to his regret not condemned by the Evangelical Church as such in the same unequivocal fashion as by the Catholic Church. In view of this he added that the witness of a truly

Christian attitude had a more powerful influence upon the Jews
than missionary preaching.[20]

From 1933 on each and every appeal and utterance from the
Judenmission was liable to misrepresentation and censure. The
'German Christians' viewed the missionary activities as a grave
encouragement of racial contamination. 'The introduction of
Jewish converts can do disastrous damage to the volkish consciousness within our Churches'.[21] The 'German Christian'
Church Government in Saxony in August 1933 banned collections
in church for the Mission, and insisted that converts of alien
blood had no claim to membership of a genuinely German Evangelical Church.[22]

A certain Pastor Dannenbaum incurred in August 1935 the
scornful wrath of the *Völkischer Beobachter* by an article of his
which that Nazi organ described as a 'tasteless hymn of praise
for the Jews calculated to make every German blush with shame'.
The remarks that caused such a disturbance were as follows:
'God spares the Jewish people for a final great act of world history.
Purified in the furnace of suffering—and who knows through what
bloody torments of anti-semitism they will yet be harassed—
they will be ripe for conversion. Recognising what potential such
a people has while placed under a curse, how marvellous must be
the blessing that they will confer upon the world, when they have
again been graciously received by God! And the day for this will
dawn! In crucifying Jesus, they came under the curse of the
divine judgement, an abomination to all peoples. When they
accept Jesus, there will be an endless time of Grace, a source of
blessing for the whole world!'[23]

It is amazing to learn that one of the foremost agencies for
Judenmission, the Society for the Promotion of Christianity among
the Jews, that had been founded as early as 1822 in Berlin, was
tolerated by the Nazis until 1941, when its closure was at length
required, and that there were those identified with the cause who
had the courage to protest openly against this order.[24]

NOTES

1. For Spener see J. F. A. de le Roi: *Die evangelische Christenheit
   und die Juden unter dem Gesichtspunkte der Mission,* Berlin, 1884,
   Band 1, pp. 206–15, and Martin Schmidt in *Kirche und Synagoge,*

ed. Karl-Heinrich Rengstorf and Siegfried von Kortsfleisch, Ban 2, pp. 90–106.

2. Quoted by Martin Schmidt. Ibid., 93–94.

3. For Callenberg see de le Roi, Vol. 1, pp. 246–69.

4. For Schultz see de le Roi, Vol. 1, 304–23.

5. For Delitzsch see de le Roi, Vol. 2, pp. 132–4 and Hans-Joachir Barkenings in *Juden und Christen*, ed. Wolf-Dieter Marsch and Ka Thieme, Mainz, 1961, pp. 210–19.

6. Franz Delitzsch in *Redet mit Jerusalem freundlich! Nachrichte über das Seminar des Institutum Judaicum zu Leipzig*, Leipzig, 188 pp. 14 and 21.

7. Ibid., 40.

8. Franz Delitzsch: *Sind die Juden wirklich das auserwählte Volk* Leipzig, 1889, p. 4.

9. Hermann Strack: *Das Institutum Judaicum Berolinense in den erste 30 Jahren seines Bestehens*, Leipzig, 1914, p. 3.

10. Hermann Strack: *Das Blut im Glaube und Aberglaube der Menschhei* Leipzig, 1900.

11. Franz-Heinrich Philipp in *Kirche und Synagoge*, Band 2, p. 313.

12. Hermann Strack: *Die Juden, dürfen sie Verbrecher von Religion wegen genannt werden?* Berlin, 1893.

13. *Das Institut Judaicum Berolinense*, 13.

14. Barkenings in ibid., 210.

15. *Protokolle der in Köln 6–9. Oktober 1900 abgehaltenen Allgemein Missionkonferenz für die Arbeit der Evangelische Kirche an Israe.* Leipzig, 1901, p. 66.

16. Ibid., 67.

17. Hans Windisch, quoted by Barkenings, ibid., 206.

18. Hans-Joachim Kraus in *Versuche des Verstehens*, p. 179.

19. *Kirchliches Jahrbuch*, 1929, p. 223.

20. *Kirchliches Jahrbuch*, 1932, pp. 484, 487.

21. Friedrich Wieneke: *Die Glaubensbewegung 'Deutsche Christen'*, p. 24

22. Gauger: *Gotthard-Briefe*, 202.

23. *Junge Kirche*, 1935, p. 762.

24. Wilhelm Niemöller: *Die Evangelische Kirche im Dritten Reich*, p. 380

The Radical Racial Anti-semites

In the main narrative consideration has been given to those who may be regarded as having had a direct influence upon the development of a religious and Christian version of anti-semitism. To make the picture reasonably complete brief sketches are here provided of various contributors to the genesis and the spread of radical racial anti-semitism in Germany in the latter part of the nineteenth century. Extensive use has been made of the valuable article by Alexander Bein—*Der moderne Antisemitismus und seine Bedeutung für die Judenfrage* in *Vierteljahrshefte für Zeitgeschichte*, October 1958, pp. 340 ff. Bein begins his article with the remark that the fact that in the 1870s a special word, 'Antisemitism', for animosity towards the Jews was coined, shows that the Jewish issue was moving into a new phase. The use of the description 'anti-semitic' served to show that the new approach was quite different from that which was based upon the mediaeval attitude. It promised that the battle was to be waged on an altogether wider front than the religious or the political. The issue would be treated as fundamentally a racial one. It also had a scientific air about it. It was found necessary before long to explain that anti-semitism was not intended to cover the whole semitic race. The Arabs were certainly not to be included. The Jews were the target.

A curious, rather gentle and melancholy work of undistinguished scholarship entitled *The Inequalities of the Human Race* by Count Artur de Gobineau was published in Paris in 1853. It proved to be the fount of all future anti-Jewish racial writings, although its author had little concern himself for the Jewish problem. He even revealed a certain respect for Jewish racial exclusiveness. Gobineau claimed that in race was to be found the source and determining factor of all that took place in history. His aim was to 'gain admission for the "science of history" into the "family of natural sciences".'[1] There was a rigid law set by nature. Any other influence such as that of religion, politics, economics, philosophy was in comparison with race of but secondary significance. With a species of 'historical chemistry'—Gobineau's own phrase[2]—it should prove possible to solve the riddle of the life and death of nations. 'Race', he declared, 'is a jealous god, it is everything.'[3] He proceeded to make a distinction between higher and lower races, arriving at the conclusion that only the white races possessed true creative power, the Aryan group being the most valuable with the Germanic or Nordic Peoples preeminent. The aristocratic race was in peril of contamination by lesser blood, and racial bastardisation was a continual threat. Nothing mattered more than the maintenance of racial purity, and true virtue was the outcome of noble uncontaminated blood. Democracy, which the aristocratic Gobineau hated, was with its conception of equality and fraternity a token of racial degeneracy. Gobineau did not himself proceed to the glorification of the Aryan Germanic race. He was profoundly pessimistic and fatalistic in his outlook. Convinced of the inexorability of racial degeneration and seemingly overwhelmed by it, his final verdict was: 'We are at the end of European Society. Its present state truly represents its death agony.'[4]

Alongside Gobineau another Frenchman, Ernst Renan, had a distinct influence. Whereas Gobineau's contribution was to bring into currency the idea of the decadence of particular races, Renan had the doubtful distinction of being the pioneer in expressly affirming the inferiority of the semitic-speaking peoples in comparison with the indo-Germanic.[5] He believed that the Jews as semites comprised 'a really inferior combination of the human race',[6] and he was to be found writing in disparaging terms of 'the religion of the wilderness, lacking in originality, weak in imagination, remotely related to everday ethics'.[7]

There were not lacking anthropologists and philologists to follow on, where Gobineau and Renan had left off, and the splendid Germanic Aryan type, tall, blond-haired, blue-eyed was contrasted with the mean, physically small and dark-haired semitic type, the latter being branded as uncreative and parasitic. All such pseudo-scientific racial surmisings that magnified the Germanic and deprecated the semitic were exactly what the radical anti-Jewish brigade were looking for to provide what

they would claim to be objective, scholarly foundation for their
hostile campaigning. The Jews by their present behaviour were
to be presented as altogether more than a nuisance or a menace.
They were to be deemed perpetually and irrevocably corrupt by
nature. Christian baptism might change their religious allegiance,
but it would not affect their racial character.

1861 saw the publication in Germany under the pseudonym of
H. Naudh of a work entitled *Die Juden und der Staat*, which that
expert on anti-Jewish publications Theodor Fritsch recognised
to be the 'classic document of anti-semitism'. In it the inseparable
relationship of Jewish blood and Jewish *Geist* was emphasised,
and it was recommended that what was characteristically Jewish
should be assessed in terms of race and not of religion. The Jewish
race 'which has invented the doctrine of the Chosen People, the
practice of whose religion consists merely in the cult of material
gain, whose conception of Right is solely determined by considerations of profit, which treats moral categories arithmetically,
converts the Family into a business-concern, and recognises
self-interest to be the very principle of its existence, while at
the same time hating to have to work was declared by the
author to be the mortal foe of every State and the enemy of
mankind'. [8]

Wilhelm Marr, about whom not much is known, in all probability invented the term 'anti-semitism'. It was certainly used
first publicly by him when he founded in 1879 the 'Antisemitic
League' and published a series of 'anti-semitic' leaflets. Marr who
was a journalist nursing a grievance at having been dismissed
from his job to suit the requirements of what he complained to
be the Jewish-controlled Press, is supposed to have been the son
of a Jewish actor, but later research has proved him to have been
of pure Aryan stock, although one of his wives was a Jewess,
and two others half-Jewish. His book entitled *The Victory of
the Jewish People over the Germanic People* was reprinted no less
than twelve times between 1893 and 1897. Influenced by Feuer-
bach and Voltaire, he regarded God as a subjective product of
our conscious life, and on such grounds attacked Christianity
along with Judaism, claiming that it was both dangerous and
futile to make a confessional issue out of the Jewish problem. The
real contrast was between Jew and German, not Jew and Christian,
and the 'line of division not accidental and remediable but eternal

and indelible'.[9] The Christian solution of conversion and baptism was a vain one, because the real offence of the Jew lay not in his religious peculiarity or his share in the responsibility for the Crucifixion, but in his biologically corrupt nature. Christianity was 'in no position to save the world from the perils of the semitic Jewish race'.[10] The only real way of rescuing the German people and the rest of the world from Jewish domination—and the Jews definitely were in his view a world power and much stronger than the Germans—and moral debasement was to refrain from hatred of the individual Jew who could not help being what he was, and to declare war upon the whole race. The Jews had already done mortal damage to the Germanic people, and the future appeared to belong to them. Marr was indeed extremely pessimisitc regarding the rot within the German State.

It was the boast of Eugen Dühring, a lecturer at Berlin University, that he was the first to give really thorough consideration to the Jewish Question as a racial issue. His work published in 1880 with the title of *The Jewish Question and its Threat to National Existence and Culture* has a right to be regarded as the standard work on racial anti-semitism. It was followed three years later by another book bearing the cumbersome title of *The Substitution for Religion of Something more Complete and the Elimination of Everything Jewish by means of the Modern Spirit of Nationalism (Völkergeist)*. It was Dühring's belief that it was misleading and outdated to treat the problem as a predominantly religious issue, a matter of Christian animosity to the people responsible for the murder of Jesus Christ and of Christian effort at conversion. The problem would in no wise be resolved, he maintained, even if all the Jews in Germany were to be baptised; rather, it would be enlarged, for they would not cease to be menacingly Jewish, and would have tremendously increased scope for the domination of social and political life. Every Jew was a member of a hostile and evil race. It was not just certain Jewish traits that were dangerous and to be condemned. The Jewish character as a whole was inherently depraved. From the very outset it had developed quite immutable attributes which he described in terms of 'quite inflexible self-seeking, the basest of cruelty, absolute shameless sensuality and most impudent hypocrisy'.[11] At the same time the Jews, in his reckoning, were fundamentally uncreative and lacking in cultural worth, feeding like parasites upon other peoples and intent upon despoiling them. Hostility against the rest of the human race had been the Jewish watchword throughout the whole of world history, and Germany at the present time was the main focal point of such venomous thirst for power. Its source was to be discovered in the peculiar and unnatural version of monotheistic religion that was in itself racial in origin, and that demanded submission to the One and Only Lord God, who was actually nought other than the image and mirror of the Jewish people themselves, and the exaltation of His Chosen People. Paradoxically it encouraged the Jew to regard himself as both 'worm' and 'serf' and also 'conqueror'.

Christianity of Palestinian origin came under much the same condemnation. It was 'itself Semitism',[12] 'offspring of the Jewish oriental racial soul',[13] and everything recorded of Jesus was 'drenched in draughts of Jewish tradition'.[14] The Christian tradition came into inevitable conflict with the Germanic character and its ideals. It was clearly futile to endeavour to conduct the struggle against the Jews with Christian concepts borrowed from Judaism. Indeed, it had to be recognised how impossible it was to be at one and the same time an intelligent convinced Christian and a serious anti-semite. 'The tables were fully turned. The Christian Church as Jew-enemy No. 1 sits together in the dock with Judaism.'[15]

The great hope for the future, so Dühring professed to believe, was to sever what by inheritance was characteristically Germanic from what was traditionally Christian. The real strength of the Germanic Race was to be realised not through the process of education and civilisation but rather by means of racial purity which would preserve the German from religious depravity and restore the vital sources of his instinctive life, thus leading to a further dynamic development of the Volk. That which was Jewish should never have been allowed to infiltrate into German life. To continue tolerating its influence would be perilous, to seek to reform it would be hopeless. For the time being a radical final settlement was out of reach. As a temporary expedient the most to be hoped for would be the calling off of emancipation, the rigid control upon Jewish influence in public life with no more participation permitted in Press and Education and a ban on Jewish-Gentile marriages, and a measure of deportation.

Dühring gave consideration, as Bein remarks, to almost everything that was to be found featured in later anti-semitic literature.[16]

An early concrete application of the concept of racial conflict is to be discovered in the anti-semitic agitation launched by Otto Böckel. A librarian in Marburg with a research interest in folk songs, and a democrat in politics, he advocated a form of national socialism, which included a popular version of anti-semitism in declared opposition to that of Adolf Stoecker and proved to be highly critical of the Church. Böckel's new movement spread like wild fire through the country districts of Hesse and Westphalia. He identified himself with the anxieties and grievances of the local peasants who complained that they were the victims of Jewish cattle-dealers and mortgage-brokers, and he enjoyed a period of extreme popularity, being hailed as the 'Hessian Peasant-King'. He advocated with racial arguments the exclusion of the Jews from all facets of life, and attacked in particular their economic overlordship. His pamphlet *The Jews— the Kings of our Time* was said to have had a circulation of half a million. In it Böckel referred to the Jews as 'this tough old alien race' which cannot be subdued either by baptism or intermarriage and which 'thinks differently and acts differently'.[17] The only solution was to separate the two different peoples by legal means, cancelling the provisions for emancipation and emphasising the mere guest-status of the Jews. Adolf Stoecker was greatly concerned that Böckel had won such esteem in Hesse, that the local clergy did not dare to oppose him, even when he was obviously preaching the very opposite of the 'Christian' version of anti-semitism, for fear that thereby they would have lost all influence in their parishes. Indeed, some of the pastors had fallen directly under his spell.[18] The central authority of the Hessian Church felt bound in 1890 to issue a circular letter rebuking those who sought to make the Jews as a whole responsible for individual Jewish misdemeanours and were prepared in the name of Christianity to preach a kind of crusade against the Jews. A Christian minister's duty was to stand firmly on the side of Right, Truth, Love and Peace.[19]

In 1887 Böckel stood successfully as an anti-semitic candidate at the Reichstag election. Two years later at Bochum an effort was made to form a united national anti-semitic party, bringing together Böckel's revolutionary socialism and the altogether more

onservative programme of the volkish anti-semites led by
Liebermann von Sonnenberg, an impecunious ex-officer, Bernard
Förster, brother-in-law of Nietzsche, and Theodor Fritsch. This
not surprisingly failed, and the latter group formed themselves
into the 'Anti-semitic German-Social Party', while Böckel and
his followers constituted themselves into the Anti-semitic People's
Party. In the election of 1893 the two groups of anti-semites
together won sixteen seats in the Reichstag. In 1894 the anti-
semitic members of the Reichstag, excluding Böckel and Ahlwardt,
managed to form themselves into the German-Social Reform
Party which is memorable for its 'Hamburg Guiding-Principles'
of 1899 which called for an official State decision that would
clearly establish who according to the law was to be reckoned a
Jew, and recommended that hereditary descent, and that alone
should be the determining consideration. This suggestion foreshadowed the eventual requirement of an 'ancestral pass' and was
accompanied by the prophecy that in the twentieth century the
Jewish question would become a world issue, and would be
jointly and finally solved by the Germans and other peoples
on the lines of complete ostracism, and if required in self-defence,
the ultimate annihilation of the Jewish people.[20] 1907 proved to
be the peak year when twenty five anti-semitic candidates were
returned, but in 1912 the number had slumped to thirteen. Those
who voted 'anti-semitic' never exceeded half a million.

Success within parliament proved to be more difficult. A
motley small band of noisy agitators unversed in parliamentary
procedure and constantly falling out among themselves, they had
no prospect whatever of promoting anti-semitic legislation. They
did, nevertheless, have the satisfaction of having permanently
won over to their cause considerable numbers of protestant
country folk. They had also a measure of success in influencing
public opinion at a higher level, and contrived to make it far
more difficult, if not in some cases almost impossible, for Jews
to gain admittance to university, join Students' Associations and
be accepted for State appointments. More sinister still was a
certain effect upon the administration of justice revealed in the
partiality shown in cases arising from anti-semitic disorders.
Virulent defamation of the Jews had a very good chance of
remaining unpunished.[21]

Most bizarre and contemptible of all the radical anti-semites of

this period was Hermann Ahlwardt. Born in 1846 in a village in
Pomerania and of humble origin, he became in 1881 Rector of
primary school in Berlin. Before long he was in serious financial
straits, and was dismissed his post in 1890, having been found
guilty of embezzlement of school funds that had been collected
for the children's Christmas party. The same year he published
pamphlet bearing the title *The Desperate Struggle between the
Aryan Peoples and the Jews*, in which he endeavoured to substantiate by wildly inaccurate evidence his belief that there was
a predatory Jewish stranglehold over the whole of German
society. He cited in particular the Army, Education, Agriculture
the Business World and the Civil Service. Certain government
departments he also claimed to be open to bribery and corruption
from Jewish sources. Ahlwardt's message was that the people
that could manage to rid itself of the Jews would be set free for
unimpeded national development, and would thereby be taking
a decisive step towards world domination. To him 'Jewry was
the Mephistopheles of world history. In dealing with the Jew
mercy was decidedly out of place'.[22] They should be declared
aliens and be excluded from all areas of German life and culture
with the prospect of eventual deportation. Much of the first part
of this intemperate work which surpassed all current anti-semitic
diatribes in its fantastic and slanderous falsifications, was auto-
biographical, providing details of his personal contracts with
Jewish money-lenders that were as uncomplimentary to him as to
his extortioners. In the second part he accused a prominent and
influential Jew of perjury that he claimed had been covered up by
influential representatives of the Government. This calumny which
was proved to be without any foundation earned him four month's
imprisonment. Almost as soon as he was free from gaol, he was
hard at it again, this time in a leaflet, *Jew-Rifles*, accusing a
Jewish manufacturer of having supplied defective arms to the
German Forces in furtherance of a sinister Franco-Jewish plot
against the Reich. This, again, was proved to be a complete
fantasy, and he was sentenced to a further five months in prison
which punishment he, however, escaped by having in the meantime been elected a member of the Reichstag. As was only to
be expected, this created a first-class scandal, but it did not
prevent him from becoming a popular hero in lower middle-class
circles in Berlin which found Stoecker too tame and proper, and

with the local peasantry to whose delight he soon proceeded to couple the Junkers with the Jews in a resounding battle-cry. By the close of the century he had become altogether too much for Böckel and other previous allies, and before long he disappeared from the public scene. An attempted come-back in 1907, with the Jesuits and the Freemasons this time as his target, proved to be a damp squib, and this most unprincipled and despicable of agitators, whom Pulzer has neatly described as having 'had only one accomplishment, the ability to rant',[23] was found guilty two years later of blackmail. He finally perished in a traffic accident in Leipzig in 1914.

This sketch of the contributions made by the radical anti-semites would be seriously incomplete without reference to Theodor Fritsch who has been described as 'the creator of practical anti-semitism'[24] and was revered by the Nazis as the *Altmeister* or supreme authority. Born in 1852, of petit bourgeois origin, he was soon caught up in the anti-semitic wave of the eighties, and after years and years dedicated to unremitting volkish and anti-semitic propaganda, was still alive in 1933 to witness the Nazi triumph. Fanatically obsessed by the notion that the Jews were the main source of all that was corrupt and evil, and that every issue had to be made subordinate to the supreme aim of upholding Germanic racial purity, and convinced that his life-work had to consist in rousing all classes in Germany to a recognition of this fact, and not permitting himself to be discouraged, when anti-semitism appeared to be on the ebb or on the way out, he became and remained for nearly half a century the leading anti-semitic publicist. An admirer writing in 1935 described him as 'the Father of anti-Judaism, the faithful guardian of the German people, like one crying in the wilderness [scarcely a happily chosen description!], the unyielding and never-tiring hero who sacrificed property and freedom and devoted everything to this holy war against Asia in Europe'[25]

In 1885, when the first outburst of anti-Jewish activity appeared to be spent, Fritsch sought to establish in Leipzig the 'German Anti-semitic Alliance' with the object of infiltrating all political parties, claiming that anti-semitism was 'a matter of Weltanschauung which can be accepted by anyone, no matter what party he belonged to'.[26] The output of pamphlets and other literature for which he was responsible was already so extensive that by

1890 it was reckoned that on average from four to five thousand copies were being daily distributed all over the place. In 1887 he published his anti-semitic catechism, which in time developed into the Handbook of the Jewish Question, with the sub-title 'The most important Facts for consideration in assessment of the Jewish People', and which by 1934 had been reprinted thirty-seven times. These 'facts' included arbitrarily chosen passages from the Old Testament and the Talmud depicting Jahweh as a monstrous, barbarous national god and Jewish 'morality' as thoroughly corrupt, deceitful, obscene and anti-social, geared to scornful hatred of the Gentile, and imputations of Jewish ritual murdering of Gentile boys, of Jewish organisations plotting for world domination, of an unholy Jewish alliance with the Church of Rome, and of Jewish responsibility for the growth of communism, pacifism and free-masonry. Painstakingly collected details were marshalled of alleged corrupt Jewish control over the Press, High Finance, the Business World, Literature, the Arts and Medicine, and statistics provided designed to prove the alarmingly high Jewish criminal record. A further section of the Handbook was devoted to quotations regardless of context from a formidable array of anti-Jewish witnesses. They included Seneca, Tacitus, Mohammed, Erasmus, Luther, Frederick the Great, Maria Theresa, Napoleon, Voltaire, Kant, Goethe, Schiller, Carlyle, Gibbon, Bismarck and Wagner.

In 1902 Fritsch began to issue his fortnightly '*Hammer*' leaflets which he advertised as 'designed for the consideration of all sorts of problems involving the Jews in a form of presentation readily comprehensible to all grades of the population right down from government ministers to the simplest working man'. Two years later he founded the '*Hammer*' Discussion and Propaganda Groups, which by 1914 were nineteen in number and grouped together in a Reich organisation.

Fritsch proved to have a quite obsessive anxiety regarding the corruption of the Germanic race by infiltration of Jewish blood. He wrote in his Anti-semitic catechism—'Esteem the corruption of noble Aryan blood with Jewish characteristics (*Juden-Art*) as an outrage upon your people. Recognise that Jewish blood persists for all time, and forms the Jew body and soul, shaping his character right down to the present generation'. In one of his 'Hammer'-blows under the title of *The Riddle of Jewish Success* he waxed eloquent upon the theme of the racial bastardy resulting from thousands of liaisons between Jews and Aryans that had resulted in hybrid births, the male Jew, he suggested, treating the Gentile woman as a 'sex-animal'. He claimed to be able to establish from police records that the Jews had a penchant for seducing Aryan maidens of tender years, and attributed to the Jew despite his unprepossessing appearance a magnetic power, not unlike that of an electric shock, of reducing his victim to quivering and trembling compliance.[28]

Alexander Bein ends his article by remarking that in the Hitler period there was really nothing left to add to what had been thought up by the racial anti-semitic theorists. All that remained was to give brutal and systematic realisation to the doctrines originated round about 1880.[29]

NOTES

1. Helmut Krausnick: *Anatomy of the SS State*, p. 4.
2. Artur de Gobineau: *The Inequalities of the Human Race*, Heinemann, 1915. Author's dedication, p. xii.
3. Quoted by Alexander Bein: *Der moderne Antisemitismus und seine Bedeutung für die Judenfrage*, *Vierteljahrshefte für Zeitgeschichte*, October 1958, p. 343.
4. Michael Biddiss: *Father of Racial Ideology—Social and Political Thought of Count de Gobineau*, Weidenfeld and Nicolson, 1970, p. 259.
5. W. ten Boom: *Die Enstehung des modernen Rassenantisemitismus* Leipzig, 1928, p. 8.
6. Ernst Renan: *Histoire générale des Langues Semitiques*, Paris, 1878, I, p. 16.
7. Bein, p. 344.
8. E. Naudh: *Die Juden und der Staat*, p. 81, quoted by ten Boom, p. 14.
9. Pulzer, 49.
10. Uriel Tal: Introduction to Johann Snoek: *The Grey Book*, p. x.
11. Eugen Dühring: *Der Ersatz der Religion durch Vollkommeneres und die Auscheidung alles Judentums durch den modernen Völkergeist*, Karlsruhe, 1883, p. 23.
12. Tal, p. xiv.
13. Kampmann, p. 300.
14. Dühring: *Der Ersatz der Religion*, p. 22.
15. Philipp in *Kirche und Synagoge*, II, 307.
16. Bein, 350.
17. Paul W. Massing: *Rehearsal for Destruction*, New York, 1949, p. 88.
18. Massing, 89.

19. Philipp, 315–16.
20. Tilgner in *Rasse Kirche und Humanum*, 289.
21. Philipp, 308.
22. Mosse: *Crisis of German Ideology*, 139.
23. Pulzer, 116.
24. *Handbuch der Judenfrage*, Leipzig, 1934, p. 5.
25. Friedrich Heer: *God's First Love*, Weidenfeld and Nicolson, 1970, p. 279.
26. Pulzer, 107.
27. Quoted in Massing: *Vorgeschichte des politischen Antisemitismus*, Frankfurt, 1959, p. 106.
28. Saul Friedländer in *Deutsches Judentum im Krieg und Revolution*, p. 64.
29. Bein, 360.

APPENDIX 4

The *Ostjuden*

There had been large-scale immigration from the East long before the First World War. A very considerable number of the estimated 2,725,000 Jews who between 1880 and 1914 quitted their former homes for other parts of the world passed through Germany, the obvious bridge in the heart of Europe between East and West. The *Hilfsverein der deutschen Juden*, a German Jewish charitable organisation, was assisting about 40,000 to 50,000 such immigrants yearly between 1903 and 1914.[1] A modest proportion of them, and many of such with reluctance, stayed put in Germany. There was also a steady trickle of Jewish students from Russia, who contrived to get to German universities and in many cases remained in Germany on conclusion of their studies. It has been reckoned that in August 1914 around 90,000 foreign Jews were to be found in Germany.[2] During the war Jews from the East were allowed into Germany, proved of considerable use in the war-effort and were obliged to stay for the duration. The total estimated figure at the end of the war came to 160,000 including 35,000 war-workers and a like number of Jewish prisoners of war and civilian internees.[3]

It was proposed in 1918 to compel those Jews who had not lived in Germany before the war to leave the country, but this was easier said than done, for many of them were without roots abroad and others just could not return whence they had come. Their numbers were rapidly swollen by a stream of Jews from all Eastern European countries where there happened to be a wave of persecution. Such immigrants pathetically believed that they would find a refuge in Germany which they understood to be the land of good order and emancipation, and were ignorant of, or paid no attention to, reports of heightened German anti-semitism. An enlightened and humane attempt was made in 1919 by Wolfgang Heine, the Prussian Minister for Home Affairs, to regularise the situation. His decree of the first of November allowed for the continued residence until further notice of all the Eastern Jews including those who had made illegal entry, provided they were 'personally unobjectionable', and were sponsored by German Jewish relief organisations, even though their continued stay might put the employment of Germans in jeopardy.[4] Unfortunately this concession was not accompanied by any careful planning for their economic integration. These Eastern Jews proved an embarrassment to the resident German Jews who were alarmed by the increase in vociferous anti-semitism and saw in the presence of the *Ostjuden* a threat to their own stability and therefore proved reluctant to offer employment to these their fellow-Jews, many of whom they indeed regarded as dangerous communists. German protests then and later at such immigration failed to recognise how 'qualitatively and quantitatively insignificant an issue was the immigration of less than 100,000 Jews into a country with a population of 63 million'.[5]

The radical anti-semites had already during the war raised the alarm that the Reich was 'threatened by a swarm of locusts' and had talked with wild exaggeration of 'a threatened mass-immigration of six million inferior mongolised human beings'.[6] Immediately the war was at its end they effectively spread the rumour that Jews from the East had engineered the downfall of Germany and the ensuing Revolution, suggesting that Russian and Polish Jews had been deliberately brought to Germany during the war disguised as workers to prepare for the Revolution with the aid of Russian-Jewish financial support. The *Schutz-und-Trutz Bund* issued in 1920 a pamphlet under the title of *What is going to become of the Ostjuden?*[7], which piously declared that 'it has continuously been a sign of German weakness to be exaggeratedly fair to aliens and unfair to one's own people'(!)[8], violently attacked Wolfgang Heine for his charitable legislation, and raised the scare of hazard to health, of further increase in the desperate housing shortage and of growth in unemployment with the robbing in particular of demobilised German soldiers of jobs. The pamphlet complained that a considerable number of the immigrants, some of them undoubtedly criminals, were already involved in highly dubious commercial practices, and demanded that the Jewish influence that underlay government policy should be completely and speedily eliminated, and that all post-war Jewish immigrants should be immediately expelled, so that Germany might be exclusively for the Germans. The authors of this pamphlet took pleasure in quoting at length from an official publication of the Democratic Party which expressed grave concern at the extent of the immigration, proving that one need not be a full-blooded nationalist or anti-semite in order to express such anxiety. It would appear that none of the major political parties showed desire to espouse the interests of the immigrants.

Adolf Hitler in his earliest printed speech made mischievous capital as follows out of the popular misgivings: 'Compare the million working men in Berlin before 1914 with what they now are. Working men as before. But what a transformation! They have become emaciated and poverty-stricken, clothed in worn out rags. Now take a look at those 100,000 Ostjuden. . . . The great majority of them have made good, and drive around in cars. Not because they are more capable . . ., but for the simple reason that these 100,000 were never from the very start prepared to co-operate loyally in promoting national prosperity, but were determined in advance to regard the whole national community as nothing other than a "forcing-bed" (*Mistbeet*) for their own advancement.'[9]

Though there were undoubtedly shady characters among the immigrants and some who sought to thrive on the black market and a few who did make their fortune, the lot of the majority, whose intentions were honest enough, was certainly not enviable. 1920–1 was a particularly unhappy period for them. Anti-Jewish riots and excesses were frequent in Berlin. In March 1920 in Berlin 250 quite innocent *Ostjuden* were arrested and interned. In April the Bavarian Government sought to expel 5,000 of them. Mishandling and expulsion of Jews was organised in Silesia. In 1921 some of the *Ostjuden* were committed to concentration camps and there were some cases of Nazi-like ill-treatment.[10] From 1921 to 1925 the *Ostjuden* were a continual subject of debate in parliament. 1925 witnessed the zenith of the immigration, and it has been calculated, though no accurate figures can possibly be arrived at, that by then between 18 and 19 per cent of the Jewish population in Germany consisted of foreign Jews.[11] The immigration did not cease in the next few years, but was largely cancelled out by the extent of further Jewish emigration from Germany to other countries, which, it should be recognised, was the intention all along of a considerable number of the *Ostjuden*.

It is possible, however, to make too much of this influx of undesired and reputedly undesirable immigrants, when considering the extensive growth of anti-semitism during the twenties. The target of the thorough-going anti-semites was ever the Jewish race as a whole. But the *Ostjuden* served their purpose admirably as the most obvious, the most characteristically alien and the most handily representative object of anti-Jewish feeling. *The Ostjuden* by reason of their different manner of behaving, their particular bearing and form of dress and their slowness and awkwardness in assimilating themselves made an altogether more vivid and disturbing impression upon the public than did the established German Jews.[12] German pride and ambition hurt by the humiliation of defeat after having hoped for conquest of territories to the East and smarting under their present treatment by the outside world were ready to unleash their feelings of discontent, of animosity and of suspicion upon the uninvited alien intruders. The anti-semites had lost no opportunity of fortifying such unfriendly emotions, and already during the war had made a myth out of the dangers that would threaten the German Reich by the flood of Jews from the East, and subsequently sought to present the immigrants as 'an obvious bolshevist bodyguard' charged with the task of implementing the Revolution.[13] Many Germans who had hitherto been reluctant and unwilling to think ill of, and join in the persecution of, the settled Jews in their midst proved to have little compunction in sharing in the prevailing unfriendliness for the sinister invaders, and in treating them as welcome scapegoats. It was, as was clearly revealed, all too tempting and all too easy to proceed to extend such an attitude of suspicion and animosity to the whole Jewish people.

NOTES

1. S. Adler-Rudel: *Ostjuden in Deutschland 1880–1914*, pp. 3–4.
2. Ibid., 21.
3. Ibid., 60.
4. Ibid., 64–6.
5. Ibid., 84.

6. Werner Jochmann: in *Deutsches Judentum in Krieg und Revolution 1916–1923*, 413.

7. *Was wird aus den Ostjuden ? Eine kritische Auseinandersetzung zur Ostjudenfrage*, published by Deutsch-volkischen Schutz-und-Trutz *Bund*, Hamburg, 1928.

8. Ibid., 20.

9. Saul Friedländer in *Deutsches Judentum in Krieg und Revolution*, 55.

10. Adler-Rudel, 115–18.

11. Wilhelm Treue in *Deutsches Judentum in Krieg und Revolution* 400.

12. Franz-Heinrich Philipp in *Kirche und Synagoge* Vol. 2, 323.

13. Jochmann 463.

Extract from a Munich Church Address

Extract from the anonymous Address by members of the Church in Munich on the subject of the duty of Christian Proclamation in the matter of the Persecution of the Jews, presented to Bishop Meiser, Easter 1943.

'As Christians we can no longer tolerate the Church in Germany keeping silent about the persecution of the Jews. In the Gospel Church all members of the congregation have a joint responsibility for the right exercise of the preaching office. Consequently we recognise our share of the blame for neglect in this respect. The next step that is now threatened, the inclusion of the so-called 'privileged' Jews in the persecution through the dissolution of marriages that are valid according to Divine Law, gives the Church the opportunity to bear such witness as God's Word demands from her against the violation of the first, sixth, seventh, eighth, ninth and tenth commandments, and at last to do what she ought to have done so long ago.

Our incentive is first and foremost the straightforward command to show neighbourly love, as Jesus expounded it in the parable of the Good Samaritan. He thereby ruled out each and every limitation of neighbourly love that makes it apply merely in the case of those holding the same faith or belonging to the same race or people. Every non-Aryan, whether he be Jew or Christian, has today in Germany 'fallen among murderers', and we are asked whether we are going to encounter him as Priest and Levite or as Samaritan. The recognition that there is a 'Jewish Problem' cannot absolve us from such a decision. On the contrary, the Church has to make use of this situation, in order to testify that the Jewish Question is primarily an Evangelical concern and not a political issue. The politically irregular and singular existence of the Jews has according to Holy Scripture its one and only ground in the fact that God has fastened upon this particular people as the instrument of His Revelation.

The Church must, therefore, just as the first Apostles did— *after* Golgotha!—testify unwearyingly to all *Jews*: 'Unto you *first* God having raised up His Son Jesus, sent Him to bless you, in turning away every one of you from his iniquities'. (Acts 3, 26). This witness the Church can accomplish convincingly for Israel, only if she simultaneously espouses the cause of the Jew who has 'fallen among murderers'.

The Church has in particular to oppose that version of 'Christian' anti-semitism in the *Congregation* itself that excuses the passivity of the Church respecting the procedure of the non-Christian world against the Jews by citing the 'merited' curse upon Israel, and thereby forgets the apostolic exhortation: 'Be not highminded, but fear. For if God spared not the natural branches, take heed lest He also spare not thee.' (Romans 11.20 ff)

Over against the *State*, the Church has to bear witness to the redemptive (*heilgeschichtlich*) significance of Israel, and to withstand to the utmost every attempt to solve the Jewish Question according to a self-manufactured political gospel involving the annihilation of Jewry, and to reveal it as an attempt to resist the God of the First Commandment. The Church must make confession that she as the True Israel is indissolubly bound up both in Guilt and in Promise with Jewry. The Church may no longer try to promote her own security in face of the attack directed against Israel. She must on the contrary testify that along with Israel she and her Lord Jesus Christ Himself are being attacked.

The witness required of the Church according to the parable of the Good Samaritan is, therefore, not, as it were, suspended because of the Jewish problem. The phenomenon of the Jews, in whom the prophetic prediction is fulfilled that they shall be 'a curse and an astonishment and an hissing and a reproach among all the nations' (Jeremiah 29:18) bears witness to the whole world of the God of the First Commandment, who through His dealing with Israel proclaims His title to dominion over the nations. The Church has to interpret this phenomenon. By means of her preaching and teaching she has to see to it that those who rule do not endeavour to evade such witness by brushing aside the phenomenon. The Church achieves this by proclaiming the Gospel of the God who has brought Israel and us out of Egypt, 'out of the house of bondage' (Exodus 20:2), and who despite all the disloyalty of those whom He has chosen from out of both Jews and Gentiles remains true to His Covenant. The Church, therefore, testifies to those who bear rule that they can only through faith in Jesus Christ become free from that which is demonic in the political gospel by which they are possessed and which they desire to realise free from all limitation of divine law. Regarding their behaviour towards Israel, the Church has, therefore, to preach to those who bear authority not only that which is contained in the second table of the commandments but also at the same time to testify that such preaching is demanded by the First Commandment, and that those who bear rule will only exercise their office aright, if they be obedient to the God of the First Commandment. That means that they prove that they can apply the law and administer justice in the right way.

The testimony of the Church against the persecution of the Jews in Germany thus becomes an exceptionally important special instance of the witness that she is required to give against all violation of the Ten Commandments by the State Authority (*Obrigkeit*). The Church has in the name of God—therefore not with political arguments as now and then has happened—to admonish the State that it 'oppress not the stranger, the fatherless and the widow' (Jeremiah 7:6), and to remind it of its task to pass right judgement in orderly and public legal procedure based upon humane laws, and of its duty to be fair in its measures for the carrying out of punishment, in its legal protection of the oppressed and in its respect for certain basic rights of its subjects.

This witness of the Church must be made publicly either from the pulpit or by means of a special word from those who hold the office of bishop, shepherd and watchman. Only so can the Church fulfil her obligation towards all those who have a legislative or executive part in the persecution, and at the same time supply the Jews concerned and the Christian congregation assailed in its faith, with the due instruction of their consciences. Everything that has hitherto been done in this matter by the Church in Germany cannot be regarded as such witness, for it has neither taken place in public nor has it been in its content correctly aligned to the genuine task of the preaching office.'

Bishop Wurm's letter to Hitler, 16 July 1943

'In the last years and right up to the present time churchmen have repeatedly endeavoured to make contact with the Reich leadership or with influential individuals holding high office in State and Party, in order to gain a hearing for matters that are of important concern in Christian circles. Their representations in writing have, however, received no answer, and their endeavours to enter into personal conversation have had no success. It might be suggested that the time has now come to keep silent and to decline to have any share of responsibility for all future happenings. Every Christian, nevertheless, bears a share of responsibility along with the present State, since he is charged to espouse the cause of Good and to bear witness against Evil. The love for my people, whose lot I as a 75 year old have for many decades sought to further, and for which I have been called upon to make hard sacrifices in my own intimate family circle,[1] impels me once again to see what can be achieved by a frank and open utterance.

Among those many men and women who have died in this war for Germany are countless Christians. Among those who in silent resignation are contending for the Fatherland and enduring heavy sacrifices are, likewise, countless Christians. On behalf of both the living and the fallen Evangelical Christians of Germany I appeal to the Führer and the Government of the German Reich. I do so as the most senior Evangelical bishop and assured of the understanding and support of wide circles within the Evangelical Church.

In the name of God and for the sake of the German people we give expression to the urgent request that the responsible leadership of the Reich will check the persecution and annihilation to which many men and women under German domination are being subjected, and without judicial trial. Now that the non-Aryans who have been the victims of the German onslaught have been very largely eliminated, it is to be feared, in the light of what has already happened in certain individual cases, that the so-called 'privileged' non-Aryans who have so far been spared are in renewed danger of being subjected to the same treatment. In particular, we would raise emphatic objection to such measures as are threatening the marriage-bond in legally unimpeachable families and the children that have been born of such unions.[2] Such intentions like the measures taken against the other non-Aryans are in the sharpest contrast to Divine Law and an outrage against the very foundations of western thought and life and against the very God-given right of human existence and of human dignity. In invoking this right so absolutely bestowed by God upon man we solemnly raise our voices in protest against countless measures that have been adopted in occupied territories. Happenings which have become known at home and are being much talked about weigh very heavily upon the consciences of countless German men and women and severely impair their strength. They are suffering more from such measures than from the sacrifices that each day brings. German Evangelical Christians have urgently to require that the nations and religious confessions brought under the dominion of the Reich shall be accorded full freedom in the practice of their religion and be guaranteed treatment that conforms to the principles of law and of justice irrespective of nationality or of confessional adherence. Evangelical Christians in Germany realise their Christian solidarity with all those who as a result of incomprehensible rulings are to their deepest distress prevented from seeking comfort in the fellowship of their faith. We do not fail to recognise the stern necessities of war. We are, nevertheless, persuaded that arbitrary measures against life, property and freedom of faith carried out by Party authorities and State departments by appeal to such necessities have done infinitely more harm than that which would have ensued from any misplaced resort to justice and clemency.

Christians in Germany have up to the present withstood attacks upon the Christian Faith and upon freedom in its application. They deplore most profoundly the many and diverse forms of suppression of freedom of faith and of liberty of conscience, the continuing repression of parental and Christian influence in the training of youth, the keeping in confinement in concentration camps of thoroughly honourable individuals, the violation of the administration of justice and the general legal insecurity resulting from it.

In speaking out in the name of countless Evangelical Christians we ask nothing for ourselves. German Evangelical Christians share in all the sacrifices that have to be made. They do not desire any special rights or preferential treatment. They do not strive after might, or want any particular power. But nothing and nobody in the world shall hinder us from being Christians, and as Christians standing for what is right before God. It is, therefore, our most earnest petition that the Reich leadership will heed this demand of ours, and prove mindful of its great responsibility for the life and future of the German people.'

NOTES

1. The deaths in 1942 of his son and of his son-in-law in the Russian campaign.
2. Reference to the proposed compulsory divorce whereby the non-Aryan partner would lose all his privileged status and the Aryan would become secure and altogether reputable.

Extract from an exposition of the Sixth Commandment

Extract from the exposition of the Sixth Commandment, 'Thou shalt not kill', published by the Twelfth Synod of the Confessional Church in Prussia, Breslau, 17 October 1943.

'17. In particular, old people depend these present days more than in former times upon our help. The incurably sick, the weak-minded, the mentally disturbed also need our succour. We have to help their families to bear the burden. We must not forget that they derive as good as no assistance from public sources. The Christian is not perturbed by public disapproval of such help being given. The Christian at all times discovers his neighbour among those who are helpless and in need of him, and that irrespective of any difference of race, nationality or religion. All human life belongs to God alone. It is sacred to him. And that includes the life of the People of Israel. Admittedly Israel has rejected God's Christ, but neither as fellow-humans or as Christians are we called upon to chastise Israel's unbelief.

18. We owe to our non-Aryan fellow-Christians the proof of our spiritual fellowship and brotherly love. To exclude them from the congregation is an offence against the Third Article of our Confession of Faith, against the right understanding of the Sacrament of Holy Baptism, against Galatians 3:28 and against that which Romans 11 teaches regarding "Israel after the flesh". Such exclusion is also inoperative from the standpoint of ecclesiastical law, for the Church as a legally constituted public body may do nothing that contradicts her essential character as the Communion of Saints.

19. We can in no wise allow others to take away from us our responsibility before God in all these decisions. Admittedly we

have in many cases no watching brief to see whether just verdicts are passed in court or whether a war is conducted justly or unjustly. In such cases the Government (*Obrigkeit*) and its officers are directly responsible before God. But where we clearly recognise that injustice is demanded from us, or that we are being prevented from doing what is right according to God's Will, we then have according to our own responsibility to do what is right in God's sight, and have to obey God rather than men (Acts 5.29). Everyone stands or falls to his own Lord. We must all appear before the Judgement-Seat of Christ (2 Corinthians 5:10). We cannot allow those who govern us to take from us our responsibility before God. God will require at our hands those whom we unjustly put to death, and fearful is the threat pronounced against those who commit murder (Revelation 21:8; 22:15).'

(*Kirchliches Jahrbuch*, 401–2)

Select Bibliography

In this Select Bibliography English publications are cited with the names of their publishers, and the place of publication is London unless it is otherwise stated.

ADAM, UWE DIETRICH. *Judenpolitik im Dritten Reich*, Düsseldorf, 1972.

ADLER, H. G. *The Jews in Germany, From the Enlightenment to National Socialism*, Indiana, U.S.A., 1969.

ADLER-RUDEL, S. *Ostjuden in Deutschland 1880–1940*. Tübingen, 1959.

ALTHAUS, PAUL. *Kirche und Volkstum*, Gütersloh, 1928.

——*Die deutsche Stunde der Kirche*, Göttingen, 1934.

——*Theologie der Ordnungen*, Gütersloh, 1934.

——*Kirche und Staat nach lutherische Lehre*, Leipzig, 1935.

——*Völker vor und nach Christus*, Leipzig, 1937.

——*Luthers Lehre von den beiden Reichen im Feuer der Kritik*, Luther Jahrbuch, Berlin, 1957.

ANDERSEN, FRIEDRICH, *Der deutsche Heiland*, München, 1921.

ANDREAS-FRIEDRICH, RUTH. *Berlin Underground*, Lutterworth, 1948.

ARENDT, HANNAH. *Eichmann in Jerusalem*, Faber and Faber, 1963.

ARNDT, INO. *Die Judenfrage im Licht der evangelischen Sonntags-blätter, 1918–1933*. Unpublished Dissertation, Tübingen, 1960.

ASMUSSEN, HANS. *Zur jüngsten Kirchengeschichte*, Stuttgart, 1961.

BAIER, HELMUT. *Die Deutschen Christen Bayerns im Rahmen des bayerischen Kirchenkampfes*, Nürnberg, 1968.

BARTH, KARL. *Theologische Existenz Heute*, München, 1933. English edition, *Theological Existence Today*, Hodder, 1933.

——*Die Kirche Jesu Christi*, Theologische Existenz Heute, No. 5, München, 1933.

——*Eine Schweizer Stimme, 1938–1945*, Zürich, 1945.

——*Die Evangelische Kirche in Deutschland nach dem Zusammen-bruch des Dritten Reiches*, Stuttgart, 1946.

BARTH, KARL. *Der Götze wackelt. Zeitkritische Aufsätze, Reden und Briefe von 1930 bis 1960*, Berlin, 1964.

BECKMANN, JOACHIM, ed. *Kirchliches Jahrbuch für die Evangelische Kirche in Deutschland, 1933–1944*, Gütersloh, 1948.

——*Kirchliches Jahrbuch für die Evangelische Kirche in Deutschland, 1945–1948*, Gütersloh, 1950.

——*Kirchliches Jahrbuch für die Evangelische Kirche in Deutschland 1950*, Gütersloh, 1951.

BEIN, ALEXANDER. *Der moderne Antisemitismus und seine Bedeutung für die Judenfrage. Vierteljahrshefte für Zeitgeschichte*, Oct.,1958.

——*Der jüdische Parasit. Vierteljahrshefte für Zeitgeschichte*, April, 1965.

BEN ELISSAR, ELIAHU. *La Diplomatie du IIIe Reich et les Juifs, 1933–1939*, Jaillard, 1969.

BETHGE, EBERHARD. *Dietrich Bonhoeffer. Eine Biographie*, München, 1967. English edition, London, 1970.

——*Geschichtliche Schuld der Kirche in Karl Herbert* ed: *Christliche Freiheit im Dienst am Menschen zum 80. Geburtstag von Martin Niemöller*, Frankfurt, 1972.

BOEHLICH, WALTER. *Der Berliner Antisemitismusstreit*, Frankfurt, 1965.

BONHOEFFER, DIETRICH. *Gesammelte Schriften*, München, Band I, 1958, Band II, 1959.

BOSANQUET, MARY. *The Life and Death of Dietrich Bonhoeffer*, Hodder and Stoughton, 1968.

BOYENS, ARMIN. *Kirchenkampf und Oekumene, 1933–1939*, München, 1969.

BRACHER, KARL DIETRICH. *The German Dictatorship*, Weidenfeld and Nicolson, 1971.

BROSSEDER, JOHANNES. *Luthers Stellung zu den Juden im Spiegel seiner Interpreten*, München, 1972.

BRUNOTTE, HEINZ. *Die Kirchenmitgliedschaft der nichtarischen Christen im Kirchenkampf, Zeitschrift für evangelischer Kirchenrecht*, Band XIII, 1967–8, 140–174.

BUCHHEIM, HANS. *Glaubenskrise im Dritten Reich*, Stuttgart, 1953.

CARGILL THOMPSON, W. D. J. *The Two Kingdoms and the Two Regiments. Some Problems of Luther's Zwei Reiche Lehre*, Journal of Theological Studies, 1969.

CHAMBERLAIN, HOUSTON STEWART. *The Foundations of the Nineteenth Century*, ed. John Lees, John Lane, 1911.

COCHRANE, ARTHUR. *The Church's Confession under Hitler,* Philadelphia, 1962.

COHN, NORMAN. *Warrant for Genocide,* Eyre and Spottiswoode, 1967.

CONWAY, JOHN. *The Nazi Persecution of the Churches,* Weidenfeld and Nicolson, 1968.

CORNU, DANIEL. *Karl Barth et la Politique,* Geneva, 1967.

DAHM, KARL WILHELM. *Pfarrer und Politik,* Köln, 1965.

DAVIES, A. J. *Anti-Semitism and the Christian Mind,* New York, 1969.

DIBELIUS, OTTO. *Das Jahrhundert der Kirche,* Berlin, 1928.

——*Nachspiel. Eine Aussprache mit den Freunden und Kritikern des 'Jahrhunderts der Kirche',* Berlin, 1928.

——*Obrigkeit,* Stuttgart, 1963.

——*In the Service of the Lord,* Faber and Faber, 1964.

Die Evangelische Kirche und die Judenfrage, Ausgewählte Dokumente aus den Jahren des Kirchenkampfes 1933 bis 1943, Genf, 1945.

DIEM, HERMANN. *Restauration oder Neuanfang in der evangelische Kirche?,* Stuttgart, 1946.

——*Karl Barths Kritik am deutschen Luthertum,* Zürich, 1947.

——*Das Rätsel des Antisemitismus. Theologische Existenz Heute,* Neue Folge, Nr. 80, München, 1960.

——*Kirche und Antisemitismus* in *Deutsches Geistesleben und Nationalsozialismus,* ed. Andreas Flitner, Tübingen, 1965.

——*Kirche und staatliche Autorität in Württemberg,* in *'Schwäbische Heimat',* December 1969.

——*Kann die Kirche Busse tun?* in *'Evangelische Korrespondenz',* October 1970.

DIPPER, THEODOR. *Die Evangelische Bekenntnisgemeinschaft in Württemberg, 1933–1945, Arbeiten zur Geschichte des Kirchenkampfes,* Band 17, Göttingen, 1966.

DORPALEN, ANDREAS. *Heinrich von Treitschke,* Yale, 1957.

DUNCAN-JONES, A. S. *The Struggle for Religious Freedom in Germany,* Gollancz, 1938.

EHRENBERG, HANS. *Autobiography of a German Pastor,* S.C.M., 1943.

EHRENFORTH, GERHARD. *Die schlesische Kirche im Kirchenkampf, 1932–1945,* Göttingen, 1968.

ELIAS, OTTO. *Der evangelische Kirchenkampf und die Judenfrage* in *Informationsblatt für die Gemeinden in den niederdeutschen lutherischen Landeskirchen*, Hamburg, July 1961.

ENGELKE, FRITZ. *Christentum Deutsch*, Hamburg, 1933.

FEDER, GOTTFRIED. *Das Program der NSDAP und seine weltanschaulichen Grundgedanken*, München, 1932.

——*Der deutsche Staat auf nationaler und sozialer Grundlage*, München, 1933.

FINK, FRITZ. *Die Judenfrage im Unterricht*, Nürnberg, 1937.

FINK, HEINRICH, ed. *Stärker als die Angst. Den sechs Millionen die keinen Retter fanden*, Berlin, 1968.

FORCK, BERNHARD. *Und folget ihrem Glaubennach. Gedenkbuch für die Blutzeugen der Bekennende Kirche*, Stuttgart, 1949.

FRANK, WALTER. *Hofprediger Adolf Stoecker und die Christlich Soziale Bewegung*, Hamburg, 1935.

FRANZ, HELMUT. *Kurt Gerstein. Aussenseiter des Widerstandes der Kirche gegen Hitler*, Zürich, 1964.

FRIEDLÄNDER, SAUL. *Counterfeit Nazi. The Ambiguity of Good*, Weidenfeld and Nicolson, 1969.

FREUDENBERG, ADOLF, ed. *Rettet sie doch! Franzosen und die Genfer Oekumene im Dienste der Verfolgten des Dritten Reiches*, Zürich, 1969.

FRITSCH, THEODOR. *Handbuch der Judenfrage*, Berlin, 1933.

GAUGER, JOACHIM. *Chronik der Kirchenwirren. Gotthardbriefe.* 3 Bände, 1933–5, Eberfeld, 1934–6.

GAUS, GÜNTHER. *Zur Person, Porträts in Frage und Antwort*, München, 1965.

GEIGER, MAX. *Der Deutsche Kirchenkampf, 1933–1945*, Zürich, 1965.

GERLACH, WOLFGANG. *Zwischen Kreuz und Davidstern. Bekennende Kirche in ihrer Stellung zum Judentum im Dritten Reich.* Unpublished Dissertation, Hamburg, 1970.

GOLDSCHMIDT, ARTUR. *Geschichte der evangelische Gemeinde Theresienstadt, 1942–45*, Tübingen, 1946.

GOLDSCHMIDT, DIETER and KRAUS, HANS-JOACHIM, eds. *Der ungekündigte Bund*, Stuttgart, 1963.

GLENTHØJ, JØRGE. *Die nicht-jüdische Nicht-Arier im Dritten Reich*, in *Junge Kirche*, 1965.

GOLLWITZER, HELMUT. *Die christliche Gemeinde in der politischen Welt*, Tübingen, 1954.

GOLLWITZER, HELMUT. *Forderungen der Freiheit. Aufsätzen und Reden zur politischen Ethik*, München, 1962.

GRÜBER, HEINRICH. *Dona Nobis Pacem, Gesammelte Predigten und Aufsätze aus 20 Jahren*, Berlin, 1956.

——*Zeuge pro Israel*, Berlin, 1963.

——*Erinnerungen aus sieben Jahrzehnten*, Berlin, 1968.

GRUENAGEL, FRIEDRICH. *Die Judenfrage*, Stuttgart, 1970.

GRUNBERGER, RICHARD. *A Social History of the Third Reich*, Weidenfeld and Nicolson, 1971.

GRUNDMANN, WALTER. *Entjüdung des religiosen Lebens als Aufgabe der Theologie*, Weimar, 1939.

GURIAN, WALDEMAR. *Antisemitismus in Modern Germany* in *Essays on Antisemitism*, ed. Koppel S. Pinson, New York, 1946.

HEER, FRIEDRICH. *God's First Love*, Weidenfeld and Nicolson, 1970.

HERMAN, STEWART. *It's Your Souls we Want*, Hodder, 1943.

HERMELINK, HEINRICH. *Kirche im Kampfe. Dokumente des Widerstands und des Aufbaus der evangelischen Kirche Deutschlands von 1933 bis 1945*, Tübingen, 1950.

HESSE, HERMANN. *Die Judenfrage in der Verkündigung heute*, Stuttgart, 1948.

HEYDENREICH, RENATE MARIA. *Erklärungen aus der Evangeliscehn Kirche Deutschlands und der Ökumene in der jüdischen Frage, 1932–1961* in *Der ungekündigte Bund*, ed. Goldschmidt und Kraus, Stuttgart, 1963.

HEYDT, FRITZ VON DER. *Die Ziele der Deutschen Christen*, Bonn, 1934.

HILBERG, PAUL. *The Destruction of the European Jews*, London, 1961.

HILLERDALL, GUNNAR. *Gehorsam gegen Gott und Mensch. Luthers Lehre von der Obrigkeit und die moderne Staatsethik*, Göttingen, 1965.

HIRSCH, EMANUEL. *Theologische Gutachten in der Nichtarierfrage* in *Deutsche Theologie*, May 1934.

HITLER, ADOLF. *Mein Kampf*, München, 1933.

HOCHHUTH, ROLF. *The Representative*, Penguin Books, 1969.

HÖHNE, HEINZ. *The Order of the Death's Head, The Story of Hitler's S.S.*, Secker and Warburg, 1969.

HOSSENFELDER, JOACHIM, ed. *Volk und Kirche. Bericht der ersten Reichstagung 1933 der Glaubensbewegung Deutsche Christen*, Berlin 1933.

HUG, HERBERT. *Das Volk Gottes. Der Kirche Bekenntnis zur Judenfrage,* Zürich, 1942.

HÜRTEN, HEINZ, ed. *Deutsche Briefe,* 2 Bände, Mainz, 1969.

JACOBS, HELENE. *Illegalität aus Verantwortung* in *Unterwegs,* 1947, Nr 3.

JASPER, RONALD. *George Bell, Bishop of Chichester,* Oxford, 1967.

JOCHMANN, WERNER. *Die Ausbreiting des Antisemitismus* in *Deutsches Judentum in Krieg und Revolution, 1916–1923,* ed. Werner E. Mosse, Tübingen, 1971.

JOFFROY. PIERRE. *A Spy for God. The Ordeal of Kurt Gerstein.* Collins, 1970.

JONG, LOUIS DE. *Niederländer und Ausschwitz* in *Vierteljahrshefte für Zeitgeschichte,* January 1969.

KAMPMANN, WANDA. *Deutsche und Juden. Studien zur Geschichte des deutschen Judentums,* Heidelberg, 1963.

KANTZENBACH, F. W. *Widerstand und Solidarität der Christen in Deutschland, 1933–1945. Eine Dokumentation zum Kirchenkampf aus den Papieren des Dr. Wilhelm Freiherr von Pechmann,* Nürnberg, 1971.

KATCHER, LEE. *Postmortem. The Jews in Germany—Now,* Hamish Hamilton, 1968.

KINDER, CHRISTIAN. *Volk vor Gott,* Hamburg, 1935.

——*Neue Beiträge zur Geschichte der evangelischen Kirche in Schleswig-Holstein und im Reich,* Flensburg, 1968.

KITTEL, GERHARD. *Die Judenfrage,* Tübingen, 1934.

KLEMPERER, VICTOR. *Die unbewältige Sprache,* Darmstadt, 1966.

KLEPPER, JOCHEM. *Unter den Schatten deiner Flügel,* Stuttgart, 1956.

KLINGLER, FRITZ, ed. *Dokumente zum Abwehrkampf der deutschen Evangelischen Pfarrerschaft gegen Verfolgung und Bedruckng, 1933–1945,* Nürnberg, 1946.

KLOTZ, LEOPOLD, ed. *Die Kirche und das Dritte Reich,* 2 Bände, Gotha, 1932.

KLÜGEL, EBERHARD. *Die lutherische Landeskirche Hannovers und ihr Bischof, 1933–1945,* Berlin, 1964, and Dokumente, 1965.

KOCH, WERNER. *Heinemann im Dritten Reich. Ein Christ lebt für Morgen,* Wuppertal, 1972.

KRAKAUER, MAX. *Lichter im Dunkeln,* Stuttgart, 1947.

KRAUS, HANS-JOACHIM. *Die evangelische Kirche* in *Entscheidungsjahr 1932, Zur Judenfrage in der Endphase der Weimarer Republik,* ed. Werner E. Mosse, Tübingen, 1965.

KRAUSNICK, HELMUT. *The Persecution of the Jews* in *Anatomy of the SS State*, Collins, 1968.

KREMERS, HERMANN. *Nationalsozialismus und Protestantismus*, Berlin, 1931.

KÜNNETH, WALTER and SCHREINER, HELMUT, eds. *Die Nation vor Gott. Zur Botschaft der Kirche im Dritten Reich*, Berlin, 2nd ed. 1934, 5th ed. 1937. (see especially Walter Künneth: *Das Judenproblem und die Kirche*, in two different versions.)

KÜNNETH, WALTER. *Der grosse Abfall*, Hamburg, 1948.

——*Politik zwischen Dämon und Gott, Eine Christliche Ethik des Politischen*, Berlin, 1961.

KUPISCH, KARL. *Quellen zur Geschichte des deutschen Protestantismus, 1871–1945, Siebenstern Taschenbuch 41/42*, München, 1960.

——*Durch den Zaun der Geschichte*, Berlin, 1964.

——*Zwischen Idealismus und Massendemokratie. Eine Geschichte der Evangelische Kirche in Deutschland von 1815–1945*, Berlin, 1963.

——*Studenten entdecken die Bibel. Die Geschichte der Deutschen Christlichen Studenten-Vereinigung*, Berlin, 1964.

——*Deutschland im 19. und 20. Jahrhundert* in *Die Kirche in ihrer Geschichte*, Handbuch ed. K. D. Schmidt and Ernst Wolf, Göttingen, 1966.

——*Adolf Stoecker. Hofsprediger und Volkstribun*, Berlin, 1970.

——*Im Bann des Zeitgeistes, Theologische Existenz Heute*, Neue Folge, 159, München, 1969.

KÜPPERS, ERICA. *Kirche und Israel. Anhang zur 'Bekennende Kirche. Martin Niemöller zum 60. Geburtstag'*, München, 1952.

KUPTSCH, JULIUS. *Christentum im Nationalsozialismus*, München, 1932.

——*Im dritten Reich zur dritten Kirche*, Leipzig, 1933.

LAGARDE, PAUL DE. *Deutsche Schriften*, Göttingen, 1886.

——*Ausgewählte Schriften*, ed. Paul Fischer, München, 1934.

LAMPARTER, EDUARD. *Evangelische Kirche und Judentum* in *Versuch des Verstehens, Dokumente jüdisch-christlichen Begegnung, 1918–1933*, ed. Robert Geis und Hans-Joachim Kraus, München, 1966.

LE SEUR, PAUL. *Adolf Stoecker, der Prophet des Dritten Reiches*, Berlin, 1936.

LEUNER, H. D. *When Compassion was a Crime. Germany's Silent Heroes, 1933–1945*, Wolff, London, 1966.

LEWY, GÜNTHER. *The Catholic Church and Nazi Germany*, Weidenfeld and Nicolson, 1964.

LOHSE, EDUARD. *Israel und die Christenheit*, Göttingen, 1960.

LÖSENER, BERNARD. *Als Rassereferent im Reichministerium des Innern. Vierteljahrshefte für Zeitgeschichte*, 1961.

LOUGEE, ROBERT. *Paul de Lagarde*, Harvard, 1962.

MACFARLAND, CHARLES. *The New Church and the New Germany*, New York, 1934.

MARSCH, WOLF-DIETER and THIEME, KARL, eds. *Christen und Juden*, Mainz, 1961.

MASCHMANN, MELITA. *Account Rendered: A Dossier on my former self*, Abelard-Schuman, London, 1964.

MASSING, PAUL. *Rehearsal for Destruction*, New York, 1949.

MAURENBRECHER, MAX. *Der Heiland der Deutschen. Der Weg der Volkstum schaffenden Kirche*, Göttingen, 1933.

MEHNERT, GOTTFRIED. *Evangelische Kirche und Politik, 1917–1919*, Düsseldorf, 1959.

MEIER, KURT. *Die Deutschen Christen*, Göttingen, 1964.

——*Kirche und Judentum*, Göttingen, 1968.

MEYER–ERLACH, WOLF. *Juden, Mönche und Luther*, Weimar, 1935.

——*Der Einfluss der Juden auf das englische Christentum*, Weimar, 1940.

MIDDENDORF, FRIEDRICH. *Der Kirchenkampf in einer reformierte Kirche. Arbeiten zur Geschichte des Kirchenkampfes*, Band 8, Göttingen, 1961.

MOSSE, GEORGE. *The Crisis of German Ideology*, Weidenfeld and Nicolson, 1964.

——*Die deutsche Rechte und Die Juden in Entscheidungsjahr 1932, zur Judenfrage in der Endphase der Weimarer Republik*, ed. Werner Mosse, Tübingen, 1965.

MÜLLER, ARNDT. *Geschichte der Juden in Nürnberg*, Nürnberg, 1968.

MÜLLER, HANS MICHAEL. *Der innere Weg der deutschen Kirche*, Tübingen, 1933.

MÜLLER, LUDWIG. *Deutsche Gottesworte*, Weimar, 1936.

MURTORINNE, EINO. *Erbischof Eidem zum deutschen Kirchenkampf, 1933–34*, Helsinki, 1968.

NEUHÄUSLER, JOHANN. *Kreuz und Hakenkreuz. Der Kampf des Nationalsozialismus gegen die katholische Kirche und der kirchliche Widerstand*, München, 1946.

NEUMANN, PETER. *Die Jungreformatorische Bewegung, Arbeiten zur Geschichte das Kirchenkampfes*, Band 25, Göttingen, 1971.

NIEMÖLLER, MARTIN. *The First Commandment, Selected Sermons, 1933–1935*, Hodge, 1937.

——*The Gestapo Defied, the last Twenty-Eight Sermons, 1936–1937*, Hodge, 1942.

NIEMÖLLER, WILHELM. *Ist die Judenfrage bewältigt?* Beiheft 2, *Junge Kirche*, 1968.

——*Wort und Tat im Kirchenkampf*, München, 1969.

——*Steglitz Synode, Arbeiten zur Geschichte des Kirchenkampfes*, Band 23, Göttingen, 1970.

——*Kampf und Zeugnis der Bekennenden Kirche*, Bielefeld, 1947.

——*Gottes Wort ist nicht gebunden*, Bielefeld, 1948.

——*Die Bekennende Kirche sagt Hitler die Währheit. Die Geschichte der Denkschrift der Vorläüfigen Leitung von Mai 1936*, Bielefeld, 1954.

——*Die Evangelische Kirche im Dritten Reich. Handbuch des Kirchenkampfes*, Bielefeld, 1956.

——*Aus den Leben eines Bekenntnispfarrers*, Bielefeld, 1961.

——*Neu Anfang 1945. Zur Biographie Martin Niemöllers*, Frankfurt, 1967.

NORDEN, GÜNTHER VAN. *Kirche in der Krise. Die Stellung der Evangelischen Kirche zum Nationalsozialistischen Staat im Jahre 1933*, Düsseldorf, 1963.

OERTZEN, DIETRICH VON. *Adolf Stoecker, Lebensbild und Zeitgeschichte*, Schwerin, 1912.

PARKES, JAMES. *Antisemitism*, Valentine Mitchell, 1963.

PFISTERER, RUDOLF. *Im Schatten des Kreuzes*, Hamburg, 1966.

PHILIPP, FRANZ-HEINRICH. *Protestantismus nach 1848 in Kirche und Synagoge*, ed. Karl-Heinrich Rengstorf and Siegfried von Kortzfleisch, Band II, Stuttgart, 1970.

PHILLIPS, PETER. *The Tragedy of Nazi Germany*, Kegan and Paul, 1969.

POELCHAU, HARALD. *Die Ordnung der Bedrängten*, Berlin, 1963.

PORTER, J. R. *The Case of Gerhard Kittel* in *Theology*, November 1947.

PRATER, GEORG, ed. *Kämpfer wider Willen. Erinnerungen des Landesbischofs von Sachsen, D. Hugo Hahn*, Metzingen, 1969.

PULZER, P. J. G. *The Rise of Political Anti-semitism in Germany and Austria*, New York, 1964.

RADDATZ, FRITZ, ed. *Summa Iniuria oder Dürfte der Papst schweigen? Hochhuths Stellvertreter in der offentlichen Kritik,* Hamburg, 1963.

RAUSCHNING, HERMANN. *Hitler Speaks,* Thornton Butterworth, 1939.

REICHMANN, EVA. *Hostages of Civilisation,* Gollancz, 1950.

——*Der Bewusstsein der deutschen Juden* in *Deutsches Judentum im Krieg und Revolution, 1916–1923,* ed. Werner Mosse, Tübingen, 1971.

REITLINGER, GERALD. *The Final Solution,* London, 1968.

RIEGER, JULIUS. *The Silent Church. The Problem of the German Confessional Witness,* S.C.M., 1944.

ROI, A. F. DE L. *Die evangelische Christenheit und die Juden unter dem Gesichtspunkte der Mission,* Berlin, 1884.

ROON, GER VAN. *German Resistance to Hitler,* London, 1971.

ROSENBERG, ALFRED. *Der Mythus des 20 Jahrhunderts,* München, 1934.

RUNES, DAGOBERT. *The War against the Jew,* New York, 1968.

RUPP, GORDON. *Martin Luther. Hitler's Cause or Cure?,* Lutterworth, 1945.

SAMUEL, MAURICE. *The Great Hatred,* Gollancz, 1943.

SASSE, MARTIN. *Martin Luther über die Juden. Weg mit ihnen!* Freiburg, 1938.

SAUER, PAUL. *Dokumente über die Verfolgung der jüdischen Bürger in Baden-Württemberg,* Stuttgart, 1966.

——*Die Schicksäle der jüdischen Bürger Baden-Württemberg während der nationalsozialistischer Verfolgungszeit,* Stuttgart, 1969.

SCHÄFER, GERHARD, ed. *Landesbischof Wurm und der nationalsozialistische Staat, 1940–1945,* Stuttgart, 1968.

SCHLATTER, ADOLF. *Wird der Jude über uns siegen?* Essen, 1936.

SCHLEUNES, KARL. *The Twisted Road to Auschwitz, Nazi Policy towards German Jews, 1933–1939,* Andre Deutsch, 1972.

SCHMID, HEINRICH. *Apokalyptisches Wetterleuchten,* München, 1947.

SCHMIDT, HEINZ. *Die Judenfrage und die Christliche Kirche in Deutschland,* Stuttgart, 1947.

SCHMIDT, JÜRGEN. *Martin Niemöller im Kirchenkampf,* Hamburg, 1971.

SCHMIDT, KURT DIETRICH. *Die Bekenntnisse und grundsätzlichen*

Äusserungen zur Kirchenfrage, 1933–1935, 3 Bande, Göttingen, 1934–6.

SCHMIDT, KURT DIETRICH. *Dokumente des Kirchenkampfes. Die Zeit des Reichskirchen ausschusses, 1935–1937. Arbeiten zur Geschichte des Kirchenkampfes,* Bände 13 and 14, Göttingen, 1964.

SCHNEIDER, GEORG. *Kirche am Scheideweg,* Stuttgart, 1935. *Neuland Gottes, von der Heimkehr der deutschen Seele,* Stuttgart, 1936.

SCHOEPS, HANS–JOACHIM. *Der Patriotismus der Juden und der Nationalsozialismus,* Berlin, 1970.

SCHOLDER, KLAUS. *Die Evangelische Kirche und das Jahr 1933* in *Geschichte im Wissenschaft und Unterricht,* November 1965.

——*Die Kapitulation der Evangelischen Kirche vor dem national- sozialistischen Staat* in *Zeitschrift für Kirchengeschichte,* 1970.

——*Die Kirchen im Dritten Reich, Beilage zur Wochenzeitung Das Parlament,* B 15/71, 10 April 1971.

SCHOLL, INGE. *Six against Tyranny,* Murray, 1955.

SHARF, ANDREW. *The British Press and the Jews under Nazi Rule,* Oxford, 1964.

SHIRER, WILLIAM. *The Rise and Fall of the Third Reich,* Secker and Warburg, 1960.

SNOEK, JOHAN. *The Grey Book.* A collection of protests against anti-semitism and the persecution of the Jews, issued by non- Roman Catholic Church leaders during Hitler's rule, Assen, 1969.

STÄHLIN, WILHELM. *Die völkische Bewegung und unsere Verant- wortung,* Sollstedt, 1924.

——*Via Vitae, Lebenserinnerungen,* Kassel, 1968.

STAEWEN, GERTRUD. *Bilder aus der illegalen Judenhilfe* in *Unterwegs,* 1947, Nr 3.

STAPEL, WILHELM. *Der christliche Staatsman. Eine Theologie des Nationalismus,* Hamburg, 1933.

——*Sechs Kapitel über Christentum und Nationalsozialisums,* Hamburg, 1933.

——*Die Kirche Christi und der Staat Hitlers,* Hamburg, 1933.

STEINERT, MARLIS. *Hitlers Krieg und die Deutschen,* Düsseldorf, 1970.

STERLING, ELEONORE. *Judenhass, Die Anfänge des politischen Anti- semitismus in Deutschland, 1815–1850.* Frankfurt, 1969.

STERN, FRITZ. *The Politics of Cultural Despair,* California, Univ. Press, 1961.

STOECKER, ADOLF. *Christlich-Sozial, Reden und Aufsätze*, Berlin, 1885.

TAYLOR, TELFORD. *Guilt, Responsibility and the Third Reich*, Churchill College Fellowship Lecture, 6, Heffer, Cambridge, 1970.

THADDEN, REINHOLD VON. *Auf verlorenem Posten?* Tübingen, 1948.

THIEME, KARL. ed. *Judenfeindschaft*, Frankfurt, 1963.

THOMAS, E. E. *Hitlerism, Communism and the Christian Faith*, Unicorn Press, 1935.

TILGNER, WOLFGANG. *Volksnomostheologie und Schöpfungsglaube, Arbeiten zur Geschichte des Kirchenkampfes*, Band 16, Göttingen, 1966. *Judentum und Rassenfrage in deutschen Protestantismus*, in '*Rasse, Kirche und Humanum*' ed. Klaus-Martin Beckmann, Gütersloh, 1969.

TUTZINGER TEXTE. *Sonderband I, Kirche und Nationalsozialismus*, München, 1969.

VISSER 'T HOOFT, W. A. *The Kingship of Christ*, S.C.M. 1948.

——*Memoirs.* S.C.M., 1973.

VOGEL, ROLF, ed. *The German Path to Israel*, Documentation, Dufour, Chester Springs, Pennsylvania, 1967.

VOGELSANG, ERIK. *Luthers Kampf gegen die Juden*, Tübingen, 1933.

VORLÄNDER, HERWART. *Kirchenkampf in Elberfeld, 1933–1945*, Göttingen, 1968.

WAGNER, MARTIN. *Die Deutschen Christen im Kampf um die innere Erneuerung des deutschen Volkes*, Berlin, 1933.

WECKERLING, RUDOLF, ed. *Durchkreutzer Hass*, Berlin, 1961.

WEIDEMANN, HEINZ. *So sieht die Kommende Kirche aus*, Bremen, 1941.

WIENEKE, FRIEDRICH. *Die Glaubensbewegung Deutsche Christen*, Soldin, 1933.

WIENER, PETER. *Martin Luther—Hitler's Spiritual Ancestor*, Hutchinson, 1944.

WOLF, ERNST. *Die lutherische Lehre von der zwei Reichen in der gegenwärtigen Forschung in Zeitschrift für evangelischen Kirchenrecht*, 1957–8.

——*Kirche im Widerstand?* München, 1965.

——*Barmen. Kirche zwischen Versuchung und Gnade*, München, 1970.

——*Volk, Nation, Vaterland im protestantischen Denken von 1930 bis zur Gegenwart* in *Volk, Nation, Vaterland*, ed. Horst Zillessen, Gütersloh, 1970.

WRIGHT, JONATHAN. *The Political Attitudes of the Protestant Church Leadership, November 1918–July 1933.* Unpublished D.Phil. Thesis, Oxford, 1969.

WURM, THEOPHIL. *Erinnerungen aus meinem Leben,* Stuttgart, 1953.

ZELZER, MARIA. *Weg und Schicksal der Stuttgarten Juden,* Stuttgart, 1964.

ZIPFEL, FRIEDRICH. *Kirchenkampf in Deutschland,* Berlin, 1965.

Index